Bloomsbury Companions

The *Bloomsbury Companions* series is a major series of single volume companions to key research fields in the humanities aimed at postgraduate students, scholars and libraries. Each companion offers a comprehensive reference resource giving an overview of key topics, research areas, new directions and a manageable guide to beginning or developing research in the field. A distinctive feature of the series is that each companion provides practical guidance on advanced study and research in the field, including research methods and subject-specific resources.

Titles currently available in the series:

Aesthetics, edited by Anna Christina Ribeiro
Analytic Philosophy, edited by Barry Dainton and Howard Robinson
Aristotle, edited by Claudia Baracchi
Continental Philosophy, edited by John Ó Maoilearca and Beth Lord
Ethics, edited by Christian Miller
Existentialism, edited by Jack Reynolds, Felicity Joseph and Ashley Woodward
Hegel, edited by Allegra de Laurentiis and Jeffrey Edwards
Heidegger, edited by Francois Raffoul and Eric Sean Nelson
Hobbes, edited by S.A. Lloyd
Hume, edited by Alan Bailey and Dan O'Brien
Kant, edited by Gary Banham, Dennis Schulting and Nigel Hems
Leibniz, edited by Brandon C. Look
Locke, edited by S.-J. Savonious-Wroth, Paul Schuurman and Jonathan Walmsley
Metaphysics, edited by Neil A. Manson and Robert W. Barnard
Philosophical Logic, edited by Leon Horsten and Richard Pettigrew
Philosophy of Language, edited by Manuel García-Carpintero and Max Kölbel
Philosophy of Mind, edited by James Garvey
Philosophy of Science, edited by Steven French and Juha Saatsi
Plato, edited by Gerald A. Press
Pragmatism, edited by Sami Pihlström
Socrates, edited by John Bussanich and Nicholas D. Smith
Spinoza, edited by Wiep van Bunge, Henri Krop, Piet Steenbakkers and Jeroen M.M van de Ven

The Bloomsbury Companion
to Epistemology

Edited by
Andrew Cullison

Bloomsbury Academic
An imprint of Bloomsbury Publishing Plc

B L O O M S B U R Y
LONDON · NEW DELHI · NEW YORK · SYDNEY

Bloomsbury Academic

An imprint of Bloomsbury Publishing Plc

50 Bedford Square	1385 Broadway
London	New York
WC1B 3DP	NY 10018
UK	USA

www.bloomsbury.com

BLOOMSBURY and the Diana logo are trademarks of Bloomsbury Publishing Plc

First published in paperback 2015

First published as *The Continuum Companion to Epistemology* 2012

British Library Cataloguing-in-Publication Data
A catalogue record for this book is available from the British Library.

ISBN: PB: 978-1-4725-8577-6
ePDF: 978-1-4725-8578-3
ePub: 978-1-4725-8579-0

Library of Congress Cataloging-in-Publication Data
A catalog record for this book is available from the Library of Congress.

Typeset by Deanta Global Publishing Services, Chennai, India
Printed and bound in Great Britain

Contents

Contributors

James Beebe *(University at Buffalo, USA)*

Kenneth Boyce *(University of Notre Dame, USA)*

E. J. Coffman *(University of Tennessee, USA)*

Earl Conee *(University of Rochester, USA)*

Andrew Cullison *(SUNY Fredonia, USA)*

Richard Feldman *(University of Rochester, USA)*

Richard Fumerton *(University of Iowa, USA)*

Sanford Goldberg *(Northwestern University, USA)*

Daniel Howard-Snyder *(Western Washington University, USA)*

Carrie Jenkins *(University of Nottingham, UK)*

Peter Klein *(Rutgers University, New Brunswick, USA)*

Jonathan Kvanvig *(Baylor University, USA)*

Jon Matheson *(University of North Florida, USA)*

Alvin Plantinga *(University of Notre Dame, USA)*

Sharon Ryan *(West Virginia University, USA)*

Gregory Wheeler *(New University of Lisbon, Portugal)*

Dennis Whitcomb *(Western Washington University, USA)*

Introduction

Epistemology: A Brief Historical Overview and Some Puzzles about Methodology

Andrew Cullison

Epistemology is the branch of philosophy that deals with questions pertaining to knowledge and related concepts such as justification or reasonable belief. In this chapter, I will sketch some of the standard methods that contemporary epistemologists typically employ to answer these questions. In doing, so I will outline what I will call the *Standard Method*. I will also sketch some challenges to this method.

Epistemology: A brief historical overview

Epistemology has experienced a bit of a renaissance within the last fifty years, and much of this renaissance can be traced back to Gettier's now famous paper showing that knowledge is not justified true belief. Epistemology looked quite different before Gettier. It was then largely taken for granted that knowledge (if we had any) was justified true belief. If, one thinks that knowledge (if there is any) is justified true belief, then it is very natural to assume that the primary questions in epistemology are: Do we have knowledge? What sorts of things count as evidence or appropriate grounds for knowledge?

For example, if you go back to Locke's *An Essay Concerning Human Understanding*—a classic work in Early Modern epistemology—he notes that the purpose of the essay is to "To enquire into the original, certainty, and extent of human Knowledge."[1]

We can see Locke's influence in terms of articulating what epistemology is through the early part of the twentieth century.[2] We can see this influence into the mid-twentieth century as well.

What's not as present in the Early Modern works are detailed discussions and debates about how best to *analyze* knowledge. What we see are questions about what sorts of things we can know *with certainty* and whether we can build on that to explain how we know other things; and whether we can then have a satisfactory response to the skeptic.

Likewise, you don't see much discussion about how best to analyze justification. Perhaps because it was likely taken for granted that justification was just having adequate grounds. The debates concerning justification seemed to be primarily about what sorts of inputs qualified as good grounds. For example, large concerns included whether *a priori* intuitions could be included as adequate grounds, and can we find a set of grounds that yield certain knowledge which can be used to help build up a system of knowledge that resists skeptical worries. We also see discussions about the nature of various kinds of inputs that border on psychology (e.g. memory, introspection, perception, objects of awareness) and whether these inputs can yield adequate grounds.

For example, a common categorization for studying Early Modern philosophers is to group them into two groups: Empiricist or Rationalist.[3] It's also common to structure a class in Early Modern philosophy by going back to Descartes and talking about how he attempts to refute skepticism and then the back and forth between many Early Moderns concerning their stance on whether *a priori* knowledge was possible or not.

Even Quine's call to naturalize epistemology can be seen as Lockean in spirit. Quine notes that "the Cartesian quest for certainty had been the remote motivation of epistemology, both on its conceptual and doctrinal side; but that quest was seen as a lost cause."[4] Quine then argues that "epistemology still goes on, though in a new setting and a clarified status. Epistemology, or something like it, simply falls into place as a chapter of psychology and hence of natural science." The proper role of this naturalized epistemology is to empirically study the nature of human cognitive inputs, which apart from the Cartesian/Lockean project of exploring the extent of our knowledge and its certainty is something that Locke would think is the proper domain of epistemology. The reason I characterize Quine's conception of epistemology as Lockean is that his view seems to be that *once* it is clear that the Cartesian project of responding to skepticism by building a system from foundations that are certain and indubitable fails, the only thing left for epistemology to consider are those aspect of the Lockean project that really do seem to be much more about psychology and studying the *nature* of various epistemic inputs.

Enter Gettier. As noted, before Gettier it was traditionally assumed that knowledge was justified true belief, and justification was traditionally understood as having good reasons or evidence. In two short pages Gettier convinced just about everyone that one could have a justified true belief that wasn't knowledge. The basic idea is that it seems possible to have justified true beliefs that are clearly not knowledge. Here's a simple Gettier case:

Sheep In The Field

Smith is walking through a field and sees what appears to be a genuine sheep. It is a very realistic looking fake sheep and Smith is fooled. He forms the belief that there is a sheep in the field. It turns out that Smith's belief is *true* because there is a real sheep in the field hidden behind a bush.[5]

Smith has a justified true belief that is clearly not knowledge. Even if Gettier wasn't the first to recognize this problem,[6] he is certainly responsible for bringing it to everyone's attention. Suddenly, there was a very new puzzle that became the center of attention.

Here is a candidate diagnosis of what happened. First, epistemology realized that there was this important component of knowledge that had *until* Gettier been overlooked. Reactions were varied. Many thought that we could patch up the analysis, and thought that perhaps there is some minor modification that will avoid the counter-example. Knowledge is justified true belief *plus* some fourth condition. But whenever someone offered a candidate fourth condition, someone showed that it didn't capture some obvious case of knowledge (or that it counted something as knowledge that obviously wasn't).

Around the same time, philosophers started to carefully scrutinize the notion of justification, and whether justification was necessary for knowledge at all. At this point, we start seeing the birth of externalism. This begins with epistemologists radically jettisoning justification from the analysis entirely. Nozick argued that knowing something is a matter of being sensitive to the truth of that proposition.[7] Goldman argued that knowing something was merely a matter of that fact being the cause of your belief in that fact.[8] Armstrong argued that there must be some law like connection between the features that lead to a person in believing P and the truth of P. None of these three accounts mention justification at all. It didn't take long for externalism to evolve.[9]

Some externalists began to think that maybe we should keep the notion of justification, but radically re-think what justification is. We typically assumed that justification was a matter of having good evidence that was accessible to us, but perhaps justification is something entirely different. Goldman who stood squarely in the classic externalism camp *also* is partially responsible for this new approach, and we begin to see externalist accounts (most notably reliabilism) of not knowledge but the justification component of knowledge.

All of this careful reflection on the structure and nature of justification began to yield new ways in which one might avoid the regress argument for skepticism. New ways to respond to skeptical arguments. It has yielded interesting results in moral and religious epistemology too. This volume is designed to focus on some of these recent developments in greater detail.

Epistemology: Methodology

There are relatively new and interesting questions about the nature of knowledge and justification that contemporary epistemologists are trying to answer. In the remainder of this chapter, I will briefly outline some of the methods that contemporary epistemologists typically employ to attempt to answer these questions, and briefly present some puzzles for this method.

Identify unifying features about obvious cases of knowledge and justification

As I noted, one central task in epistemology is to try and understand the nature of various epistemic properties (or relations) such as *knowledge, justification, warrant, reasonable,* and *rational.* A common method to do this is to begin with obvious cases of knowledge (or justification, or reasonable belief) and perhaps some obvious cases where knowledge is absent or lacking. We then try to abstract some general features that the obvious cases have in common. So a person might start with the following lists:

Propositions I Know
I am typing.
I have two hands.
2 + 2 = 4.
George Washington was the first president of the United States.

I am hungry.

Propositions I Do Not Know

Thomas Jefferson was the first president of the United States.

There is a Pink Elephant in the Room.

There is an even number of grains of sand on St Pete Beach.

One obvious similarity among items on the known list is that they are true and I believe them. I don't believe any of the propositions in the "I Do Not Know" category. If we just focused on those similarities, we might construct the following analysis of knowledge:

True Belief Analysis

S knows that P = df. P is true and S believes P.

Now that we have our analysis, we can test it. We can search for obvious cases of knowledge that it rules out, or obvious cases of non-knowledge that it includes. It doesn't take long to realize that the True Belief Analysis is unsatisfactory. Lucky guesses that result in firmly held beliefs would qualify as knowledge according to the True Belief Analysis. Whatever knowledge amounts to—it is reasonably clear that these kinds of cases shouldn't qualify as knowledge.

Once we realize that our first attempt at an analysis fails, we can return to our list, add any obvious cases that were brought to our mind when we were testing the first analysis, and search for some other property that we may have overlooked.

In this case, we have overlooked some salient differences. The obvious cases of knowledge have something in common in addition to true belief; they are also obvious cases of reasonable or rational belief. Epistemologists call this third feature *justification*. Historically, something like this analysis was taken for granted by most philosophers going back to Plato.[10] As we noted earlier, Gettier's attention to this analysis drastically altered the shape of contemporary epistemology. However, in this section, my purpose is merely to illustrate what one of the standard methods in epistemology is. It is not much different from methods you see in other areas of philosophy. Many areas of philosophy have certain complex concepts or properties that they focus on. In ethics it might be *rightness* or *wrongness*. In metaphysics it might be *personhood* or *mereological simple*. In aesthetics it might be *art* or *beauty*. A common method in each of these areas is to start with obvious cases where something has the property we are interested in and try to determine what features these obvious cases have in common. We try to construct an analysis on the basis of those unifying features.

Epistemologists employ the same method with respect to other interesting epistemic concepts such as *justification*. For example, a traditional view about the nature of epistemic justification is evidentialist. According to evidentialism, justification essentially depends on having good supporting evidence. Recently there has been a huge shift away from the classical evidentialist picture. So one of the contemporary debates that will receive a lot of attention in this volume is about the nature of epistemic justification. Some think that *internal evidence* is an important component. Other epistemologists (e.g. Reliabilists and Proper Functionalists) think that *internal evidence* is not an essential component of the concept of justification. Despite their differences, many classical evidentialists, reliabilists, and proper functionalists often argue for their views by coming up with intuitively obvious cases of justification, and arguing that their theory best captures those intuitions about those cases. Notice that much of the disagreement between proper functionalists, reliabilists, and evidentialists in this book center around how well each theory does with respect to preserving intuitions about allegedly obvious cases of justification.

Preserve ordinary language uses of the terms "knows" and its cognates

Another method that is sometimes relied on in epistemology is to examine *ordinary language* uses of the term "knows" and its cognates, and construct theories that best capture patterns of linguistic use of those terms. Suppose we learned that people only tend to use "knows" in situations where the stakes for being wrong are not very high. However, when the stakes for being wrong *are* very high they are much less likely to attribute knowledge to themselves or some agent in the scenario.

Some would argue that this suggests that there is some practical constraint on the application of "knows," which in turn suggests that an adequate theory of knowledge will incorporate a practical constraint in their theory of knowledge.

Consider the following examples from Jason Stanley:

> *Low stakes.* Hannah and her wife Sarah are driving home on a Friday afternoon. They plan to stop at the bank on the way home to deposit their paychecks. It is not important that they do so, as they have no impending bills. But as they drive past the bank, they notice that the lines are very long, as they often are on Friday afternoon. Realizing that it isn't very important that there paychecks are deposited right away, Hannah says, "I know the bank will be open tomorrow,

since I was there just two weeks ago on Saturday morning. So we can deposit our paychecks tomorrow morning."

High stakes. Hannah and her wife Sarah are driving home on a Friday afternoon. They plan to stop at the bank on the way home to deposit their paychecks. Since they have an impending bill coming due, and very little in their account, it is very important that they deposit their paychecks by Saturday. Hannah notes that she was at the bank two weeks before on a Saturday morning, and it was open. But, as Sarah points out, banks do change their business hours. Hannah says, "I guess you're right. I don't know the bank will be open tomorrow."[11]

Philosophers like Stanley note that there is something *linguistically appropriate* about both assertions. We need a theory that captures the appropriateness of these assertions.

This may not be much different from the method outlined in the previous section, but I keep it separate for two reasons. The first reason is that some epistemologists talk about preserving intuitions about cases, while others talk about capturing ordinary language use. Second, even if many epistemologists think that these methods are two sides of the same coin, there is conceptual room for thinking that these are different methods. For example, it could be that people use the word "knows" in a certain way, without having intuitions about cases and it could be possible that *philosophers* construct theories that capture this usage without themselves having intuitions about cases. Maybe one shouldn't be in the business of capturing ordinary language unless there were some reason to think that ordinary language tracked intuitions about cases, but the point is that these are descriptively distinct phenomena. If it turns out that they are two sides to the same coin, then consider this another example of how philosophers construct theories by preserving intuitions about cases. You'll see discussion of appeals to this method in this book.[12]

Capture other desiderata concerning the connection between knowledge and other concepts

A third method in epistemology involves developing theories that explain intuitions that we have about the connection between knowledge and other concepts or properties. Conversely we might rule epistemic theories out because they entailed that there was no connection between some epistemic property and some other property (when intuitively there is such a connection). Here are some examples.

A. Knowledge and value

Some philosophers claim that knowledge is valuable in a way that *mere* true belief is not. This goes back to Plato, but the connection has recently been pressed into service to argue against contemporary epistemological theories.

Jonathan Kvanvig calls this the *Meno* Problem, and has argued that reliabilism (for example) fails to explain why knowledge in more valuable than mere true belief, because *reliably formed true beliefs* are no more valuable to the believer than mere true beliefs, knowledge must be something other than *reliably formed true belief.*[13]

B. Knowledge and norms of assertion

Other philosophers claim that *knowledge* is a norm of assertion. In other words, if you do not know some proposition P, then you ought not assert P.[14]

Similarly, some philosophers claim that there is a connection between knowledge and practical reasoning. In other words, if you know P then you can use P as a premise in practical reasoning. It is regarded by some philosophers to be a strike against an account of knowledge or justification if it conflicts with either of these two claims about the connection between knowledge and other norms.

C. Closure

Many epistemologists think that knowledge is closed under logical implication. Roughly, that if you know that P and you know that P entails Q then you know that Q. With a few exceptions, this is a widely held principle. If it turns out that a theory conflicts with closure, it is generally regarded as a bad consequence for that theory.

For example, Richard Feldman says,

> I believe that some version of the closure principle, restricted to known consequences, is surely true. Indeed, the idea that no version of the principle is true strikes me, and many other philosophers, as one of the least plausible theses to come down the philosophical pike in recent years.[15]

And it isn't just that closure is intuitively plausible. Other epistemologists argue that closure is essential to making sense of the idea that we can come to know things via deduction.

Many epistemologists argue that it is a strike against a theory of knowledge or justification if it conflicts with a plausible closure principle, and we'll see some examples of that in this volume.

D. Justification is normative

The above examples all involve assessing a theory based on whether or not it preserves intuitions about connections between knowledge and some other important concept. We see similar strategies involving justification. For example, some claim that the justification component of knowledge is a *normative* notion. It is a little difficult to explain what the normative/nonnormative distinction is, but it seems similar to the ought-is distinction in ethics. One might describe the facts about what is the case. Bob is causing Tim pain because Bob thinks it is funny. That's a pure description about what is the case. One might say that Bob's actions are *morally wrong*—that's a normative predicate that presumably picks out a normative property.

A lot of epistemologists think that there is a similar normative/nonnormative distinction in epistemology. If an analysis of justification fails to respect the idea that justification is a normative notion, it is not uncommon to find philosophers willing to reject it.

Richard Foley notes,

> It is an understatement to suggest that there is no agreement among epistemologists as to how to analyze the concept of epistemic justification. But a surprising number of philosophers with radically different approaches to analyzing justified belief seem to agree that the concept of epistemic justification is in some sense a normative concept. The issue is potentially significant because the alleged normativity of epistemic justification has been used to attack prominent analyses of justification.[16]

E. Justification and the truth connection

Another intuition that many epistemologists appeal to is that there is a connection between justification and truth. One common way to introduce the notion of epistemic justification is with the following kind of case:

The Baseball Hitter

Imagine a batter knows that if he believes he will get a hit, he has a better chance of getting a hit. However, he also knows that statistically his overall chances of getting a hit (even when he believes he will get a hit) are about 3 in 10.

Should the batter believe that he is going to get a hit? You may feel pulled in two directions on this one. In one sense, he should. It will be in his practical interests to believe. In another sense, however, it seems that he shouldn't. He doesn't have good reasons to believe that it is *true* that he will get a hit. We can call the former sense of justification *practical justification*. We can call the latter sense, *epistemic justification*. This distinction also highlights something that a lot of epistemologists think we should think about epistemic justification. Namely that there is *some* connection between justification and truth.

As Marian David notes, "Epistemologists of all persuasions tend to invoke the goal of obtaining truth and avoiding error. This goal seems to be of special importance to epistemology. No other goal is invoked as frequently as this one."[17]

David has extracted a couple of apt quotes from Alston and BonJour. I'm using David's versions of the quotes because of the way he simplifies them.

> [Epistemic Justification] has to do with a specifically *epistemic* dimension of evaluation. Beliefs can be evaluated in different ways. One may be more or less prudent, fortunate, or faithful in holding a certain belief. Epistemic justification is different from all that. Epistemic evaluation is undertaken from what we might call "the epistemic point of view" That point of view is defined by the aim at maximizing truth and minimizing falsity in a large body of beliefs . . . For a belief to be justified is for it, somehow, to be awarded high marks relative to that aim. . . . Any concept of epistemic justification is a concept of some condition that is desirable or commendable from the standpoint of the aim at maximizing truth and minimizing falsity. . . .[18]

> What makes us cognitive beings at all is our capacity for belief, and the goal of our distinctively cognitive endeavors is truth: We want our beliefs to correctly and accurately depict the world . . . The basic role of justification is that of a *means* to truth, a more directly attainable mediating link between our subjective starting point and our objective goal . . . If epistemic justification were not conducive to truth in this way, if finding epistemically justified beliefs did not substantially increase the likelihood of finding true ones, then epistemic justification would be irrelevant to our main cognitive goal and of dubious worth . . . The distinguishing characteristic of epistemic justification is thus its essential or internal relation to the cognitive goal of truth. It follows that one's cognitive endeavors are justified only if and to the extent that they are aimed at this goal, which means very roughly that one accepts all and only those beliefs that one has good reasons to think are true.[19]

Conclusion

I think that is a fair characterization of a popular conception of what epistemologists are up to, and I think it is a fair characterization of a popular method for coming to answer those questions. Let's call this the *Standard Method*. There are, however, many challenges to the standard picture. While much of epistemology deals with developing and examining the merits of theories about the nature of knowledge and justification, another large project in epistemology wrestles with several challenges to the standard picture.

Problems for the standard method

Skepticism

One major challenge to the Standard Method is skepticism. Proponents of the Standard Method often start with the assumption that we have knowledge and rational beliefs. They also assume that we have some rough idea as to when we have knowledge and when we have justified beliefs in some large class of what they'll call *obvious cases*. The skeptic thinks that we're not entitled to that assumption.

There are numerous reasons that have been raised for taking skepticism seriously. One is the infinite regress. The basic idea is that in order to be justified in believing something or know something, you must have a reason to believe it. But it seems that you should know or be justified in believing whatever that reason is. A puzzle looms. If for each justified belief you have, you need some further justified belief, then it looks like we're going to need an infinite number of beliefs. But that's impossible, so we must not have any knowledge or justified beliefs. There are four options. You could accept *Infinitism* and maintain that you really can in some sense have an infinite number of reasons that ultimately justifies your beliefs. You could accept *Coherentism* which will accept that all beliefs need additional supporting beliefs and reasons, but that you don't need an infinite number because there is a way in which all of your beliefs can be justified by being in some sense *mutually supporting*. This seems to permit some kind of epistemic circularity, but many argue that the kind of circularity involved is not epistemically bad. The last non-skeptical alternative is *Foundationalism*. The foundationalist maintains that there is a special class of beliefs, foundational beliefs that are justified, but these beliefs are not justified based on inferences from other beliefs or reasons. This book contains a chapter devoted to discussing each of these non-skeptical responses to the regress argument.

The regress represents just one skeptical strategy. There are more. Another popular version of the skeptical challenge invites you to consider the possibility that you're the victim of some massive deception tricked into thinking you're in the real world. Perhaps you are in a very long dream. Perhaps you are being deceived by an evil demon. Perhaps you are a bodiless brain-in-a-vat hooked up to a super-computer. How can you rule these possibilities out? The world would look exactly like this if one of those alternatives were true. Historically, this is perhaps one of the central challenges in epistemology, and epistemologists have spent an enormous amount of intellectual effort trying to respond to this challenge. Of course, there is an entire chapter devoted to discussing recent responses to this kind of challenge. I direct the reader to Richard Fumerton's discussion of skepticism in this volume.

Skepticism about intuitions

Another problem for the Standard Method is that it seems to rely very heavily on intuitions about cases. Any reason that one might have to be worried about reliance on intuitions would be reason to worry about the Standard Method. There are, at least, two.

First, beliefs based on intuition seem like they are not based on experiential evidence at all. They are *a priori.* But *a priori* knowledge is a puzzling sort of knowledge. Many are doubtful that it is even possible to have genuine *a priori* knowledge. It is particularly difficult to understand how one could have robust *a priori* knowledge about the world around us, or of substantive philosophical theses (as opposed to more mundane tautologies like *golden trumpets are trumpets*).[20] The problem of *a priori* knowledge is an ancient philosophical problem. In fact, as we noted above, it was a central issue in epistemology before Gettier.

There is a much more contemporary challenge to the use of intuitions in epistemology (and philosophy in general). There is a very recent movement in philosophy called *Experimental Philosophy.* We often talk about what the folk intuitions *are* about a given thought experiment. Experimental philosophers are actually going out there to empirically test whether or not philosophers engaged in the standard method are right about what the folk intuitions are. They are also looking to see if folk intuitions are influenced by factors that would give us any reason to distrust using intuitions to construct our philosophical theories. The philosophical community seems pretty divided over whether the current results do give us good reasons to give up relying on intuitions when constructing our epistemological theories.[21]

Feminist epistemology

Feminist epistemology raises a serious challenge to the Standard Method of doing epistemology in (at least) three distinct ways. One charge is that there is just much more that the epistemologist could be doing than what the Standard Method seems to do. The Standard Method of doing epistemology seems to assume that what we're doing when we do epistemology is try to understand the nature of knowledge and justification. It also assumes that understanding the nature of knowledge and justification involves attempting to provide satisfactory analyses of both concepts.

One way in which feminist epistemology challenges this traditional picture is from the outside. The idea is that contemporary epistemology has missed an important component to understanding the nature of knowledge. The idea is that knowledge seems to be *socially constructed* and how knowledge is constructed may depend in part on issues related to gender. Consider an analogue. How the government operates and how goods are distributed is a social construction in the following sense. People, collectively, are the determiners of how the government operates and how goods are distributed. Given that, it makes sense to ask if one group's values are getting disproportionate consideration.[22] If knowledge is a social construction, like a government, then it makes sense to raise similar concerns about whether or not one group's values and interests are getting disproportionate consideration in the construction of knowledge.

Another way in which feminist epistemology challenges the traditional picture is from within. As we noted, traditional epistemology, starts with intuitive judgments about cases. These intuitive judgments about cases are *where we start*. From there we develop a theory about what knowledge is (or what justification is). The problem is that where we start may in part be a function of where we're coming from. If gender, for example, plays any role in what our intuitions are about cases—then we have some prima facie reason to be skeptical about relying on the standard method and its results. In fact, the experimental epistemology movement seems to have really gained momentum by testing for precisely this.[23]

Since justification is normative and we often talk about epistemic value, a third way in which feminist epistemology might challenge the traditional picture has to do with thinking about how differences in gender or circumstances might affect or influence what one has to say about normative issues in epistemology or epistemic value.

Consider a parallel to feminist critiques of ethics and political philosophy. One of the driving motivations for feminist theory is the fact that ethical and political considerations seems to supervene on what sorts of things are valuable or what sorts of things are valued by society. However, what things have value and what sorts of things are valued seems to supervene on what the dominant group values and what they have traditionally valued for some long duration of time. If considerations about what is or is not valuable play any role in our epistemological theorizing, then it would be very natural for someone raising feminist critiques in ethics or political philosophy, to raise the same concerns in epistemology.[24]

Epistemic relativism

Proponents of the Standard Method traditionally assume that there are objective epistemic facts. Most proponents of the Standard Method appear to assume from the outset that there are objective matters of fact about what a person is justified in believing or what a person knows in a given situation. An alternative picture is that there really are no mind, independent epistemic facts about what one knows or what one ought to think. Perhaps there is a distinctively Western way of appraising a body of evidence. Perhaps there is a distinctively Eastern way of approaching a body of evidence. Perhaps there is a distinctively *religious* way of approaching a body of evidence. Perhaps the epistemic standards that one accepts could vary based on other features such as race, gender, age, or socioeconomic factors. A common view of among epistemic relativists is that people may have these different ways of approaching evidence, and the epistemically appropriate thing to do is to believe whatever is in accordance with the epistemic standards you accept. But there is no mind-independent fact of the matter as to *which* epistemic standards you should accept. No standard is objectively any better than any others standard.

The reasons for this are parallel to the reasons that have been offered for thinking that relativism is true with respect to other normative fields such as ethics.

Outline of the chapters

This brief historical introduction and discussion about methodology, sets the stage for the rational for this book. Earl Conee surveys a wide range of post-Gettier developments related to the Nature of Knowledge. He discusses Weatherson's recent claim that we ought to consider returning to the traditional analysis because of other theoretical virtues that analysis exemplifies. He discusses Williamson's claim that knowledge is unanalyzable. He also discusses an early version of contextualism, Kornblith's naturalized epistemology, and virtue epistemology.

As I noted, post-Gettier epistemology has focused quite a bit on the nature *and* structure of epistemic justification. I thought it was important to have a companion that devoted substantial space to this particular shift. There are three chapters that each take a position on the *structure* of epistemic justification written by leading defenders of each approach. Daniel Howard-Snyder discusses foundationalism. Jonathan Kvanvig discusses coherentism, and Peter Klein discusses infinitism.

The next three chapters focus on the debate between *internalism* and *externalism*. Rather than have a general internalism vs externalism chapter, I thought it would be better to have overviews of paradigmatic internalist and externalist analyses of justification/warrant. Reliabilism and proper functionalism are the two main externalist theories. Sandford Goldberg surveys the current debate surrounding reliabilism. Alvin Plantinga and Kenneth Boyce survey proper functionalism. One of the paradigmatic internalist theories of epistemic justification is evidentialism. Richard Feldman and Andrew Cullison survey some of the main arguments for and against evidentialism.

I noted that discussion of *a priori* knowledge seemed to drop off after Gettier. For example, in his review of Bon Jour's book on *In Defense of Pure Reason,* Albert Casullo noted that it is the "only available book-length treatment of epistemological issues related to the a priori." Since then, there has been a resurgent interest in the *a priori*. Carrie Jenkin's entry in this volume surveys some puzzles related to the a priori and offers a summary of her novel account of a priori knowledge that aims to provide an account of a priori knowledge for the empirically minded philosopher. The basic idea is that a priori knowledge is empirically adequate, because concept possession is empirically grounded.

The remaining chapters focus on discussions that are to some extent departures from traditional epistemology and in some cases are challenges to it.

Richard Fumerton surveys some of the recent work on skepticism focusing largely on skepticism about justification. Jonathan Matheson articulates a plausible version of an argument for epistemic relativism. He considers some ways in which we might respond to the epistemic relativism challenge and then defends his favored solution.

Another pair of recent trends in epistemology that are related is contextualism and subject-sensitive invariantism. A tacit background assumption of many epistemic theories is that the meaning of the word "knows" is invariant across conversational contexts. It doesn't shift in meaning like an indexical such as "I" or "She" would. It's also not context sensitive the way that "Tall" or "Flat" might be. Contextualism rejects this. Contextualism argues that the word "knows" does behave more like a context sensitive term. And that shifts in meaning can occur when a person is entertaining the possibility of error. Contextualists argue that we can appeal to this kind of context sensitivity to respond to skeptical worries.

Subject-sensitive invariantists argue that we can preserve the above benefits of contextualism without embracing the linguistic thesis, if we acknowledge that whether or not someone knows something can depend on apparently non-epistemic facts. As I noted earlier, Stanley argues that there are pairs of cases that support this view that knowledge can depend on the practical stakes for being wrong. E. J. Coffman's chapter gives us an exposition of both Contextualism and Subject-Sensitive Invariantism and critically discusses the motivations for each view.

Another recent trend worth noting in the history epistemology is the explosion of literature that brings formal elements of logic and calculus to bear on classic epistemological puzzles and problems. The movement is called *formal epistemology*. Some might view formal epistemology as a challenge to the Standard Method. As Gregory Wheeler notes in his chapter in this volume, "There is, after all, plenty of epistemology that is not informed by formal methods, and plenty of epistemologists seem committed to keeping it that way. Giants have made their mark with little more than commonsense and a smidgeon of logic." In his chapter, Wheeler sets out to answer the question "Why be formal?" and argues that contemporary epistemologists ought to add more formal tools to their tool-kit. His defense is two-pronged. He notes that significant progress has been made in other disciplines by introducing formal models, and that by analogy it is reasonable to suspect that progress might be made in epistemology. He then offers two examples about how applying formal tools and using formal models actually does seem to illuminate some classic epistemological problems.

The above-mentioned chapters survey some core issues in epistemology, but there are a wide range of interesting new directions.

As I noted earlier, one very recent and controversial trend is experimental philosophy. Experimental philosophy brings the resources and methods of social science to bear on philosophical questions. One very popular method is to survey populations to learn more about the sources of intuitions and philosophical judgments. Some argue that the Standard Method's reliance on intuitions has been called into question by some of this recent empirical research. James Beebe explains what experimental epistemology is, discusses some of the recent important results in experimental epistemology, and critically discusses some objections to the experimental epistemology program.

Another new direction in epistemology is a growing interest in *epistemic value.* Dennis Whitcomb offers some highlights of what he calls the *value turn* in epistemology. He discusses three motivations for the value turn, and then briefly surveys three branches of the value turn.

Finally, it is curious that the concept *wisdom* has not received substantive attention in contemporary epistemology. Philosophy means *love of wisdom* and *wisdom* seems like it's some kind of epistemic concept. Recently, however, there has been a growing interest among contemporary epistemologists. In her essay, Sharon Ryan surveys some candidate accounts of wisdom including her own. After discussing why she is dissatisfied with them, she offers and defends a new account of wisdom.

Notes

1 Locke. *Essay I,* 1, 2.
2 See, e.g., Baldwin's entry on Epistemology in the *Dictionary of Philosophy and Psychology* (1901, 333–5) for a very Lockean characterization of epistemology.
3 See, e.g., Baird, F. and Kaufmann, W. *Modern Philosophy,* 2nd edn (Prentice-Hall, ix). It's also worth noting that Martinich, Alhoff, and Vaida make rationalism (and the distinction between rationalism and empiricism) a primary focal of their Early Modern textbook. See A. Martinich et al., *Early Modern Philosophy: Essential Readings with Commentary* (Oxford: Blackwell, 2007, 1).
4 Quine (1969, 74).
5 It should be noted that this is not one of Gettier's original examples, but I use this because it is a bit more straightforward than some of the original examples.
6 There is some reason to suspect that Plato was aware of the fact that knowledge was not justified true belief, and Russell also comes up with an example.

7 Nozick (1981).

8 Goldman (1967).

9 Armstrong (1973).

10 See Theatetus 101.

11 These examples come from Stanley (2005a, 3–4). I'm not listing all of Stanley's examples here. I don't think it is necessary for the purposes of this chapter to go through all of Stanley's examples.

12 See, e.g., Coffman's discussion of contextualism and subject-sensitive invariantism in this volume. See also Beebe's exposition on experimental epistemology.

13 See Kvanvig (2003) for a detailed application of this strategy.

14 See Williamson (2002).

15 Feldman (1995, 1).

16 Fumerton (2001, 49) (in Steup 2001).

17 David (2001, 151) (in Steup 2001).

18 Alston 1985, 83–4 from David p. 151.

19 BonJour 1985, 7–8 from David p. 151.

20 See Jenkins for a recent account of a priori knowledge.

21 See Beebe in this volume for a recent discussion of this.

22 In fact, some (Nelson 1993) have argued that the standard method is fundamentally misguided because knowledge is fundamentally a property that a *community* bears to a proposition rather than fundamentally a property that an individual bears to a proposition.

23 Beebe's exposition of experimental epistemology in this volume discusses recent experimental work suggesting that gender might influence intuitions about classic epistemological thought experiments.

24 While this volume does not have a separate chapter devoted to feminist philosophy, it is worth noting that the experimental epistemology chapter does a good job of highlighting and drawing out one major concern that a feminist critique of the Standard Method might raise. The chapter by Whitcomb in this volume also highlights the recent "Value Turn" in epistemology. This chapter highlights a wide range of ways in which questions about what is epistemically valuable are increasingly being recognized as important to epistemology. This gives major traction to another feminist critique of traditional epistemology. It's very easy to see how a feminist critique of a particular area can be raised when questions about what's valuable are central to that area. Also, the chapter on epistemic relativism takes seriously ideas about varying epistemic standards and what we should think about the nature of epistemic facts that feminist epistemologists have raised.

References

Alston, W. P. 1985 (1989). "Concepts of Epistemic Justification," The Monist 68. Reprinted in "Epistemic Justification: Essays in the Theory of Knowledge." Ithaca, NY: Cornell University Press.

Armstrong, D. M. 1973. *Belief, Truth and Knowledge.* CUP Archive.

BonJour, L. 1985. *The Structure of Empirical Knowledge.* Cambridge, MA: Harvard University Press.

David, M. 2001. "Truth as the Epistemic Goal." In Steup (2001).

Feldman, R. 1995. "In Defence of Closure." *The Philosophical Quarterly* 45: 487–94.

Fumerton, R. 2001 "Epistemic Justification and Normativity", in Steup (2001), 49–60.

Goldman, A. 1979. "What is Justified Belief?" In G. Pappas, ed., *Justification and Knowledge.* Dordrecht: D. Reidel, pp. 1–23.

Kvanvig, J. 2003. *The Value of Knowledge and the Pursuit of Understanding.* Cambridge: Cambridge University Press.

Nelson, L. H. 1993. "Epistemological Communities." *Feminist Epistemologies.*121–60.

Nozick, R. 1981. *Philosophical Explanations.* Cambridge, MA: Belknap Press.

Quine, W. V. (1969), "Epistemology Naturalized" in Ontological Relativity and Other Essays. New York: Columbia.

Stanley, J. 2005a. *Knowledge and Practical Interests.* Oxford: Oxford University Press.

Williamson, T. 2002. *Knowledge and its Limits.* New York: Oxford University Press.

1

The Nature of Knowledge

Earl Conee

Background

Factual knowledge is knowledge of a fact. A fact is a truth. Thus, one necessary condition for having factual knowledge (hereafter just "knowledge") is that what is known is true. Knowledge is a cognitive relation to a fact. To cognize a fact is at least to take it to be true, or in other words, to believe it. Thus, another condition on factual knowledge is believing the known fact. Some true beliefs are mere hunches that are borne out, or accurate guesses. These true beliefs are not known to be true. In contrast, when a true belief is accepted from a perspective that enables the person to be aware of its factual character, it is knowledge. A perspective like this is one that indicates conclusively to the person that the belief is true. What does this indicating is traditionally called justification for the belief. Thus, knowledge requires having justification for a belief that is true.

According to the traditional conception, these three conditions are sufficient as well. That is, it is not just obvious that whenever someone has a justified true belief, the person knows the belief to be true. But neither does knowledge obviously require something more.

In 1963 Edmund Gettier offered examples of justified true beliefs that are not known.[1] Here is a somewhat embellished version of one of them.

E1. Smith has ample evidence to regard Jones as a Ford owner. Smith has observed Jones driving an impeccable vintage Ford for years and Smith has frequently heard Jones expressing his joy about owning it. Smith's other close friend is Brown, who has been traveling throughout Europe. Smith has no definite information about where Brown is now. On a whim, Smith uses his justified belief about Jones owning a Ford to infer something about an arbitrary European location for Brown:

D. Either Jones owns a Ford or Brown is in Barcelona.

Smith sees that D has to be true, given that Jones owns a Ford. D is thus quite well justified for Smith. But it turns out that D is true only because Brown happens to be in Barcelona. In a shocking development, unsuspected by Smith, Jones's prized Ford has been seized by creditors.

D is a truth that Smith is justified in believing. Only D's second disjunct makes it true, though. Smith has no indication of this truth. It seems quite clear that Smith does not not know D for a fact. It is contrary to what he has excellent reason to think about why D is true.

Kindred examples of justified true belief without knowledge proliferated, illustrating what became known as "the Gettier problem." In fact, decades earlier Bertrand Russell had described an example that makes for another illustration.[2] Here is a somewhat embellished version.

> E2. In order to find out the time, Robinson checks a public clock that is celebrated for its beauty and reliability. The clock is right, but only by coincidence. In an unprecedented breakdown, the clock stopped exactly twelve hours before. So Robinson's checking happens to occur at the exact time on which the clock is stuck. Still, since Robinson is familiar with the clock's esteemed status and has no reason to suspect the breakdown, he is justified in relying on the time displayed by the clock.

Robinson has a justified true belief as to what the time is, but he does not know it. No one knows the time just by consulting a clock that has long been stopped.

A common initial reaction to such examples is to suspect that the justification involved is not strong enough for knowledge. For instance, in E1 Smith's justification for believing D depends on his justification for his false belief that Jones owns a Ford. Thus, his grounds for that belief allow it to be untrue. It might be thought that this failure to guarantee the truth of the belief that is supposed to be justified creates the problem.

Not so. Here is a variant of E1 where Smith has a justification guaranteeing the truth of what it justifies.

> E3. Smith has the same strong grounds for his false belief that Jones owns a Ford. Now Smith infers something else. He has begun to study formal logic. He has heard a thesis about logical implication that interests him, though he has not yet found out whether the thesis is true. It is this:
>
> L. If one proposition logically implies another, then anything that implies the one implies anything that the other implies.

Thinking about L, Smith infers the following from his belief that Jones owns a Ford:

D2. Either Jones owns a Ford or L is true.

Smith knows enough logic to see the validity of this inference.

Smith has legitimately inferred D2 from a justified belief. But as in E1, Jones does not own a Ford. It is only L, the unjustified disjunct in D2, that makes D2 true. Though Smith does not realize this, L is a truth of logic. A justification "guarantees" the truth of a proposition when it is impossible for the person to have the justification without the proposition being true. In this sense, any justification at all for D2 guarantees its truth. D2's second disjunct is a logical truth that L could not be untrue and its inevitable truth ensures the truth of D2 as a whole. So Smith's justification for D2 guarantees its truth. Yet Smith does not know D2. Thus, even requiring a justification to guarantee the truth of what it justifies does not make justified true belief sufficient for knowledge.

None of the Gettier examples suggest that justified true belief is unnecessary for knowledge. The early research on the topic largely focused on finding a fourth condition, a condition that is also necessary for knowledge and is not met in the Gettier examples. Multiple promising approaches to solving the Gettier problem were developed. Some of them supplemented the justification condition and some replaced it. New problem cases challenged each approach. No consensus on a solution emerged.

Renewal

In the last decade of the twentieth century and on into the new millennium, knowledge has received renewed attention in epistemology. The focus of most of this work is not on the Gettier problem, though usually it is addressed in one way or another. Several exciting ideas about the nature of knowledge have emerged. We will consider five of them in the remainder of this chapter.

Ultratraditionalism for a new reason

Exposition

Brian Weatherson points out that the idea that justified true belief is necessary and sufficient for knowledge has considerable theoretical appeal.[3] There is unity and simplicity in the conjunction of these three conditions. Also, the conditions are jointly met in an enormous variety of cases where there is knowledge and at least one of the conditions is not met in an enormous variety of cases where there is not knowledge. What stands in the way of identifying knowledge with justified true belief are the intuitive judgments about Gettier cases. Weatherson makes the radical suggestion that perhaps these intuitive judgments are overridden by the theoretical virtues of the justified true belief account of knowledge.

Weatherson does not advocate ruthlessly abandoning intuitive judgments for the sake of having a simple theory of knowledge. He holds that one of the basic theoretical desiderata is to accommodate as many intuitions about the phenomenon as possible. Some such theoretical factor that can at least counterbalance simplicity is mandatory, if the justified true belief theory itself is to have a chance. The rival theory that mere true belief is knowledge has an advantage in simplicity over the justified true belief theory, and the belief-only theory is even simpler. What most clearly disqualifies these rivals is their drastically poorer showing by the test of intuitive judgments about examples.

Weatherson does hold that simplicity considerations can outweigh some contrary intuitions, particularly if there is a good explanation available of a mistake that gives rise to the contrary intuitions. He focuses on a certain sort of simplicity involving a type of naturalness. He suggests that justified true belief is a "natural property." This naturalness is not defined, but the idea can be sketched out as follows. A natural property is a real part of the framework of the universe and not just a classification that happens to suit human interests. The fundamental properties of physics, such as charge and mass, are the clearest examples of natural properties. Biological classifications like having lungs and engaging in photosynthesis also qualify. In contrast are classifications made significant by contingent human activities, such as the property of being a coin and the property of being a frequently discussed person. Nearer the extreme are properties exemplified by assortments, such as the things that have the disjunctive property of being either an animal or a symphony, and the yet more diversely exemplified property of being neither an animal nor a symphony.

Weatherson's proposal is this. Justified true belief is a conjunction of properties that is natural enough for us to have singled out the combination with the term "knowledge." There is no comparably natural combination of properties that as closely accords with our inclinations to attribute knowledge. The conditions on knowledge that have been offered as solutions to the Gettier problem are all considerably less natural and not considerably better at matching intuitive judgments about knowledge.

Doubt

This proposal stands in need of an explanation for the mistake made by the many who find the Gettier cases convincing. The proposal asserts that no other natural enough combination of properties comes close enough to matching our intuitively made knowledge attributions. But this does not explain why so many deny knowledge in the particular circumstances of the Gettier cases, in spite of recognizing the presence of the purportedly most natural combination of justified true belief.

Also, the proposal seems to underrate the theoretical assets of some rivals. For instance, a simple version of one early fourth condition is this:

R. The justification for any known proposition does not justify anything untrue.[4]

Adding R to justified true belief appears not to make for any significant unnaturalness. R uses only the properties of justification and truth that are already included, employing them in a simple logical combination of quantification and negation. Yet adding R does a lot better with intuitive judgments. The standard Gettier examples all involve a justified falsehood. In E1, E2, and E3, for instance, there are the justified falsehoods that Jones owns a Ford and that the public clock is working. So requiring R disqualifies the justified true beliefs in those examples from being knowledge. Thus, by Weatherson's standards for evaluating theories, this four-condition account seems to outdo the justified true belief theory.[5]

Contextual infallibility

Exposition

David Lewis proposes a theory of knowledge that has as a principle aim to accommodate two sorts of data.[6] The first sort of data tells us that ordinary people know a great many ordinary beliefs, and that experts know a great deal more. This knowledge extends from the simplest facts of perceptual observation to the findings achieved by advanced science. The other sort of data is less familiar to nonphilosophers. It includes the fact that there are skeptical arguments that successfully describe possibilities of our actual beliefs being massively in error. For instance, there is the Cartesian possibility of an extremely powerful evil demon who is deceiving us to a maximal extent. Lewis holds that we cannot "eliminate" these possibilities. That is, there is a chance, however slight, that we are in fact making all of these errors. Yet Lewis finds it clear that knowledge requires no chance of error. So apparently this latter data tells us that we know nearly nothing, at most.

Remarkably, Lewis seeks to reconcile the conflict between these two sorts of data with a theory of knowledge that consistently accommodates both. The theory has two importantly different components. One states a certain sort of condition on knowledge. Anyone who can be correctly said to know something does so by meeting an appropriate version of the condition.

The other main component of Lewis's theory consists in claims about how knowledge is rightly attributed. Lewis holds that different versions of his condition on knowledge are made applicable by certain aspects of the situations where knowledge is attributed.

The condition on knowledge is fairly straightforward. The idea is roughly that knowing a proposition consists in having evidence that guarantees its truth. Lewis develops the idea as follows: Someone's "basic evidence" is the ultimate data that the person has to go on, in order to find out what is true. In Lewis's preferred view, our basic evidence consists in our perceptual experiences and memories, but his theory allows other forms of basic evidence, such as intuitive impressions or innate inclinations to believe. The possibility of a proposition is "eliminated" by someone's basic evidence when it is impossible for the person to have the same basic evidence with that proposition true. In these terms, the condition for knowledge is this:

LK. S knows P iff S's basic evidence eliminates every possibility in which not-P.

LK might seem to be a single unambiguous necessary and sufficient condition for knowledge. But according to Lewis, it is not. He understands the term "every" in LK to be subject to various restrictions, depending on its context of use. As Lewis puts it, his theory is to be understood as though a certain whispered qualification were added to LK—every last not-P possibility is eliminated by the basic evidence, *except for the not-P possibilities that we are properly ignoring.*

Explaining this qualification is the second component of Lewis's theory. The second component consists in claims about what determines correct knowledge attributions. This part of the theory is an instance of an approach to knowledge that arose in the 1980s, attributor contextualism. In the whispered qualification of LK, the "we" who may properly ignore possibilities are those who attribute knowledge of P to S. Attributor contextualism holds that part of what makes a "knowledge" attribution correct is the context in which the attribution is made. Different sizes count as "small," depending on whether it is being used in a discussion of plants or planets. According to Lewis, "knowledge" attributions are likewise dependent on the context of the attribution. Some differences in the contexts in which someone is said to "know" P affect which not-P possibilities it is proper for the attributor to ignore.

Lewis proposes several rules as those that govern which possibilities an attributor can properly ignore. Three of the rules are of special interest here. One is the following:

> Rule of Actuality. An actual truth is never a properly ignored possibility.

In conjunction with LK, the Rule of Actuality has the effect of requiring anything that is correctly said to be a known proposition to be true. An untruth could not be known, because its true negation would always stand as a possibility not properly ignored—no basic evidence eliminates any truth because the evidence and the truth are both actual.

> The second especially interesting rule is this.

> Rule of Resemblance. Possibilities that saliently resemble any that are not properly ignored are themselves not properly ignored.

This second rule is thought by Lewis to account for the absence of knowledge in Gettier cases. For instance in E2, the public clock example, there is a salient possibility that the clock has the same reading while it is stopped, although the clock reading is incorrect because the time is in fact earlier. This possibility perfectly resembles actuality in its having Robinson see the same clock stopped at the same time. Robinson's basic evidence does not eliminate this possibility because it would give him the same perceptual experiences while he had the same memories. Since this is an uneliminated possibility that the Rule of Resemblance makes it improper for us to ignore, it would not be true for us to say that Robinson knows the time.

> The last rule of special interest is this.

> Rule of Attention. Possibilities that are not in fact being ignored, because we are paying attention to them, are not properly being ignored.

The Rule of Attention is used by Lewis to explain the data concerning skeptical arguments. The rule tells us that when we are paying attention to skeptical possibilities, such as the possible existence of a maximally deceptive evil demon, we are not properly ignoring these possibilities. So any proposition that could be true, along with our having our basic evidence and this demon possibility holding, is not eliminated by our basic evidence. Hence, by LK—including its whispered qualification—we do not know any proposition that is untrue anywhere among those uneliminated, not-properly-ignored possibilities. This makes for a chance that those propositions are actually untrue. All of our ordinary external world beliefs are untrue somewhere among such possibilities of our pervasive deception. So under circumstances in which we are attending to skeptical possibilities, as in an epistemological examination of skeptical arguments, we do not correctly attribute to anyone knowledge of any of those ordinary beliefs. As Lewis puts it, "That is how epistemology destroys knowledge."

Lewis adds immediately: "But it does so only temporarily." Mostly, the Rule of Attention does not keep skeptical possibilities from being properly ignored, since mostly we are not attending to them. Lewis's other rules for proper ignoring also allow that we are usually properly ignoring these possibilities. This enables Lewis to use LK to affirm the other main type of data for his theory. According to LK with its whispered qualification, on the usual occasions when skeptical alternatives are properly ignored, we do indeed know a lot.

Doubt

One problem for Lewis's theory of knowledge is that the basic evidence gets a free pass. Any fact that must obtain whenever the basic evidence exists is automatically known, according to the theory. This is true because the basic evidence, entirely apart from what is properly ignored, eliminates the negations of such facts. Yet this seems insufficient for us really to know all such facts.

For instance, suppose that our basic evidence includes our perceptual experiences. Suppose too that they are physical in nature. In particular, suppose that every possible situation in which such experiences exist involves electrochemical events. If so, then according to LK it is automatically known by all who have perceptual experiences that there are electrochemical events. It does not matter whether they have considered this proposition or whether they are even able to understand it. It does not matter whether they have been given reasons to doubt that such events exist, reasons to which they have no counter. The actual entailment by the basic evidence that electrochemical events exist is all that LK requires for knowledge of this. Yet it seems not to be that easy to know such facts.

It might be doubted that there are any such hidden necessary consequences of our basic evidence. Even if not, there is a related problem for the theory. Suppose again that our perceptual experiences are part of our basic evidence.

E4. Smith is given strong reason to doubt that he is undergoing the experience of feeling warm. Manifestly expert neuroscientists assure Smith that their brain scanning equipment reveals him to be the victim of a peculiar illusion. The illusion makes it appear to him that he is feeling warm when he is not. In fact, though, the experts are deceiving Smith about this. He actually is having the experience of feeling warm.

With the impressive sort of counterevidence that Smith has in E4, he has serious reason to doubt that he is feeling warm. Yet he is in fact feeling that way and the feeling is part of his basic evidence. So according to LK, Smith knows that he is feeling warm in E4. That is problematic, because it seems that knowledge of basic evidence, like all other knowledge, can be prevented by having reasonable doubts about it.

Naturalistic antitraditionalism

Exposition

Hilary Kornblith holds that knowledge is best understood to be a kind of natural phenomenon, like aluminum and digestion.[7] Accordingly, just as with other natural kinds, knowledge is rightly studied by the methods of natural science.

The sort of natural kind that Kornblith takes knowledge to be is a homeostatic cluster of properties. These clusters are properties that strongly tend to be present together because their combined presence is mutually supporting.

To identify the cluster of properties that constitute the natural kind of knowledge, Kornblith looks to work by cognitive ethologists. He finds them making knowledge attributions both to explain individual animal behavior, such as that of a particular piping plover, and to explain general species behavior, such as navigational success by the dolphin. He hypothesizes that what unites the cases to which this knowledge is attributed, particularly in explanations of species success, is the presence of true beliefs that are attuned to their environment. On this basis, Kornblith proposes that knowledge turns out to be reliably produced true belief.

In making this proposal about knowledge as it is found in nature, Kornblith does not merely report findings of the empirical research he cites. First, there is the question of which empirical research to study, in order to find scientific facts about the knowledge that epistemologists seek to understand. Cognitive ethologists are not the only scientists to use the term "knowledge" in their work.

Others include computer scientists, cognitive psychologists, and sociologists. Only if all of these scientists study a single natural phenomenon to which they apply the term is it safe to look for the scientific candidate for knowledge in just one line of scientific research, such as ethology.

Second, in the animal research that Kornblith cites, the scientists do not say that they have discovered animal knowledge and it turns out to be reliably produced true belief. They are never cited as using the word "reliable" or any synonym. Instead, the scientists are cited as making knowledge attributions on the basis of individual and species-wide behavior, such as a piping plover luring a potential predator away from a nest and the success of the dolphin at successfully navigating migratory pathways. Some scientists are also cited as making evolutionary claims about the adaptive development of mechanisms of perception and information storage. It is Kornblith's contention that reliably produced true belief best explains the ethological attributions of knowledge, especially in the accounts of species-wide behavior that has apparent evolutionary advantages.

Thus, in arguing for his view about what knowledge is, Kornblith relies on empirical hypotheses of its own. One of them is that the presence of a certain trio of properties—reliably produced true belief—explains some scientifically discovered facts about behavior and evolution. Another empirical hypothesis of Kornblith's is that this trio forms a homeostatic cluster to which the scientists are referring when attributing knowledge and knowledge-entailing processes such as perception.

Doubt

Here are some concerns about this view: First, other combinations of properties may give a better explanation of the relevant evolutionary successes than the threesome that Kornblith offers. For instance, instead of the evolutionary success resulting from having true beliefs produced by a mechanism that reliably produces truths, the success may be better explained as resulting from beliefs produced by a mechanism that reliably produces safety-enhancing beliefs. True belief would be a common output of this sort of mechanism, because safety-enhancing beliefs are often true ones. But a reliably accurate mechanism need not best promote survival. For instance, a mechanism for believing so as to flee at any sudden sign of a predator may not yield reliably true beliefs, because of frequent false alarms. Yet it may be safer and not otherwise too costly. If so, then this sort of mechanism is potentially better for survival than one reliably delivering truths. The latter may be too dangerous. So perhaps what was actually selected for is belief that is reliably safety enhancing rather than reliably true. At least, this is an empirical question that the research Kornblith cites leaves open.

Second, some reliably produced true beliefs seem to be Gettier cases. For instance, in E1 Smith's reasons for D, his belief that either Jones owns a Ford or Brown is in Barcelona, consist in his observations of Jones's Ford owner-like conduct and ownership claims, plus Smith's legitimately inferring D from the proposition, supported by these observations, that Jones owns a Ford. This sort of rational basis of strong observational backing and good inference seems reliably to lead to true beliefs. Yet we are disinclined to attribute to Smith knowledge of D. Thus, the view that reliably produced true belief is knowledge does not fit with this knowledge-withholding inclination. In the animal examples that Kornblith mentions there are no Gettier cases. But they can easily arise among animals.

> E5. A bird flees following its perception of a threatening motion. A gust of wind happened to move a tree branch almost exactly when and where an unperceived predator was launching an attack on the bird.

To the extent that birds appear to have justified beliefs, it appears that in E5 the bird has a justified true belief about a threat, but not knowledge of it. Kornblith gives no reason for thinking that in a case like E5 cognitive ethologists would attribute knowledge of a threat to the bird, merely because it is a reliably formed true belief. He gives no empirical reason for thinking that there is not some other homeostatic cluster which is present whenever ethologists would attribute knowledge, while being absent in Gettier cases. In short, the cited empirical research gives no distinctive support to the view that knowledge is just reliably formed true belief.

More fundamentally, it may be that the knowledge that epistemologists seek to understand is not a kind that is found in nature and studied by empirical science. Instead, the knowledge of philosophical interest may be relevantly like the mathematical relation of addition. Many sorts of supplementations and accumulations in nature are rightly called "additions"—as when new cells are grown by an organism, more sand is heaped on a sand pile, and so forth. But the arithmetical relation of addition is not a natural kind that is shared by the "additions" in nature. Sometimes many water droplets "add" together to form one big drop. This empirical fact does not refute the arithmetical fact that many added together never sum to one. These "additions" in nature are not instances of mathematical addition. They are similar enough to justify using the same term. The differences are usually harmless enough to yield no confusion or error.

Similarly, various lines of empirical research have as their subject something rightly called "knowledge." But this may be true in virtue of sufficient similarities of one or more empirical phenomena to the knowledge that is of epistemological interest, while there are differences that are sufficiently harmless in practice. For instance, perhaps "knowledge" that is of some empirical interest requires only true belief formed with a reliability that is sufficient for some sort of practical success, while the knowledge of epistemological interest requires some high level of justification. At least, the empirical research that Kornblith discusses is compatible with this sort of possibility.

Nonnaturalistic antitraditionalism

Exposition

Timothy Williamson sees no good reason to think that knowledge has any analysis into constituent necessary and sufficient conditions.[8] He notes the general failure to find acceptable analyses of philosophically important concepts. He also notes that the proposed solutions to the Gettier problem have their own counterexamples with no sign of a developing success.

On the positive side, Williamson makes an extensive and impressive case for the conclusion that knowledge is a mental state. This is not the uncontroversial thought that knowing includes being in the mental state of believing. The claim is that the whole state of knowing is a mental state, just like fearing and imagining.

This conclusion is initially questionable, because typically what is known is some fact that obtains in the environment external to the knower. This being so, it is easy to think that knowing any such fact is partly external, in virtue of the state including as relation to an external fact. In contrast, it seems that mental states are altogether internal.

Williamson argues powerfully that knowledge does not factorize into an internal mental component in conjunction with an external component. So the attractive thought about internal and external parts of knowledge cannot be spelled out in that way, if Williamson's argument is successful.

Suppose that knowledge is a mental state. Williamson sees as one payoff a new objection of a traditional argument for external world skepticism. The traditional argument goes as follows: For any of our true external world beliefs, there is a possible situation in which we are mentally the same, and yet the belief is false. These possible situations are supposed to be illustrated by skeptical scenarios, such as our being a victim of a deceptive demon or a mad scientist brain manipulator. Yet knowledge requires our having some way to tell what is true. Being able to tell what is true is a mental capability. So if it is possible for us to be mentally the same as we actually are, while any given external world belief is false, then we cannot tell whether or not it is true. Hence, we do not have knowledge of any external world belief.

If knowledge is a mental state, though, then this sort of skeptical reasoning has a problem. It seems to assume that we can hold fixed our entire mental condition and proceed to investigate what propositions we can tell to be true. Only the latter propositions are eligible to be our knowledge. But holding fixed of the mental before determining what is known cannot be done, if our knowledge is included in the mental. If it is, then for any of our true external world beliefs that are in fact known by us, there is no possible situation in which we are in the same mental states without this knowledge.

Williamson contends that the most that the skeptic can show with skeptical scenarios is that there are possible situations in which we have false external world beliefs that are indiscriminable by us from situations in which we have knowledge of the external facts. Willaimson contends that this lack of discriminability does not show that we lack knowledge. He proposes that knowledge is clearly not always discriminable by the knower from false belief. Someone might go from knowing who is President to falsely believing it, in virtue of an as-yet-undisclosed assassination.

Another of Williamson's important contentions about knowledge is the claim that the evidence that any given person has is identical to the person's knowledge (E = K). Again we confront an initially questionable thesis. Some of our evidence seems to consist in our being in various perceptual states without our knowing propositions that assert that we are in them, if only because we do not often form beliefs in propositions about our experiences. And it seems initially that the knowledge that is at the outermost limits of what our evidence enables us to know depends on our evidence rather than providing us with any. Yet these appearances may be deceptive. Williamson argues extensively and impressively for the E = K thesis.

Suppose that E = K. If so, then we have a new objection to another skeptical argument. The argument goes much the same as the previous one, except that it is addressed to our evidence rather than to our entire mental condition: We know only what our evidence enables us to tell to be true. In skeptical scenarios we have the same evidence that we actually have, while our actual external world beliefs are false. So we cannot tell by our evidence that these beliefs are true. Hence, we do not know the truth of our external world beliefs.

Here the skeptical argument seems to assume that we can hold fixed our evidence and separately investigate what it enables us to know. Yet if $E = K$, then this separation is not possible, since our evidence consists in all that we know. So this assumption is not true.

Doubt

The skeptic might try to retrench. The skeptic might revise the first argument and hold that it is our *apparent* mental condition that must give us such knowledge as we can have. The thought would be that those appearances are all that we have to go on ultimately, beyond mental differences that are indiscernible to us, and so the appearances are ultimately what must enable us to tell what is true. The skeptic might revise the second argument and hold that it is our *apparent* evidence that must give us such knowledge as we have, since what appears to us to be our evidence is our only ultimate means for telling what is true. It is worth pondering whether the resulting versions of the skeptical arguments restore their force.

It is also worth pondering whether our mental condition, or our evidence, must have been different, were a belief to have been false, in order for it to give us what we need from it in order to know that the belief is true. Perhaps we do not need this sort of "telling difference." Perhaps we need only that they support the truth of the beliefs strongly enough. And perhaps they do this supporting, whether or not the beliefs are true. If so, then the skeptical arguments fail at that point in any case.

More exposition

Although Williamson denies that knowledge has any analysis, he does offer an informative account of what knowledge is. Unlike the justified true belief analysis and proposed solutions to the Gettier problem, Williamson's account is not intended to offer separately necessary conditions for knowledge that are jointly sufficient. It is supposed to provide a necessary equivalent of knowledge that illuminates it. Here is the account in a few words, to be explained immediately below:

WA. Knowledge is the most general factive stative propositional attitude.

Here is what WA means. Propositional attitudes are mental relations to propositional contents, such as believing and wondering. A factive attitude is one that has only factual propositions as contents, such as being glad that something is so, or being disappointed that something is so. A stative attitude is a mental condition rather than a change. Stative attitudes are illustrated by having something a memory, in contrast to actively recalling, and by being sorry, in contrast to coming to regret. Lastly, what Williamson means, by saying that knowledge is "the most general" stative factive propositional attitude, is that knowledge is the one that is implied by all of the others. That is, each stative factive propositional attitude, such as being content about some fact or resenting some fact, implies knowing that fact.

One asset that Williamson attributes to WA is of considerable interest. It is clear that having knowledge is often important to us. Williamson contends that WA provides an explanation of this importance. Here is the explanation:

> On this account, the importance of knowing to us becomes as intelligible as the importance of truth. Factive mental states are important to us as states whose essence includes a matching between mind and world and knowledge is important to us as the most general factive stative attitude.[9]

More doubt

This explanation seems problematic. The factive nature of knowledge is important to us. But knowledge matters more to us than a belief we have that happens to be true. Yet all of our true beliefs have the asserted importance of being "states whose essence includes a matching between mind and world."[10]

The rest of the explanation seems not to describe anything that makes knowledge matter more. First, that knowledge is a state seems evaluatively neutral. Our being in some state seems no more important to us than our undergoing an event or process.

Second, the status of knowledge as a propositional attitude is a neutral classificatory fact. Knowledge shares this classification with curiosity and doubt. It has no apparent importance to us on its own.

Finally, KA asserts that knowledge is maximally "general," meaning that the other factive stative propositional attitudes all entail knowledge of their contents. This generality too seems not to aid our understanding of what makes knowledge matter to us. The generality implies something interesting about the other factive stative propositional attitudes—they entail knowing their contents.

But what makes knowledge itself matter to us is something for which knowledge is sufficient. This importance that knowledge brings with it cannot be identified by specifying some of the things that are sufficient for knowledge.

Virtue

Exposition

John Greco explains knowledge in terms of the exercise of intellectual virtue. His theory addresses the Gettier problem directly.[11] It is one of two problems that his theory of knowledge is intended to solve. The other one is the lottery problem. That problem can be illustrated as follows:

> E6. You know that you have just one ticket in a fair lottery of a million tickets with just one winner. This knowledge is an extremely strong probabilistic justification for the conclusion that your ticket is not the winner. You believe on this probabilistic basis, that your ticket is not the winner. You are right.

It seems clear that in E6 you do not know that your ticket is not the winner. Yet it seems to be a justified true belief, and unlike Gettier cases there is no surprising fact that is hidden to you about the truth of the matter. So why are not such lottery beliefs known? This is the lottery problem.

Greco's theory of knowledge has two distinctive elements. One is a version of attributor contextualism. The other consists in conditions for knowledge that Greco's theory requires to be met by any true knowledge attribution. Interplay between these two elements is supposed to solve the Gettier problem and the lottery problem.

Greco offers three conditions as necessary and sufficient for knowledge. Here they are:

> GK. S knows p iff
>
> 1. S's believing p is *subjectively* justified, in that S's believing p is a result of dispositions that S manifests when S is trying to believe the truth,
>
> 2. S's believing p is *objectively* justified, in that the dispositions that result in S's believing p make S reliable in believing p, that is, the dispositions that result in S's believing p constitute intellectual abilities, or powers, or virtues, and
>
> 3. S believes the truth regarding p *because* S is reliable in believing p, that is, the intellectual abilities (or powers or virtues) that result in S's believing p are

an important necessary part of the total set of causal factors that give rise to S's believing the truth regarding p.[12]

In fewer words, GK amount to this. S knows p when S comes to believe the truth concerning p as a result of exercising an intellectually virtuous disposition that S employs in seeking truth, and a causal explanation of why it is a true belief essentially and importantly includes the fact that it results from this disposition.

It will be helpful in understanding Greco's position to see that GK, on its own, solves neither the Gettier problem nor the lottery problem. In our Gettier case E1, for instance, Smith quite reasonably infers the true disjunction D: either Jones owns a Ford or Brown is in Barcelona. Though it is not obvious just what intellectual virtues Smith employs here, it is clear that this conclusion is well reasoned. It is also pretty clear that reasoning that manifests the same dispositions will rarely lead to false beliefs. E1 meets condition 3 of GK as well. An important necessary part of a causal explanation of Smith's having the true belief in D is the intellectually virtuous thinking he employed. Had he not done that, he would not have gotten the preliminary Ford ownership belief and gone on to believe D.[13] At least, the three conditions of GK are as clearly met in E1 as they are in the following example of knowledge.

> E7. The facts are almost exactly as in E1. They differ just enough so that, while things are the same from Smith's perspective, Jones does own a Ford. Jones avoided its seizure by creditors by getting a loan that was denied him in E1. Smith uses the same intellectual virtues in inferring D. In this case D is true in part because, as Smith quite reasonably thinks, D's first disjunct is true.

In E7 as in E1, virtuous thinking plays a crucial causal explanatory role in gaining a true belief. Nothing in the three conditions of GK differentiates a Gettier case like E1 from a case of knowledge like E7.

In the same way, lottery cases meet the three conditions. In E6, our example of your belief that you lost a million-ticket lottery, the probabilistic basis that led to your belief is an eminently virtuous and reliable sort of belief forming basis. And this basis plays as prominent and central a role in your acquiring your true lottery belief as does any excellent though fallible reasoning in routine cases of knowledge. So the three conditions of GK do not disqualify the lottery belief from being knowledge.

Greco's solution to the two problems does not deny these things. Instead, Greco suggests that a solution can be found not in GK, which is what knowledge itself requires, but rather in the standards that we employ in our knowledge attribution practice. He proposes that our practice of knowledge attribution serves the further function of awarding credit to the person for getting a true belief.

Greco proposes that one standard we have for awarding this credit is that our noticing an instance of chance in the relevant thinking undermines it. This standard is crucial for his solution to the Gettier and lottery problems.

> CS. When an element of chance in someone's thinking that leads the person to a true belief becomes salient to us, this chance undermines any grounds for our giving credit to the person for the true belief.

In Greco's view, we give this credit whenever we attribute knowledge. So in his view whenever CS applies, it requires us not to attribute knowledge.

> Here is an analogy.

> E8. Jones won the championship match of a tennis tournament. But Jones did not play well in the tournament. Remarkably, he won each match by forfeit. In each case, his opponent was playing better and leading, but the opponent had to forfeit owing to a medical emergency. (This highly suspicious sequence of mishaps was thoroughly investigated and found to be coincidental.)

Jones won the championship. This is a sufficient condition for the term "champion" to apply to Jones. But that term connotes a sort of praise. The term suggests, without strictly requiring, an excellence of performance that Jones did not exemplify. That may well make us quite reluctant to call "the champion" someone who won by luck that Jones had.

Similarly, Greco proposes that attributing knowledge does not just ascribe to someone a state that meets the GK conditions. Attributing knowledge also serves to convey a sort of credit for the true belief. Greco further proposes that CS is one rule we use in determining whether to award this credit.

CS readily applies to lottery cases. In such cases, we are thinking about a belief that is about an outcome of a fair lottery. This makes it conspicuous to us that from the point of view of the believer, the win-or-lose property of the ticket is a matter of chance. According to CS, a salient chance involved in the thinking leading to the belief undermines anything otherwise creditable about the true belief. Thus, given that we are constrained by CS, it is no wonder that we do not attribute knowledge to the lottery beliefs.

In Gettier cases, the virtuous intellectual dispositions that the protagonists employ might incline us to credit them for their true belief. But when we focus on how it is accidental that their virtuously formed beliefs are true—the happenstance that makes for a Gettier case—any inclination we have to credit them for their true beliefs is overridden. By CS, the chance involved has us withhold the credit. Consequently, governed by CS we do not attribute knowledge.

Doubt

Two aspects of Greco's proposals about knowledge deserve some critical attention.

For one thing, we might wonder whether each of the three conditions in GK is really necessary. The first condition requires the knower to have sought the truth and to be disposed in certain ways to do so. But couldn't someone who was never a truth seeker gain knowledge, by being irresistibly shown the truth of some fact? And couldn't someone happen to learn a fact, despite having bad standards for what dispositions to employ in a search for truth that did not operate in gaining the knowledge?

The second condition of GK requires an intellectually virtuous disposition to be a reliable one. But couldn't an intellectual virtue happen to be prone to false beliefs, while still giving us knowledge in cases where it gains us true ones with no relevant accident? For example, it might be that lengthy and complicated mental arithmetical calculations are unreliable because they are error-prone, even when they are fastidiously executed. Couldn't this virtuous sort of calculation nonetheless give us knowledge in flawless instances?

The third condition of GK requires the true belief to be explained by the virtue. But suppose that a belief exists because it gives emotional solace. This believing thus would not be explained by intellectual virtue. Yet the person might also have virtuously acquired conclusive evidence for the truth of the belief. In the absence of a Gettier problem, wouldn't that acquisition give the person knowledge of the consoling fact?

Here is a doubt about the second part of Greco's theory involving CS. Suppose that we ponder some manifestly fictitious circumstances in which one losing ticket in some enormous lottery is believed by the subject not to win, purely on the basis of the odds. We have no plan to discuss the example and no other interest in whether or not actually to award any credit. Suppose too that we are not participants in our imagined scenario. So we are not concerning ourselves with whether in those circumstances we would award credit to the subject. Yet we seem to be as inclined as ever to not find knowledge by the subject of the lottery belief. Apparently, we are determining whether or not to think of the belief as knowledge entirely by our best judgment about whether or not the belief would have what it takes to be known. No additional function of our attributing knowledge appears to be at stake. If not, then no knowledge attribution constraint like CS solves the lottery problem. The same seems to go for our thinking about Gettier cases. If so, then correct solutions to these problems involve conditions on knowledge itself, rather than conditions on its proper attribution.

Conclusion

The innovative ideas about knowledge that we have considered are refreshing and thought provoking. They do confront problems of their own. The traditional conception of knowledge, as justified true belief plus some further condition that solves the Gettier problem, remains in contention.

Notes

1 Edmund Gettier, "Is Justified True Belief Knowledge?" *Analysis* 23 (1963) 121–3.
2 Bertrand Russell, *Human Knowledge: Its Scope and Limits* (New York: Allen and Unwin, 1948, 154). It is not clear that Russell intended the true belief in his example to be justified as well. On the following page, Russell discusses requiring strong evidence as a way to supplement a true belief account so as to avoid its problems. He does not raise any doubt about the sufficiency of this requirement by referring back to his example. In any event, when Russell's example is slightly supplemented with explicit justification for the belief, as in E2 below, it is a helpful Gettier case.
3 Brian Weatherson, "What Good Are Counterexamples?" *Philosophical Studies* 15 (2003) 1–31.
4 This is the basic idea behind Roderick Chisholm's approach in *Theory of Knowledge,* second edition (Englewood Cliffs, NJ: Prentice-Hall, 1977, 109).
5 A serious cost of this fourth condition is that it disallows some intuitive cases of knowledge. In E1, Smith does know that Jones has long driven a Ford and asserted his pleasure in its ownership. Yet Smith's justification for this knowledge—his relevant memories of Jones—seem also to support to Smith the falsehood that Jones owns a Ford. Given this, R disallows the knowledge by Smith of Jones's driving a Ford and asserting pleasure in owning one.
6 David Lewis, "Elusive Knowledge," *Australasian Journal of Philosophy* 74 (1995) 549–67.

7   Hilary Kornblith, "Knowledge in Humans and Other Animals," *Philosophical Perspectives* 13 (1999) 327–46.

8   Timothy Williamson, *Knowledge and Its Limits* (Oxford: Oxford University Press, 2000), chapter 1 "A State of Mind," and chapter 9 "Evidence."

9   Ibid., 39–40.

10 Williamson argues that unlike knowledge, true belief is not a *mental* state (ibid., 27–30). But his claim concerning what gives knowledge importance does not include that the states are mental. Anyway, it is irrelevant to the importance of knowledge to us whether the match is *within* a mental state that has content about the external world, or *between* the mental state of belief and its external world content. Also, if Williamson means "essence" quite literally, as something without which the actual state could not have existed, then in general a true belief does not have a mind/world match in its essence. Generally, the same belief could have existed while false. But what seems important to us about the match is that it is actually present, not that the same state could not possibly have lacked it. Necessarily, if a belief is true, then the match is present. So any contingently true belief does have this importance to us.

11 John Greco, "Knowledge as Credit for True Belief," in Michael DePaul and Linda Zagzebski, eds, *Intellectual Virtue: Perspectives from Ethics and Epistemology* (Oxford: Oxford University Press, 2004, 111–34).

12 Ibid., 16–17.

13 It is not really necessary that Smith used his actual disposition, in that other dispositions could have gotten him to believe the disjunction. But the crucial point is that it is as causally necessary in this case as it is in the maximally similar disjunctive knowledge case. So GK does not distinguish the two.

2

Foundationalism

Daniel Howard-Snyder

Foundationalists distinguish basic from nonbasic beliefs. At a first approximation, to say that a belief of a person is *basic* is to say that it is epistemically justified and it owes its justification to something other than her other beliefs, where "belief" refers to the mental state that goes by that name. To say that a belief of a person is *nonbasic* is to say that it is epistemically justified and not basic.[1] Two theses constitute *foundationalism:*

a. *Minimality.* There are some basic beliefs.
b. *Exclusivity.* If there are any nonbasic beliefs, that is solely because they (ultimately) owe their justification to some basic belief.

Those who affirm minimality but reject exclusivity endorse *minimal foundationalism.*[2] Those who affirm exclusivity but reject minimality endorse either *epistemic nihilism,* the view that there are no justified beliefs, or some non-foundationalist epistemology such as coherentism or infinitism.

In this chapter I aim to characterize the notion of a basic belief more precisely and to assess some arguments for and against foundationalism. In the process, I hope to exhibit the resilience and attractiveness of both. Several preliminary remarks are in order before I begin.

Preliminary remarks

First, foundationalism is about *epistemic* justification as opposed to moral, legal, prudential, and other sorts of justification. As might be expected, what distinguishes epistemic from other sorts of justification is controversial. Nevertheless, I'll be thinking of it as a positive normative status enjoyed by a belief just when it is held in such a way that in virtue of holding it in that way it has a good chance of being true. There are competing theories of what that way is. Everything I have to say will, I hope, be consistent with each of them. (I will leave the qualifier "epistemic" in "epistemic justification" tacit hereafter.)

Second, although I have characterized the basic–nonbasic distinction in terms of justification, I might have characterized it in terms of another positive epistemic status, for example, rationality, warrant, or knowledge. Foundationalism says that, for any positive epistemic status, some of our beliefs have it and some of them have it without owing it to other beliefs of ours.

Third, foundationalism is not a theory of justified belief since it does not specify the conditions under which a belief is justified. Rather, it is a theory about the *structure* of a system of justified beliefs, a theory of how the beliefs in a system of beliefs must be related to each other if some of them are justified. It says that any system of justified beliefs requires basic beliefs, which stands in contrast with other theories, notably coherentism and infinitism.

Fourth, we must distinguish a belief's *being justified* from someone's *justifying* it. The first denotes a property, the second an activity. Moreover, one's belief can be justified even if one has not justified it. Consider an analogy. Suppose you challenge me with respect to how I have raised my children over the years. I would justify my behavior by exhibiting how it was justified. Similarly, suppose you challenge me with respect to my belief that God exists. I would justify it by exhibiting how it was justified. In each case, I display a property my behavior and belief had prior to justifying it, namely it's being justified.

Finally, foundationalism concerns a belief's being justified, not justifying it. It is not a theory about the structure of the activity of justifying beliefs; it is a theory about the structure of a system of beliefs at least some of which are justified. Philosophers sometimes forget this fact.[3]

Characterizing basic beliefs more precisely

I said above that, at a first approximation,

> S's belief B is *basic* = df B is justified and B owes its justification to something other than S's other beliefs.

There are at least two reasons to characterize basic belief more precisely.

The first reason has to do with epistemic overdetermination. Suppose I hear a baby crying nearby and, at the same time, I am informed by a reliable source that a baby is crying in the next room. Now suppose, just for the sake of illustration, that my baby belief owes its justification to its sounding to me as if a baby is crying as well as an inference from my belief that my informant told me a baby is crying. In that case, given our initial characterization of basic belief, it is nonbasic; after all, it owes its justification to my other beliefs, at least in part. This misrepresents foundationalism, however. For, when the foundationalist calls a person's belief "basic" she means to say that there are conditions sufficient for its justification that do not include his other beliefs. These conditions could be satisfied even if he bases his belief on other beliefs of his as well, as in the case of my baby belief. As William Alston observes, "Overdetermination is an epistemic as well as a causal phenomenon. What fits a belief to serve as a [basic belief] is simply that it doesn't *need* other justified beliefs in order to be justified itself."[4]

The second reason has to do with distinguishing foundationalism from its traditional alternatives, notably coherentism, the view that some beliefs are justified solely because they are members of a coherent system of beliefs.[5] But given my characterization of basic belief, coherentism is a version of foundationalism. For on coherentism, *every* justified belief of a person owes its justification entirely to something other than her other beliefs, something that is alone sufficient for its justification, namely membership in a coherent system of beliefs.[6]

It is better, therefore, to say:

S's belief B is *basic* = df B is justified and B owes it justification at least in part to something other than S's other beliefs or the coherence of her belief system, something that is by itself sufficient for B's justification.

However, this characterization rules out what we might call *brute basicality,* the view that basic beliefs are justified but do not owe their justification to anything.[7] If the foundationalist wants to allow brute basicality (and perhaps she doesn't), a better characterization is this:

S's belief B is *basic* = df B is justified and B does not owe its justification wholly to (i) S's other beliefs or (ii) the coherence of her belief system, or (iii) a combination of both.

If S's belief B is justified but does not owe its justification to anything, then, *a fortiori,* it doesn't owe its justification wholly to (i), (ii), or (iii). One might ask, however: if brute basicality is allowed, why not *brute nonbasicality,* the view that nonbasic beliefs are justified but do not owe their justification to anything either? Here the foundationalist must put her foot down. For if both are allowed, the basic–nonbasic distinction vanishes—no foundationalist will allow that.

The capaciousness of foundationalism

Foundationalism is a capacious canopy under which a vast variety of epistemological flora and fauna flourish. It is customary to exhibit this fact by recounting the numerous views about what sorts of beliefs are basic, how it is that basic beliefs are related to nonbasic beliefs, and how experience can justify basic empirical beliefs. One might also display the variety of substantive foundationalist theories, varieties of reliabilism, evidentialism, proper functionalism, epistemic duty theory, and so on, in addition to showing how what's important about systemic coherence can be accounted for through a foundationalist-friendly defeasibility theory. A less common way to exhibit the capaciousness of foundationalism is to show how easily it absorbs its critics.

To illustrate this last way, consider Ernest Sosa, who famously argued that an appeal to intellectual virtue provided a way beyond the impasse between foundationalism and coherentism.[8] *En route* to this conclusion, Sosa claimed that "*All* foundationalism based on sense experience is subject to a fatal dilemma."[9] What is this "fatal dilemma"? Suppose we believe that the apple before us is red on the basis of its looking red to us. If experience can justify basic belief, then there is some specific principle of experiential justification relating that particular sort of experience to that particular sort of belief, for example, if something looks red to you, then your belief that it is red is defeasibly justified. And there will be other such principles, says Sosa, regarding a plenitude of actual and possible sense modalities. Each specific principle of experiential justification faces the following dilemma: either it is derived or it is fundamental. If it is derived, "then it would be quite unphilosophical to stop there." If it is fundamental, then "we would open the door to a multitude of equally basic principles with no unifying factor." So, each specific principle of experiential justification is either an unphilosophical stopping point or there are many such ununified principles.[10]

Does Sosa's dilemma suffice to dispose of *experiential foundationalism*, the view that sensory experience can justify basic empirical belief? Hardly. As for the second horn, suppose there is no unifying factor for the multitude of equally basic principles of experiential justification, say, in the way some ethicists think there is no unifying factor for the multitude of equally basic prima facie duties.

What would be objectionable about throwing open the door to them? As for the first horn, suppose there is some unifying factor. Why can't the foundationalist avail herself of one of the many theories about it or develop a new one? But my main point is this. After rejecting experiential foundationalism, Sosa sketched in three dense paragraphs how an appeal to intellectual virtue can provide an "alternative to foundationalism of sense experience."[11] It is difficult to discern any such thing there; however, we later learn that experience *can* justify belief after all, provided the belief is formed because of "a stable and reliable disposition to form beliefs about the environment on the basis of experiential inputs."[12] This is no "alternative to foundationalism of sense experience"; it is an instance of it. Sosa is a foundationalist, not unlike many other critics.[13]

On the very idea of a basic belief

Some philosophers find the very idea of a basic belief perplexing, so much so that they doubt there can be such a thing. In this section I assess three arguments to that effect.

Argument 1. If your belief is basic, it is justified. In general, your belief is justified only if you have a good reason for it. However, that's the case only if you justifiedly believe the premises of a good argument for it. Of course, your belief in these premises will typically be dispositional and not occurrent—still, you must believe them. But given that you do, your belief owes its justification to these other beliefs of yours. So your belief is basic only if it owes its justification to them, which is a contradiction.[14]

We might worry about the question-begging condition on what counts as a good reason for belief, but three other concerns are more instructive.

First, let's distinguish necessary and constitutive conditions. The fact that two and two is four is a necessary but not a constitutive condition of your existence—it is not that even partly in virtue of which you exist, it is not that to which you owe your existence, not even in part. Likewise, the fact that two and two is four is a necessary but not a constitutive condition of your belief being justified—it is not that even partly in virtue of which your belief is justified, it is not that to which your belief owes its justification, not even in part. Now suppose your belief is justified only if you justifiedly believe the premises of a good argument for it, as Argument 1 says. Then a necessary condition on your belief being justified is your believing those premises. Even so, it does not follow that a constitutive condition on your belief being justified is your believing those premises; so it does not follow that your belief owes its justification to these other beliefs of yours.

Second, even if it were required that your belief owes its justification to these other beliefs, it might also owe its justification to something foundationalist-friendly and sufficient for justification. At best, this requirement implies that each basic belief is epistemically overdetermined by a good argument for it, which is compatible with its being basic.[15]

Third, Epistemic Nihilism threatens. The two main premises entail that your belief is justified only if you justifiedly believe the premises of a good argument for it. Since this entailment is perfectly general and reiterative, you cannot justifiedly believe anything unless you justifiedly believe infinitely many propositions of the required sort. But you can't believe infinitely many propositions of that sort. Thus, the two main premises entail that you justifiedly believe nothing. Response: although I cannot occurrently believe infinitely many propositions of the required sort, I dispositionally believe them since I am disposed to believe infinitely many propositions of that sort, just as I am disposed to believe that one and one is two, one and two is three, two, and two is four, and so on *ad infinitum*. Reply: Dispositional belief is not the disposition to believe and, even if it were, you are no more disposed to believe infinitely many propositions of the required sort than you are to believe infinitely many sums since infinitely many members of both sets outstrip your grasp and you cannot believe what you cannot grasp.[16]

Argument 2. If your belief can be basic, you can have a justified belief that is not supported by any other beliefs of yours. But that's impossible: "you could not possibly so much as host the target belief without a lot of the relevant supportive beliefs." So your belief cannot be basic.[17]

Notice that the term "supported by" is ambiguous. It might express the relation of *justificatory support,* where X justificatorily supports Y if and only if Y owes its justification (at least in part) to X, or it might express the relation of *existential support,* where X existentially supports Y if and only if Y would not exist in the absence of X. In order to avoid equivocation, let's consider two versions of the argument, one for each relation.

Justificatory support version. If your belief can be basic, you can have a justified belief that does not owe its justification to any other belief of yours. But you can have no such thing. Therefore, your belief cannot be basic.

This argument fails because the second premise is synonymous with the conclusion.

Existential support version. If your belief can be basic, then you can have a justified belief without having any other beliefs that existentially support it. But you can have no such thing. Therefore, your belief cannot be basic.

This argument has much more going for it. The second premise is true, I think. That's because, in general, no belief of yours, justified or not, can exist in the absence of certain other beliefs of yours. Why? Because when you form a belief, you apply at least one concept. But you can apply a concept only if you have a grasp of it, at least somewhat, and that requires the ability to discriminate between things to which it applies and doesn't apply. A disposition to perfect application is unnecessary; but with respect to a wide variety of things to which it does and doesn't apply, you must be disposed to apply it correctly. This capacity to discriminate consists in, among other things, the possession of certain beliefs, expectations about how things to which the concept applies would tend to behave under various conditions, as well as beliefs about its interrelations with other concepts. Call such beliefs *concept-possession beliefs.* In general, no belief of yours can exist in the absence of its requisite concept-possession beliefs.

But what about the first premise? Why suppose that if your belief can be basic, you can have a justified belief without having any other beliefs that existentially support it? The assumption here is that if your belief cannot exist in the absence of certain other beliefs of yours, then it must owe its justification to them as well. But why suppose that's so? Nothing in the story about concept-possession beliefs reveals why. Moreover, if the justificatory relation holds between your belief and some non-doxastic state of yours, then, given some foundationalist-friendly facts relating those states to your belief, it can be justified without owing its justification to its existentially supporting beliefs. We might ask what those facts are. Foundationalists answer differently. It is no part of my brief here to defend an answer. I aim only to exhibit at a more abstract level how basic belief survives the existential support requirement.[18]

Argument 3. If your belief is basic, it is justified. Your belief is justified, however, only if you can justify it. To be sure, you need not in fact justify it, but you must be able to do so. But you can do that only if you have what it takes to justify it, and that requires having other justified beliefs to which to appeal in justifying it. In that case, your belief owes its justification to them. So your belief is basic only if it owes its justification to other beliefs, which is a contradiction.

I am inclined to deny that being justified entails being able to justify, for three reasons.

First, think of analogues. Your action can be morally justified even if you can't justify it. Indeed, consider any sort of justification and it can be justified in that way even though you can't justify it. Why should epistemic justification be any different?

Second, counterexamples are a dime a dozen. The ability to justify a belief involves the ability to give a good argument for it. Philosophers are too prone to take for granted the skill and conceptual sophistication needed to do that, neither of which are shared by the class of all those who have justified beliefs. We need not think only of higher nonhuman animals in this regard. Even though young children lack the conceptual sophistication and skill to give good arguments, many of their beliefs are still justified. Or consider cases in which those who can ordinarily argue in the required way temporarily lose that capacity. Normal, mature adults can experience mental "seizures"—episodes that render them cognitively tongue-tied and temporarily render them unable to give good arguments. The causes of such episodes are various but include shyness, insecurity, anger, shock, and the like. Even mature, philosophically adept adults who are not in the grip of a mental seizure are sometimes unable to produce a good argument for what they believe, even though their belief is justified.[19]

Third, Epistemic Nihilism looms. For if your belief is justified only if you can justify it and you can justify it only if you have other justified beliefs to which to appeal in justifying it, then your belief is justified only if you have other justified beliefs to which to appeal in justifying it. Since this implication is perfectly general and reiterative, you cannot justifiedly believe anything unless you justifiedly believe infinitely many propositions of the required sort, which you can't do. Response: While your belief is justified only if you are able to justify it, you can possess that ability at a particular time even if you don't then have beliefs to which to appeal in justifying it, in which case no regress arises.[20] Reply: That's like supposing you are able to throw a football at a particular time even if you don't then have arms. In general, you are able to do something at a particular time only if you then have what it takes to do it. But suppose I'm wrong. In that case, the regress is avoided but only at the expense of denying the main premise of Argument 3. The ability to justify threatens basicality only if it requires that you already hold beliefs to which to appeal.

On experiential foundationalism

According to Donald Davidson, experience cannot be a "reason" or an "epistemological basis" or a "ground or source of justification" of a belief; indeed, the very idea of experience justifying belief is "unintelligible."[21] Strong words, these. Is he right? Here's what he says:

> The relation between a sensation and a belief cannot be logical, since sensations are not beliefs or other propositional attitudes. What then is the relation? The answer is, I think, obvious: the relation is causal. Sensations cause some beliefs and in this sense are the basis or ground of those beliefs. But a causal explanation of a belief does not show how or why the belief is justified.[22]

Davidson speaks of "sensations" but his intended target is any "attempt to ground belief in one way or another on the testimony of the senses: sensation, perception, the given, experience, sense data, the passing show."[23] I'll use "experience." So what's his argument? There seem to be two.

First argument: experience causes beliefs; but a causal explanation of a belief does not show how or why it is justified; so experience cannot justify belief.

This argument fails. For although the fact that experience causes belief cannot explain how and why it justifies belief, no foundationalist ever said it did. Rather, a belief owes its justification to an experience that caused it only under certain noncausal conditions, for example, only if

1. it's not possible to have it while the belief is false, or
2. one would not have it if the belief were false, or
3. one would have it if the belief were true, or
4. it makes the belief very likely to be true, or
5. one is nonnegligently unaware of any defeaters, or
6. one has not violated any epistemic duty in believing on the basis of it, or
7. one satisfies the relevant epistemic duty to believe on the basis of it, or
8. the best explanation of one's having it is that the belief is true, or
9. it is evidence for the belief, or
10. one is able to justify believing on the basis of it, or
11. it furnishes one with certain demonstrative contents, one's grasp of which provides one with a reason for the belief, or
12. it is the input of a reliable belief-forming process, or
13. it is the input of properly functioning cognitive capacities that are aimed at truth and reliable in the environments for which they were designed, or
14. one exhibits intellectual virtue in holding the belief on the basis of it.

The list goes on and on.

Second argument: if a belief owes its justification to some other mental state, it confirms it, and so it has propositional content.[24] But experience lacks propositional content. So experience cannot justify belief.

We might note that many philosophers think that experience has propositional content.[25] But even if it doesn't, and even if justification requires confirmation (a view not universally held), experience can nevertheless confirm a belief. Even if my feeling pain lacks propositional content, it renders it likely *in excelsis* that my belief that I am in pain is true; and even if the wall's appearing smooth to me lacks propositional content, it makes it much more likely than not that my belief that it appears smooth and my belief that it is smooth are true. And so on. Even if the probability calculus applies only to propositions, it doesn't follow that only propositions can probabilify; better to infer that the calculus is limited in the scope of its application.[26]

On behalf of foundationalism

What might be said on behalf of foundationalism? Two things, I think.

First, as for minimal foundationalism, it certainly seems as though some of our beliefs are justified but not by our other beliefs. Suppose I just spent the last 13 hours hiking the 31 miles from Cajon Pass to Inspiration Point on the Pacific Crest Trail carrying a 30-pound pack. I ache all over and I feel hungry. I then justifiedly believe that I feel achy and hungry. Are there some other beliefs from which I infer these things? It seems not. Or suppose I skirt Mt Baden-Powell, hiking on Highway 2 instead of taking the route over the peak. I justifiedly believe that I am hiking the road in order to avoid the icy north face. That's my reason for hiking the road. There seem to be no other beliefs of mine from which I infer that this is my reason. Or suppose that while I'm hiking I imagine what my boys are doing at school: playing tag at recess, writing in their journals, doing math, and so on. I justifiedly believe that this is what I'm imagining. Do I infer it from something else I believe? It seems not.[27]

Something similar can be said about other beliefs of ours. Suppose the sign in front of me says "No vehicles allowed." I justifiedly believe that the sign says this. Are there some other beliefs from which I infer that this is what it says? It seems not; I believe it simply because of the way it looks to me. My friend said this morning that she was headed back to the trail. I justifiedly believe she said this. There seems to be no other belief of mine from which I infer this. I simply recall her saying it.[28]

Of course, in each such case, there could be some hidden inference on which I base my belief. Perhaps I really inferred that I feel achy and hungry from the way I rummage in my pack for some Ibuprofen and a Snickers bar. Perhaps I really believe my reason for walking the road is to avoid the icy chutes because I reason that if I were to walk the road, that's why I'd be walking the road now, and I'm now walking the road. Perhaps I really believe the sign says "No vehicles allowed" on the basis of my belief that its saying that is the best explanation of my visual experience. And so on for each and every case where it seems I'm making no inference at all.

What should we make of the hidden inference hypothesis? Like other hypotheses that posit hidden mental goings-on, we can't rule it out. Even so, we can't simply neglect how things seem. And things seem congenial to minimal foundationalism.

The second thing to be said on behalf of foundationalism is that it provides a satisfying solution to the epistemic regress problem. Suppose S is one of us, a typical adult, and suppose that her belief that q is justified. Furthermore, suppose she believes that q on the basis of an inference from two other beliefs of hers, her belief that *if p, then q* and her belief that *p*. Finally, suppose her belief that q owes its justification to these other two beliefs of hers via this inference.

A simple question arises: How can this be? How can S's belief that q owe its justification to her other two beliefs via her inference?

Could it be that it owes its justification to them even though neither is justified—the unjustified justifier option? Or could it be that it owes its justification to them since they are justified and they owe their justification to some further beliefs of hers, and so on, so that, ultimately, it owes its justification to itself—the circular justification option? Or could it be that it owes its justification to them since they are justified and they owe their justification to some further beliefs of hers, and they in turn to some others, and so on, for infinitely many non-repeating beliefs of hers—the infinite regress option? According to the foundationalist, each of these options is untenable. The unjustified justifier option is ruled out by the platitude that no belief can owe its justification to another belief from which it is inferred unless the other belief is justified. The circular justification option is ruled out by the truism that no belief can owe its justification to itself. The infinite regress option is ruled out by the fact that we cannot hold infinitely many beliefs of the required sort.[29]

That leaves one option: S's belief that q owes its justification to her two beliefs and they in turn owe their justification, ultimately, to something other than her other beliefs—the basic belief option.[30]

Coherentists, of course, will reject this argument. S's belief that q may well be justified, alright; and she may have come to believe q on the basis of an inference from the contents of her other two beliefs, both of which are justified.

But it cannot be the case that her belief owes its justification to her other two beliefs via that inference. Why? Because a belief is justified solely by virtue of its membership in a coherent system of beliefs and never by virtue of an inference from other justified beliefs. Inferential justification is impossible.

This is not the place to develop concerns about coherentism. Suffice to say that, by my lights, it fails on two counts. First, it implies the rejection of all inferential justification. Second, it lacks the resources to connect what it is in virtue of which a belief is justified, that is, membership in a coherent belief system, with its being held in such a way that in virtue of holding it in that way it has a good chance of being true.[31]

Others have objected to the regress argument for foundationalism in other ways, especially to versions of it according to which experience can justify basic belief and thereby stop the regress. The most famous of these objections is the Sellarsian Dilemma.[32]

The Sellarsian Dilemma

There are different versions of the Sellarsian Dilemma. I will consider two.

The first goes like this: Either an experience has propositional content or it doesn't. If it does, it is in need of justification itself. If it doesn't, it cannot contribute to the justification of a belief. But an experience can end the regress by justifying a belief only if it can contribute to its justification and it is not in need of justification itself. So, an experience cannot end the regress by justifying a belief.[33]

Consider the second premise: in need of justification *for what*? If the answer is "in need of justification to be justified," the claim is that if one's experience has propositional content, then it is justified only if one justifies it. But this claim is true only if it is also true that, in general, for *any* mental state, if it has propositional content, it is justified only if one justifies it—and that's false.

It is better to understand the second premise as a way of saying that if an experience has propositional content, then it is the sort of thing that is either epistemically justified or unjustified. This makes sense. For suppose an experience has propositional content. Then, given the present understanding of the second premise, it follows that an experience is the sort of thing that is either justified or unjustified, and so it cannot end the regress—for if it is justified, the regress continues, and if it is *un*justified, it cannot justify the belief.[34]

But is it true that if an experience has propositional content, then it is the sort of thing that is either justified or unjustified? No. For if it was true, then having propositional content would suffice to make every mental state that has it either justified or unjustified—and it doesn't. For example, my imagining life as a Tahoe ski bum has propositional content but is neither justified nor unjustified, and the same goes for wondering, entertaining, desiring, and the like.

The first version of the Dilemma has a false premise; still, it raises a vexing question: What is it about a mental state in virtue of which it is the sort of thing that is either justified or unjustified while other mental states are neither?[35] I propose that it is its being assertive. Only assertive mental states are either epistemically justified or unjustified. Let me explain.

Some mental states are assertive in that they are partially constituted by something like an assertion. Just as when one asserts a proposition, one typically thereby commits oneself to its truth and is thereby evaluable by certain linguistic norms that govern assertion, norms that render it either linguistically justified or unjustified, so when one believes a proposition, one thereby commits oneself to its truth and is thereby evaluable by certain epistemic norms that govern belief, norms that render it epistemically justified or unjustified. Other mental states, however, are nonassertive. Desire is a paradigm case. When one desires that something be the case, one does not thereby commit oneself to the truth of a proposition, and so one is not evaluable by the norms that govern assertive mental states.[36]

One might object. On my proposal, the line between assertive and nonassertive mental states is the line between those that are either justified or unjustified and those that are neither justified nor unjustified. But, the objection goes, being in doubt about a proposition is a mental state that is either justified or unjustified even though it is nonassertive. When one is in doubt, one is not thereby in a state that is partially constituted by a commitment to the truth of what it is that one is in doubt about.[37]

Reply: I agree that when one is in doubt about a proposition, one is not thereby in a state that is partially constituted by a commitment to the truth of *that* proposition. But it does not follow that when one is in doubt about a proposition, one is not thereby in a state that is partially constituted by a commitment to the truth of *some* proposition. I submit that when one is in doubt about a proposition, one's doubt is partially constituted by a belief to the effect that one's grounds for it are no better or worse than one's grounds for its denial. It is this belief that partially constitutes being in doubt about a proposition and in virtue of which being in doubt about a proposition is assertive, contrary to the objection. It is this belief in virtue of which being in doubt is the sort of state that is either justified or unjustified.[38]

Much more needs to be said about my proposal; it must wait for another occasion.

Suppose I'm right, however. Then a second version of the Sellarsian Dilemma presents itself: Either an experience is assertive or isn't. If it is, it is either justified or unjustified. If it isn't, it cannot contribute to the justification of a belief. But an experience can end the regress by justifying a belief only if it can contribute to its justification and it is neither justified nor unjustified. So, an experience cannot end the regress by justifying a belief.

What should we make of this line of thought?

The second premise is a logical consequence of my proposal, which I am now supposing is true. That leaves the third premise: if an experience is nonassertive, it cannot contribute to the justification of a belief. This premise is dubious, but before I explain why, I need to address a pressing question.

Suppose that experience *really is* assertive. Then, given the second premise, it follows that experience is either justified or unjustified, in which case it cannot end the regress. So: is experience assertive? Or, more accurately, is *all* experience assertive?

It seems not. Purely qualitative states lack propositional content, in which case they are nonassertive. But what about other sorts of experience, for example, the sensory experience involved in visual perception? It is a vexed question in the philosophy of perception to which I can hardly do justice here whether *all* sensory experience has propositional content, notably sensory experience involved in object perception. (Fact perception has propositional content, of course.) Suffice to say that if the sensory experience involved in object perception lacks propositional content, as many philosophers believe, then, like purely qualitative states, some sensory experience is nonassertive.[39] But suppose, just for the sake of argument, that all sensory experience has propositional content, including the sensory experience involved in object perception.

Even so, it is not clear that it is assertive. For, first, it bears repeating that propositional content does not suffice for assertiveness. Second, we can recognize that we are having a sensory experience while believing its propositional content is false without feeling anything like the dissonance that would attend that recognition if sensory experience were assertive. Let me explain.

Consider three different kinds of cases.

Case 1. We believe that p while we believe that not-p, and we recognize that this is the case.

This doesn't happen very often to us, fortunately. But when it does, the dissonance we feel is severe. We scramble to find some way to modify one of the beliefs or back off both of them. For in believing that p, we commit ourselves to its truth, and in believing that not-p, we commit ourselves to its falsehood; consequently, when we recognize that we are in this position, we can't stand it. We feel that something has to give.

Case 2. We want it to be the case that p while we believe that not-p, and we recognize that this is the case.

This happens all too often to us, unfortunately. But when it does, although we may well feel frustration, we don't feel anything like the sort of dissonance we feel in Case 1. That's because desire is a nonassertive state. In wanting it to be the case that p, we don't commit ourselves to the truth of p.

Case 3. It phenomenally looks to us as if p while we believe that not-p, and we recognize that this is the case.

This happens more often than the first case but much less often than the second. To illustrate, consider a known illusion. Imagine that before you there is a straight stick half submerged in a clear beaker of water and you know this. Visually, it looks to you as if the stick is bent and yet, at the very same time, you believe that it is not bent, and you recognize that this is the case.

Now here's my argument. If its phenomenally looking to you as if the stick is bent were an assertive mental state, you would be in a position like Case 1. For if its looking to you as if the stick is bent were assertive, you would be committed to the truth of the proposition that the stick is bent by virtue of its looking bent to you while, at the very same time, you were committed to the falsehood of that proposition by virtue of believing that it is false. You, in short, would suffer dissonance of the sort exemplified in Case 1, the sort that attends recognition of holding contradictory beliefs. However, if its looking to you as if the stick is bent were a nonassertive mental state, you would be in a position like Case 2. For if its looking to you as if the stick is bent were nonassertive, you would not be committed to the truth of the proposition that the stick is bent and so you would not be committed to the truth of the denial of what you believe. You, in short, would enjoy a lack of dissonance of the sort exemplified in Case 1. So which is Case 3 more like, Case 1 or Case 2? In my own case, I can attest that I feel no dissonance whatsoever. It seems, therefore, that its looking to me as if the stick is bent is nonassertive. I suspect that others are like me in this regard. If so, then, on the plausible assumption that if its looking to me as if the stick is bent is nonassertive in the illusory case, it is nonassertive in the veridical case, it follows that, in general, the stick's looking bent is nonassertive. *Mutatis mutandis,* the same goes for other sensory experiences, at least those that can figure in illusions—even if they have propositional content.

Much more needs to be said about this argument and the more general issue of whether sensory experience is assertive; it must wait for another occasion.

I now return to the second premise of the second version of the Sellarsian Dilemma, the claim that if an experience is nonassertive, it cannot contribute to the justification of a belief. Is it true? Here we need to distinguish two cases: being nonassertive while having propositional content and being nonassertive while lacking propositional content. In the first case, the claim at issue is that if an experience is nonassertive while having propositional content, it cannot contribute to the justification of belief. In the second case, the claim at issue is that if an experience is nonassertive while lacking propositional content, it cannot contribute to the justification of belief. If at least one of these claims is false, the foundationalist will have the elbow room to theorize about how experience can justify belief—even if experience is nonassertive. The truth is both seem false.

As for the first claim, it's difficult to even begin to see what to say on its behalf. So long as an experience has propositional content, even the critics of experience justifying belief will admit that it can do what they deem experience cannot do if it lacks propositional content, notably enter into confirmation relations, nonarbitrarily support one belief rather than another, and play a role in the practice of giving reasons. The nonassertive/propositional combination seems to be open to the foundationalist as she theorizes about how experience can justify belief.

As for the second claim, the claim that if an experience is nonassertive while having propositional content, it cannot contribute to the justification of belief, consider two arguments.

Argument 1. If an experience is nonassertive while lacking propositional content, it is arbitrary whether it justifies one belief rather than another. But if it is arbitrary whether it justifies one belief rather than another, it cannot contribute to the justification of a belief. So if an experience is nonassertive while having propositional content, it cannot contribute to the justification of belief. To illustrate: suppose I feel a sharp, burning pain across my right shin as I hike the southern ridge down to Bird Spring Pass. Naturally, I believe that my right shin hurts. But if the pain in my right shin lacks propositional content, why suppose it justifies my belief that my right shin hurts rather than my belief that the price of rice in China is currently 55 Yuan a bag? And the same goes for object perception. If the wall's appearing smooth to me lacks propositional content, why suppose it justifies my belief that the wall is smooth rather than my belief that disjunctive syllogism is valid? Absent propositional content, an experience isn't fit to justify one belief rather than another.[40]

By way of reply, at least three suggestions deserve exploring. First, certain external relations between the experience and the target belief might nonarbitrarily pin down its justifying that belief rather than others. For example, perhaps the wall's appearing smooth to me confirms my belief that it is smooth rather than others because the wall's appearing smooth is related in a law-like fashion to the truth of the content of my belief but not that of others. Second, certain internal relations between the experience and the target belief might nonarbitrarily pin down its justifying that belief rather than others. For example, perhaps the wall's appearing smooth to me has a representational structure that, although lacking in propositional content, maps onto the content of my belief in such a way that it does not map onto that of others. Third, suppose that the wall's appearing smooth to me has the nature attributed to it by the Theory of Appearing: it is a relation between me and the wall that is an essential component of my conscious perceptual experience of the wall and, as such, is not reducible to theoretically more fundamental categories or conditions, whether propositional, representational, or conceptual. In that case, on the plausible principle that if X appears F to me, then, absent defeaters, my belief that X is F justified, the wall's appearing smooth to me can justify my belief that the wall is smooth rather than other beliefs because the propositional content of my belief and not the others "registers" or "reads off" what is presented there in my conscious experience.[41] The upshot of these three suggestions is that even if experience is nonassertive while lacking propositional content, it remains to be seen whether it is arbitrary that it justifies one belief rather than another.

Argument 2. If an experience is nonassertive while lacking propositional content, it cannot provide an articulable reason for holding the belief. But if an experience cannot provide an articulable reason for holding the belief, it cannot contribute to its justification. So, if an experience is nonassertive while lacking propositional content, it cannot contribute to the justification of belief.[42]

Which premise deserves our attention depends on what sort of thing we take a reason for holding a belief to be. In common parlance, a reason for holding a belief is anything offered on its behalf, where it's left open what sorts of things might be so offered. In academic philosophy, however, it's often not left open: only propositions are reasons, we are told.

Suppose we go with common parlance. Then the second premise seems true and the first is better expressed as the claim that if experience is nonassertive while lacking propositional content, it can provide nothing articulable for holding a belief. But is that right?

I don't think so. Consider again my belief that I feel pain in my right shin. Suppose you ask me what reason I have to hold it. I answer: "My reason is the pain I feel in my right shin." If the claim under consideration is true, I have provided nothing articulable for holding my belief. But surely I have. For although I have not expressed a proposition but only used a noun clause to identify my reason, that suffices for providing something "articulable" for holding my belief—I did use words to pick it out, after all. (What if I had answered, "My reason is *that* I feel pain in my right shin"? Would that be a good reason? Surely not. But what other proposition would?)

Mutatis mutandis, we can say the same for beliefs about sensory experience, for example, my belief that the wall before me appears smooth. Suppose you ask me what reason I have to hold it. I answer: "My reason is its appearing smooth." If the claim under consideration is true, I have provided nothing articulable for holding my belief. But surely I have.

What about my belief that the wall *is* smooth? Suppose you ask me what reason I have to hold it. I answer: "My reason is the wall's appearing smooth." Does the gap between its *being* smooth and its *appearing* smooth make it the case that I have provided nothing articulable for holding my belief? I think not, at least not if we allow that I provided something articulable for holding the beliefs in the first two cases, as I think we should.

Now let's turn to academic philosophy. Then the first premise is true and the second is better expressed as the claim that if an experience cannot provide an articulable proposition for holding the belief, it cannot contribute to its justification. Is this true?

I think not. Even though the pain I feel in my right shin cannot provide an articulable proposition for holding my belief that I feel pain there, it can contribute to its justification by virtue of making the content of my belief vastly more likely than its denial. Likewise, even if the wall's appearing smooth cannot provide an articulable proposition for holding my belief that it appears smooth or my belief that it is smooth, it can contribute to the justification of both beliefs by virtue of making the content of each belief vastly more likely than its denial.

That's not to say that nothing more is needed for its justification, but it certainly seems that this counts as a contribution and a significant one at that.

I am under no illusion that I have defended foundationalism adequately in this chapter. That would take quite a bit more work than I am up to. I hope, however, to have taken a significant step toward exhibiting its resilience and attractiveness.

Notes

1   Basic beliefs are sometimes called "foundationally," "directly," "immediately," or "noninferentially" justified. Nonbasic beliefs are sometimes called "nonfoundationally," "indirectly," "mediately," or "inferentially" justified.

2   For example, Pryor (2005).

3   For example, Klein (1999, 2003, 2004, and 2005) and Kvanvig (2007).

4   Alston (1989b, 45). Cp. Alston (1989c, 64). Failure to recognize epistemic overdetermination has led to specious objections, e.g., Haack (1993), whose anti-foundationalism relies entirely on her stipulation "that basic beliefs get their justification *exclusively* from something other than the support of further beliefs" (31). Cf. Howard-Snyder and Coffman (2007, 539–40), my emphasis.

5   BonJour (1985, 92). This is sometimes called *pure* Coherentism. Sometimes further conditions on the system of beliefs are added, e.g., BonJour adds that it must "contain laws attributing a high degree of reliability to a reasonable variety of cognitively spontaneous beliefs" (141). And sometimes it is assumed that experience has propositional content and that their contents bear on the coherence of the relevant system. These qualifications are not relevant to my purposes.

6   Cp. Plantinga (1993, 77ff): "Coherentism, therefore, is a special case (a *very* special case) of foundationalism" (80). Perhaps Sosa would agree: Sosa (1980, 18).

7   As Dennis Whitcomb observed in conversation.

8   Sosa (1980, 23).

9   Ibid., 24, my emphasis.

10   Ibid., 20–3.

11   Ibid., 23.

12   The words of Sosa's sympathetic commentators in Greco and Turri (2009). Cp. Sosa on competently taking experience into account and virtue reliabilism: (2009a, 100ff; 2009b, 37–8, 160).

13   Perhaps even Klein. See Howard-Snyder and Coffman (2007, 552).

14   BonJour (1985, 32).

15 I leave it to the reader to apply these first two concerns to other arguments I discuss later.

16 Audi (1994). For more on BonJour's antifoundationalism, see Howard-Snyder (1998). I should note that he has since converted to foundationalism.

17 Sosa (2003, 208–09). Others who argue in this way say that there cannot be a justified belief that does not *depend* on other beliefs of the person who has it, e.g., Davidson (1986a, 311), and Lehrer (1990, 73–5), on which see Howard-Snyder (2002, 546–53), and Howard-Snyder (2004, 52–61). For more on Lehrer's antifoundationalism, see Howard-Snyder (2004).

18 Howard-Snyder and Coffman (2007, 557–62). Cp. Alston (1989b, 63–4), and Audi (1993, 151).

19 Alston (1989b, 70) and Alston (1989e, 335).

20 Perhaps Adam Leite thinks this: Leite (2004, 239).

21 Davidson (1986a, 307).

22 Ibid., 311.

23 Ibid., 310.

24 The logical relation specified in the quotation is confirmation: Davidson (1986b, 331). Cp. Everitt and Fisher (1995, 84).

25 Such as those indicated in Le Morvan (2008).

26 For more on Davidson's anti-experiential-foundationalism, see Howard-Snyder (2002).

27 Cf. Pryor (2005, 184–5).

28 Cf. Ginet (2005, 142–3).

29 I concede that a god with justified beliefs who can hold infinitely many beliefs of the sort in question need not have a system of beliefs that is structured in a foundationalist fashion. That's why argument in the text begins: "Suppose S is one of us, a typical adult . . ." Consequently, my third preliminary remark at the outset of this chapter must be qualified. Cf. Cortens (2002).

30 Critics of the regress argument for foundationalism sometimes represent the regress problem as a regress of "giving reasons for" a belief, e.g., Klein (2005), or a regress involving "defending" a belief by "citing" reasons for it, e.g., Kvanvig (2007). This is a mistake. Foundationalism is about the structure of a system of justified beliefs, *not* the structure of justifying a belief.

31 See, e.g., BonJour (1985) and Kvanvig (2007).

32 Sellars (1956). For my take on Klein's anti-experiential-foundationalism, see Howard-Snyder (2005) and Howard-Snyder and Coffman (2007).

33 Cf. BonJour (1985) chapter 3, and Howard-Snyder (1998).

34 Don't confuse being *positively* *un*justified with being *non*justified.

35 Matthias Steup suggests that (Sellars suggested that) it is the possibility of error in virtue of which a mental state is either justified or unjustified (Steup and Sosa 2005, 129). This can't be right, for two reasons. First, some mental states are such

that it is impossible that they are in error but they are nevertheless either justified or unjustified, e.g., beliefs whose propositional contents are necessary truths. Second, some mental states are such that it is possible that they are in error by virtue of having a propositional content that's false or contingently true but they are nevertheless neither justified nor unjustified, e.g., desires whose propositional contents are false or contingently true. Leite suggests that it is the believer's possession of the ability to justify her belief (Leite 2004, 238). This can't be right either. The class of those with justified beliefs is larger than the class of those able to justify their beliefs since, e.g., the former but not the latter includes young children, certain impaired adults, and higher nonhuman animals.

36   I leave for another occasion whether representational states that lack propositional content are assertive or nonassertive.

37   I said *being in doubt about,* not *doubting that.* The latter, but not the former, involves a strong inclination to believe that the object of one's doubt is false. They must not be confused.

38   In this connection, being in doubt resembles propositional hope. If you hope that p, you are not thereby in a state that is partially constituted by a commitment to the truth of p, but your hope is either epistemically justified or unjustified. That's because it is partially constituted by a belief to the effect that p is possible, in which case your hope is assertive and so justified or unjustified.

39   Philosophers such as those indicated in Le Morvan (2008).

40   Pryor (2005, 192–3).

41   Alston (1999, 198–201).

42   McDowell (1994, 165–6); cf. Pryor (2005, 193–4).

References

Alston, W. 1989a. *Epistemic Justification: Essays in the Theory of Knowledge.* Ithaca, NY: Cornell University Press.

— 1989b. "Has Foundationalism Been Refuted?" In Alston 1989a: 39–56.

— 1989c. "What's Wrong with Immediate Knowledge?" In Alston 1989a: 57–78.

— 1989d. "Epistemic Circularity." In Alston 1989a: 319–49.

— 1999. "Back to the Theory of Appearing." *Philosophical Perspectives* 13.

Audi, R. 1993. "The Foundationalism–Coherentism Controversy: Hardened Stereotypes and Overlapping Theories." In R. Audi, ed., *The Structure of Justification.* New York: Cambridge University Press, pp. 117–64.

— 1994. "Dispositional Beliefs and Dispositions to Believe." *Nous* 28: 419–34.

BonJour, L. 1985. *The Structure of Empirical Knowledge.* Cambridge, MA: Harvard University Press.

Cortens, A. 2002. "Foundationalism and the Regress Argument." *Disputatio* 12: 22–37.

Davidson, D. 1986a. "A Coherence Theory of Truth and Knowledge." In Ernest LePore, ed., *Truth and Interpretation: Perspectives on the Philosophy of Donald Davidson*. Oxford: Blackwell Publishing, pp. 307–19.

— 1986b. "Empirical Content." In Ernest LePore, ed., *Truth and Interpretation: Perspectives on the Philosophy of Donald Davidson*. Oxford: Blackwell Publishing, pp. 320–32.

Everitt, N. and Fisher, E. 1995. *Modern Epistemology*. New York: McGraw Hill.

Ginet, C. 2005. "Infinitism Is not the Solution to the Regress Problem." In M. Steup and E. Sosa, eds, *Contemporary Debates in Epistemology*. Oxford: Blackwell Publishing, pp. 140–9.

Greco, J. and Turri, J. 2009. "Virtue Epistemology." In Edward N. Zalta, ed., *The Stanford Encyclopedia of Philosophy*. Available at: http://plato.stanford.edu/entries/epistemology-virtue/

Haack, S. 1993. *Evidence and Inquiry*. Oxford: Blackwell Publishing.

Howard-Snyder, D. 1998. "BonJour's 'Basic Antifoundationalist Argument' and the Doctrine of the Given." *Southern Journal of Philosophy* 36: 163–77.

— 2002. "On an 'Unintelligible Idea': Donald Davidson's Case against Experiential Foundationalism." *Southern Journal of Philosophy* 40: 523–55.

— 2004. "Lehrer's Case against Foundationalism." *Erkenntnis* 60: 51–73.

— 2005. "Foundationalism and Arbitrariness." *Pacific Philosophical Quarterly* 86(1): 18–24.

Howard-Snyder, D. and Coffman, E. J. 2006. "Three Arguments against Foundationalism: Arbitrariness, Epistemic Regress, and Existential Support." *Canadian Journal of Philosophy* 36: 535–64.

Klein, P. 1999. "Human Knowledge and the Infinite Regress of Reasons." *Philosophical Perspectives* 13: 297–325.

— 2003. "Skepticism." In Edward N. Zalta, ed., *The Stanford Encyclopedia of Philosophy*. Available at: http://plato.stanford.edu/archives/fall2003/entries/skepticism.

— 2004. "What *IS* Wrong with Foundationalism is that it cannot Solve the Epistemic Regress Problem." *Philosophy and Phenomenological Research* 65: 166–71.

— 2005. "Infinitism is the Solution to the Regress Problem." In M. Steup and E. Sosa, eds, *Contemporary Debates in Epistemology*. Oxford: Blackwell Publishing, pp. 131–40.

Kvanvig, J. 2007. "Coherentist Theories of Justification." In Edward N. Zalta, ed., Available at: http://plato.stanford.edu/entries/justep-coherence/

Lehrer, K. 1990. *Theory of Knowledge*. Boulder, CO: Westview Press.

Leite, A. 2004. "On Justifying and Being Justified." *Philosophical Issues* 14: 219–53.

Le Morvan, P. 2008. "Sensory Experience and Intentionalism." *Philosophy Compass* 3(4): 685–702.

McDowell, J. 1994. *Mind and World*. Cambridge, MA: Harvard University Press.

Plantinga, A. 1993. *Warrant: The Current Debate*. New York: Oxford University Press.

Pryor, J. 2005. "There is Immediate Justification." In M. Steup and E. Sosa, eds, *Contemporary Debates in Epistemology*. Oxford: Blackwell Publishing, pp. 181–202.

Sellars, W. 1956. "Empiricism and the Philosophy of Mind." In H. Feigl and M. Scriven, eds, *Minnesota Studies in the Philosophy of Science, Volume I: The Foundations of Science and the Concepts of Psychology and Psychoanalysis*. Minneapolis: University of Minnesota Press, pp. 253–329.

Sosa, E. 1980. "The Raft and the Pyramid: Coherence versus Foundations in the Theory of Knowledge." In P. French, T. E. Uehling, Jr. and H. Wettstein, eds, *Midwest Studies in Philosophy*, Volume V, Minneapolis: University of Minnesota Press, pp. 1–25.

— 2009a. *A Virtue Epistemology*. New York: Oxford University Press.

— 2009b. *Reflective Knowledge*. New York: Oxford University Press.

Steup, M. and Sosa, E., eds, 2005. *Contemporary Debates in Epistemology*, Oxford: Blackwell Publishing.

3

Coherentism

Jonathan Kvanvig

Coherentism is the primary alternative to foundationalism in the history of epistemology. Both approaches are positions concerning the structure of knowledge or justification, and both arise primarily in response to the regress argument for skepticism. I will begin by characterizing the regress argument and the way in which coherentism arises as a response to it. After doing so, I will focus on the primary objections to coherentism and the primary tasks facing the view, beyond that of responding to objections.

Coherentism and regress

The regress argument begins by insisting that what we know and have good reason to believe must have a basis of some sort that accounts for this positive status, and the standard form of the argument requires that such a basis involve some chain of supporting reasons. Once this beginning point is granted, the question arises concerning the nature of this chain of reasons. Here, the skeptic notes that there are three possibilities: either the chain is infinitely long, or it stops at some point, or it turns back on itself, proceeding in a circle. The skeptic then attempts to show that all three options are problematic, arguing that an infinitely long chain involves a vicious regress of reasons that cannot justify anything, that any stopping point would be arbitrary and unjustified thereby ultimately leaving the original belief with only arbitrary support, and that circular reasoning cannot justify anything. The positions targeted by these arguments are infinitism, foundationalism, and coherentism. Defenders of each approach argue that the skeptical stance taken on their favored approach is not correct.

Coherentists, in particular, argue that it is a mistake to think of their position as involving the fallacy of circular reasoning. Though an attempt to avoid the regress argument for skepticism by endorsing circular reasoning would count as a version of coherentism, coherentists have not taken this approach. Instead, coherentists are best understood as objecting to the regress argument at an earlier step, maintaining that the initial premise of the regress argument is mistaken. That step claims that knowledge and justification require some chain of supporting reasons, and coherentists typically insist that such a requirement is mistaken. They claim that such a requirement involves a linear conception of reasons, whereas positive epistemic status involves a holistic conception of reasons on which the support for any given belief arises out of its holistic relationship to an entire system of information.

Thus, whereas foundationalists prefer the metaphor of a building which rests on a suitable foundation of some sort, coherentists prefer the metaphors of a web of belief, with all parts of the web hanging or falling together, or a ship at sea having to be rebuilt enroute, regardless of where the problems are found. These metaphors suggest a picture of positive status that depends on the structural integrity of the entire entity in question, and thus that such status is best conceived of as a holistic characteristic of the system in question.

In short, then, coherentists agree with foundationalists and skeptics that the infinitist option involves a vicious regress, and side with the skeptic that there is no adequate nonarbitrary stopping point to a chain of reasons of the sort that foundationalism requires. Though it is possible to adopt these stances by endorsing circular chains of reasons, typical coherentists favor a holistic conception of reasons so that justification involves a relationship between a target belief and an entire system of information.

From schematic to substantive coherentism

Such a characterization of coherentism does little to identify the substance of the view, however. Instead, it identifies the region of logical space in which coherentism is found, leaving the larger project of clarifying the central elements of coherentism untouched. One way to summarize this point is to say that the response to the regress argument above identifies coherentism in schematic form only, whereas a full defense of the view will require moving from schematic to substantive coherentism.

To do so, coherentists need to discharge two primary obligations. They must first say what the relation of coherence involves, and they must identify which system of information is the relevant system for implying positive epistemic status for its members.

The standard answer among coherentists to the second question is that the system of information in question is the system of beliefs of the individual whose beliefs are being evaluated. Thus, a standard slogan among coherentists is that nothing can justify a belief except another belief, or that there is no exit from the circle of beliefs.[1]

There is, however, another line of thought among coherentists that suggests a less restrictive viewpoint. Coherentists often object to foundationalism by claiming that there is no given or uninterpreted element in sensory experience, and by claiming that mere experience by itself cannot justify anything because experience is always in need of interpretation.[2] One way to honor these points is to insist that only beliefs can justify other beliefs, but a weaker way to do so focusing on this idea that nothing less than interpreted experience can justify anything. If this latter route is taken, the important question to answer is the question of what interpreted experience involves. On this point, coherentists might insist on a distinction between mere awareness and perceptual experience. That is, coherentists might deny that perceptual experience can be reduced to sensory awareness, and that perceptual experience itself needs to be understood in conceptual terms so that every perceptual experience has propositional content and that the subject of such an experience must have a concept for each representational item of the proposition in question.[3] On such a view, the relevant system of information includes not only beliefs of the individual in question, but also experience and its contents as well.

The primary concern regarding this option of including experiences in the relevant system of information is that it may commit a theorist to foundationalism, in which case it cannot be endorsed by coherentists. In particular, the worry is that by appealing to experience in any form, a theorist has to endorse the central foundationalist element that some beliefs have intrinsic warrant or self-warrant. Foundationalists maintain that if it appears to me that it is raining, this appearance generates some degree of intrinsic or self-warrant for my belief that it is raining, whereas no such self-warrant or intrinsic warrant arises if I infer that it is raining from believing that the weatherman on TV is telling the truth about current conditions.

Such a concern, though plausible, is mistaken. Central to foundationalism is the view that some beliefs have intrinsic warrant or self-warrant, and typical foundationalists claim that such warrant arises out of the relationship between experience and foundational beliefs. Coherentists may maintain, not that this relationship between experience and belief is sufficient for such beliefs to have some degree of warrant, but rather that it is necessary. In one way, this point is already implicit in the distinction between experience and awareness noted earlier, for any interpretation of the sort involved in an experience having propositional content may be appropriate or inappropriate, and the notion of appropriateness here is an epistemic notion of propriety that coherentists typically use to insist that a legitimate stopping point for foundationalism has not yet been found. Moreover, the natural coherentist story to tell about which interpretations of experience are appropriate is a holistic one, concerning background knowledge in terms of which the interpretation arises. So the mere fact that coherentists might appeal to interpreted experience in their explanation of the relevant system of information does not turn their view into a form of foundationalism.

The other major issue for coherentists is the nature of the coherence relation itself. On this issue, coherentists have not been as helpful as one could wish. Early proposals included the bizarre suggestion that a system of information coheres just in case every member of the system entails every other member. Such a proposal severely restricts the range of justified beliefs, since contingent propositions are not entailed by necessary ones, and yet it is obvious that some of our contingent beliefs are justified.

A slightly weaker requirement interprets coherence in terms of entailment by the rest of the system of information in question. This proposal is an advance over the prior one, since it allows for the possibility of justified contingent beliefs. Even so, it isn't adequate to the defeasible justification involved in learning. I can learn that my wife is at the store from overhearing my daughter tell her to get milk and eggs in addition to the items on her list of grocery supplies, but none of my information here or elsewhere in my belief system entails that she is at the store. Nonetheless, I am justified in believing that she is, in spite of this lack of entailment.

More sophisticated accounts of coherence aimed at recognizing the defeasible and probabilistic nature of much of our justification came into the literature on coherentism in the work of C. I. Lewis.[4] Lewis claimed that coherence among independent witnesses enhanced the probability of truth (when each source has some degree of initial credibility), and thus thought of coherence as involved probability relations as well as logical ones, with both probability and coherence relevant to the question of which of our beliefs are justified. Lewis was no coherentist, of course, and the point about the need for initial credibility of the sources is essential to understanding why he was a foundationalist rather than a coherentist, but the point to note is the introduction of the language of probability into discussions concerning the nature of coherence, an influence on the literature that is still present in current discussion.

After this introduction of the language of probability into discussions of coherence, one direction of influence led to versions of Bayesian coherentism, which clarify coherence solely in probabilistic terms. According to such an approach, a system of (partial) beliefs is coherent if it is probabilistically consistent. Such an approach involves replacing the psychological notion of belief with that of a degree of belief. For those who follow the more traditional path involving the notion of belief itself, one quite popular approach is in terms of coupling the language of coherence with that of explanation, and the most detailed account of coherence along this path is developed by Laurence BonJour, and it incorporates explanatory connections as one element among several.[5] In particular, BonJour's account involves the following five features:

1. logical consistency
2. probabilistic consistency
3. the range of inferential connections between beliefs
4. the inverse of the degree to which the system is divided into unrelated, unconnected subsystems of belief and
5. the inverse of the degree to which the system of belief contains unexplained anomalies. (pp. 95, 98)

As BonJour admits, this account is far from complete, but even if we had more detail on how the items on the list function together, this account of coherence is at the systemic level only. One important fact about the justification of our beliefs is the variability among our beliefs regarding their degree of justification. Some are justified while others are not, and within each class, some are more justified than others. An account of coherence that applies only at the systemic level cannot explain this variability.

On this score, Bayesian coherentism offers hope. If justification for a degree of belief involves probabilistic coherence within a system of (partial) beliefs, then we can distinguish different levels of justification for a given proposition in terms of what degree of belief is probabilistically consistent within that system. So suppose p and q are propositions and S is a person, and, given S's system of partial beliefs, S can only remain probabilistically consistent by believing p to degree 0.8 (on a scale from 0 to 1 inclusive) and q to degree 0.9. In such a case, q is more justified for S than is p.

While this approach has an advantage over a merely systemic account of coherence, it has a cost as well. The notion of probabilistic coherence it employs restricts the relevant system of information to the system of partial beliefs, thus eliminating interpreted experience from relevant system of information relative to which justification arises.

A full defense of coherentism thus would need to make advances on the current options available in terms of the relevant system of information as well as the nature of the coherence relation itself. Problems for coherentism are not limited to this lack of development, however, and we turn in the next section to the primary arguments used by those who reject coherentism.

Arguments against coherentism

The primary arguments against coherentism can be grouped into three categories. There are objections deriving from the nature of coherentism as a holistic view, arguing that coherentists cannot properly explain what it is to base a belief on other beliefs or experiences. There is also the longstanding objection that coherentists cut off justification from the world, sometimes called the input problem and sometimes called the isolation problem. And there are problems concerning the truth connection, one well-known example of which is the alternative systems objection. I will discuss each of these in turn.

The basing relation difficulty

If justification is conceived of in terms of linear chains of reasons, then it may be fairly easy to explain the difference between someone who bases their belief on the reasons that justify the belief and someone who believes the same thing, has the reasons in question for that belief, but believes on some other basis. The fundamental difference between the two is this: to properly base the belief in question, it must be based on the item preceding it in the chain of reasons that justifies the belief in question. The issue of exactly what is involved in basing a belief on a reason might still be a difficult question to answer, but identifying which particular item this relation must relate the target belief to is not difficult.

Once we adopt a holistic account of justification, however, this simple answer is no longer available. If we tried the same approach, we would require the basing relation to hold between the target belief and that which justifies that target belief. But, by hypothesis, that which justifies the belief is the entire system of information in question, typically interpreted to involve at least all of the beliefs of the person in question. The result is a strange and awkward view: justified beliefs must be based on everything in one's system of beliefs. Since the notion of basing is an explanatory or causal notion concerning the psychology of the person in question, this result has all the appearance of a *reductio*: how can the entire system of beliefs play a causal or explanatory role in the story of how I base my belief that I'm officially married on my beliefs and memories concerning a ceremony, official signings of documents, etc.? There may be a large component of my belief system that is involved here, but it isn't very plausible to think that my belief that New Zealand is closer to Australia than Texas, plays a role in the psychological story of why I believe that I'm officially married.[6]

To respond to this objection, coherentists need to deny that the basing relation is a relation between a target belief and that which justifies that target belief. One way to do this is to distinguish between features of the belief system that are essential for that system to justify the belief in question and those features that are inessential. According to holistic coherentists, no part of a system of information is sufficient in itself to justify a belief, but some parts can be essential to the story of justification even if insufficient. By distinguishing parts of the system in this way, a coherentist can maintain that the basing relation is best understood as a relation between a target belief and items in the system of information that are essential to the justification of that belief, even though it takes the entire system to explain the nature of justification.[7]

The isolation objection

A second major objection to coherentism claims that coherentists cut off, or isolate, the story of justification from the story of the world, leaving the concept of justification too independent from reality itself. In some cases, this concern arises because coherentists typically insist that justification is solely a relation among beliefs. Conceived in this way, one can imagine cases where experience continues to vary across time, but a belief system (assumed for the sake of argument to be fully coherent) is frozen. Thus, Plantinga's example of a person initially in the middle of climbing a mountain, having a fully coherent set of beliefs while doing so, but having that set remain the same after descending the mountain and then experiencing a Mozart opera.[8] If coherence is a relation solely on a system of beliefs, one can object that such a system might be fully coherent and yet be cut off from the world in virtue of eliminating the role of experience, understood in the obvious way to be the avenue by which we enter into contact with reality, from the story of justification.

As we have seen, however, there is no good reason for coherentists to rule out experience from the story of justification. At most, they have a reason to rule out uninterpreted experience, but when experience involves propositional content, that is, interpretation, the relevant system of information with respect to which justificatory status is assessed can legitimately be included. When it is included, this version of the isolation objection is simply mistaken: justification is not cut off from the world in virtue of the discounting of experience from playing a role in the story of justification.

This input problem, however, threatens a large variety of coherentist theories. The usual coherentist response is to try to find some necessary effect by experience on the system of beliefs, perhaps in the form of spontaneous beliefs as found in BonJour.[9] The problem with such attempts is that the connections posited seem at best necessary only in the causal or nomological sense. Perhaps it is nomologically necessary that we have some beliefs based in experience, and perhaps it is nomologically necessary that individuals who have experiences must have those experiences reflected in the system of beliefs at least in normal cases. Even if these claims are granted, however, they are not modally strong enough, since the account of justification in question is intended to be metaphysically necessary, covering all possible cases of the justification of belief, whether nomologically possible or not. So, as long as cases like Plantinga's are logically or metaphysically possible, the problem for coherentism remains even if experience and belief bear certain important nomological connections.

Even so, since coherentism should not be understood as a theory that requires that coherence be a relation only on a system of beliefs, the isolation objection does not threaten coherentism as such. Even so, it does threaten a major subtype, one adopted by most of the major coherentist approaches in the literature.

Problems concerning the truth connection

Issues related to the truth connection arise initially when one notes that a good piece of fiction will display exceptional coherence in spite of having no connection at all to what is actually true. A traditional way of putting this concern is in the language of the alternative systems objection, according to which nearly any belief can be justified by simply embedding it in the right system of information.

In one way, this objection is simply misplaced. One of the platitudes about justification is that it is perspectival, that what a person is justified in believing is a function of their total perspective on the world. In light of this platitude it should not surprise us that many claims are justified for twenty-first century westerners that were not justified for folk in the Middle Ages or even twenty-first century non-westerners. Moreover, if we interpret the objection to mean that if a given individual were to have sufficient control over their system of beliefs, any belief could be defended by making enough adjustments elsewhere in the system, that point too is not obviously objectionable. It is a fact of epistemic life that recalcitrant experience does not carry with it any definitive pointer as to which elements in our belief system need to change in light of the experience. So the mere fact that adjustments to a system can be made in a variety of ways is part of the reality of epistemic life, rather than a basis for an objection to theories that accommodate such a point.

What would be a problem is if individuals with suitable control over their systems of belief were to be irrationally motivated to preserve certain cherished beliefs by making outlandish and extensive changes to a belief system when simpler changes could have been made. As should be obvious, however, there is nothing in coherentism as such that requires it to count such an individual as justified in making such changes. To hang onto cherished beliefs is to be motivated in certain non-epistemic ways to hold and retain a given belief, and even if such beliefs cohere with a system of information, they will have a hard time passing the tests for a properly based belief, since the non-epistemic motivation will interfere with basing the belief on the elements in the system of information that are essential for the justification of that belief.

Hence, when put in the language of the alternative systems objection, worries concerning the truth connection are not decisive against coherence theories. But forcing worries about the truth connection into the language of the alternative systems objection would be a mistake, for the heart of the concern is not about alternative systems at all, but about the fact that justification is supposed to be a guide to truth and the worry is that coherence itself is not an indicator of likelihood of truth.

One version of this concern traces to Lewis's endorsement of coherence as a guide to truth. Lewis thought that agreement among independent witnesses with some degree of initial credibility raises the likelihood of truth, and Lewis-inspired treatments of the notion of coherence in terms of probability appear to be promising approaches to addressing concerns about the truth connection.

Recent work, however, has questioned this idea, relying on formal impossibility results about the connection between coherence and likelihood of truth.[10] The significance of the impossibility results depends, of course, on the plausibility of the regimenting of coherentism that is required to obtain the results. On this score, it is far from clear that such regimenting has revealed anything like the essence or core of coherentism. In fact, the notion that coherence needs to truth-conducive is only one way for coherentists to respond to the problem of the truth connection. Suppose, for example, we understand truth-conduciveness in this way: for any two sets of statements where the first is at least as coherent as the second, then the first is at least as probable as the second.[11] One might wonder why a coherentist should prefer this kind of formal regimentation to weaker ones which require only that changes in coherence are reflected in changes in justificatory status.[12] One way to formalize such a result would be to appeal to the Bayesian notion of confirmation-conducivity. If one set of statements is positively correlated and another is not, then the first is more coherent than the second (where a set of statements is positively correlated just when the probability of the conjunction of the members of the set is greater than the product of each of the individual members). More generally, we might want variations in coherence to track variations in degree of correlation, rather than probability itself. Careful coherentists will want this relationship to be *ceteris paribus* only, since connections between probability and coherence may only be one factor to consider in assessing the overall coherence of a set, and these two points in combination avoid the best-known impossibility results.[13]

There is much more work to be done on the formal side here, but whatever the results, their significance is muted to a significant degree. First, there is the general problem for Bayesians of not having an idea of how to model the inclusion of interpreted experiences. When it comes to beliefs and partial beliefs, one constructs a model in terms of the propositional content of such beliefs, but one can't adopt this approach for experience as well, since we sometimes rationally believe the opposite of what experience reveals (as when we know that conditions are deceptive). Second, it is not clear what amount of formalization can be defended regarding the topic in question. In order to prove impossibility results, the informal notion of coherence has to be formalized, and whatever precisifications are involved will be controversial.

Moreover, there is a general problem with the usual formulations of the truth condition that deserve attention. Casual formulations often maintain that justification must be understood in terms of the best guide to truth, but this formulation cannot be accepted as it stands. First, taken at face value, it threatens most foundationalist theories as well as coherentist theories, so it would not count as some special problem that coherentists face. Second, it has a special difficulty in explaining why we are more justified in accepting a scientific theory than we are in accepting the conjunction of its empirical consequences. It is a theorem of the probability calculus that if A entails B, then the probability of A is less than or equal to the probability of B, so if justification is understood in terms of the best guide to truth, the safer bet would typically favor not accepting the theory itself but only the conjunction of its empirical consequences. Third, casual formulations ignore the new evil demon problem. It is intuitively obvious that denizens of the relevant demon worlds have roughly the same justified beliefs that we do, since they could be us, and yet nearly all of their justified beliefs are false. So a casual statement of the truth connection ignores this important fact about justification.

There is, however, one special concern for coherentists regarding the connection to truth, arising out of the lottery and preface paradoxes. In each case, the central conclusion of concern to coherentists is that these paradoxes show that justified inconsistent beliefs are possible, and this point conflicts with the idea that whatever else coherence involves, a minimal condition for it is consistency. Here the problem is that coherentists have too strong a truth connection, restricting justification to systems of information that might have only true members, whereas the lessons of the paradoxes seems to be that such a requirement is too strong. In the lottery paradox, we imagine the lottery big enough that it is justified for you to think that your ticket will lose. The same grounds for this conclusion apply to the other tickets as well, so one can deduce that no ticket will win. Hence, the combination of justified beliefs is inconsistent. In the preface paradox, conscientious authors express humility in their prefaces, noting the obvious fact that in spite of our best efforts, we make mistakes. If we suppose that all the claims in the text are justified, this expression of humility in the preface generates an inconsistency.

This problem of justified inconsistent beliefs is a special problem for coherentists not faced by other theories of justification.[14] One might try to avoid it by compartmentalizing beliefs systems and requiring consistency only within subcompartments,[15] but such a suggestion faces the enormous difficulty of specifying how to carve out the subcompartments appropriately. There is, however, another approach that coherentists might take, appealing to the idea that the kind of justification they intend to characterize is one responsive to the platitude that justification is what knowledge looks like from the inside. On the basis of this platitude, coherentists may insist that the kind of justification relevant to an account of the nature of knowledge is one thing, and there may be other notions of justification, even alethic notions clarifiable in terms of the goal of getting to the truth and avoiding error, that are not. So they may claim that ordinary alethic justification is present in lottery and preface cases, but that ordinary alethic justification is not the epistemic justification they intend to characterize.

In order to defend this line, coherentists need to explain what distinguishes epistemic justification from ordinary alethic justification. There are two ways to do so, one stronger and the other weaker. The stronger version maintains that when we are epistemically justified in believing a claim, we also have justification for concluding that we know the claim in question. One way to argue for this claim is to argue that each of the standard four conditions for knowledge are amenable to such a requirement. Thus, one might argue that if we justifiably believe *p* in the epistemic sense, then we have good enough evidence to conclude that we believe *p* and that *p* is true (the first would seem to be supportable by the first-person authority we each possess regarding the contents of our own minds, and the second would seem to be a consequence of the nature of truth). The key elements for this approach would then be to show that we have good enough evidence to conclude that we are justified in believing *p* when we are, and good enough evidence to conclude that we are ungettiered.

To show the former, coherentists need an argument for the claim that if there is justification of the epistemic sort for *p*, then there is justification that there is justification for *p* (call this the "JJ principle"). This claim is one endorsed by access internalists, who maintain that justification is something that, when we have it, we can detect it by reflection alone. But the claim is independent of access internalism. In fact, one way to think about the relationship between access internalism and the JJ principle is that access internalism is what you get when you try to operationalize that principle, that is, when you try to say what would happen in behavioral terms when attempting to detect whether you are justified in believing a given claim. So access internalism should be thought of as just a special case of a class of theories that endorses the JJ principle. Such a conclusion gives resources to coherentism for defending the JJ principle since many of the objections to this style of theory are really objections to access internalism rather than to the JJ principle itself.

A full defense of the JJ principle would be beyond the scope of this chapter, and it is here that the distinction between weaker and stronger ways of distinguishing ordinary alethic justification from epistemic justification is significant. Defending the JJ principle is only necessary for the stronger way of drawing the distinction, and the weaker way focuses on a feature of the kind of justification necessary for knowledge that is related to the Gettier problem. Knowing involves justification for closure to further inquiry, confirmed by the fact that it makes little sense to say, "I know that it is raining outside, but I think I should go check to make sure," or to say, "I know today is Thursday, but further inquiry regarding today's date is probably appropriate." Just imagine a news conference in which the athletic director says, "We, together with the NCAA, have investigated all relevant charges of impropriety in the operation of our basketball program, and as a result, we now know that all of the charges are false and that our program is completely clean. But the investigation will continue . . ." Such a remark would be utterly bizarre, and the reason it would be bizarre is because knowledge involves a legitimate closure of investigation. In particular, it involves an inquiry that is of sufficient quality that it licenses the conclusion that any further learning could undermine one's present opinion only by presenting one with misleading information.

This way of putting the point should not be confused with a stronger way of endorsing the present claim about the relationship between knowledge and further learning. One may be tempted here to say that inquiry adequate for knowledge licenses one to conclude that further learning could only confirm one's present opinion, but that it is too strong. It is too strong because of the possibility of misleading pockets of information. A simple statistical case will suffice as an example. Suppose statistical knowledge is possible, and that one's sample of tosses has given one knowledge that a given die is unlikely to come up a six when tossed. It is consistent with such knowledge that were one to investigate further, that any finite string of sixes could result on future tosses of the die. Were further inquiry to occur and such an improbable sequence of events happen, one's opinion would have to change in order to be rational. What is licensed by one's present body of evidence on the assumption that this body of evidence is strong enough to put one in a position to know, however, is not the conclusion that no further learning could rationally undermine present opinion, but rather the weaker claim that any further learning that would rationally undermine present opinion would involve misleading information.

This feature by itself is sufficient to distinguish ordinary alethic justification from epistemic justification. In the lottery case, closure of inquiry is not legitimated by the quality of one's evidence for the claim that your ticket will lose. That is why it is fully appropriate to check the newspaper tomorrow to see what the winning ticket number is. Moreover, the expression of epistemic humility at the heart of the preface paradox involves a recognition of the difficulty and complexity of the subject matter of the book, sufficient to warrant further checking by anyone reading the book, including the author! So the closure of inquiry that is central to the kind of justification needed for knowledge is not present in these cases, and hence the kind of justification that is present is only ordinary alethic justification.

For those preferring the stronger response, the response that attempts to show that when epistemic justification is present, there is justification present for the claim that we know, the above point can be used in the following way. One would only need to tie the notion of misleading information to the defeasibility theory to complete the response. It is well-known that knowledge is different from undefeated justified true belief, since some defeaters are misleading. If one's total evidence confirms that further investigation could undermine present opinion only by uncovering misleading information, then one's total evidence confirms that further learning could at worst reveal only misleading defeaters. Hence, if one is epistemically justified in believing *p*, one is justified in concluding that one's justification is ungettiered, that is, that one's justification is defeated at most by misleading defeaters. Adding the point to the defenses already pointed to regarding the other three conditions, the defender of the stronger approach would now have achieved the advertised result of arguing for the claim that ordinary alethic justification falls short of epistemic justification since only the latter involves justification for the claim that one knows.

Either the weaker or stronger routes gives a general coherentist strategy for dealing with the type of justified inconsistency involved in sets of statements of more than one member. There is, however, another type of justified inconsistent belief, one involving only a single proposition. For example, Frege was justified in accepting the comprehension axiom, in spite of the fact that it leads to Russell's paradox.

The best coherentist strategy for dealing with this problem involves noting that it is not so much an epistemological problem as it is a problem in the philosophy of mind. The problem is, at bottom, how to characterize the contents of representational states such as beliefs. The standard model here takes belief to be a relation between a person and a proposition having wide content (so that the sentences "I am tired" and "JK is tired" express the same proposition), but such an account is widely recognized to be unable to explain the cognitive significance of representational states. Addressing the problem of cognitive significance requires resources that go beyond this simple dyadic account of belief. One promising new approach is in terms of the variety of two-dimensional semantics that are being developed,[16] but there is also the possibility of resurrecting a Fregean approach to propositional content in terms of the sense or meaning of the terms involved in the sentences in question, or adding a third relatum to the standard view, where the third element is designed to solve the problem of cognitive significance.[17] In each case, the emendations to the standard view will involve representational and semantic features beyond those involved in wide-content propositions, and these additional features will provide coherentists with the resources needed to address the problem of justified inconsistent individual beliefs. For patterns of inference and explanation that count as fully justified will need to be explained on anyone's theory in terms that go beyond wide-content propositions, so the additional resources involved in solving the problem of cognitive significance can be used by coherentists to explain why, even though in terms of the wide-content proposition expressed, a belief is inconsistent, a focus on the representational features involved in the patterns of inference and explanation that are justified for a person will involve a focus on representational features beyond wide-content propositions, and there is reason to expect these features to involve consistency even when the wide-content proposition is inconsistent.

Conclusion

Thus, in spite of the variety of problems and challenges facing coherentism, its current lack of popularity, in contrast to its heyday in the mid-twentieth century, should not be viewed as a sign that it is an all-but-dead theory. Coherentists have much yet to explain and explore, but the problems raised for the theory do not show that the path ought to be abandoned in favor of more promising approaches.

Notes

1   See, e.g., Donald Davidson, "A Coherence Theory of Truth and Knowledge," in Ernest LePore, ed., *Truth and Interpretation: Perspectives on the Philosophy of Donald Davidson* (New York: Oxford University Press, 1989); and Keith Lehrer, *Knowledge* (Oxford: Clarendon Press, 1974) for such claims.

2   See, e.g., Wilfrid Sellars on the myth of the given and Keith Lehrer on the "prick of sense," especially p. 188.

3 For clarification and defense of such a view, see John Bengson, Enrico Grube and Dan Korman, "A New Framework for Conceptualism," unpublished ms available at: https://netfiles.uiuc.edu/dzkorman/www/Conceptualism.pdf

4 C. I. Lewis, *An Essay on Knowledge and Valuation* (LaSalle, IL: Open Court, 1946).

5 Laurence BonJour, *The Structure of Empirical Knowledge* (Cambridge, MA: Harvard University Press, 1985).

6 The source of this objection is John Pollock's *Contemporary Theories of Knowledge* (Totowa, NJ: Rowman & Littlefield, 1985).

7 An account along these lines is developed in Jonathan L. Kvanvig, "Coherentists' Distractions," *Philosophical Topics* 23 (1995) 257–75.

8 Alvin Plantinga, *Warrant: The Current Debate* (Oxford: Oxford University Press, 1992, 82).

9 Laurence BonJour, *The Structure of Empirical Knowledge* (Cambridge, MA: Harvard University Press, 1985).

10 See, e.g., Erik Olsson, *Against Coherence: Truth, Probability, and Justification* (Oxford: Oxford University Press, 2005); and Luc Bovens and Stephan Hartmann, *Bayesian Epistemology* (Oxford: Oxford University Press, 2004).

11 This is the Lewis-inspired connection underlying the impossibility result proved in chapter 1 of Bovens and Hartmann, *Bayesian Epistemology* (Oxford: Oxford University Press, 2004).

12 Some formal results within this general approach that can help coherentists on this point can be found in Dietrich, F. and L. Moretti. "On Coherent Sets and the Transmission of Confirmation." *Philosophy of Science* 72(3), 403–24; and in Moretti, L. "Ways in which Coherence is Confirmation Conducive." *Synthese* 157(3), 309–19.

13 The first idea can be found in Brandon Fitelson's review of Bovens and Hartmann, *Bayesian Epistemology, Mind* 114 (April 2005), 394–99; and the second idea can be found in Michael Huemer's review of Olsson, *Against Coherence, Notre Dame Philosophical Reviews,* published May 10, 2006. Available at: http://ndpr.nd.edu/review.cfm?id=6583.

14 The *locus classicus* of this objection is Richard Foley, *The Theory of Epistemic Rationality* (Cambridge, MA: Harvard University Press, 1986, 96–102).

15 A suggestion first made by Wayne Riggs and first published in William G. Lycan, *Judgment and Justification* (Cambridge: Cambridge University Press, 1988).

16 For a nice overview of these approaches, see David Chalmers, "Two-Dimensional Semantics," forthcoming in LePore and Smith, eds, *Oxford Handbook for the Philosophy of Language,* a draft of which is available at: http://consc.net/papers/twodim.pdf.

17 See, e.g., Nathan Salmon, *Frege's Puzzle,* 2nd edn (Atascadero, CA: Ridgeview, 1986).

4

Infinitism

Peter D. Klein

Introduction

The purpose of this chapter is to explore and defend infinitism—one of the three non-skeptical solutions that is available for addressing the epistemic regress problem. That problem has a long history. Aristotle discusses it, but its most familiar formulation, and the one that still provides a basis for the current thinking about the regress problem, was described by Sextus Empiricus in his discussion of the arguments directed against those (the "dogmatists") who thought reasoning could provide a basis for assenting to a proposition.[1] Sextus's depiction of the argument has been recast in many forms and, contrary to its original intent, it is often employed to defend foundationalism or coherentism. This chapter will develop and defend an alternative to the foundationalist and coherentist solution to the regress by arguing that both rely upon a truncated account of justification. Armed with a more robust and accurate account of justification, the most viable solution to the regress argument is the infinitist one.

The chapter is divided into five sections:

1. The Epistemic Regress Argument
2. Outline of the Four "Solutions" to the Regress Problem
3. The Initial Plausibility of the Foundationalist Solution
4. The Problems with the Foundationalist and Coherentist Solutions
5. Sketch of Infinitism and Replies to some Objections.

The epistemic regress argument

The classical statement of the regress argument is given by Sextus Empiricus in Chapter 15 of his *Outlines of Pyrrhonism*:

The later Skeptics hand down Five Modes leading to suspension, namely these: the first based on discrepancy, the second on the regress *ad infinitum,* the third on relativity, the fourth on hypothesis, the fifth on circular reasoning. That based on discrepancy leads us to find that with regard to the object presented there has arisen both amongst ordinary people and amongst the philosophers an interminable conflict because of which we are unable either to choose a thing or reject it, and so fall back on suspension. The Mode based upon regress *ad infinitum* is that whereby we assert that the thing adduced as a proof of the matter proposed needs a further proof, and this again another, and so on *ad infinitum,* so that the consequence is suspension [of assent], as we possess no starting-point for our argument. The Mode based upon relativity . . . is that whereby the object has such or such an appearance in relation to the subject judging and to the concomitant percepts, but as to its real nature we suspend judgment. We have the Mode based upon hypothesis when the Dogmatists, being forced to recede *ad infinitum,* take as their starting-point something which they do not establish but claim to assume as granted simply and without demonstration. The Mode of circular reasoning is the form used when the proof itself which ought to establish the matter of inquiry requires confirmation derived from the matter; in this case, being unable to assume either in order to establish the other, we suspend judgement about both.[2]

The five modes discussed by Sextus include three that portray the alternative accounts of the structure of reasoning that the "dogmatists" believe are available for settling a disputed question.[3] They are the mode of hypothesis in which the regress terminates in a belief for which no further reason is needed, the mode *ad infinitum* whereby every reason needs a further reason, and the mode of circular reasoning in which a reason appears twice in the chain of reasons. The other two modes, relativity and discrepancy, are designed to provide a general recipe for disputing all claims that are offered as being beyond dispute. For either those claims are based upon the contents of perception (and those contents are subject/context relative) or upon accepted beliefs (but those beliefs are not universally accepted by either the "ordinary people" or the experts—i.e. philosophers). Thus, neither appealing to perception nor appealing to what is generally accepted will settle matters. Reason must be brought to bear and Sextus reported that the recognition of the limitations of reasoning led to the suspension of judgment regarding disputed propositions.

Although many contemporary epistemologists employ the regress argument to motivate one or another form of what Sextus would have called "dogmatism" by embracing one of the horns of the trilemma implicit in Sextus's argument, these epistemologists would not use the labels that Sextus does to name their views because each appellation smacks of arbitrariness. For example, a contemporary foundationalist would not use "hypothesis" as a term to describe his/her view because that brings with it the connotation of arbitrariness, and, as we will see, the contemporary foundationalist (as well as the archetypal foundationalist that Sextus has in mind, namely Aristotle) holds that the basic propositions are not mere hypotheses that need to be subjected to further justification. Rather, they are deliveries of our senses or other reliable epistemic mechanisms (e.g. memory, reason) which are properly accepted unless there is some countervailing evidence. Coherentists would abjure using the label "circular reasoning" because that, too, brings with it the connotation of arbitrariness. Finally, as we shall see, infinitists would be careful not to label or explain their view in a way that would imply the viciousness often accompanying an infinite series.

Sextus's depiction of the three models of reasoning depends upon an unarticulated but extremely plausible principle of inferential justification that we can call the Inherence Principle (IP):[4]

IP: If a belief, b, acquires justification in virtue of a reason, r, having been given for b, then r has to be justified.

The contrapositive of IP seems equally intuitively plausible: If r is not justified, then a belief b cannot acquire justification in virtue of r being given as a reason for b. I say that the regress argument depends upon IP because, as we will see, if IP were false, then Sextus's regress argument supporting skepticism contains no good basis for rejecting any of the three "dogmatic" solutions to the regress problem. First, if IP were false, no good reason has been presented for rejecting infinitism because if a belief, b, could be justified in some important respect on the basis of a reason, r, having been given for b without it being the case that r is justified in that respect, then there is no need for a "starting point."[5] That type of justification can arise by giving a reason. Second, IP provides Sextus with the basis for discarding the foundationalist solution to the regress when coupled with the modes of relativity and discrepancy. Those two modes are used to show that the "hypothesis" offered as a starting point by the foundationalists is not justified and, hence, the hypothesis cannot transfer justification to other beliefs. Arbitrariness in, arbitrariness out. Finally, circular reasoning is rejected because r would have to be justified before being able to transfer the justification (perhaps through intermediate beliefs) to b and b would have to be justified before being able to transfer justification (perhaps through intermediate beliefs) to r. Thus, if circular reasoning is permitted, no account of the origin of justification has been provided. An analogy might help to make that clear: Imagine some basketball players standing in a circle passing the ball to each other. The basketball can be transferred from one player to another, but how the basketball got there in the first place remains mysterious. In sum, whichever account of reasoning is endorsed by the "dogmatist," IP (coupled with the modes of discrepancy and relativity) is available to show that the chosen account of reasoning cannot account for the origin of justified beliefs.

Outline of the four "solutions" to the regress problem

The **skeptical** "solution" is to embrace the argument's conclusion, namely, that reasoning cannot resolve disputes. There are many important nuances here that would have to be explored if a full understanding of the skeptical "solution" were one of the goals of this chapter. For example, it would have to be determined whether a skeptic could endorse either the conclusion of the regress argument (and its premises) or the probative power of the argument without violating both his/her own practice of withholding judgment concerning what is nonevident (i.e. whatever requires an argument in order to be affirmed) when the very outcome of the argument calls into question the probative power of reasoning. I do think there are ways to show how the Pyrrhonian Skeptic can employ the argument as a response to dogmatism without embracing dogmatism, but that would take us too far afield.[6]

A good way to understand each of three non-skeptical contemporary "solutions" to the regress problem is to focus on IP and the different stances each view takes to IP.

Foundationalists accept the principle. Good reasoning can transmit justification but because IP precludes reasoning from initiating justification, the foundationalist says that there are (or, given that the skeptical solution is not acceptable, must be) some beliefs that are justified but not in virtue of inheriting justification through reasoning from other beliefs. For example, a foundationalist could claim that perceptual beliefs are justified in virtue of their causal history and the circumstances in which the belief arises. If I come to believe that the ball is red by seeing the red ball in good light, then my belief that the ball is red is at least prima facie justified. Then, through reasoning, the justification could be transferred to other beliefs if the reasoning were done properly.

Coherentists take a more revisionist tact. They do not have to advocate a kind of circular reasoning as envisioned by IP because they do not hold that justification is a property whose primary bearers are individual beliefs. Instead of justification being transferred from one belief to another, they would hold that individual beliefs obtain a positive epistemic status in virtue of being members of a set of beliefs that are sufficiently coherent (plus, possibly, some other features). That is, the individual beliefs do not obtain their justification (or at least not all of their justification) from other justified beliefs. They are justified, at least in part, in virtue of being members of a set of propositions that are coherent (and perhaps have other properties as well). They need not deny IP when the so-called "local" reasons are being provided for a belief. One belief can bolster another's justification by providing some evidence for it. Nevertheless, at least some prima facie justification arises in the first place in sets of beliefs.

Infinitists deny IP. They hold that at least some positive epistemic status is gained by a belief, b, if a reason is provided for it. Reasoning does not merely transmit epistemic properties, it can enhance the epistemic status of a belief. Thus, by providing a reason, r, for b, b becomes more justified than it was before the reason was provided. It is crucial to note that this can happen even if no reason for r had yet been located and/or provided. In such a case, r would not be transferring a property that it already has. Rather, when a person, S, has a reason, r, for a belief, b, that belief has thereby acquired some positive epistemic property, call it "reason enhanced," which b lacked before S had the reason. The point is that b can become reason-enhanced even though r is not (yet) reason-enhanced.

The initial plausibility of the foundationalist solution

We will return to the coherentist and infinitist solutions, but it is fitting to begin with foundationalism because that approach has dominated epistemology from the Greeks to contemporary philosophy.

Suppose, for the moment, that IP is correct. The question remains: If a belief, b, inherits justification from r, and r inherits justification from r1 and r1 acquires it from r2, etc., then how does justification originate? The answer that has dominated epistemology is that there are some beliefs that do not acquire their justification from reasoning. They are justified in virtue of something other than reasoning. For example, it could be claimed, a la Chisholm, that basic beliefs play a distinctive role in Socratic questioning;[7] or it could be claimed that there is good phenomenological evidence that some beliefs merely record the contents of our sense experience and such beliefs could not be wrong, or it could be claimed that basic beliefs are characterized by their ability to be (what I will call) "conversation stoppers." There are other proposed definitive characteristics of putative basic beliefs, but the most frequently cited property of basic empirical beliefs, at least since Aristotle, is their etiology which begins with sensation. That is, if the belief has the right kind of causal pedigree in which reasoning plays no essential justificatory role, it is at least prima facie justified. Here is a crucial passage from Aristotle's *Posterior Analytics*:

> We have already said that scientific knowledge through demonstration is impossible unless a man knows the primary immediate premises . . . Therefore we must possess a capacity of some sort . . . and this at least is an obvious characteristic of all animals, for they all possess a congenital discriminative capacity which is called sense-perception. But though sense perception is innate in all animals, in some the sense-impression comes to persist, in others, it does not . . . and when such persistence is frequently repeated a further distinction at once arises between those which out of persistence of such sense-impressions develop a power of systematizing them and those which do not. So out of sense-perception comes to be what we call memory, and out of frequently repeated memories of the same thing develops experience; for a number of memories constitute a single experience. From experience again—i.e., from the universal now stabilized in its entirety within the soul, the one beside the many which is a single identity within them all—originate the skill of the craftsman and the knowledge of the man of science, skill in the sphere of coming to be and science in the sphere of being. (PA 99b20–100a9)

It is worth noting that Aristotle takes the contents of the so-called basic beliefs that provide the foundation for all scientific knowledge to be the first principles of a science which define the essential properties of the type of object under study. This is quite different from beliefs about individual objects and their properties which are typically cited by modern and contemporary (empiricist) foundationalists. But that difference in the content of the so-called basic beliefs illustrates my point that it is the etiology of the belief—rather than the content—that many foundationalists will point to as the distinguishing feature of basic beliefs. The claim is that if the etiology of the belief does not include reasoning from other beliefs and the belief is justified, then the beliefs are basic beliefs.

The following quotation from Alvin Goldman is typical of contemporary foundationalists who propose that the etiology of a belief determines whether it is a justified basic belief:

> In characterizing the causal process relevant to the justifiedness of a perceptual belief, I have thus far followed Feldman in considering the process *from experience to belief*. . . . An alternative treatment, however is available to process reliabilism. The relevant process might be a more external one, not *from experience to belief* but *from receptor stimulation (to experience) to belief*. This more extended process has potential advantages because of what might transpire between receptor and stimulation and experience. . . . Thus, we should leave the door open to either type of process—the more or the less extended process—as the optimal choice from the perspective of process reliabilism.[8]

Although the contents of the purported immediately justified beliefs depicted by Goldman and Aristotle are not similar, one being about specific objects and their properties the other being about universal and essential properties of natural kinds, respectively, the underlying structures of their views are similar. If the etiology of a belief does not include reasoning or inference but does include what are taken to be truth-conducive processes, the belief is justified and can provide the basis for reasoning that can confer justification upon nonbasic beliefs. To generalize, foundationalism holds that there is some property, call it "F," in virtue of which some beliefs are justified, but in such a way that their justification is not at all dependent upon reasoning from other beliefs.

Regardless of the various F's that are proposed as the distinguishing characteristic of basic propositions, foundationalists can claim two principal virtues of their account of justification: (1) it explains how a belief can be justified but not in virtue of another belief and (2) it explains how such a basic belief can transmit justification through reasoning to a hitherto unjustified belief. Thus, foundationalism provides us with a schema for solving the regress problem. Or does it?

The problems with the foundationalist and coherentist solutions

The Pyrrhonians thought that foundationalism was unable to adequately address the regress problem because there are just too many actual and potential disagreements over the content of the so-called foundational beliefs. Both the beliefs that are commonly accepted as well as the beliefs based upon the testimony delivered by our senses can be challenged, and without an unchallengeable reply to these challenges, the so-called foundational beliefs were seen to be mere hypotheses that require further justification. Recall the modes of relativity and discrepancy. Even if some so-called basic beliefs were accepted by all members of my epistemic community, there are other epistemic communities (including my own at other times) that would not, or at least might not, accept the same beliefs. To privilege my community over those other actual or potential communities is nothing but epistemic hubris. Even simple perceptual beliefs like "this looks red" or "this seems hot" can't be foundational beliefs on which to base other beliefs because they are relative to a perceiver or to the circumstances in which the perception arose. That is, one could grant that something looks red to some subject, S1, at one time, but point out that it looks orange to that same subject at another time or that it looks blue or colorless to another subject, S2, etc. Those beliefs are merely about how things look to particular subjects in particular circumstances and because those appearances can vary, they cannot serve as basic propositions that can be employed to settle an issue.

Now there are some initially promising replies available to the Pyrrhonian objections to foundationalism. For example, we could argue that the "real" properties of an object are those which play a significant role in explaining the differences in the perceptions of the object on various occasions. Thus, we can take the ways things look to be useful evidence for beliefs about how things are. And we could distinguish between relative expert communities and nonexpert ones. For example, if there are two groups that held different opinions about the cause of the tragic earthquake in Haiti on January 12, 2010—one thinking it was God's punishment for some religious transgression by the Haitian people and another group thinking it was the result of tectonic plate shifts[9]—we could determine which group is better able to predict future earthquakes (or retrodict past ones).

Those are initially promising responses, and perhaps they can be fleshed out so as to successfully answer the Pyrrhonian objections to foundationalism. But the important point to note is that the giving or reasons need not stop with the citing of the so-called basic beliefs. Once raised, questions about the epistemic status of the so-called basic beliefs need to be addressed if a practicing foundationalist is to be entitled to maintain his/her degree of credence in the basic beliefs. Indeed, I think there is a very general way of showing that the foundationalist, as well as the coherentist, purported solution to the regress problem fails.

The regress problem is essentially this: Is there some belief in the chain of beliefs, offered as reasons, that is immune to further interrogation? The issue is not whether we do stop giving reasons for our beliefs. Of course, we do. The issue is not whether there are commonly held beliefs which are accepted by an epistemic community that, when deployed, typically put an end to the need to provide further reasons. Of course, there are. Rather, the issue is whether there is ***always*** some legitimate basis for questioning the offered "basic" belief which did stop, or at least could have stopped, the "regress."[10] I will argue that there is always such a legitimate basis for requiring further reasons.

Let me begin by pointing out that most discussions in which reasons are offered never arrive at the types of beliefs that the foundationalists think are basic, but nevertheless those conversations do end—and nonarbitrarily so. Typically, contemporary foundationalists take beliefs about our sensations, memories, or intuitions as the proper stopping points, and surely it is true that sometimes such propositions properly end conversations. But there are many other beliefs which seem equally well suited to stop conversations. Here are some snippets of conversations with their stopping points:

Do you know when "Saturday Night Live" starts tonight?
Yes, it starts around 11:30.
What reason do we have for believing that?
It says so right here in the TV Guide.

Do you know how many planets there are?
Yes, there are at least eight; nine, if you count Pluto.
What reason do you have for believing that?
I've been told that by people who study such things and I've read it a bunch of times in reliable sources.

Do you know how old you are?
Yes, 70.
What reason do you have for believing that?
I was born in September, 1940, and it's now October, 2010.

Do you know what's going to happen to that car?
Yes, it will soon be my son's car?
What reason do you have for believing that?
I own it and I will give it to him.

None of those stopping points are what the foundationalists would have cited as basic beliefs. Nevertheless they stop conversations just as well as the so-called basic beliefs. Indeed, they represent types of beliefs which probably stop conversations more often than the so-called basic beliefs that foundationalists would single out. So what is special about the foundationalist's stopping points? Presumably, the foundationalist would hold that the so-called basic propositions are immune to further questions, whereas the stopping points above are clearly not immune—although they typically are not challenged. It is the purported immunity to further challenge that distinguishes the foundational propositions from the non-foundational stopping points.

Other philosophers have pointed to the fact that what we can call "conversation stoppers" varies from one context to another.[11] If we want to know whether a certain formation in football is legitimate, we check the rule book. If we want to know whether the deal on a used car is good, we check the Kelley Blue Book. If we want to know whether someone feels dizzy, we ask them, etc. Foundationalists could grant that there are stopping points other than the ones they would typically cite, but what they would claim—in fact, must claim if they are to be true to their creed—is that all conversation stoppers other than the privileged ones offered by foundationalists are merely convenient stopping points on the way to the privileged ones.

However, I think it is rather easy to show that the so-called basic beliefs are not in principle any more immune to further interrogation than the conversation-stoppers employed in the examples given earlier. Consider a favorite candidate for a basic belief—a belief about how things appear:

> The ball is red.
> What reason do you have for believing that?
> It looks red to me and I am not aware of anything unusual in the circumstance.

Often only the first conjunct is given as the reason and for the sake of simplicity, let's focus on that one.[12] Is "it looks red to me" immune from further challenge? No! I could be asked whether I am a good detector of how colors appear? Of course, I'm not usually asked that question because it is usually taken for granted that I am a good apparent color detector—just as it is usually assumed that I am a good detector of my intentions, or that I remember when I was born, or that experts know how many planets there are.

But all of the conversations could continue if the standard or "criterion," as it was referred to by the Pyrrhonians, is challenged.[13] I could explain why the standard is truth conducive. For example, I could cross-check my memory of when I was born by citing what I have been told and what my birth certificate says, or I could explain the basis on which the experts are selected. And, most importantly, I could explain why I believe that I and almost everyone else is a good detector of apparent colors.[14] I could offer a basis for believing that there is no way I could to be wrong about apparent colors because I am merely reporting how things seem to me rather than how they actually are. And in so doing, there is no risk of error because no sense can be made out of the claim that there is a difference between how things seem to seem to me and how they seem to me. The lack of that difference explains why I cannot be wrong in making claims about how things seem to me. I have, or so it could be claimed, privileged access to my "mental contents."

Perhaps if this reasoning were carefully developed, it would be good enough to justify my reports about the contents of my experiences. Let me grant that. The point remains that without those reasons available, the implicit claim that I am entitled to my belief that the ball looks red would be groundless.

Let me generalize this point.[15] Suppose a foundationalist is practicing what she preaches, and after giving several reasons for a belief she eventually arrives at what she takes to be a basic belief, b. The challenge begins by asking her why she is stopping at that point. She answers that b is basic and needs no further reason. Then she is asked: "What is it about b that makes it immune to further questioning?" Now, if she has no answer for that, it certainly looks like she should lower her credence in b because she would be in the epistemically awkward position of claiming that b doesn't need a reason but being unable to point to a property of b that gives it this privileged status.

Suppose that she answers that b is foundational because it has some property, say F, in virtue of which it is foundational. Her claim is that possessing F is sufficient to make b justified and, thus, no reason for b need be given. Indeed, she might grant that there are reasons for believing b, but claim that b is justified to the extent necessary without her marshaling those reasons. Then, the next challenge is obvious: Is F truth conducive? In other words, is it true that if b has F, then b is likely to be true? There are only three possible answers: "Yes, it is truth conducive." "No, it is not truth conducive." "I don't know whether it is truth conducive or not." I take it that the only response that would entitle her to continue to believe b with the same degree of credence is the first one. The "no" answer would undercut her reason for believing b needs no justification, and the agnostic answer would indicate that her reasoning has floundered and, as the Pyrrhonians would say, her acceptance of b is arbitrary.

Again, my point is not that there won't be good answers. There probably are good answers. My point is rather that the so-called foundational beliefs are not immune to further interrogation. Even if they are not usually challenged, they—just like all the other conversational stoppers—can be challenged. They might be challenged less often than many other stoppers; but they can be, and once that happens, if we are to be epistemically responsible agents, the challenges require an answer because without one, there is a suspicious arbitrariness in holding them.

Now, it might be objected that the request for a reason either for thinking that b is a basic belief or for thinking that b's having F is truth conducive is a request to *show* that we are justified in believing b, but in order to *be* justified in believing that b, it is not required that we *show* that we are justified in believing that b. That is, it could be claimed that all that is required for S to be justified in believing that b is that b's having F *is* truth conducive; it is not further required that we either believe that F is truth conducive or have good reasons for believing that b's having F is truth conducive.[16]

The plausibility of this objection depends an ambiguity in the expression "the belief that p is justified" which stems from an ambiguity in the constituent expression "belief that p." "Belief that p" can be referring either to the *propositional content* of a belief-state, as in "the belief that p is true," or to the *belief-state itself,* as in "she had the belief that p for many years." So, the expression "S is justified in believing that p" can mean that S has adequate reasons for p even if S has no belief-state with p as its content. That type of justification is called "propositional justification." But when the belief-state itself is being referred to, rather than the content of the state, then the expression "S is justified in believing that p" means that the belief-state with p as its content is one that S is entitled to, and it typically implies that S has that belief.[17] That type of justification is called "doxastic justification."[18] I have been using "belief" throughout the chapter to refer to the belief-state rather than the propositional content. In particular, in the general argument given earlier, the claim is that the so-called basic belief states are not privileged in the way foundationalists claim.

I grant that any argument that conflates propositional justification of p with propositional justification of "p is propositionally justified" would be subject to the objection under consideration here. S can have adequate evidence for p without having adequate evidence for "p is justified." But if S has no good answer to the question about whether F is truth conducive, she is much less entitled to the belief-state than she would be if she had such an answer. Indeed, meta considerations are, in general, relevant in determining whether S is entitled to a belief. For example, suppose S's epistemic equipment (e.g. senses, memory, and reason) were working in a way that typically led to falsehoods, then even though a proposition, p, might be justified because S had adequate evidence for p, S is, ceteris paribus, less entitled to the belief-state than S would be were his/her epistemic equipment working properly.

Note that I have not claimed that if S lacks a reason for thinking that b's possessing F is truth conducive, she has no entitlement at all to the belief. I am willing to grant part of what the foundationalists claim, namely that b's possessing F is truth conducive. My point is that S's locating and providing reasons for thinking that b's possessing F is truth conducive provides the belief with another type of justification—the reason-enhanced kind.

I assume that, ceteris paribus, having a reason for believing something is epistemically better than not having one. At the core of epistemology is the presupposition first enunciated by Plato in the *Meno* that knowledge is the most highly prized form of true belief.[19] There are at least two epistemically good-making features a belief, b: (1) the etiology of the belief-state should be truth conducive, (2) when challenged the person holding b should have a reason, r, for thinking that the propositional content of b is true. No doubt, there are other epistemically good-making features of beliefs that contribute to the value of knowledge beyond those two.[20] The point here is simply that having a reason is epistemically better than not having one.[21] Locating a reason and providing it can add a type of reason-enhanced justification to a belief that hitherto was non-reason enhanced. So, reasoning can generate an important type of justification. In other words, IP is false.

I will suppose that *circular* reasoning cannot increase the entitlement we have for a belief. Aristotle and the Pyrrhonians were right about that. If p is in the chain of reasons that I give for my believing that p, the reasoning is inert and cannot provide any kind of entitlement, because the reasoning makes use of a belief whose very credentials are at stake.

But contemporary coherentism does not endorse circular reasoning. Rather contemporary coherentists hold that justification is a property that emerges in sets of beliefs when those sets are coherent and possibly have other properties. The best example of this view that I know of was developed by Laurence BonJour.[22] These coherentists take justification, or at least one feature of it, to be a property of sets of beliefs and, thus, the coherentist thinks that IP—the inheritance principle—neglects an important way in which justification arises. Individual propositions do not inherit their primary epistemic status from other beliefs. Rather, the justificational status of any belief in the set results from its being a member of a set of beliefs that are coherent (plus, perhaps, other properties of the set of beliefs).

Although this emergent form of coherentism avoids the circularity objections developed by Aristotle and repeated by the Pyrrhonians, Ernest Sosa has pointed out that emergent coherentism is actually a form of foundationalism because all of the beliefs in the coherent set are justified in virtue of being members of a set of beliefs whose propositional content has the requisite structure.[23] All members of the belief set are justified in virtue of being members of the set. They do not inherit their justification from the other members. Of course, some of the propositional contents of the beliefs might be more important to the coherence of the set, but they are all basic beliefs because they are (at least prima facie) justified merely in virtue of being a member of a coherent set of propositions (that, possibly, has additional required features). In standard foundationalism, the F property—the property that characterizes a so-called foundational belief— is a property of individual beliefs, and set of beliefs are justified in virtue of each member of the set being justified. Emergent coherentism reverses the "in virtue of" relationship. That is, each proposition in the set of propositions is justified in virtue of being a member of a set of justified propositions. The F property is "being a member of a set of coherent beliefs."

Once it is recognized that this is a form of foundationalism, the general argument against foundationalism can be applied to emergent coherentism. The general question addressed to the practicing foundationalist was this: Is the F property truth conducive? Applying that to coherentism the question becomes: Is coherence truth conducive?[24] If the practicing coherentist cannot provide a reason for thinking that coherence is truth conducive, his/her beliefs lack an important epistemic good-making feature and some recalibration of the degree to which she is entitled to the beliefs is required. The crucial point is that without a reason for thinking that coherence is truth conducive, the set of beliefs lacks the reason-enhanced quality and each member falls short of being the most highly prized form of belief, that is, it falls short of being knowledge.

The upshot of this section is that neither foundationalism nor coherentism can provide a good solution to the regress problem because there simply are no beliefs, whether individual or in sets, that are immune to further interrogation.

Infinitism: A sketch and defense against objections

If foundationalism and coherentism cannot provide a solution to the regress problem, the only non-skeptical solution is infinitism. But that view has been seen virtually by all philosophers, as a non-starter. As Aristotle and later the

Pyrrhonians asked rhetorically, "How can a finite mind produce an infinite number of beliefs?" Further, how can infinitism account for the origin of justification? Mustn't there be some starting point?

We will be in a better position to address those questions after we examine what infinitism claims, and equally important, what it does not claim.

Infinitism holds (1) that there are no privileged beliefs that are immune to further challenge and (2) that any belief backed by more reasons in the chain of reasons is better justified than one that includes only a portion of the chain of reasons. That is not to claim that any belief is better justified than another belief if there are, say six, reasons in the former chain and only three in the later. The shorter set of reasons might be stronger. It is merely to claim that each belief for which a reason is located is epistemically better justified than it was before the reason was located. But even that flies in the face of what seemed like a plausible epistemic principle. Recall IP:

> **IP:** If a belief, b, acquires justification in virtue of a reason, r, having been given for b, then r has to be justified.

Infinitists deny that principle. They will say that when a reason, r, is given for a belief, b, which hitherto had no reason, the belief b is epistemically better justified than it had been before the reason was located and provided. But if that is the case, then IP is false because a reason for r might not yet have been either located or provided. Put another way, if justification is a many-splendored epistemic property, then some of the good-making properties might be transferred through reasoning, but it does not follow that all of them are transferred through reasoning. One good-making epistemic property of a belief arises when a reason is located and provided. A reason, r, can enhance the epistemic status of a belief, b even when b itself has not been reason-enhanced. Reasoning is not merely a process by which some facets of justification are transferred, rather it can generate one of the good-making features of justification.

How far do we have to go in providing reasons in order for a true belief to rise to the level of the most highly prized type of true belief—knowledge? I don't think there is a general answer to that question. It will depend upon many factors and it is important to note that some of those factors are competing. For example, the goal that our beliefs be consistent will often conflict with the goal of comprehensiveness. Generally, the question is: How *epistemically* important is it that the propositional content of a belief be true? If it's not very important, then probably the giving of reasons can stop rather early in the process. For example, if adding a particular belief does little to increase coherence or to provide comprehensiveness, then it would probably be better epistemic management to stop at a relatively short set of reasons. On the other hand, if the candidate belief would be relatively central to the belief system, for example, if it would increase coherence and comprehensiveness significantly, then it would be more incumbent on us to seek further reasons. How much time and effort should be spent on locating and providing reasons for our beliefs is a matter of employing good time-and-effort management rules governing our epistemic practices.

The crucial point here is that infinitism does not require an epistemic agent to "traverse an infinite series" of reasons in order for a belief to be sufficiently justified so as to constitute knowledge. No belief is immune to further interrogation, *pace* the foundationalist, but it is not necessary to continue the search for reasons beyond what is required of a responsible epistemic agent. As we push back the artificial barrier to further inquiry erected by the foundationalists by their categorizing a belief as "basic," we increase the degree of justification for the belief. But at some point we have increased the degree of justification sufficiently for the belief to constitute knowledge until a new challenge arises.

Infinitism can satisfy many of the basic insights motivating all the other "solutions" to the regress problem. The Pyrrhonian Skeptics held that reason cannot settle matters once and for all—and infinitism can grant that. No belief is immune to further interrogation.[25] The foundationalists hold that there are appropriate stopping points in any discussion or reasoning process—and infinitism can grant that. Good epistemic management practices dictate that. Coherentists think that coherence is a good-making feature of our belief sets—and infinitism can grant that.

But while granting all of those intuitions, infinitism departs from all three views in significant ways. The Pyrrhonian Skeptics seem to have held that reasoning cannot increase the justification of a belief. Infinitists think it can. The Pyrrhonian Skeptics and the foundationalists subscribe to IP. Infinitists hold that an important type of justification is not transferred from the reason to the belief for which it is the reason. The problem with foundationalism, including the one-step coherentist variety, is that unless the practicing foundationalist can provide reasons for thinking (1) that she is a good basic belief detector, and (2) that the distinguishing features of the so-called basic beliefs are truth conducive, stopping the regress at the so-called basic beliefs is, as the Pyrrhonians argued, merely an arbitrary hypothesis. In order to avoid that arbitrariness, the foundationalist must provide further reasons and relinquish the claim that the so-called basic beliefs have the privileged status that had previously been granted to them. It is now time to turn to some objections:

1. **The finite mind objection:** Probably the most important objection to infinitism, and the one that has seemed insurmountable, has been the so-called "finite mind objection." BonJour puts it this way:

> Perhaps the most obvious way to argue against this alternative [infinitism] is not to claim that such a regress would necessarily be vicious, but rather to raise the question of whether such a picture, even if unobjectionable in the abstract, could possibly represent an accurate account of how the empirical knowledge of ordinary, finite human knowers is actually justified (as opposed to an account of how such knowledge might have been possible for cognitive beings with different and superior capacities). For if construed as a claim about actual human knowers, the infinite regress view clearly entails the dubious thesis that any person who has any empirical knowledge at all literally possess an *infinite* number of empirical beliefs. And surely, the argument continues, this is impossible for a creature with only a finite mental capacity and a finite brain.[26]

I hope it is now clear why that objection misses the mark. Justification comes in degrees and it is not necessary to produce an infinite set of reasons in order for a belief to be justified to the degree necessary for knowledge. Of course, in some cases withholding a belief will be the appropriate epistemic practice whenever we have tried and always failed to locate a reason for a belief. Perhaps there is no good reason for the belief and some major recalibration is called for—even to the point of denying or withholding the belief. But there is no need to locate and provide an infinite series of justificatory reasons in order for a belief to be justified to the extent required for knowledge.

2. **The objection that infinitism is nothing but a form of foundationalism that has unjustified propositions at the base:**[27] This objection misses the mark for two reasons. First, infinitism does not claim that the temporary stopping points in the progress of reasoning are not at all justified. Those beliefs could have the kind of justification that arises in virtue of the etiology of the belief. Second, the beliefs that, as of any given point in the production of chain of reasons, lack the kind of justification that arises when reasons are provided might acquire that reason-enhanced type of justification when challenged. Of course, we might not (at least at the moment) locate a reason, and then some recalibration is required.

3. **The objection that infinitism is a form of skepticism because nothing is ever finally settled:** Infinitism is committed to the claim that no belief is immune from interrogation and, thus, it is committed to the view that nothing is finally settled. But that does not entail that we lack knowledge

unless knowledge requires that we have settled the matter once and for all. And there seems to be no reason for holding that requirement for knowledge.

4. **The something from nothing objection:** This objection is that in order for a belief to be justified by another belief which is offered as a reason, the reason must itself be justified. Otherwise it looks like the justification arises from nothing. This is just restating IP and it fails to take note that a type of justification arises as we produce reasons for our beliefs. Because there are other important epistemic good-making features of a belief, producing such reasons is not sufficient for the belief to rise to the level of the most highly prized form of belief, but making a belief reason-enhanced does add a crucial good-making feature in the array of features required for the most highly prized form of true belief.

Notes

1 See the *Posterior Analytics,* especially 72b5–73a20, and the *Metaphysics,* especially 1011a1–a14.

2 Sextus Empiricus, *Outlines of Pyrrhonism* (Cambridge, MA: Harvard University Press, 1976, I: 164–9).

3 Modes were general recipes for responding to the dogmatists. So, e.g., the mode *ad infinitum* was designed to respond to the infinitist and the mode of circular reasoning was designed to respond to a person who thought that circular reasoning was a way of responding to the persistent request for a reason for whatever belief was advanced.

4 Richard Fumerton endorses an even stronger principle. He says:

> To be justified in believing one proposition P on the basis of another proposition E, one must be (1) justified in believing that E and (2) justified in believing that E makes P probable. (Richard Fumerton, "Metaepistemology and Skepticism," Boston and London: Rowman & Littlefield, 1995, p. 58)

Because of the second conjunct, this is a stronger principle than IP. While the second conjunct is controversial, the first conjunct is almost universally accepted. For a discussion of the second conjunct, see Peter Klein, "Foundationalism and the Infinite Regress of Reasons," *Philosophy and Phenomenological Research,* 58.4 (1998) 919–25.

William Alston, whose defense of foundationalism strikes me as the best extant account, implicitly employs IP in his development of foundationalism and his rejection of infinitism. In speaking about foundational beliefs he says, ". . . each branch [of the justification] terminates in an immediately justified belief that is justified without the necessity for further justified beliefs. Hence justification is transferred along each branch right back to the original belief" (p. 54). His rejection of infinitism goes as follows:

> If there is a branch with no terminus, that means that no matter how far we extend the branch, the last element is still a belief that is mediately justified, if at all. Thus as far as this structure goes, wherever we stop adding elements, we still have not shown that the conditions for mediate justification of the original belief are satisfied. Thus the structure does not exhibit the original belief as mediately justified. (p. 54)

See William Alston, *Epistemic Justification* (Ithaca, NY and London, England: Cornell University Press, 1989). It's interesting that Alston himself slips between a proposition *being* mediately justified and showing that it is justified in this objection to infinitism. Later, we will see that Alston in this very same essay claims that some of the objections to foundationalism conflate that important distinction. Further, one wonders why, if this depiction of infinitism were correct (and I will give some reasons for thinking that it is at least misleading), the existence of an infinite chain would not be sufficient to make all beliefs in the chain mediately justified. And, hence, the theory does, indeed, show how a belief can be mediately justified. It would be mediately justified *iff* there exists an infinite chain of the appropriate type.

5   Unless otherwise explicitly mentioned, I am using "belief" here, and throughout this chapter, to refer to belief states rather than to the propositional contents of beliefs. As we shall see, this is an important distinction.

6   See my "Epistemic Justification and the Limits of Pyrrhonism," *Pyrrhonism in Ancient, Modern, and Contemporary Philosophy,* Diego Machuca (ed.) (Dordrecht, Holland: Springer, 2011, 79–96).

7   See Roderick Chisholm, *Theory of Knowledge,* 2nd edn (Englewood Cliffs, NJ: Prentice Hall, 1977, 16–33). There Chisholm writes as follows about the regress:

> We might try to continue *ad indefinitum,* justifying each new claim that we elicit by still another claim. Or we might be tempted to complete a vicious circle . . . But if we are rational beings, we will do neither of these things. For we will find that our Socratic questions lead us to a proper stopping place. . .

Let us say provisionally that we have found a proper stopping place when the answer to our question may take the following form:

> What justifies me in thinking that I know that a is F is simply the fact that a is F. (p. 19)

8 Alvin Goldman, "Immediate Justification and Process Reliabilism," in Quentin Smith, ed., *Epistemology: New Essays* (Oxford and New York: Oxford University Press, 2008, 76–7).

9 See the following for a video clip in which the minister, Pat Robinson, said that the earthquake in Haiti was the result of a bargain made with the devil! http://www.youtube.com/watch?v=f5TE99sAbwM

10 I put "regress" in quotation marks because I think progress is being made when we supply reasons, and "regress" brings with it a pejorative connotation.

11 See, e.g., Michael Williams, *Unnatural Doubts* (Cambridge, MA and Oxford, England: Blackwell Publishers, 1991) and Ludwig Wittgenstein, *On Certainty* (New York: Harper & Row, 1972).

12 For a recent evidentailist account of the so-called basic beliefs along the lines sketched here, see E. Conee, and R. Feldman, "Evidence," in *Epistemology: New Essays,* op. cit., 84–104. They write this (where E_1–E_n are experiences):

> Here are two important intuitive epistemic features of E_1–E_n. First, they can be evidence for a proposition without one's having evidence for them. So, they can stop a regress of justification . . . Second, E_1–E_n are elements of the interface of one's mind with the world. (p. 92)

Earlier in speaking about "scientific evidence" they had said that the reason we have for believing something based upon such evidence required that we "know, or at least have reason to believe" that the evidence is an indicator of the truth of the proposition. One wonders why they did not apply that to the case of E_1–E_n. That is, wouldn't our reason for thinking that p be that we have experiences E_1–E_n and that those experiences are indicators of p? Then, it is obvious how the "regress" would continue: what makes you think the E_1–E_n are indicators of p? Even further, why wouldn't we have to have an answer to this question, if asked: Are you a good detector of E's? If we didn't "know, or at least have reason to believe" that we were good detectors of E's, would we be entitled to appeal to them as stoppers of the regress? Conee and Feldman say that if we required answers to those questions, we would end up with an "intolerable infinite regress" (p. 95), but, of course, that question-begging answer will not suffice here.

13 I think this is just what the Pyrrhonians were arguing. See, e.g., Sextus Empiricus, *Outlines of Pyrrhonism* (Cambridge, MA: Harvard University Press, 1976, I: 114–18).

14 I say almost everyone else because there are some people who lack any color sensations.

15 The general argument here against foundationalism is a recasting of a similar argument first developed by Laurence Bonjour, *The Structure of Empirical Knowledge* (Cambridge, MA and London, England: Harvard University Press,

1985, 30–3). Here, I try to blunt the criticism of this style of argument that it conflates a belief being justified with showing that a belief is justified by employing the distinction between propositional and doxastic justification.

16 William Alston makes this important distinction and argues that it is sufficient for foundationalism that the basic proposition be justified; it is not further required that we be justified in believing that it is justified or that we show or establish that it is justified. See *Epistemic Justification,* op. cit., pp. 39–56, especially pp. 55–6, and "Level-Confusions," *Midwest Studies in Philosophy* 5 (1980) 135–50 and "Two Types of Foundationalism," *Journal of Philosophy* 73(7) (1976) 165–85.

17 I will use "doxastic justification" to include the condition that S has the belief. But I think nothing essential hinges on that. The reply to the objection under consideration here does not depend upon taking doxastic justification to include that condition. For S would be not be as entitled to the so-called basic belief (even if S lacked that belief) if S had no reason to think that b's having F is truth conducive as S would be if S had a reason to think that F is truth conducive.

18 I believe that Roderick Firth was the first to introduce this crucial distinction. See his "Are Epistemic Concepts Reducible to Ethical Concepts?" in A. Goldman and J.Kim, eds, *Values and Moral* (Dordrecht, Holland: D. Reidel, 1978, 215–29).

19 Plato, *Meno* 97a–98b.

20 For example, the belief and the reasons for it might have to be at least consistent with other beliefs that we hold. I have argued against such coherence requirements elsewhere, but for the purposes of this chapter I can and will grant that there are many good-making features as the reader wishes so long as it is granted that, ceteris paribus, a reason-enhanced belief is epistemically better than a belief lacking a reason. I have argued elsewhere that (1) coherence is not truth conducive, and (2) that weakly inconsistent sets could be such that all members are justified. For (1) see "What Price Coherence?" (with Ted Warfield), *Analysis* 54.3 (July 1994) 129–32 and "No Help for the Coherentist," (with Ted Warfield) *Analysis* 56.2 (April 1996) 118–21. For (2) see "Virtues of Inconsistency," *Monist* 68(1) (1985) 105–35.

21 Note that I have not required that the cause of the belief include the belief that is offered as a reason. It just might be that the etiology of the belief is, at least in some cases, quite distinct from the chain of reasons which are cited for the belief. Whether the etiology often, or occasionally, or never coincides with the reasons strikes me as an empirical matter and it is best left to cognitive scientists. Whatever they discover, it will still be true that, ceteris paribus, we are epistemically better off having (non-overridden) reasons for our beliefs than we are if we lacked reasons.

22 Laurence BonJour, *The Structure of Empirical Knowledge,* op. cit., especially 87–110. There BonJour refers to this view as involving nonlinear justification.

23 Ernest Sosa, "The Raft and the Pyramid," *Midwest Studies in Philosophy* 5 (1980)
    3–25.

24 I think it is worth noting that BonJour correctly claims that one of the standard
    objections to coherentism is that there is no reason to believe that mere coherence
    is truth conducive. In order to address that objection, BonJour requires that the
    coherent sets contain "observational" beliefs. I think that is a tacit recognition
    that the practicing coherentist must have a reason for thinking that coherent sets
    are truth conducive. No doubt they will claim that satisfying the requirement that
    some of the beliefs satisfy the observational requirement makes coherence truth
    conducive. Nevertheless, my point remains: the "regress" has continued.

25 It might be thought that there is an exception to this. Beliefs with analytic
    propositions as their content seem, at first glance, immune to this generalization.
    For the sake of argument I could grant that and limit the generalization to beliefs
    with a nonanalytic content. But I think even such beliefs are subject to further
    interrogation. Take one of the simplest: the belief that a is a. It strikes me that
    even that belief is subject to interrogation. For example: Are you a good detector
    of beliefs with identities as their propositional content? And what is it about
    identities that makes them true? Again, the point is not that there are no good
    answers to those questions. There are. The point is that even these beliefs are
    subject to interrogation.

26 Bonjour, op. cit., p. 24. BonJour, an architect of coherentism, does go on to say this
    about the argument quoted above: "Though it is difficult to state in a really airtight
    fashion, this argument seems to me an adequate reason for rejecting alternative
    (2) [the infinitist position]" p. 24. Alston, an architect of foundationalism writes
    something similar about the regress argument he had just presented. He says, "I do
    not claim that this argument is conclusive; I believe it to be open to objections in
    ways I will not be able to go into here. But I do feel that it gives stronger support to
    foundationalism than any other regress argument." Alston, *Epistemic Justification,*
    op. cit., p. 55. I can't resist a slight ad hominem here: Perhaps the reason that the
    regress argument is neither airtight nor conclusive is that infinitism is correct!

27 For full discussion of this objection, please see Michael Bergmann, "Is Klein an
    Infinitist about Doxastic Justification?" *Philosophical Studies* 134.1 (May 2007)
    19–24, and my reply "How to Be an Infinitist about Doxastic Justification,"
    Philosophical Studies 134.1 (May 2007) 25–9. Also see the "debate" between Carl
    Ginet and me in *Contemporary Debates in Epistemology* (Malden, MA and Oxford,
    England: Blackwell, 2005), Steup, M. and Sosa, E. eds, pp. 131–56.

5

Evidentialism

Richard Feldman and Andrew Cullison

What is evidentialism?

Evidentialism is the view that epistemic justification depends on evidence and evidence alone. That is, one is justified in believing a proposition if and only if one's evidence adequately supports that proposition.

Generic Evidentialism

S is justified in believing P = df. S's total evidence adequately supports P.

Versions of evidentialism can differ in how they characterize evidence, what it is to have evidence, what sorts of things count as evidence, and what it is for evidence to support a proposition adequately. A common view among evidentialists is that one's evidence is constituted by mental states (e.g. sense perceptions, rational intuitions, introspective awareness of one's mind, etc.). It is also a common view among evidentialists that for one to have a mental state as evidence, one must have some kind of awareness of it, although evidentialists will disagree as to how aware of the evidence one must be. Evidentialism of this sort is often identified as a species of internalism.

It wasn't until Gettier convinced everyone that knowledge was not justified true belief that epistemologists fully realized that this connection between knowledge and evidence or justification and evidence might be accidental. That is, they realized that justified true beliefs need not amount to knowledge, and they focused more explicitly on the implications of the fact that justified beliefs might be false. But evidentialism holds that the connection between evidence and justification is necessary. This is perhaps the best way to characterize the fundamental difference between classical evidentialism and rival views such as reliabilism and proper functionalism. Traditional evidentialism holds that there is a necessary connection between a body of evidence and the doxastic attitudes one is justified in adopting based on that evidence. The other views deny this, even if they are consistent with the fact that people typically do have evidence for beliefs that are justified. For example, reliabilists, who hold that beliefs are justified provided they result from a process that reliably leads to truth, might explain why evidence is often present in cases of justification by noting that *for us* basing beliefs on supporting evidence is a reliable process. Proper functionalists, who hold that beliefs are justified when they result from the proper function of the cognitive system, can say something similar. It may be that in most (or even all) cases of *actual* justified belief, the properly formed beliefs are based on supporting evidence. However, the fundamental reason these are justified is that *for us* forming beliefs based on certain inputs like perceptions are part of the proper function of cognitive systems.

In favor of evidentialism

Reasons requirement

Evidentialism seems to be the default view. There is an intuitive sense that reasonable belief should be based on good reasons, and it is very natural to say that *good reasons* just are *supporting evidence.* Evidentialism fits well with the standard practice of gathering evidence for beliefs. It fits well with the practice of challenging knowledge claims by asking people what their evidence is for their beliefs. It also fits well with the practice of defending beliefs. When people try to articulate *why* they are justified in believing something, they list evidence that they have.

Intuitive judgments about cases

Another reason to favor evidentialism is that it best explains intuitive judgments about cases. In any case where it is plausible to suppose that two subjects differ with respect to what they are justified in believing, there is a difference in the supporting evidence the subjects have. Whenever someone becomes *more* justified in believing something, the person seems to also have *more* or *better* supporting evidence. Feldman and Conee offer a series of examples that illustrate this. Here are two:

> **Example 1:** Bob and Ray are sitting in an air-conditioned hotel lobby reading yesterday's newspaper. Each has read that it will be very warm today and, on that

basis, each believes that it is very warm today. Then Bob goes outside and feels the heat. They both continue to believe that it is very warm today. But at this point Bob's belief is better justified.

Comment: Bob's justification for the belief was enhanced by his experience of feeling the heat. He had a mental change which, so to speak, "internalized" the actual temperature. Ray just had the forecast to rely on.

Example 2: After going outside and feeling very warm, Bob goes back in and tells Ray of the feeling. Here are two versions of the relevant details:

(2a) Bob is in fact a pillar of integrity, but Ray has no reason to think so. As far as Ray can tell, it is just as likely that Bob is trying to deceive him as that Bob is telling the truth.

(2b) Bob is a pillar of integrity, and Ray has observed and recalls many examples of Bob's honesty and none of dishonesty.

In example (2b) Ray's belief that it is very warm becomes more strongly justified after he hears from Bob. In example (2a) hearing Bob does not affect the strength of Ray's justification for his belief.

Comment: Bob's honesty, something out of Ray's ken in (2a), has become "internalized" by Ray in (2b). Bob's integrity made no justificatory difference to Ray's belief until it was suitably brought into Ray's mind.[1]

These examples were originally introduced to defend mentalism, a species of internalism that says that epistemic justification supervenes on mental states. However, they can be used to defend evidentialism too. It seems that the primary difference in both cases that explains the differences in justification is internal evidence that the subjects have (or lack).

The second example also helps motivate the thesis that external factors that might make it objectively probable that the believer's belief is true do not effect justification unless the believer has evidence that they obtain.

Many other examples can be produced to display the merits of evidentialism.

Problems with competing theories

A related reason to favor evidentialism is that evidentialism handles some key examples far better than its main rivals. In this section, we will briefly present two rival theories: reliabilism and proper functionalism and discuss some of these cases. There are, of course, numerous other rivals not surveyed here.

Reliabilism

Reliabilism is (roughly) the thesis that a belief is justified if, and only if, it is formed by a belief-forming process that is a member of a reliable belief-forming process type. Reliable processes are ones that regularly lead to true beliefs. One problem for reliabilism centers on cases in which there are internal duplicates whose faculties differ drastically in reliability. This is called "The New Evil Demon Problem."

New Evil Demon

> Brian lives in the real world. Brain is Brian's unfortunate brain-in-a-vat twin. He is hooked up to a super-computer and is being *tricked* into thinking he is Brian in the real world. He has all of the same apparent perceptions, memories, intuitions, and beliefs. Brian and Brain are internal duplicates.[2]

It seems that Brian and Brain are *equally* justified in believing the propositions they believe. However, since Brain is forming beliefs that are caused by systematically *unreliable* processes, reliabilism is committed to the thesis that Brain is unjustified in believing almost all of the propositions about the external world that Brian is justified in believing.

This objection to reliabilism relies on the assumption that the processes Brain, the demon's victim, uses are unreliable. This seems clearly true, since Brain's beliefs about the world are so often false. However, it should be noted that reliabilists have proposed solutions to this problem, arguing in favor of ways of assessing reliability other than the relatively natural one presupposed in the objection.[3]

Another puzzle for reliabilism is the generality problem. The basic idea is that any particular belief-forming process will be an instance of many different belief-forming process types, some reliable and some unreliable. For example, suppose Bob is in a dark room and Bob forms the belief that there is a glass on the table based on looking at it. The particular token belief-forming process is a member of many different types:

a. Vision
b. Vision-in-a-dark-room
c. Vision-from-5-feet-away
d. Vision-from-5-feet-away-in-a-dark room

The physical process in Bob's brain that leads to his belief can also be classified in highly specific or more general ways, so it is an instance of many of these types as well.

It is unclear which process is the relevant process type to assess for reliability. This makes it unclear what implications reliabilism has, even in simple cases of perception. Reliabilists have proposed several different ways in which they might select the relevant type. It remains to be seen whether any response will prove adequate.[4]

Proper functionalism

Proper functionalism is sometimes discussed as a view about warrant and sometimes discussed as a view about justification.[5] We will be concerned with discussing it as a view about justification. According to the proper functionalist about justification, justification is a matter of forming beliefs in accordance with a design plan that is aimed at acquiring true beliefs. While the view mentions *a design plan,* the view is supposed to be theologically neutral. That design plan may come from God (if there is one) or via natural selection and evolution (if there is no God).

One difficulty for proper functionalism bears some similarity to the New Evil Demon problem. Imagine an internal duplicate of Brian who suddenly materializes out of the swamp as a result of an accidental combination of unusual events. This duplicate has no design plan, since he neither is a result of divine creation nor of evolution. However, given his similarity to Brian, it appears that his beliefs are just as well justified as Brian's. Proper functionalism appears to imply otherwise. This suggests that justification is a function of evidence, not of belief formation according to plan.

Proper functionalism also appears to classify some obvious instances of unjustified belief as justified. Imagine a deity who wants to create creatures who form true beliefs about rat terriers based on appearances of tabby cats. He sets up a world with creatures that form beliefs contrary to their appearances when they have perceptions of tabby cats. Suppose he sets up the world so that they are often right when they do this. It seems that this deity has successfully aimed his creatures at true beliefs by making his creatures hold unjustified beliefs in a small set of isolated cases. Proper functionalism, however, entails that these beliefs are justified.

Once again, defenders of the theory do have avenues to explore in its defense against both of these problems.[6]

Objections to evidentialism

Epistemic responsibilism

Kornblith argues that the manner in which evidence is gathered is relevant to justification.[7] If someone engages in epistemically irresponsible practices, then the person may not be justified in believing a proposition even if their evidence supports it. The idea is that a person whose evidence supports a proposition may nevertheless not be justified in believing that proposition if the belief arose through disreputable means such as avoiding relevant evidence, failing to seek important information, and the like.

Evidentialists can respond by noting that there are two ways in which these cases of irresponsibility can be fleshed out. In one way of fleshing the cases, the person has evidence of the irresponsibility. If subjects have reason to believe that they've been irresponsible evidence gatherers, or the fact that they are ignoring data from other experts, then they have evidence that is relevant to the proposition. This evidence can counteract the support their other evidence provides for the proposition, making belief not justified by evidentialist standards. If, instead, subjects have no information about any irresponsibility on their part, then it becomes much less clear that this impacts their justification. That is, they seem to be justified in believing as they do, since there is nothing to which they have access that indicates that the proposition in question is not true. There is nothing unreasonable about believing what is supported by the evidence one does have and failing to take into account contrary evidence that one does not realize one has missed.

Practical reasons for belief

Some argue that people can be justified in believing propositions even when the evidence supports their denial. Consider the following case:

> Baseball Batter
>
> Joey Votto gets a hit about 1 out of every 3 times at bat. This is a great average in baseball, but the likelihood that he will get a hit in a particular time at bat is very low. You might initially think that it would be unreasonable for Votto to believe he will get a hit in a particular time at bat. However, suppose you learn that Votto recently read "The Power of Positive Thinking in Baseball" and discovered that batters who believe they are going to get a hit are statistically more likely to get a hit. You might think that it would be a good idea for Votto to try to think positively and believe that he will get a hit, despite the evidence to the contrary. Hence, you might conclude that belief is justified in this case, in spite of the evidence. (It's important to note that the evidence about positive thinking only shows that it makes it more likely that one will get a hit, not that it makes it more likely than not.)

Evidentialists reply by noting that this confuses two different sorts of justification. The fact that you may find yourself of two minds here suggests that there are two different sorts of justification. In one sense, it seems that Votto shouldn't believe that he will get a hit. After all, the evidence indicates that he won't. Call that the *epistemic* should. Corresponding to this is a sense of "justified" according to which the belief is not justified. That's the sense that evidentialism is about. That's the sense that is relevant to things like knowledge and truth. There is another sense in which you might think that Votto *should* believe that he's going to get a hit, but that sense is more *practical.* It would be in Votto's practical interest to adopt the belief that he's going to get a hit. So, we might say that Votto has good *practical reasons* to believe that he's going to get a hit. Evidentialists can admit that beliefs sometimes have practical utility. But this has no bearing on their epistemic justification. It may have something to do with some notion of practical or prudential justification.

Pragmatic encroachment

There are, however, ways in which philosophers have argued that practical considerations matter *even for* the epistemic justification.

Consider the following two cases.

Low Stakes

You're on a train. You're wondering whether it goes to Oxford. You ask a passenger, who says "Yes." But it is of no real importance to you whether it stops there, since you are headed for a destination beyond that point.

High Stakes

You're wondering whether or not the train goes to Oxford. You ask a passenger, who says "Yes." However, in this case, it's really important that you get to Oxford. If you don't, you'll miss an important job interview. You decide that it would be best to double-check with the conductor.

Intuitively, your evidence is the same in both cases—the passenger's testimony. Intuitively, you're justified in believing that the train goes to Oxford in the first case. However, it seems reasonable for you to double-check in the second case. This suggests that you are not justified in believing in the second case *merely* on the basis of this testimony. After all, if you were justified in believing, then there should be no need to check.[8]

Evidentialists have a few different things to say about these cases. First, evidentialists might try to preserve the judgment that there is a difference in justification here by arguing that the amount of evidential support required for justification shifts based on the practical stakes. This would depart from the spirit of classical evidentialism, but notice that supporting evidence would still be required in every instance of justified belief. The evidential support relation would just be a bit more complicated. Roughly, the idea would be to require *more* supporting evidence for a belief when the practical stakes are raised.

An alternative view is to deny that the need to check has any bearing on whether or not the belief is epistemically justified. The mere fact that a belief is justified does not guarantee that it is true, and so one might think that when the stakes are extremely high, you can have strong practical reasons to gather more evidence before acting on a belief that is well enough supported to be justified.[9]

Inexplicable knowledge

There are cases of what one might call *inexplicable knowledge* where people come to have highly reasonable beliefs but are unable to identify what it was about the situation that led them to form that belief. For example, in one study people were asked to look at several photographs of faces.[10] They were asked, for each photo, to try and determine whether the person in the photograph was happy or sad. People were remarkably good at this. However, when asked what it was about the face that led them to believe this, they could not identify a relevant feature. In many cases they were *wrong*. Many said that the position of the mouth was the key factor. But this is in fact not the cue people use (even if they don't realize what they are doing). The most likely hypothesis is that people made accurate judgments on the basis of the pupil size of the persons in the photographs. But these people weren't consciously aware of pupil size, so the idea that their justification depends on evidence they are aware of seems false.

However, we think it is reasonable to suppose that in these cases there *are* still evidential differences that these subjects are aware of (e.g. a seeming that this person is happy or the general way the person looked) that explains *why* they formed the belief they did. And these factors could serve as the evidence for the belief that this person is happy. In other words, the happy people did look different than the unhappy people—they did seem happy. This is true even if the subjects could not correctly explain what it is about the appearance that had this effect.

Stored beliefs

Some have argued that evidentialism cannot account for the fact that people have a large stock of justified stored beliefs.[11] Stored beliefs are beliefs that are not occurrent and before one's mind. For example, most people in the United States are *right now* justified in believing that George Washington was the first president of the United States. However, most of those people are likely not entertaining that proposition at this particular moment.

Other examples of stored beliefs might be facts about what happened in your recent past. Bob might be justified, throughout the entire day, in believing that he had eggs for breakfast even though Bob might not entertain that proposition for most of the day.

The problem is that when people are not reflecting on these propositions, they are also probably not reflecting or immediately aware of whatever mental states might *justify* those propositions. But if evidentialism requires supporting evidence that one is in some sense *aware* of, then evidentialism cannot explain how these stored beliefs are justified.

Evidentialists have a few possible responses to offer. One is to argue that people do have justifying evidence for these stored beliefs. If it makes sense to talk about stored beliefs, then it will also make sense to talk about stored evidence. A stored belief is likely just a disposition to form an occurent attitude (belief) toward a proposition when it is entertained. But part of the *reason* people might have those dispositions is that when they entertain those propositions *good reasons* to believe them will also become occurent. The reason it is reasonable for Bob to believe that he had eggs for breakfast is that if he *were* to reflect on what he had for breakfast, good evidence that he had eggs (e.g. an apparent memory of having had eggs) would become occurent. This stored evidence justified his stored belief. It is true that there are difficult questions about exactly which stored beliefs can justify other beliefs. Further clarification of this issue remains an open question for evidentialists.

Another option for evidentialists is to maintain that *strictly speaking* these stored beliefs are not justified. They only become justified once they become occurent along with the requisite evidence. Talk of these stored beliefs being justified is just shorthand for certain kinds of counterfactuals that may be true about the situation.

Necessary connections and semantic externalism

Classical evidentialists hold that there is a necessary connection between one's total evidence and the doxastic attitudes that one is justified in adopting. This is more precisely captured as the *same evidence principle*.

Same Evidence Principle

If A and B have the exact same total body of evidence, then A and B are justified in believing the same propositions to the same extent.

Michael Bergmann, however, has raised some worries about the same evidence principle.[12] Imagine beings who are wired differently from us, so that the phenomenal sensations they get when they feel a smooth ball are the phenomenal sensations we get when we smell fresh baked bread. Imagine further that when they smell fresh baked bread they get the phenomenal sensations we get when we feel a smooth ball. This is basically like a case of spectrum inversion, but the qualia are being switched across tactile and olfactory inputs.

Call the phenomenal qualia that we get when we feel a billiard ball SMOOTH. You might think that SMOOTH is (for us) evidence that we're holding a billiard ball, but that SMOOTH for these other creatures is evidence that there is fresh baked bread, nearby. These judgments conflict with the same evidence principle.

One problem with the way Bergmann spells out the case, initially, is that these creatures will not have the same total evidence as us. The Same Evidence Principle is a thesis concerning what your total evidence supports. To get a pair that generates a successful counterexample to the Same Evidence Principle, we need them to be complete internal duplicates. For example, presumably when these creatures *feel* smoothness, they often do things like *see* bread and *eat* bread. So their total evidence is not the same, and thus the example does not count against the principle.

We could try to make it a simple case of spectrum inversion. Imagine someone who is internally identical to you, but is spectrally inverted with respect to red and green. When they come look at green objects, they have the sorts of phenomenal qualia that you have when you look at red objects. You might think that being appeared to red-ly justifies you in thinking that there is something red, but that being appeared to red-ly justifies them in thinking that there is something green. However, even here the total evidence is slightly different. When you were first learning colors and you were appeared to red-ly, people told you that you were looking at a red object, but when your inverted spectrum counter-part was appeared to red-ly, they were told that they were looking at a green object. These different histories could lead to different current (remembered) evidence. So it's not clear that you have the same total evidence. A related point is that, on this version of evidentialism, the red appearance all by itself is *not* evidence for the proposition that there is something red present. Rather, it is an essential part of a larger body of evidence supporting that conclusion, where that larger body includes the key evidence resulting from the training just described as well as any other relevant information one may have.

The closest we can come to having genuine *internal* duplicates that appear to be justified in believing different propositions would be a case that looks very much like a Twin Earth case. Imagine a pair of individuals, Oscar and Twoscar. Oscar and Twoscar are, in some very important sense, perfect internal duplicates. They appear to speak the same language and, for our purposes, let's assume they have the same internal experiences. However, Twoscar lives on Twin Earth. On Twin Earth, the clear, potable liquid that Twoscar drinks and that fills the rivers and oceans of Twin Earth is not H20; it has a completely different chemical composition—XYZ. Call the stuff on Twin Earth that is composed of XYZ *twater.* While this thought experiment is used to motivate *content* externalism in philosophy of language and philosophy of mind,[13] it has been argued that it also has serious epistemological implications. One might think that Oscar's total evidence justifies him in believing that he is drinking water and Twoscar's total evidence justifies him in believing that he is drinking twater. If they are internal duplicates and have the exact same total evidence, then we have a reason to reject evidentialism.[14]

This seems like the clearest way to formulate an objection to the Same Evidence thesis, but now there are two plausible options for the evidentialist. First, one could deny that content externalism is true. The Twin Earth thought experiments were designed to argue that beliefs have content that is external to the mind. The reasoning is that Oscar and Twoscar are internally identical, and so they should believe the exact same propositions if content internalism is true. But not everyone is persuaded by Twin Earth thought experiments. There are content internalists who argue that Oscar and Twoscar really don't believe different propositions. Any plausible defense of this view could be embraced by the evidentialist.

Another option for evidentialism would be to preserve semantic externalism. However, some of the most plausible options for preserving semantic externalism involve invoking something like narrow content as a mediator.

One example is *Ways-Millianism.* According to Ways-Millianism, belief is a mediated relation between a person and a proposition. Persons believe propositions in virtue of standing in relation to some third thing, a way of believing. One view of what ways are is that they are mentalese sentences (or something like what content internalists call *narrow content*). If this version of semantic externalism were true, then the evidentialist can maintain that there will still be a necessary relation between a person's internal evidence and what *ways* they are rational in accepting. So something very much like the Same Evidence thesis will be preserved—the same evidence won't always justify internal duplicates in believing the same propositions, but it will always justify people in accepting some similar internal mentalese sentence (or way).

Truth connection objections

Some epistemologists argue that an adequate account of justification will explain the intuitive idea that there is some connection between justification and truth. Some argue that this truth connection is best fleshed out in terms of *truth conducivity* or *probability*. Many allege that reliabilism or proper functionalism are in a better position to explain this connection. For example, reliabilism holds that if a belief is formed by a reliable process, then it is objectively probable or likely that the belief is true. Hence, according to reliabilism justified (i.e. reliably formed) beliefs are likely to be true.

Evidentialists who endorse the necessity thesis will have to deny the truth of any version of the thesis that all or most justified beliefs are true. They will have to acknowledge that there are possible cases in which most justified beliefs are false. However, this result is one that they will welcome. This was made plain in the discussion of Brian and Brain earlier on. In that case, it was argued, Brain was in an unfortunate situation in which forming justified beliefs largely leads him away from the truth. But this seems to be exactly the right result. To believe what is true in Brain's situation would be to believe without basis in an unsupported and far-fetched (but true) account of his situation.

It's important to note that evidentialists need not claim that there is *no* connection to the truth. Intuitively, there is some connection. What evidentialists must deny is that the truth connection should be understood in terms of objective likelihood.[15]

The problem of the speckled hen

Another objection to evidentialism is based on *The Problem of the Speckled Hen*. Imagine a person who is looking at a hen with three speckles and justifiably forms the belief that the hen has three speckles. Next, imagine a person who has a visual experience of a hen with forty speckles. These examples pose a puzzle for evidentialists. If a visual experience of three speckles is sufficient to justify the first person in believing that the hen has three speckles, then a visual experience of forty speckles should be sufficient to justify the second person in believing that the hen has forty speckles. But it seems clear that a "forty speckle appearance" does not justify a belief that the hen has forty speckles. If this is correct, there must be some difference between these two cases that goes beyond what experiential evidence is present in both cases. Evidentialists need to explain the difference. Reliabilists will say we can reliably form beliefs about small quantities based on looking, but not large quantities. Proper functionalists might say that we were designed to form beliefs about small quantities, but not large quantities.

However, evidentialists have the resources to respond here. The problem of the speckled hen foists a particular conception of evidence on the evidentialist. However, there is arguably more to the evidence than just the raw visual experience. In addition to the raw visual data containing three spots, there is a kind of awareness or seeming *that* the experience contains three spots. This is absent in the case of forty speckles. Furthermore, in realistic cases, people have information about their reliability, or their apparent reliability, in forming the relevant beliefs. This is evidence that evidentialists can appeal to.

Other examples help to clarify the point. Were a normal person to see three toothpicks on a table before him, he could immediately tell that there were three toothpicks there. But if there were 142 toothpicks, he would not be able to tell this. Now, imagine someone with the remarkable ability to *immediately* identify that there are 142 toothpicks before him.[16] It's difficult to believe that there is absolutely no internal difference between this person and someone who lacks the ability. One likely candidate difference is that there is a kind of meta-awareness or seeming about *what* is represented in the visual field. In addition, there are likely differences in background evidence that can play a role. Hence, evidentialists may have adequate responses to these kinds of examples.

Conclusion

Evidentialism is one of the most plausible theories of epistemic justification available. It is independently plausible and it captures intuitive judgments about cases better than the main competing theories. Furthermore, evidentialism is not vulnerable to the main objections that have been offered against it.

Notes

1 Feldman and Conee (2001, 236).
2 See Cohen (1984) for one of the original presentations of this problem.
3 For example, Comesana (2002) argues that the relevant world for assessing Brain's reliability is not Brain's world, but our world.
4 See Goldberg's chapter in this volume for more discussion of these issues.
5 For example, Plantinga (1993a, 1993b, 2000) argues for proper functionalism about warrant. Bergmann (2006) argues for proper functionalism about justification.
6 See Bergmann (2006, 144–9).
7 Kornblith (1983).
8 Two prominent defenses of the idea that persons could have the same evidence but differ in terms of what they know based solely on the practical stakes are Hawthorne (2005) and Stanley (2005). However, for a careful extension of this idea to epistemic justification see Fantl and McGrath (2007) and (2009).
9 We refer the reader to Coffman's piece in this volume for more discussion of these pragmatic encroachment views.
10 For discussion of this example, see Kornblith (2003).
11 Goldman (1999, 278).
12 Bergmann (2006, 114).
13 Putnam (1973, 1996) presents these cases to argue against semantic internalism, the view that semantic content is entirely internal to the mind.
14 The more general issue here is that there is a prima facie conflict between semantic externalism and epistemic internalism. Goldberg (2007) contains several essays that discuss this problem, in particular Brown (2007), Conee (2007), and Fumerton (2007).
15 See Conee (1992) for an account of the truth connection that an evidentialist could endorse.
16 Consider Dustin Hoffman's character in *Rain Man*.

References

Bergmann, M. A. 2006. *Justification without Awareness: A Defense of Epistemic Externalism*. New York: Oxford University Press.

Braun, D. 2006. "Names and Natural Kind Terms." *The Oxford Handbook of Philosophy of Language*. Oxford: Oxford University Press, pp. 490–515.

Brown, J. 2007. "Externalism in Mind and Epistemology." In S. Goldberg, ed., *Internalism and Externalism in Semantics and Epistemology*. Oxford: Oxford University Press, pp. 13–24.

Cohen, S. 1984. "Justification and Truth." *Philosophical Studies* 46(3): 279–95.

— 2002. "Basic Knowledge and the Problem of Easy Knowledge." *Philosophy and Phenomenological Research* 65(2): 309–29.

Comesana, J. 2002. "The Diagonal and the Demon." *Philosophical Studies* 110(3): 249–66.

Conee, E. 1992. "The Truth Connection." *Philosophy and Phenomenological Research* 52(3): 657–69.

— 2007. "Externally Enhanced Internalism." In S. Goldberg, ed., *Internalism and Externalism in Semantics and Epistemology*. New York, NY: Oxford University Press, pp. 51–67.

Conee, E. and Feldman, R. 1998. "The Generality Problem for Reliabilism." *Philosophical Studies* 89(1): 1–29.

Fantl, J. and McGrath, M. 2009. *Knowledge in an Uncertain World*. New York: Oxford University Press.

— 2007. "On Pragmatic Encroachment in Epistemology." *Philosophy and Phenomenological Research* 75(3): 558–89.

Feldman, R. 2004. *Evidentialism: Essays in Epistemology*. Oxford: Oxford University Press.

Feldman, R. and Conee, E. 1985. "Evidentialism." *Philosophical Studies* 48(1): 15–34.

— 2001. "Internalism Defended." *American Philosophical Quarterly* 38(1): 1–18.

Fumerton, R. 2007. "What and about What Is Internalism?" In S. Goldberg, ed., *Internalism and Externalism in Semantics and Epistemology*. Oxford: Oxford University Press, pp. 35–50.

Goldberg, S. C. 2007. *Internalism and Externalism in Semantics and Epistemology*. Oxford: Oxford University Press.

Goldman, A. I. 1999. "Internalism Exposed." *The Journal of Philosophy* 96(6): 271–93.

Hawthorne, J. 2005. *Knowledge and Lotteries*. Oxford: Oxford University Press.

— 2003. "Roderick Chisholm and the Shaping of American Epistemology." *Metaphilosophy* 34(5): 582–602.

Kornblith, H. 1983. "Justified Belief and Epistemically Responsible Action." *The Philosophical Review* 92(1): 33–48.

Plantinga, A. 1993a. *Warrant and Proper Function*. New York: Oxford University Press.

— 1993b. *Warrant: The Current Debate*. New York: Oxford University Press.

— 2000. *Warranted Christian Belief*. New York: Oxford University Press.

Putnam, H. 1973. "Meaning and Reference." *The Journal of Philosophy* 70(19): 699–711.

— 1996. "The Meaning of Meaning." *Readings in Language and Mind* 157.

Stanley, J. 2005. *Knowledge and Practical Interests*. Oxford: Oxford University Press.

6

Reliabilism

Sanford Goldberg

Introduction

In the most general sense, "reliabilism" is a label that covers any epistemological theory which holds that the epistemic properties of a given belief—for example, whether the belief is justified, or whether (if true) it amounts to knowledge—are determined, on the whole, by the reliability with which the belief was formed and sustained. Depending on how the notion of reliability itself is understood, various distinct epistemological theories fall within this general category. For example, here we might find those theories of knowledge that place a heavy emphasis on such things as *sensitivity* (one wouldn't have formed the belief in question if it had been false), *safety* (not easily would one have formed a false belief on this occasion), and other anti-luck conditions. The development of epistemological theories of this sort has gone hand-in-hand with the development of the so-called externalist movement in epistemology. Such theories oppose traditional (internalist) epistemological theories, according to which knowledge requires having something like reflectively accessible reasons or evidence for one's beliefs. Externalist theories deny that knowledge requires this; and reliabilist versions of externalism deny this by appeal to their conception of knowledge as a matter of the relevant modal properties of the belief, that is, whether it was sensitive, safe, or what-have-you.

However, "reliabilism" is often used in epistemology in a more narrow sense, as a label for a specific externalist view known as Process Reliabilism. Developed originally by Alvin Goldman in a series of seminal articles and books from the 1970s through the 2000s, Process Reliabilism has become one of the leading epistemological theories. It is distinguished from more "internalist" rivals by its view that the causal history of a belief is the key factor in the determination of justification and knowledge; and it is distinguished among externalist theories in the role it ascribes to reliability, and in particular to the reliability of the process (or method) by which the belief was formed and sustained. In this entry, we will focus mainly on reliabilism in this more narrow sense.

Process Reliabilism as a theory of doxastic justification

The "externalist" revolution in epistemology (of which the Process Reliabilist theory of justification is a part) can be seen as a reaction to the familiar Gettier Problem. A very traditional view about knowledge held that knowledge is justified true belief (JTB), with justification understood to be a matter of the subject's basing her belief on good reasons or evidence. Gettier (1963) showed that a belief can satisfy these conditions and yet be such that its truth is only a matter of luck.[1] Since virtually all epistemologists agree that if a belief's truth is only a matter of luck it does not amount to knowledge, the existence of Gettier cases is standardly taken to show that JTB does not suffice for knowledge. Hence the Gettier Problem, which is the problem of determining how an account of knowledge ought to handle Gettier cases. More traditional epistemologists propose to do so merely by tacking an anti-luck condition onto the traditional JTB account. On such a view, knowledge is JTB whose truth is not a matter of luck, where justification still involves something like good reasons or evidence. Externalist epistemology, by contrast, is motivated by the idea that once we specify the anti-luck condition, we will see that knowledge does not require justification in the sense understood by tradition (good reasons or evidence). Early externalist theories, especially causal and truth-tracking views, held that knowledge does not require justification in *any* sense. Some subsequent externalist theories, however, were less radical: they agreed with tradition that knowledge requires justification, but proposed accounts of justification that were meant as (externalist) alternatives to the traditional reasons-based account. Process Reliabilism about justification falls into this latter category.

As a theory of justification, Process Reliabilism is best understood to be a thesis regarding doxastic justification. We can think of doxastic justification, somewhat abstractly and schematically, as that property a belief has whereby, given how (the basis on which) it was formed, the belief itself meets a certain threshold of goodness with respect to the twin aims of acquiring truths and avoiding errors. Where traditional theories of justification held that this sort of goodness was a matter of the belief's being based on good reasons or evidence,

Process Reliabilism holds that it is a matter of the belief's having been formed and sustained by a reliable process.[2] To a first approximation, a belief-forming process (really: process-*type*) φ is reliable iff it produces a preponderance of true beliefs when employed in normal circumstances. Most people interpret this as a matter of φ's having the *propensity* to produce a preponderance of true beliefs in the circumstances: even if φ has not yet produced any beliefs, it is reliable so long as it would produce a preponderance of true beliefs. Others, however, prefer a strict frequency interpretation.

Belief-forming processes themselves are cognitive processes that take a range of inputs and transform them into beliefs. Some processes, such as perception, take as their inputs something other than beliefs. Goldman (1986) termed these "belief-*independent*" processes. To a first approximation, a belief produced by a belief-independent process is said to be doxastically justified if and only if it was produced by a reliable belief-forming process. However, not all belief-forming processes are belief-independent; some take as their input one or more of the subject's other beliefs. Goldman (1986) termed these "belief-*dependent*" processes. Process Reliabilism regards their assessment to be a more complicated affair. To a first approximation, a belief formed through a belief-dependent process Q is doxastically justified if and only if (i) for each of the beliefs Q took as its input on this occasion, the input-belief was produced by a reliable process; and (ii) Q itself is conditionally reliable. (A belief-dependent process is conditionally reliable when it is reliable *given true inputs*.) To see why the reliabilist endorses this more complicated account, consider a case in which you come to believe something through wishful thinking, and then, taking that belief as a premise, go on to reason from there to acquire other beliefs. It would seem that no matter how good a reasoner you are, the degree of doxastic justification of the beliefs you acquired through reasoning can be no better than the degree of doxastic justification of those beliefs you used as premises in that reasoning.

It is worth noting, if only in passing, that some Process Reliabilist theories of justification also acknowledge yet another category of beliefs: those formed through a belief-forming *method*.[3] Where a belief-forming process is part of a subject's innate cognitive endowment, a belief-forming method is something that is acquired through learning or acculturation. Examples include the algorithms that children are taught in school (e.g. the algorithm for computing sums or products) as well as the variety of technologies (instruments, thermometers, gauges, calculators, computers, and so forth) that we use as we go about acquiring information. According to the view developed in Goldman (1986), in order for a methods-acquired belief to be doxastically justified, it is necessary not only that the method itself be reliable but also that the subject acquire the method in a metareliable fashion (i.e. through a process that, as employed in normal circumstances, would select a preponderance of reliable methods).

As noted earlier, Process Reliabilism holds that a belief-forming process (process-type) is reliable just in case it produces (would produce) a preponderance of true beliefs when employed in the relevant circumstances. But what are the relevant circumstances? That is, under what sorts of circumstance must a process φ have a propensity to produce a preponderance of true beliefs if it is to count as reliable in the sense relevant to doxastic justification? This question must be addressed, since a given process might be reliable with respect to one range of circumstances while it is unreliable with respect to another range of circumstances. Take perception, for example. Arguably, most perceptual processes are highly reliable. But it is imaginable (even if it is not the case) that there are planets on which our perceptual systems would not be reliable: if we used them there, we'd acquire a preponderance of false beliefs.

Different versions of Process Reliabilism result depending on one's views regarding relevant circumstances. Let us understand a "normal environment" for a process-type φ to be those types of environment in which φ is or would be employed in belief-formation by a cognitively healthy subject. We can then distinguish at least five distinct proposals regarding which circumstances are relevant to reliability:

Indexical Reliabilism (IR)

Process φ is reliable if and only if it produces a preponderance of true beliefs when employed in normal environments within the world of the subject under assessment.

Actualist Reliabilism (AR)

Process φ is reliable if and only if it produces a preponderance of true beliefs when employed in normal environments in *this* world, the *actual* world— whatever world the subject under assessment happens to reside in.

Normal-Worlds Reliabilism (NWR)

Process φ is reliable if and only if it produces a preponderance of true beliefs when employed in normal environments in those worlds that conform to *what we take to be* the most basic features of the actual world.

Evolutionary Reliabilism (ER)

Process φ is reliable if and only if it produces a preponderance of true beliefs when employed in normal environments prevalent at the time at which (and on the world on which) φ evolved.

Transglobal Reliabilism (TR)

Process φ is reliable if and only if it produces a preponderance of true beliefs when employed in normal environments in those worlds that are compatible with the character of the subject's sensory experiences to date.

Of these IR is perhaps the most natural view; in any case it is the version of Process Reliabilism that is typically the target of reliabilism's critics (for which see below). AR was suggested by Goldman (1986) and is in the spirit of a very similar proposal by Ernest Sosa.[4]

NWR was suggested by Goldman (1986) in reaction to certain problems facing his earlier IR proposal. ER bears some affinities to recent work by Tyler Burge (2003) and is currently being pursued by Peter Graham. TR was developed by David Henderson and Terry Horgan (2007), although it has some affinities with views developed in Sosa (2007 and 2009). Each of these views has its virtues and its drawbacks; we will return to this after we consider various objections to Process Reliabilism.

Several kinds of arguments have been made on behalf of the Process Reliabilist account of doxastic justification. Here we highlight three: First, some argue that reliability is the fundamental notion for understanding other epistemic vocabulary, including vocabulary that is employed by theories that are not reliabilist in nature. Second, some argue that Process Reliabilism is to be preferred to more "internalist" approaches to justification in being able to acknowledge the connections between the concept of justification, on the one hand, and the concept of truth, on the other. And third, some argue that Process Reliabilism is unique in capturing a plausible notion of *immediate justification* (the sort of justification associated with basic beliefs and the foundationalist's response to the regress of reasons challenge). We take these up in order.

In several of his seminal papers and books, Goldman has argued that the various epistemological concepts that other epistemologists use to analyze the concept of justification make essential use of the concept of reliability. Consider for example the notion of evidence, which is often used to analyze the concept of justification. It is plausible to think that, at least to a first approximation, evidence is a kind of reliable indication: E is evidence for Q only if E's obtaining is a reliable indication of Q's obtaining. Similarly with "good reasons": suppose you believe that p, and that you do so on the basis of reason r. Your belief is justified only if r is a good reason. But a plausible hypothesis is that your reason is good only if your having that reason is a reliable indication of the truth of what you believe. Analogous points might be made with other epistemological notions.

The second sort of argument defends Process Reliabilist accounts of justification on grounds pertaining to the connection between justification and truth. The connection is seen in the following, which is thought by many to express a conceptual truth:

> JTC A belief that is doxastically justified is more likely to be true than is a belief that is not doxastically justified.

If reliability is the core of the notion of doxastic justification, then JTC's truth is indeed trivial, since by definition a belief that is reliably formed is more likely to be true than is a belief that is not reliably formed, at least when the belief in question is produced in the relevant circumstances (see above). (Goldman [1979] presents a variant on this sort of argument, in which the reliabilist account of justification is defended on grounds pertaining to the connection between justification and knowledge.)

This argument from the connection between justification and truth is related to another familiar (if still controversial) way to argue for externalist accounts in epistemology, generally, and Process Reliabilist versions in particular. According to this related argument, externalist (and so Process Reliabilist) accounts can be used as part of a strategy for resisting skepticism. Arguments of this sort are typically presented in defense of externalist theories of knowledge rather than justification.[5]

One final argument made on behalf of Process Reliabilist accounts of justification is that such accounts appear uniquely positioned to capture a notion of *immediate justification*. To see the need for a notion of immediate justification, consider the so-called regress of reasons argument in traditional discussions of epistemic justification. If pressed to respond to queries or challenges to one's beliefs (or claims to know), one would offer one's reasons for believing as one does. However, one's reasons, just like one's beliefs, more generally, might also be challenged. When they are, one would have to offer one's reasons for thinking that one's original reasons were good. But this process could continue, *ad inifinitum*. Assuming that one's reasons cannot continue on indefinitely (contrary to Klein 1999), it appears that there are only two options available for thinking about the structure of one's justifications. One possibility is that one's reasons form an interlocking circle, so that when one traced one's reasons out far enough, one would eventually come back to a belief or reason one employed earlier. This view, which is associated with coherence theories of justification, is regarded by many epistemologists to be subject to devastating objections. The other possibility is to acknowledge that at a certain point one's reasons give out. If one continues to hold that such reasons can be good despite not being supported in this way, then one is committed to the view that some of our beliefs or reasons are "immediately justified," that is, justified in a way that is not mediated by the epistemic status of anything else. (Such beliefs are often called "basic beliefs," as they are basic in the order of justification.) But one might worry about the category of basic beliefs: how can it be that there can be beliefs whose justification does not depend in any way on one's other beliefs or reasons? What could make a belief justified in this way? Process Reliabilism offers an answer to these questions: a belief is basic when it is formed through a belief-independent belief-forming process; and a basic belief enjoys immediate justification when the process in question is a reliable one.[6]

This Process Reliabilist account of basic belief and immediate justification has certain advantages over more traditional "internalist" accounts. Those accounts held that a mental state was basic when it was a direct result of a "taking" of what was "given" in our sensory experience of the world—as when one forms the belief that there is presently a red patch before one, on the basis of a certain sensory experience. But there are two familiar difficulties facing this suggestion. The first can be presented in the form of a dilemma. Either this "taking" of what is "given" is itself a cognitive state, or it is not. If it is a cognitive state, then it might go wrong and so would appear to require justification—in which case it cannot be basic after all. But if it is not a cognitive state, then it is not clear how it can be something that can itself be justified, or justify other things in its turn. Either way, the proposal appears unworkable. A second, related difficulty with the traditional account of basic belief can be seen in the proposal's attempt to say how a belief can be justified merely by being a "taking" of what is "given" in sensory experience. The idea is supposed to be something like this: when one's mental state (belief or what-have-you) is a mere "taking" of the "given," its justification is a matter of *the fit* between what is taken from sensory experience and what is given in that experience. But it would seem that the mere fact of a fit is not sufficient for justification. This is one of the lessons of the case of the speckled hen. Suppose that one sees a speckled hen, and that one's experience represents the hen as having exactly 53 speckles. This experience fits with the belief that the hen has exactly 53 speckles. Yet it would seem that this fact alone does not yield doxastic justification for one's belief that the hen has exactly 53 speckles. After all, one might have been guessing as to the exact number of the speckles; and even if one wasn't, the fact that one got it right still might be too much a matter of good fortune to count as justified. Notice that a Process Reliabilist account of justification does not face similar problems: it holds that one's belief as to the number of speckles is doxastically justified if but only if that belief was formed through a reliable process.[7]

Process Reliabilism as a theory of knowledge

In addition to Process Reliabilist theories of doxastic justification, there have also been Process Reliabilist theories of knowledge. The Process Reliabilist theory of knowledge (like its theory of justification) is best understood against the backdrop of the traditional JTB analysis discussed earlier. According to that analysis, S knows that p if and only if (i) S believes that p, (ii) p is true, and (iii) S is justified in believing that p. We noted earlier that the JTB approach is called into question by Gettier cases, which show that JTB cannot be sufficient for knowledge. It is worth noting that this result holds even if we endorse a Process Reliabilist account of justification.

To see this, suppose that you are very good at recognizing a certain actor by his face: you can pick him out of a crowd, so to speak. The perceptual process by which you do this is highly reliable. Suppose further that, at the supermarket one day, you spot him, and form the belief that it is the actor in question. As it happens, you are right. But suppose that, unbeknownst to you, the supermarket has employed a number of look-alikes that day who were so similar in appearance that had you encountered any one of them you would have been fooled. And suppose finally that it was only lucky that you encountered the actor himself: had you just lifted your head from your grocery list a moment sooner, you would have encountered one of the look-alikes. In this case it seems that your true belief formed through a reliable process is nevertheless too lucky to count as knowledge. Even a Process Reliabilist will need to address the Gettier Problem.

It has been common for Process Reliabilist accounts of knowledge to try to formulate another notion of reliability to handle Gettier cases. On such a view, a subject S knows that p if and only if (i) S believes that p, (ii) p is true, and (iii*) S's belief that p was formed through a process that was suitably reliable, where the reliability here involves satisfying the reliability requirement on doxastic justification, but it also involves satisfying an additional reliability requirement in addition to that. Process Reliabilist accounts of knowledge aim to spell out this additional reliability requirement.

To understand what more is needed, it is helpful to return briefly to the sort of reliability requirement on doxastic justification. A process-type is reliable in this sense when it produces (would produce) a preponderance of true beliefs when operating under normal conditions, that is, the sorts of conditions in which that process is employed by cognitively healthy subjects. Processes that satisfy this reliability requirement might be called "globally" reliable: they can be expected to produce a preponderance of truths across the variety of circumstances in which that process is standardly employed. The case of the above-mentioned look-alikes, however, suggests that for knowledge the process through which the subject's belief was formed must be not merely *globally* reliable, but also reliable in *the specific circumstances* in which she presently finds herself. We might thus formulate this additional requirement as follows: the process must be such that it can be expected to produce a preponderance of truths when applied in the present situation and in situations that are relevantly like the present one. Call a process that satisfies this condition "locally reliable" (in the present context). The process employed in the look-alike case fails this condition: if the subject in that case were to rely on the perceptual appearances *in situations like the present one,* where there are indistinguishable look-alikes throughout the store and where the subject could easily have come across one of them, that process is likely to lead to a good deal of error. Thus we might say that a Process Reliabilist account of knowledge holds that S knows that p if and only if (i) S believes that p, (ii) p is true, and (iii″) S's belief that p was formed through a process-type that was both globally and locally reliable in the circumstance. Arguably, something in this vicinity is the proposal in Goldman (1986); and others, including McGinn (1984) and Henderson and Horgan (2007), have formulated something in the vicinity as well. It is worth underscoring, however, that not all Process Reliabilists about knowledge endorse the distinction between global and local reliability (see, e.g. Greco 2010), and in any case there are challenges awaiting anyone who does make this distinction.[8]

One final point is worth noting in connection with the Process Reliabilist account of knowledge. Suppose that a belief's being formed through a process that is both globally and locally reliable in the context in question does not ensure that the belief is true: a belief can be formed through such a process and yet still be false. In that case, the Process Reliabilist cannot solve the Gettier Problem by appeal to the analysis in (i)–(iii″). For we will then be able to construct a Gettier case through the following recipe (which borrows heavily from Zagzebski 1994). To begin, take a case satisfying conditions (i)–(iii″). Next, imagine a case just like the first one except that the belief formed is false. (The possibility of such a case is guaranteed so long as a belief's being locally and globally reliable does not entail its truth.) Finally, imagine a case just like the previous one except a helpful element of luck ensures that the belief turned out true after all. The result will be a Gettier case: a true belief that is both locally and globally reliable fails to amount to knowledge, owing to the presence of a knowledge-undermining element of luck. It would appear, then, that Process Reliabilist accounts of knowledge face a forced choice: either such an account must formulate a notion of local reliability that entails the truth of the belief; or else it must allow that (i)–(iii") are not jointly sufficient for knowledge after all (although they might be individually necessary).

Objections to Process Reliabilism

There are various objections that have been leveled against Process Reliabilism. Most of these take aim at Process Reliabilism's account of justification; but since that account is assumed by most Process Reliabilist theories of knowledge, these objections carry over. In what follows we discuss four main objections: the "New Evil Demon" Problem, the Problem of Reliable Clairvoyance, the Generality Problem, and the "Bootstrapping" Problem (also known as the Problem of Easy Knowledge).

According to the Process Reliabilist account of doxastic justification, a belief is doxastically justified if and only if it is formed (and sustained) through a reliable belief-forming process-type. (Here we restrict our attention to those beliefs formed through belief-independent processes.) According to such a view, the reliability of process-type is both necessary and sufficient for doxastic justification. The first two objections we will consider challenge the necessity claim and the sufficiency claim, respectively.

Let us start with the objection which alleges that reliability in belief-formation is not *necessary* for a belief to enjoy doxastic justification. Stewart Cohen (1984) famously pressed this objection with his "New Evil Demon" Problem for reliabilism. The scenario Cohen envisages is the twenty-first century version of Descartes' Evil Demon scenario. As Descartes envisaged the scenario, an Evil Demon as powerful as he was evil aimed to deceive Descartes in every possible way, and so the Demon filled Descartes' mind with impressions as of interacting in a world of other people and middle-sized dry goods, leading Descartes to form beliefs about interacting with other people and things—when in fact all of these beliefs were false (all that Descartes "perceives" are the illusions placed in his mind by the Demon). In Cohen's version, there is an Evil Brain Scientist who has hooked up a Brain-in-a-Vat (BIV) to various electrodes, and stimulates the BIV so as to give it the impression of having various "experiences"—experiences that in fact are indistinguishable from the experiences that you (a normally embodied subject in the actual world) have. Thus, although the BIV is in fact in an otherwise-empty world, it has experiences as of interacting with other people and with things in the environment, just as you do. And on this basis the BIV forms various beliefs about the world around it, just as you do. Of course, unlike your beliefs, the BIV's beliefs about the world are systematically false. For this reason, its belief-forming processes are all highly unreliable. Despite this, there is a strong intuition that the BIV's beliefs should be exactly as doxastically justified as your corresponding beliefs are. Since your beliefs (it would seem) are highly justified, so too are the BIV's beliefs. If so, reliability is not a necessary condition on doxastic justification.

There would appear to be only two ways to resist this argument. The first would be to bite the bullet, and allow that the BIV's beliefs are (unreliably formed and so) doxastically unjustified. Goldman (1988) offers a version of this response. In it he tries to blunt the force of the New Evil Demon Problem by acknowledging a sense of "justification" (which he calls "weak justification") on which the BIV's beliefs are justified, even as (here Goldman bites the bullet) they fail to be justified *tout court* (strongly justified). The only alternative to this way of resisting the argument is to deny that the BIV's beliefs are unreliably formed. What sort of case can be made for such a denial? Well, consider that the impression that the BIV's beliefs are unreliably formed is strong if we assume, with Indexical–World Reliabilism, that assessments of reliability ought to take place in the BIV's own world: since that world is empty except for the vat and the BIV, the BIV's beliefs about that world, to the effect that it contains people and things, are systematically false. But suppose we reject Indexical–World Reliabilism, and hold instead that the assessment of the reliability of the BIV's processes should proceed as follows: unhook the "experience"-producing electrodes from the BIV, attach the BIV to sensory receptors of the sort that are used by normally embodied subjects, and then assess the reliability of the BIV's processes in the *actual* world. It would then turn out that the BIV's processes were reliable after all (assuming, of course, that these processes operate like yours do). Is there any version of Process Reliabilism that would countenance this way of assessing the reliability of the BIV's processes? Well, perhaps Actual-World Reliabilism would. But many epistemologists—Process Reliabilists as well as their critics—worry about the chauvinistic attitude of Actual-World Reliabilism: why favor our world when it is not the BIV's? Alternatively, Henderson and Horgan (2007) advertise their version of Transglobal Reliabilism as yielding the result that the BIV's beliefs are reliably formed; but it remains to be seen whether that version of Process Reliabilism will be seen as attractive in other respects.

The New Evil Demon Problem aims to show that reliability is not necessary for doxastic justification. A second type of objection aims at showing that reliability is not *sufficient* for doxastic justification. The most familiar argument of this sort is from Larry Bonjour (1980). He imagined a case involving a reliable clairvoyant whose clairvoyance caused in her the strong conviction regarding the President's whereabouts, where these convictions were highly reliable. Bonjour distinguished various versions of the case. In one of them, the subject herself had doubts about the reliability of these sorts of beliefs. In another, the subject herself was agnostic about the reliability of these sorts of beliefs. In yet another, she gave the matter of this reliability no thought whatsoever. Bonjour argued that in none of these cases should we credit her clairvoyance-based beliefs with doxastic justification. This is perhaps clearest in the case in which the subject is imagined to have doubts regarding the reliability of her clairvoyance beliefs: forming a belief through clairvoyance when one had doubts about the reliability of this process seems irrational, and presumably irrationally formed beliefs are not doxastically justified. But Bonjour argued that, whether or not the subject actually has doubts about the reliability of her clairvoyance, she ought to have such doubts; and he regarded this as showing that in the other cases he described the clairvoyance beliefs should not count as doxastically justified either. Since by hypothesis her clairvoyance is a reliable belief-forming process, Bonjour concluded that reliability is not sufficient for justification.

Bonjour's example of the reliable clairvoyant is one of several examples in the literature aimed at establishing the insufficiency of reliability for doxastic justification. Reliabilist responses to this sort of objection have been of two sorts. The main sort of response has been to add a "no defeaters" condition, or something that plays the role of such a condition, into the account. A defeater here is taken to be a proposition that is such that either the subject believes the proposition, or she should believe the proposition, where in virtue of the existence of such a proposition, the subject's reliability-generated justification is defeated.

The challenge to this sort of reply is to propose such a condition in a way that is not *ad hoc*. Goldman (1979 and 1986) attempted to build in (an analogue of) a no-defeaters condition in something like the following way: doxastic justification requires not only that one's belief was formed and sustained through a reliable belief-forming process but also that there be no belief-forming process available to the subject through which she would come to believe either (i) that the proposition she believes is false, or (ii) that the process through which she formed the original belief was unreliable. Still other attempts to formulate a reliabilist-friendly "no-defeaters condition" have been made as well.

A second response to these sorts of cases has been to restrict the reliable process-types that are justification-conferring. Some, most recently Peter Graham, have endorsed the view that only "naturally evolved" processes count. One worry for this sort of view concerns the possibility of an analogue of the "swampman" scenario originally envisaged (for a different purpose) by Donald Davidson. Imagine that lightning strikes a swamp and it just happens to create a duplicate of you: someone whose mental life is as like yours as is possible for a distinct individual. Since this individual has no "naturally evolved" mental faculties, the present view must deny that it has any doxastically justified beliefs; but this seems an unhappy implication, since its beliefs, after all, are very like yours, and yours are doxastically justified. An alternative, more recent proposal for restricting the set of processes whose reliability confers justification is offered by Lyons (2008). His proposal is that only basic beliefs, which he restricts to include only those produced by a cognitively innate module, get their justification straight from the reliability of the process involved. Lyons' view would appear to depend on the outcome of a more completed cognitive science, but even here it is worth noting that many neurobiologists are skeptical whether there are any cognitive modules in the sense relevant to Lyons' discussion.

Moving on, we next consider what many regard as the most important objection facing a Process Reliabilist theory of doxastic justification: the Generality Problem.[9] Recall that the Process Reliabilist thesis is that a belief is doxastically justified iff it is formed by a reliable belief-forming process-type. But a given belief is formed through many, and arguably infinitely many, different process-types. Suppose you look out the window, see a tree rustling in the wind, and so form the belief that this is an oak tree. What was the relevant process-type through which you formed that belief? Here are several possibilities:

1. vision-based recognition of a tree
2. vision-based recognition of an oak tree
3. vision-based recognition of an oak tree exploiting sensory information regarding the shape of its leaves
4. vision-based recognition of an oak tree exploiting sensory information regarding the shape of its leaves on such-and-such a date at exactly such-and-such a time

(Variations are easily imaginable.) Notice that these process-types will likely differ in their reliability: the first is presumably very reliable, the second less so (and will depend on how good you are at distinguishing oaks from other sorts of trees). The fourth one may well count as perfectly reliable (if your belief is true) or perfectly unreliable (if your belief is false), since it looks like that process-type will only ever produce this particular belief. Admittedly, this last result might be avoided if we endorse a propensity account, as opposed to a strict frequency account, of reliability. Still, the problem remains: assuming that justification is determined by reliability and that reliability regards the relevant belief-forming process-type, we need a principled way to select the relevant process-type—on pain of not really having a fully developed theory of justification on our hands. What is more, an adequate account of how we should perform this selection will have to satisfy various constraints: it must enable us to see process-types as employable on more than one occasion; the process-types in question must not be *ad hoc* (as 4 above is *ad hoc*); and it must yield independently plausible verdicts regarding justification. The Generality Problem is the problem of saying how we are to select the relevant process-type in each case, in such a way as to satisfy all of these conditions.

There have been several attempts to address this problem. Perhaps the most popular involves the suggestion that the relevant type is to be decided by scientific (cognitive) psychology. More specifically, the relevant kind is the natural kind under which the process-type falls under relevant cognitive-psychological generalizations. On this view, process individuation follows taxonomy in cognitive psychology. However, insofar as there can be various cognitive psychological kinds, and various generalizations, in play in a given situation, further specification is called for. Goldman's view is that the relevant process is "the *narrowest* type that is *causally operative* in producing the belief token in question." (1986, 51; italics in original) Other specifications are possible.

An alternative response to the Generality Problem, owed to Heller (1995), appeals to the context-sensitivity of judgments regarding reliability. This response acknowledges that, given any case, there is no description of the relevant process that counts as "the" type for the purpose of computing reliability. But it denies that this is a fatal flaw for Process Reliabilism. For in place of the idea that there is a single correct description of "the" process-type that was employed in a given case, the context-sensitivity proposal offers the idea that decisions as to "the" type employed are to be decided by taking into account the interests of those doing the assessing (and perhaps the practical and theoretical perspective of the subject under assessment). This will yield different reliability results in different contexts of assessment; but that is considered a design feature of the proposal, not a flaw. The result is a "contextualist" account of (reliabilist) justification.

Nor are these the only replies to the Generality Problem. Wunderlich (2003) rejects the call for a single reliability score, and proposes instead that we assess reliability by assigning to each belief a reliability vector consisting of a set of ordered pairs each of which gives the reliability score of a particular process-type. Beebe (2004) proposes to use a familiar statistical method to identify the broadest "objectively homogenous" subclass of processes among the class of processes that satisfy a set of necessary conditions on the relevant cognitive process. And Comesaña (2006) questions whether the reliabilist is the only one who suffers from a version of the Generality Problem. On the contrary, he suggests that any theory of justification will do so as long as it employs a notion of a belief's being based on something. (If this is correct, the Generality Problem is a problem for virtually everyone, and so cannot be the basis for preferring one theory of justification over another.)

The final objection to Process Reliabilism to be considered here is the "Bootstrapping" or "Easy Knowledge" Problem. Richard Fumerton (1994) offered perhaps the first description of the problem. Fumerton noticed that while early proponents of Process Reliabilism typically endorsed what this theory has to say about our perceptual beliefs—namely, that they enjoy doxastic justification so long as they are reliably formed—nevertheless a good many Process Reliabilists recoiled at the idea of endorsing what this theory has to say about our higher order beliefs regarding the reliability of perception itself. Fumerton saw this as a case of bad faith: given that a process is reliable, it would seem that nothing would prevent a subject from using that process to confirm its own reliability. Take the case of perception: one can employ perception to arrive at reliable belief about the perceptual world, and then use one's reliable beliefs about the perceptual world, together with the fact that the process of perception provided one with those beliefs, to confirm (through induction) the reliability of the process of perception itself. Fumerton's point, of course, was that if this seems like an illegitimate thing to do, this is a flaw in Process Reliabilism, since from a reliabilist point of view it seems that this procedure is unexceptionable.

The problem Fumerton raised was further developed (under the label "the Bootstrapping Problem") by Vogel (2000) and Cohen (2002) (under the label "the Problem of Easy Knowledge"). Vogel pointed out that, using a procedure much like the one described by Fumerton, one can confirm the reliability of a reliable speedometer by doing nothing more than reading the speedometer. Since the speedometer is reliable, one's beliefs about the speed of the car (formed through relying on the speedometer) are reliable, hence count as knowledge. But then one can use this knowledge of one's speed, together with one's reliable beliefs (hence knowledge) about the readings of the speedometer, to confirm that the speedometer is reliable. Vogel's point, like Fumerton's, was that if this seems too good to be true, this is so much the worse for Process Reliabilism. Cohen's "easy knowledge" problem is similar (although Cohen did not assume that the problem is only a problem for Process Reliabilism).

Recent attempts to respond to the Bootstrapping Problem typically argue that some forms of bootstrapping are legitimate (on pain of a radical form of skepticism), and then use this as a basis (i) to frame the question as one of distinguishing the legitimate forms from the illegitimate forms of bootstrapping, and (ii) to show that reliabilist epistemology is only committed to the legitimacy of the former. One popular suggestion on this score, found in Henderson and Horgan (2007) (but compare also Sosa's characterization of "reflective knowledge," most recently in his 2007 and 2009 works) is to distinguish those belief-forming process-types that are under what Henderson and Horgan call "suitable modulational control." To a very first approximation, a process-type is under suitable modulational control when the following conditions hold: first, the process-type is part of a cognitive system that is itself sensitive to the conditions under which the employment of that process-type in belief-formation would likely lead one to form false beliefs; and second, the subject's reliance on that process-type in belief-formation is regulated in such a way that, when the subject is in such "dangerous" conditions, it regularly happens that she does not, in fact, rely on the process-type in forming beliefs. A good example of this phenomenon is vision. Forming beliefs through vision is a highly reliable belief-forming process, but it is likely to lead one astray under certain conditions (poor lighting, obstructed view, great distance from the viewed object, etc.) Of course, most human subjects are aware of this, and so do not rely on vision in these circumstances. The process of visual belief-formation would thus appear to be under "suitable modulational control." Building on this, one might think that bootstrapping is legitimate so long as the process-type in question is one that is under "suitable modulational control." For what such control ensures is that the subject would not likely rely on that process were she to be in a context in which that reliance would lead her astray. This criterion would distinguish the case of perception from the case of the speedometer: whereas subjects are sensitive to the conditions under which the perceptual system is likely to mislead, the same cannot be said for Vogel's subject who is relying on the speedometer: if that speedometer had been malfunctioning she still would have relied on it.[10] If this reaction is warranted, it yields the result that, unlike our use of speedometers or thermometers, which can't be used in this bootstrapping way, we can use perception to justify our belief in the reliability of perception—an anti-skeptical result that some epistemologists might actually find attractive.

An extension: Testimony

As an epistemological theory, Process Reliabilism can be (and has been) applied to beliefs of various sorts. One sort of case that has received a good deal of recent attention concerns beliefs acquired through another's say-so. How should a Process Reliabilist epistemology assess such beliefs?

The issue can be approached by considering whether another person's testimony ought to be regarded in the same way that other sensory inputs are treated. Consider for example what is involved in perception. There is an input into one's perceptual system. This input is then transduced into information, which is then processed by the subject's cognitive system, at the end of which the subject forms a perceptual belief. Here the belief-forming process is initiated at the point at which the subject receives the sensory input. In particular, the sequence of worldly events that eventuate in the subject's receiving that input, but which take place *prior* to the subject's receiving that input, are not themselves considered part of the belief-forming process in play. On the contrary, these events are considered mere causal antecedents.[11] The question is whether this is the proper model for thinking about the linguistic signal and the belief-forming process in play in testimonial belief-formation.

An affirmative answer is supported by an assumption that many Process Reliabilists have made about the nature of belief-forming processes, to the effect that every belief-forming process is a process that takes place *entirely within the head of a single subject*.[12] If this individualism about processes is endorsed, then it appears that, at the very least, testimonial belief-formation shares with perceptual belief-formation the feature whereby the process involved is initiated at the point at which the subject receives the relevant (here linguistic) input. One might think, then, that insofar as a Process Reliabilist theory makes this individualistic assumption, the theory will regard perception as the right model for thinking about testimonial belief-formation. It is worth noting, however, that another option is available for the proponent of Process Reliabilism even after she has endorsed the individualistic assumption. She might think that, while testimonial belief-formation is (like perceptual belief-formation, and indeed like belief-formation generally) an individualistic process, testimonial belief-formation is unlike perception in that it is a belief-dependent process. On such a view, the input into the testimonial belief-forming process is not the sensory/linguistic signal itself; it is rather the hearer's belief to the effect that the speaker asserted that p, together with other beliefs that the hearer brings to bear on the question of the credibility of the assertion.

Recently, both the perceptual model and the preceding belief-dependent model of testimonial belief-formation have been called into question by Goldberg (2010). Goldberg proposes instead that memory is the best model for thinking about testimonial belief-formation. In memorial belief, the subject relies on herself as a source, in two senses: first, she aims to preserve information that she herself acquired at an earlier time, and so relies on herself as a source of *information*; but second, she depends on herself to have originally acquired that information in a reliable way, and so relies on herself as a source of *doxastic justification*. This is seen in standard Process Reliabilist accounts of memorial justification. According to these accounts, a memorial belief is doxastically justified if and only if (i) the belief itself was originally acquired in a reliable way, and (ii) the process of memory itself is conditionally reliable. This model makes explicit the point that, given the sort of reliance on oneself (one's past self) that is in play in memory cases, the process involved in memorial belief-formation should be regarded as temporally extended to include the processes in play when the belief was originally acquired. Goldberg's proposal is that testimonial belief-formation ought to be treated in like fashion: in testimonial belief-formation a hearer is relying on another speaker both as a source of information and also as a source of doxastic justification, and so the process-type that is involved should be seen as extending to include all of the processes that informed the speaker's testifying as she did.

The claim that testimonial belief-formation is an "interpersonally extended" process—one that takes place in at least two heads—is a radical departure from the individualistically oriented versions of Process Reliabilism. But it is worth underscoring that it does embrace one core feature of the Process Reliablist conception of doxastic justification. In particular, as noted in Goldman (1979), Process Reliabilism is committed to the idea that doxastic justification is a matter of the goodness of the cognitive process(es) through which information is acquired and transformed along the way to belief-formation and belief-sustainment. The anti-individualistic proposal mentioned earlier endorses this conception, but holds that the cognitive processes that are involved when we rely on the word of others includes cognitive processes that take place in their heads as well.[13]

Notes

1 Roughly speaking, any case that illustrates this phenomenon is called a "Gettier case."

2 See Goldman (1979).

3 See Goldman (1986).

4 See his contribution to Sosa and Bonjour (2003).

5 See, e.g. Goldman [1986: 55–7] and Greco [2000], where arguments of this sort are suggested on behalf of a Process Reliabilist account of knowledge; but one might also hope to formulate a version of this sort of argument for externalism, including Process Reliabilism, about justification as well.

6 See Sosa [1980] for an early version of this sort of argument; and see Lyons [2008] for a variant on this sort of argument.

7 This point is emphasized in Sosa 2009.

8 See Gendler and Hawthorne (2005).

9 See Feldman and Conee (1998).

10 Indeed, it is precisely for this sort of reason that Goldman [1986] distinguished methods-formed beliefs as a class, and made the conditions on justification regarding such beliefs more stringent.

11 This sort of view is explicit in Goldman (1979, 1986).

12 For a brief discussion and defense of such a view, see Goldman [1986] and Alston [1994].

13 See Lackey [2008] for another theory that regards reliability in the testimony consumed as a necessary condition on doxastically justified testimonial belief, albeit without going so far as to endorse the "interpersonally extended" account of testimonial belief-formation.

References

Alston, W. 1994. "Belief-Forming Practices and the Social." In F. Schmitt, ed., *Socializing Epistemology*. Maryland: Rowman & Littlefield, pp. 29–52.

Beebe, J. 2004. "The Generality Problem, Statistical Relevance, and the Tri-level Hypothesis." *Noûs* 38(1): 177–95.

Bonjour, L. 1980. "Externalist Theories of Empirical Knowledge." *Midwest Studies in Philosophy* 5: 53–73.

Burge, T. 2003. "Perceptual Entitlement." *Philosophy and Phenomenological Research* 67(3): 503–48.

Cohen, S. 1984. "Justification and Truth." *Philosophical Studies* 46: 279–95.

— 2002. "Basic Knowledge and the Problem of Easy Knowledge." *Philosophy and Phenomenological Research* 65(2): 309–29.

Comesaña, J. 2006. "A Well-Founded Solution to the Generality Problem." *Philosophical Studies* 129: 27–47.

Feldman, R. and Conee, E. 1998. "The Generality Problem for Reliabilism." *Philosophical Studies* 89: 1–29.

Fumerton, R. 1994. *Metaepistemology and Skepticism*. Maryland: Rowman & Littlefield.

Gendler, T. and Hawthorne, J. 2005. "The Real Guide to Fake Barns: A Catalogue of Gifts for Your Epistemic Enemies." *Philosophical Studies* 124: 331–52.

Gettier, E. 1963. "Is Justified True Belief Knowledge?" *Analysis* 23: 121–3.

Goldberg, S. 2010. *Relying on Others: An Essay in Epistemology*. Oxford: Oxford University Press.

Goldman, A. 1979. "What is Justified Belief?" In G. Pappas, ed., *Justification and Knowledge*. Dordrecht: D. Reidel, pp. 1–23.

— 1986. *Epistemology and Cognition*. Cambridge: Harvard University Press.

— 1988. "Strong and Weak Justification." *Philosophical Perspectives* 2: *Epistemology* 51–69.

Greco, J. 2000. *Putting Skeptics in Their Place*. Cambridge: Cambridge University Press.

— 2010. *Achieving Knowledge*. Cambridge: Cambridge University Press.

Heller, M. 1995. "A Simple Solution to the Problem of Generality." *Noûs* 29(4): 501–15.

Henderson, D. and Horgan, T. 2007. "The Ins and Outs of Transglobal Reliabilism." In Goldberg, S. ed., *Internalism and Externalism in Semantics and Epistemology*. Oxford: Oxford University Press, pp. 100–30.

Klein, P. 1999. "Human Knowledge and the Infinite Regress of Reasons." *Philosophical Perspectives* 13: 297–325.

Lackey, J. 2008. *Learning from Words*. Oxford: Oxford University Press.

Lyons, J. 2008. *Perception and Basic Beliefs*. Oxford: Oxford University Press.

McGinn, C. 1984. "The Concept of Knowledge." *Midwest Studies in Philosophy* 9: 529–54.

Sosa, E. 1980. "The Raft and the Pyramid: Coherence versus Foundations in the Theory of Knowledge." *Midwest Studies in Philosophy* 5: 3–25.

— 2007. *A Virtue Epistemology*. Oxford: Oxford University Press.

— 2009. *Reflective Knowledge*. Oxford: Oxford University Press.

Sosa, E. and Bonjour, L. 2003. *Epistemic Justification*. London: Blackwell.

Vogel, J. 2000. "Reliabilism Leveled." *Journal of Philosophy* 97(11): 602–23.

Wunderlich, M. 2003. "Vector Reliability: A New Approach to Epistemic Justification." *Synthese* 136: 237–62.

Zagzebski, L. 1994. "The Inescapability of the Gettier Problem." *Philosophical Quarterly* 44(174): 65–73.

7

Proper Functionalism

Kenneth Boyce and Alvin Plantinga

Introduction

Warrant is that, whatever precisely it is, which makes the difference between knowledge and true belief.[1] Proper functionalism with respect to warrant is the view that (i) it is a necessary condition for a belief's being warranted that it arise by way of cognitive proper function and (ii) any adequate analysis of warrant centrally involves that notion. There can be proper functionalist theories of other epistemic concepts besides warrant; unless said otherwise, however, when we use the term "proper functionalism" it will be proper functionalism about warrant to which we are referring. In this chapter, we will describe proper functionalism about warrant and point to some of the reasons for it. We will also respond to some objections leveled against this view and say a few words about how it is related to other issues in epistemology.

Motivations for proper functionalism

Some preliminary remarks

The notion of proper function appealed to in proper functionalist analyses of warrant is that found in the biological sciences (as when a biologist says that the average human heart functions properly when it beats 70 times per minute).[2] Of particular import, the concept of proper function presupposes the notion of a *design plan*—something that specifies the way in which a thing is *supposed to work*.[3] We need not initially take the notions of *design plan* and the *way in which a thing is supposed to work* to entail *conscious* design or purpose.[4] In central and paradigm cases, however, design plans do indeed involve the thing's having been designed by one or more conscious designers who are aiming at an end of some sort.

Roughly (far too roughly to be of any serious use), proper functionalism maintains that a belief's being warranted is a matter of its being produced by a properly functioning cognitive faculty, one whose aim (as specified by the design plan) is the formation of true beliefs. That is, a belief's being warranted is a matter of its being produced by way of truth-aimed cognitive proper function. But why think anything like that? Why hold such a view? An easy way to see some of the motivations is to look at how it circumvents many of the problems that bedevil alternative theories. It is our conviction that any attempt to provide an analysis of warrant that does not acknowledge the central role of cognitive proper function will inevitably flounder.

The failure of internalist theories

According to internalist theories, what primarily determines whether a belief has warrant (or warrant-like status) are factors or states that are in some sense internal to the believer. (An externalist, by contrast, denies this.) More specifically, it is a matter of factors or states to which the believer has some sort of special epistemic access. Perhaps they are factors that a subject can tell are present by reflection alone; or perhaps they are factors that the subject can be certain are present; or perhaps she cannot be culpably mistaken concerning their presence.[5]

These days, in light of the Gettier problem, nearly all parties agree that no strictly internalist conditions are jointly sufficient for warrant. That is because standard Gettier cases show that no matter how well things are going for a believer from an internalist point of view, her beliefs may still be true "just by accident," and therefore not items of knowledge. However, many theories of warrant remain substantially internalist in character, maintaining that whether a belief is warranted for an individual is mostly a matter of that individual's satisfying various internalist conditions, in conjunction with some (admittedly hard to specify) externalist condition needed to mollify Gettier. Here we will argue that no such substantially internalist theory of warrant can succeed as long as it does not recognize the need for a proper function condition.

In standard Gettier cases, though everything is going well for a believer from an internalist perspective, her beliefs lack warrant because something about her cognitively external environment is amiss. It is tempting, therefore, to think that a substantially internalist analysis of warrant can pacify Gettier merely by adding some (admittedly hard to specify) condition to the effect that things in the believer's cognitively external environment are not awry. This temptation evaporates, however, when we attend to Gettier cases (or at least cases that are *Gettier-like*) in which, though everything is going right from an internalist perspective, the problem lies not in the believer's environment, but in the believer herself.

Consider, for example, a case that Chisholm attributes to Meinong: An aging forest ranger lives in a cottage in the mountains. There is a set of wind chimes hanging from the bough just outside the kitchen window; when these wind chimes sound, the ranger forms the belief that the wind is blowing. As he ages, his hearing (unbeknownst to him) deteriorates; he can no longer hear the chimes. He is also sometimes subject to small auditory hallucinations in which he is appeared to in that wind-chimes way; and occasionally these hallucinations occur when the wind is blowing.

We can stipulate that, on these occasions, the ranger meets whatever plausible internalist conditions for warrant one might like to propose.[6] But clearly, on such occasions, the aging forest ranger's beliefs have little by way of warrant for him. And this is so in spite of the fact that there is nothing amiss in his cognitively external environment. Rather, the problem is due to cognitive malfunction on the part of the ranger himself. Examples of this sort can be multiplied as well as made more specific to various internalist proposals.[7] We take such counterexamples to illustrate that any substantially internalist analysis of warrant that omits a proper function condition will find itself subject to Gettier-like counterexamples.

The failure of reliabilism

It's not just substantially internalist accounts of warrant that flounder on account of omitting a proper function condition. Externalist theories that ignore the role of cognitive proper function also do so to their peril. Here we will support that charge by focusing on reliabilist theories of warrant.

Reliabilism comes in at least two styles. The first sees warrant in terms of origin and province: a belief is warranted for one if it is produced and sustained by a reliable belief-producing mechanism. The second sees warrant as a matter of *probability*; a person is said to know a (true) proposition A if he believes it, and if the right probability relations hold between A and its significant others. Of course, these two different styles of reliabilism can be (and have been) developed with considerable sophistication. And we can't hope to address all the nuances of these developments here.[8] But the thing to see is that on either of these styles of reliabilism, a true belief can have those properties that (according to the theory) confer warrant-like status *by accident,* in the way that precludes them from having warrant.

Consider reliabilism of the second style. For definiteness, let the reliabilist view in question be the view that a belief, B, has warrant just in case it is causally sustained in virtue of S's obtaining, where S is a particular state of affairs, and the objective conditional probability (appropriately relativized to background conditions) of B given that S obtains is sufficiently high.[9] Now consider the case of the Epistemically Serendipitous Brain Lesion. Suppose that Sam suffers from a serious abnormality—a brain lesion, let's say. This lesion wreaks havoc with Sam's noetic structure, causing him to believe a variety of propositions, most of which are wildly false. It also causes him to believe, however, that he is suffering from a brain lesion. Further, Sam has no evidence at all that he is abnormal in this way, thinking of his unusual beliefs as resulting from an engagingly original turn of mind.

Since, in this case, Sam's belief that he has a brain lesion is causally sustained in virtue of its being the case that he has a brain lesion and since the objective conditional probability that Sam has a brain lesion given that *Sam's having a brain lesion* obtains is sufficiently high (unity!), it follows from the view we are considering that Sam's belief is warranted. But, obviously, Sam's belief that he has a brain lesion is not warranted.

Consider a paradigmatic reliabilist theory of the first style. According to such a paradigmatic reliabilist theory (minus a few bells and whistles) a belief is warranted for an individual just in case it is produced by a token of a sufficiently reliable type of belief-forming process.[10] Now, adapt The Case of The Epistemically Serendipitous Lesion described earlier. There is a rare but specific sort of brain lesion (we may suppose) that is always associated with a number of cognitive processes, most of which cause its victim to hold absurdly false beliefs. One of the associated processes, however, causes the victim to believe that he has a brain lesion. Suppose that Sam suffers from this disorder and accordingly believes that he has a brain lesion. Add that he has no evidence at all for this belief (also add, if you like, that he has much evidence against it; but then add also that the malfunction by the lesion makes it impossible for him to take appropriate account of this evidence). Then the relevant type of belief-forming process (while it may be hard to specify in detail) will certainly be highly reliable; but the resulting belief—that he has a brain lesion—will have little by way of warrant for Sam.

What these examples illustrate is that no mere causal or reliability condition is sufficient for warrant.[11] It is possible for such conditions to be met, for the resulting belief to be true, and yet, owing to a lack of cognitive proper function, for the agent to have acquired a true belief merely by accident. So reliabilist theories of warrant, like substantially internalist theories, ignore the need for a proper function condition to their detriment.

The upshot: Proper function and non-accidentality

We have seen how views of warrant that fail to acknowledge the need for proper function—whether substantially internalist or paradigmatically externalist—face Gettier problems. That is, these views are subject to counterexamples in which a true belief fulfills all of the specified conditions for warrant and, yet, manages to fulfill them "merely by accident." The lesson to be learned, we take it, is that a necessary condition for a belief's being warranted is that it be formed by way of cognitive proper function.

We also take there to be a stronger lesson to be learned. What examples of the above sort illustrate is that, for any merely internalist, merely causal, or merely reliabilist conditions (or any combination thereof), it is possible for a belief to satisfy those conditions "merely by accident" (in the sense at issue in Gettier cases). Furthermore, in many of these sorts of counterexamples, it seems that the only way to *explain why* it is that the relevant beliefs satisfy those conditions merely by accident is to appeal to the fact that they do so in a way that is accidental *with respect to the belief-forming mechanisms specified by the believer's cognitive design plan*. And so it seems that the notion of non-accidentality that pertains to our concept of knowledge is one that cannot be analyzed merely in terms of the meeting of certain internalist, causal, or reliability conditions (or combinations thereof). Rather, it is a concept that must be analyzed in terms that make reference to a cognitive design plan. And so the above examples seem to show not only that cognitive proper function is necessary for warrant, but that the notion of cognitive proper function is centrally involved in the concept of non-accidentality that any adequate analysis of warrant must capture.

Formulating a proper functionalist analysis of warrant

We concluded from our consideration of the examples offered in the previous section that cognitive proper function is *necessary* for warrant. Though necessary, however, it is easy to see that it is not sufficient (not even nearly sufficient) for warrant. First, not all aspects of the design of our cognitive faculties need to be aimed at the production of *true* belief; some might be such as to conduce to survival, or relief from suffering, or the possibility of loyalty, and so on. What confers warrant is one's cognitive faculties working properly, or working according to the design plan, *insofar as that segment of the design plan is aimed at producing true beliefs.*

Still more is required. For suppose a well-meaning but incompetent angel—one of Hume's infant deities, say—sets out to design a variety of rational persons, persons capable of thought, belief, and knowledge. As it turns out, the design is a real failure; the resulting beings hold beliefs, but most of them are absurdly false. If one of these beings were to happen upon a true belief, it would merely be by accident. The beliefs of these beings, therefore, lack warrant.

What must we add? That the design plan is a *good* one—more exactly, that the design governing the belief in question is a good one; still more exactly, that the objective probability of a belief's being true, given that it is produced by cognitive faculties functioning in accord with the relevant module of the design plan, is high. Even more exactly, the module of the design plan governing its production must be such that it is objectively highly probable that a belief produced by cognitive faculties functioning in accord with that module (in a congenial cognitive environment) will be true or verisimilitudinous.

Even the above conditions are not enough. It is at least broadly logically possible that beings with a good design plan might find themselves in environments radically different from the environments for which they were designed; environments in which the ways of belief formation specified by their design plan are wildly unreliable (though they would be reliable in the environment for which they were designed). If so, the beliefs of these beings, though fulfilling all of the previously mentioned conditions, would, nonetheless, lack warrant. So we need to add that the beliefs in question must be produced in the right sort of cognitive environment,[12] the sort of cognitive environment for which their faculties were designed.

As we have seen, the condition that a belief comes about by way of cognitive proper function is not sufficient (not even nearly sufficient) for warrant. But we maintain that something in the neighborhood of the conditions specified above being jointly fulfilled *is* sufficient (or at least nearly sufficient) for warrant. Accordingly, we offer the following as a first approximation to an adequate analysis of warrant:

A belief B has warrant for S if and only if the relevant segments (the segments involved in the production of B) are functioning properly in a cognitive environment sufficiently similar to that for which S's faculties are designed; and the modules of the design plan are (1) aimed at truth, and (2) such that there is a high objective probability that a belief formed in accordance with those modules (in that sort of cognitive environment) is true; and the more firmly S believes B the more warrant B has for S.[13]

The above, as was just said, is merely a first approximation. Many amendments and refinements are required (some of which we will mention later on).[14] However, for current purposes, this first approximation will do.

Objections to proper functionalism

Sadly enough, in spite of the luminous obviousness of proper functionalism, not everyone is on board. Many objections have been proposed.[15] We can't hope to address them all in the space allotted here; we will confine ourselves to addressing what we consider to be two of the most important kinds of objections raised against the view.

Swampman

First, objections according to which there are counterexamples to the claim that cognitive proper function is necessary for warrant, counterexamples in which there are beings who have warranted beliefs but who nevertheless, owing either to poor design or lack of design altogether, fail to exhibit cognitive proper function. A paradigmatic example of such a purported counterexample has been put forward by Ernest Sosa.[16]

Sosa adapts, for his own purposes, Donald Davidson's "Swampman" scenario. In that scenario, by sheer accident, a lightning strike results in the formation of a molecule-for-molecule duplicate of Donald Davidson out of the materials of a nearby swamp. As Sosa envisions the scenario, this "Swampman" exits the swamp having various perceptual experiences, and forming beliefs as a result, in the same way that Davidson himself would have. According to Sosa, "it . . . seems logically possible for . . . Swampman to have warranted beliefs not long after creation if not right away." But it also seems that Swampman (having been created just by accident) has no design plan and therefore is not properly functioning.

It's not clear, however, that the Swampman scenario that Sosa envisions *is* (broadly) logically possible (is it possible for a person to be created just by accident in this way?). So it is at least not clear that we are offered a genuine counterexample to proper functionalism here.[17] But suppose that it is possible. It is also at least conceivable that an entity acquires a design plan by accident. Or, in any case, it is not immediately clear that a being has a design plan only if it acquired one as the result of intentional design. It seems that biological systems have design plans (there are ways, e.g. that the heart is "supposed to" function) even though, if naturalism and the theory of evolution are both true, these systems were not intentionally designed. So perhaps we may think of Sosa's Swampman case as a case in which a creature acquires a design plan by accident, or at least not by way of intentional design.

But suppose we grant Sosa's case is logically possible and that in it Swampman is not properly functioning. Having granted this, it is no longer clear that, in Sosa's scenario, Swampman has genuinely warranted beliefs. Certainly, if Wilma, an ordinary human being, forms the belief that there is a tree in front of her by way of veridical perception of a tree, in the way that human beings ordinarily form such beliefs, then (provided her cognitive environment is Gettier-free), we are inclined to say that Wilma's belief is warranted. We are inclined to say this because we take it for granted that such a belief-forming process is an epistemically appropriate one for ordinary human beings like Wilma to have. We take it for granted that she forms her belief in the way that human beings are "supposed to" form such beliefs.

It is far from obvious, however, that we are entitled to take if for granted that Swampman's belief-forming processes are epistemically appropriate in the way that Wilma's are. Since, by what has been granted, Swampman's beliefs are not formed by way of cognitive proper function (or by way of cognitive malfunction, for that matter), it is not clear that there are any ways in which it can be said that Swampman is "supposed to" form the beliefs that he does. It seems plausible that if Swampman forms true beliefs, even by way of reliable belief-forming processes, that he does so merely by accident (since he does not form his beliefs appropriately; there is no way of forming beliefs that are appropriate for him). And so, upon reflection, it seems plausible to regard the cases in which Swampman forms true beliefs as Gettier cases (or at least as relevantly analogous to Gettier cases). And for that reason, it is plausible to deny that Swampman's beliefs have warrant.[18]

Gettier problems

Here's a Gettier-style counterexample to the first approximation of a proper functionalist analysis offered in the section "Formulating a Proper Functionalist Analysis of Warrant." It is an amalgamation of examples provided by Richard Feldman, Peter Klein, and Robert Shope (the narration is from Plantinga's first person perspective):

> I own a Chevrolet van, drive to Notre Dame on a football Saturday, and unthinkingly park in one of the many places reserved for the football coach. Naturally his minions tow my van away and, as befits such *lèse majesté,* destroy it. By a splendid piece of good luck, however, I have won the Varsity Club's Win-a-Chevrolet-Van contest, although I haven't yet heard the good news. You ask me what sort of automobile I own; I reply, both honestly and truthfully, "A Chevrolet van." My belief that I own such a van is true, but "just by accident" (more accurately, it is only by accident that I happen to form a true belief); hence it does not constitute knowledge. All of the non-environmental conditions for warrant, furthermore, are met. It also looks as if the environmental condition is met: after all, isn't the cognitive environment here on Earth and in South Bend just the one for which our faculties were designed? What is important about the example is this: it is clear that if the coach's minions had been a bit less zealous and had *not* destroyed my van, the conditions for warrant outlined above would have obtained and I would have known that I own a Chevrolet van. In the actual situation, however, the one in which the van is destroyed, my belief is produced by the very same processes functioning the very same way in (apparently) the same cognitive environment. Hence, on the original account, either both of these situations are ones in which I know that I own a Chevrolet van, or neither is. But clearly one is and one isn't.

Upon reflection, it is easy to see that there are many cases of this sort. There is Bertrand Russell's pre-Gettier case, for example, in which one glances up at a clock that has stopped 12 hours ago and forms a true belief about what time it is. There is also, for another example, the case in which one glances across one's lawn and believes truly that it is Paul standing in his driveway, unaware that Paul's identical twin Peter (who one does not even know exists) is currently visiting. In all of these cases, the global environment in which one finds oneself is the one we enjoy right here on Earth, the one for which we were designed by God or evolution. Yet, in each of these cases, one's beliefs are robbed of warrant because of some local environmental anomaly. And so, the original account requires amendment.

Call the sort of global environment alluded to above, the one which we enjoy on Earth and the one for which our cognitive faculties were designed, the "maxi-environment." This environment would include such features as the presence of light and air, the presence of visible objects, of other objects detectable by our kind of cognitive system, of some objects not so detectable, of the regularities of nature, of the existence of other people, and so on. There is also a much less global kind of cognitive environment. For any belief B and (more relevantly) the exercise E of my cognitive powers issuing in B, there is a much more specific and detailed state of affairs we might call its "cognitive mini-environment." We can think of a cognitive mini-environment of a given exercise of cognitive powers E as a *state of affairs* (or proposition)—one that includes all the relevant epistemic circumstances obtaining when that belief is formed (though diminished with respect to whether E produces a true belief). Let "MBE" denote the mini-environment with respect to a particular exercise of cognitive powers, E, issuing in the formation of a particular belief, B. To be on the safe side, let MBE be as full as you please, as large a fragment of the actual world as you like.

Now, what's relevant here is that some cognitive mini-environments—for example, those of the Notre Dame van case, the clock that stopped, Peter's visit to Paul—are *misleading* for some exercises of cognitive faculties, even when those faculties are functioning properly and even when the maxi-environment is favorable. It is clear, therefore, that S knows p, on a given occasion, only if S's cognitive mini-environment, on that occasion, is not misleading with respect to a particular exercise of cognitive powers producing the belief that p. So what the original account of warrant requires is an addition to the effect that the relevant mini-environment not be misleading. What must be added to the other conditions of warrant, then, is a *Resolution Condition*:

(RC) A belief B produced by an exercise of cognitive powers has warrant sufficient for knowledge only if MBE (the mini-environment with respect to B and E) is favorable for E.

What does "appropriateness" or "favorability" or "non-misleadingness," for a cognitive mini-environment consist in? Can we say anything more definite?

In the above cases (the Notre Dame van case, the case of Peter's visiting Paul, the case of the stopped clock), the problem is that the relevant exercises of cognitive powers lack sufficient resolution in the cognitive mini-environment. One cannot, while sitting in the Notre Dame stadium, distinguish its being the case that one still owns the van one drove to campus this morning from its being the case that one's van was unexpectedly destroyed. Similarly, one can't, from across the street, distinguish Paul from his identical twin Peter. And, one can't tell, just at a glance, that the clock is stopped. In each case in which one has a belief, B, produced by a given exercise of cognitive powers, E, there are some states of affairs that E is competent to detect in the relevant cognitive mini-environment, MBE, and some which it is not. So consider the conjunction of circumstances C contained in MBE such that C is detectable by E; call this state of affairs DMBE.

With these notions on hand, Plantinga earlier proffered the following, tentative suggestion of what it is for a mini-environment to be favorable:

> (FC) MBE is favorable just if there is no state of affairs S included in MBE but not in DMBE such that the objective probability of B with respect to the conjunction of DMBE and S falls below r,

where r is some real number representing a reasonably high probability.[19] In the Twin case, for example, a state of affairs S such that B is not probable enough with respect to the conjunction of DMBE and S would be Peter's being in the vicinity as well as Paul, and being indistinguishable from him across the street. In the Notre Dame van case, S is the state of affairs of one's van having been destroyed by the coach's over-zealous minions, etc.

However, this proposal won't quite do. While the original proper functionalist account countenanced as warranted true beliefs that clearly weren't items of knowledge, the current proposal excludes beliefs that do seem to count as items of knowledge. This is illustrated by the following counterexample from Thad Botham:

> Consider a version of the identical twin case where we stipulate that Paul is an only child, thereby removing Peter from the scene. In addition, the moment before you believe the proposition "There's Paul," his uncle—unbeknownst to you—lies to a friend, telling her that Paul has an identical twin brother who's visiting Paul at that very moment and that he just spoke with each of them on the telephone. Paul's uncle asserts this falsehood while in London, thousands of miles away. In this case, you know the proposition "There's Paul." However, the objective probability of your belief is not reasonably high given DMBE together with the state of affairs S—viz., its being the case that Paul's uncle just told a friend that Paul has an identical twin who is presently in the vicinity of Paul. Thus, by (FC) your MBE is unfavorable with respect to E, which together with (RC) entails that you do not have knowledge. But you do know that it is Paul.[20]

Perhaps there is an answer here. In each of the above cases, there are certain states of affairs which are, so to speak, "taken for granted" by E when it issues in B, but which are not included in DMBE. For instance, in the Notre Dame van case, it is taken for granted by E that matters haven't changed with respect to Plantinga's owning the Chevy van—not merely with respect to his owning *a* Chevy van, but with respect to his owning *that* Chevy van. In the case of the stopped clock, it is taken for granted that the clock on the wall is functioning properly. In the twin case, it is taken for granted that there is no one visually indistinguishable from Paul in the vicinity, etc.

It is difficult to say just what this property of being taken for granted consists in. It is not a matter of one's having any particular *belief* that the relevant state of affairs obtains (in some of these cases, that belief may well be absent). Nor is it obviously a matter of B's being, in some way, *based upon* what is taken for granted. Nevertheless, we seem to have an intuitive grip on the notion. And perhaps that is enough. Provided that it *is* enough, we might try replacing (FC) with the following:

> (FC') MBE is favorable just if for every state of affairs, S, such that S is taken for granted by E in the issuing of B, there is no state of affairs S˙ such that S˙ is included in MBE but not in DMBE and such that S˙ precludes S.

This may work. Induction suggests, however, that still another counterexample will rear its ugly head. Even if one were to appear, however, proper functionalism would be no worse off in this respect (i.e. that of not having a fully adequate solution to the Gettier problem) than any other extant theory of knowledge. There would also be some reason to think it is better off in this respect than many of its rivals. As we argued in the first section, the notion of cognitive proper function must be centrally involved in any adequate analysis of the concept of non-accidentality required to circumvent Gettier counterexamples. And so it appears that any successful solution to the Gettier problem will be one in which the notion of proper function plays a central role.

Further directions

So far we have been defending a particular kind of proper functionalist account of warrant. However, there is no reason that the notion of cognitive proper function can't play a significant role in other projects in epistemology. We have already noted, for example, that substantially internalist theories and reliabilist theories of warrant flounder insofar as they ignore the importance of cognitive proper function. But perhaps these theories might be significantly strengthened (while retaining their spirit) by supplementing their proposed analyses with a proper function condition. Investigating such prospects would make for a worthwhile project, one that we commend to others.

Another worthwhile project, and one that is currently a flourishing research program in epistemology, is that of virtue epistemology. According to John Greco, "the central idea of virtue epistemology is that, Gettier problems aside, knowledge is true belief which results from one's cognitive virtues," where "a cognitive virtue . . . is an ability [or 'cognitive faculty'] to arrive at truths in a particular field, and to avoid believing falsehoods in that field, under the relevant conditions."[21] Greco classifies proper functionalism, as well as Ernest Sosa's Goldman-inspired brand of reliabilism, as a paradigm instance of virtue epistemology.[22] Sosa himself concurs with this assessment, maintaining that his own view, some of Alvin Goldman's more recent views, and proper functionalism are all properly seen as "varieties of a single more fundamental option in epistemology, one which puts the explicative emphasis on truth-conducive intellectual virtues or faculties, and is properly termed 'virtue epistemology.'"[23]

We agree that proper functionalism is correctly regarded as a version of virtue epistemology. Or rather, as we would like to put it, the various views that fall within the scope of virtue epistemology should really be thought of as varieties of proper functionalism! That is because virtue epistemology of any stripe presupposes a notion of cognitive proper function. Virtue epistemology centrally involves an appeal to cognitive virtues, understood as cognitive faculties or cognitive abilities. It is this appeal that is supposed to help evade counterexamples to reliabilism, such as *The Case of the Epistemically Serendipitous Brain Lesion*. Sosa, for instance, responds to the latter by holding that a belief is warranted only if it is produced by a faculty, and a brain lesion isn't a faculty. This seems right. But the notion of a faculty itself involves the notion of proper function. A faculty or power—perception, or memory, or reason in the narrow sense, or digestion, or one's ability to walk, is precisely the sort of thing that can function properly or improperly. Indeed, this is just the difference between the brain lesion and a faculty: the concepts of proper and improper function don't apply to the brain lesion. It isn't functioning either properly or improperly in producing the belief it does: it isn't that sort of thing. So, the relevant notion of a cognitive faculty required by the virtue epistemologist presupposes the notion of cognitive proper function. Insofar as it does, we can see different views within virtue epistemology as varieties of proper functionalism.

So far we have described how proper functionalism is interestingly related to programs in epistemology that are primarily concerned with the concept of *warrant*. It is also possible, however, to develop proper functionalist theories of other significant epistemic properties besides warrant. Michael Bergmann, for example, has offered an interesting and promising proper functionalist theory of epistemic justification. We will close this section with a brief summary of some of the details and merits of Bergmann's theory.

In order to be clear about what the advantages of a proper functionalist theory of epistemic justification might be, it would be helpful to have a clear notion of just what property the term "epistemic justification" is meant to pick out. Unfortunately, in spite of the extensive literature on the concept of epistemic justification, it is difficult to say, exactly, what epistemic justification is, or even whether there is a single property being referred to in these debates.[24] We can say at least this much; the concept of justification is a transparently normative concept. And perhaps we can understand this concept (where this concept shows up in many of these discussions) as the kind of rational normativity involved in warrant. In particular, what seems relevant here is rational normativity *downstream* from experience (i.e. forming appropriate beliefs, in response to experience, irrespective of the way in which the subject's experience is connected with the world).[25] From the standpoint of proper functionalism, this kind of normativity is to be analyzed in terms of truth-aimed cognitive proper function. And Bergmann proposes just such an analysis.

Before we describe Bergmann's analysis in more detail, however, it will be helpful to give a quick overview of some of the difficulties faced by alternative theories of justification.[26] Not only is the concept of justification a normative one; it is also (at least insofar as it is a concept of the kind of normativity involved in warrant) a concept that involves the notion of truth-aptness.[27] That is, there is some connection between a belief's being produced in accordance with the norms required for justification and its being likely to be true. What norms of belief formation are truth-apt also depends, however, to a large extent, on the kinds of environments in which believers find themselves. It is appropriate, for example, for human beings to believe that ordinary objects continue to exist, even when they are not being perceived. But it is not difficult to imagine a cognitive environment in which this norm fails to be truth-apt. Or, for another kind of example, Goodman's New Riddle of Induction shows that our ways of making inductive projections are, at best, merely contingently reliable; in different kinds of cognitive environments, it would have been the case that projections involving predicates like "grue" and "bleen" would have been truth-apt whereas projections involving "green" and "blue" would not have been. And so which epistemic norms are the truth-apt ones is a contingent matter, one that depends on the nature of the relevant cognitive environment. But since the concept of justification at issue is (at least something in the neighborhood of) the concept of rational normativity *downstream* from experience, it also seems that whether or not a belief is justified is independent of environmental factors upstream.

Understandably then, it is difficult to find a theory of justification that successfully accommodates all of the above features (normativity, truth-aptness, environmental independence). The difficulty of accommodating all of these features is made especially vivid by "The New Evil Demon Problem," originally put forward by Keith Lehrer and Stewart Cohen, as a problem for reliabilist theories of justification.[28] Consider a population of beings, just like ourselves, who form their beliefs downstream from experience in just the ways that we do, but who (unlike us) are victims of a Cartesian demon who renders their belief-forming processes unreliable. From many reliabilist theories of justification, it follows that these beings have far less by way of justified belief than we ourselves do (since most of their beliefs are not formed in a truth-reliable manner).

Intuitively, however, it seems that their beliefs are justified to the same extent that our beliefs are. Their living in a demon world is an epistemic misfortune, to be sure, one that robs most of their beliefs of warrant. Nevertheless, surely the beliefs they have are still the appropriate ones for beings like them to hold in their circumstances; surely their beliefs are at least justified! One might think that an easy fix here is simply to jettison reliabilist theories of justification and maintain that which norms of belief formation are necessary and sufficient for justification is a non-contingent matter that does not depend on the epistemic congeniality of the environment. However, adopting such a theory seems to sever justification from truth-aptness, since, as we have already pointed out, which epistemic norms are truth-apt varies across different kinds of cognitive environments.

Bergmann's analysis of the concept of justification, by contrast, readily accommodates the notions of normativity, truth-aptness, and environmental independence involved in that concept. (Roughly) according to the analysis of justification that Bergmann provides, a belief is justified just in case it fulfills all of the proper functionalist conditions mentioned in the analysis proposed in the section, "Formulating a Proper Functionalist Analysis of Warrant," absent the environmental condition.[29] Bergmann argues that this analysis of justification accommodates the intuition that beings like ourselves living in a demon world have justified beliefs to the same extent that we do. For, provided that these beings have a cognitive design plan comparable to ours and they are properly functioning, many of their beliefs are justified, even though their ways of forming beliefs are, for the most part, unreliable. This analysis also, as Bergmann points out, accommodates the intuition that justification is connected with truth-aptness. For, insofar as the beings living in a demon world fulfill Bergmann's conditions for justification, the manner in which they form their beliefs would be truth-apt if they were placed in the environment for which their cognitive faculties were designed.[30]

Insofar as these advantages adhere to Bergmann's proper functionalist theory of justification, they also adhere to proper functionalism about warrant (since the concept of justification, as we have characterized it, is a concept closely related to the rational normativity required for warrant). And so the advantages that Bergmann claims for his own theory also serve to illustrate another way in which proper functionalism about warrant accounts for features of that concept that alternative theories leave out. Thus, the advantages of Bergmann's proposal offer additional support for our claim that any adequate analysis of warrant will centrally involve the concept of truth-aimed cognitive proper function.[31]

Notes

1   See Plantinga (1993a, 3), for the original characterization of warrant along these lines. We are grateful to Trenton Merricks for pointing out that the definition found there contains a misprint. The definition of 'Warrant' found in Merricks (1995, 841), and reproduced here reflects Plantinga's original intentions.

2   See Plantinga (1993b, 5–6).

3   More precisely, we might think of a design plan as a set of triples specifying circumstance, response, and purpose or function. See Plantinga (1993b, 22–4), for a fuller discussion.

4   Although, for an argument that there can be no naturalistic account of these notions, see Plantinga (1993b), chapter 11.

5   Here we offer a rough and ready characterization of internalism, one according to which internalism (or at least any paradigmatic case thereof) is to be identified with access internalism. As far as our current purposes are concerned, this characterization might as well be taken stipulatively.

6   We take it to be a necessary condition for the internalist conditions being plausible that they do not straightforwardly preclude the possibility of auditory perceptual knowledge.

7   There are many cases of the sort found in Plantinga (1993a). There are, for a few examples, Chisholm's dutiful epistemic agent who, whenever he is appeared to redly, always believes that nothing is appearing redly to him (pp. 44–5). Pollock's cognizer who by virtue of malfunction has the wrong epistemic norms (pp. 169–70), and the Coherent but Inflexible Climber (p. 82).

8   See Plantinga (1993a), chapter 9 for much more involved discussion of various reliabilist views.

9   This simplified reliabilist account is *loosely* based on the much more sophisticated reliabilist account offered in Dretske (1981) and discussed in Plantinga (1993a, 192–7).

10 For a classic and paradigmatic exposition of such a reliabilist view, see Goldman (1979).

11 See Plantinga (1993a), chapter 9 for a much more detailed argument for this claim.

12 Here, as well as elsewhere, we are ignoring complications that arise from cases in which there is a difference in how a belief is produced and how it is sustained.

13 This is the first approximation given in Plantinga (1993b, 19).

14 See Plantinga (1993b), chapter 2 for some proposed refinements. See also our discussion later concerning what needs to be added to this analysis in order to avoid Gettier problems.

15 For a whole host of them, from a number of leading epistemologists, see Kvanvig (1996).

16 See Sosa (1993, 54). For similar purported counterexamples to proper functionalism, see Taylor (1991, 187–8), Feldman (1993, 47–8), and BonJour (2002, 225).

17 For more on this issue, see the exchange between Sosa and Plantinga in Sosa (1993, 55–7), and Plantinga (1993c, 76–8).

18 Bergmann (2006, 147–9), in defense of a proper functionalist theory of justification, makes similar points concerning Sosa's Swampman scenario.

19 Plantinga (2000, 160).

20 See Botham (2003, 435–6). We have slightly altered the quote by omitting various subscripts that Botham uses.

21 Greco (1993, 414).

22 Ibid., p. 413.

23 Sosa (1993, 64).

24 See Alston (2005), chapter 1.

25 Note that this is *not* the deontological concept of justification discussed in Plantinga (1993a), chapter 1. It is more akin to what is there called "broad justification" (see p. 11). It should also be noted that this way of picking out the relevant concept of justification differs from the one that Bergmann himself provides (for Bergmann's own way of picking it out, see Bergmann 2006, 1–9).

Nevertheless, we think that this characterization of justification gets at the same sort of thing that Bergmann is interested in.

26 What follows is, for the most part, a summary of many of the points found in Bergmann (2006), chapter 5.

27 On the seemingly puzzling connection between justification and truth, see Cohen (1984).

28 Lehrer and Cohen (1983, 192–3).

29 Bergmann also adds a no-defeater condition (see Bergmann 2006, 133).

30 Bergmann (2006, 141–3).

31 Special thanks are owed to Andrew Moon for helpful suggestions concerning the organization and content of this chapter. Further thanks for helpful suggestions are also owed to Sarah Boyce, Justin McBrayer, Philip Swenson, Patrick Todd, and Chris Tucker.

References

Alston, W. P. 2005. *Beyond "Justification": Dimensions of Epistemic Evaluation*. Ithaca, NY: Cornell University Press.

Bergmann, M. 2006. *Justification without Awareness: A Defense of Epistemic Externalism*. New York, NY: Oxford University Press.

BonJour, L. 2002. "Internalism and Externalism." In Paul K. Moser, ed., *The Oxford Handbook of Epistemology*. Oxford: Oxford University Press, pp. 234–63.

Botham, T. M. 2003. "Plantinga and Favorable Mini-Environments." *Synthese* 135: 431–41.

Cohen, S. 1984. "Justification and Truth." *Philosophical Studies* 46: 279–95.

Dretske, F. I. 1981. *Knowledge and the Flow of Information*. Cambridge, MA: The MIT Press.

Feldman, R. 1993. "Proper Functionalism." *Nous* 27: 34–50.

Goldman, A. J. 1979. "What is Justified Belief." In George S. Pappas, ed., *Justification and Knowledge*. Dordrecht, Holland: D. Reidel Publishing, pp. 1–23.

Greco, J. 1993. "Virtues and Vices of Virtue Epistemology." *Canadian Journal of Philosophy* 23: 413–32.

Kvanvig, J. 1996. *Warrant in Contemporary Epistemology*. New York: Rowman & Littlefield.

Lehrer, K. and Cohen, S. 1983. "Justification, Truth, and Coherence." *Synthese* 55: 191–207.

Merricks, T. 1995. "Warrant Entails Truth." *Philosophy and Phenomenological Research* 55: 841–55.

Plantinga, A. 1993a. *Warrant: The Current Debate*. Oxford: Oxford University Press.

— 1993b. *Warrant and Proper Function*. Oxford: Oxford University Press.

— 1993c. "Why We Need Proper Function." *Nous* 27: 66–82.

— 2000. *Warranted Christian Belief*. Oxford: Oxford University Press.

Sosa, E. 1993. "Proper Functionalism and Virtue Epistemology." *Nous* 27: 51–65.

Taylor, J. E. 1991. "Plantinga's Proper Functioning Analysis of Epistemic Warrant."
Philosophical Studies 64: 185–202.

8

Skepticism and Justification

Richard Fumerton

Introduction

A large part of epistemology is shaped by the attempt to refute skepticism. Contemporary externalists, for example, often recommend their accounts of knowledge and justification for the alleged advantages such accounts have in turning back the threat of skepticism. In what follows we shall examine more closely the ways in which one might respond differently to skeptical arguments given one's metaepistemological views (one's views about the nature of knowledge and justification).

Before evaluating skeptical arguments and responses to them, though, it is important to make a number of important distinctions. We might begin by distinguishing skepticism concerning the possibility of knowledge from skepticism concerning the possibility of justified belief. The knowledge skeptic claims of some class of propositions that they cannot be known. The skeptic concerning justified beliefs claims of some class of propositions that they cannot be justifiably believed. Within both sorts of skepticism, we can distinguish global and local versions. The global skeptic concerning knowledge claims that we cannot know *anything*. The local skeptic concerning knowledge claims only of some subclass of propositions that we cannot know their truth.

Global skepticisms have often been derided for being self-refuting. The strongest sort of self-refutation occurs when an argument's conclusion entails that one or more of the premises is false. So if the conclusion of my argument is that all premises of all arguments are false, the argument is self-refuting in this sense. We can, however, introduce the notion of an *epistemically* self-refuting argument. An argument is epistemically self-refuting with respect to knowledge/justification if the conclusion of the argument entails that one cannot know/justifiably believe one or more of the premises. (To avoid certain technical problems one might qualify the above characterization of epistemic self-refutation by characterizing the entailment in question as in some sense relevant. If one assumes that it is possible to be justified in believing through argument a proposition that is necessarily false (perhaps by relying on testimony), the conclusion of the argument will (trivially) entail everything.

Now one might well worry that any argument for global skepticisms with respect to knowledge and justification will be epistemically self-refuting. If the conclusion of a skeptical argument is that no one knows/justifiably believes anything, then it follows from the conclusion that no one could know the premises of the argument that leads to that conclusion. But one can only know/ justifiably believe the conclusion of an argument on the basis of its premises if one can know/justifiably believe the premises. In addition to this sort of epistemic self-refutation, one might also legitimately worry about arguments that question the legitimacy of an inference, when the argument employs the reasoning under skeptical attack.

It would be a mistake to dismiss the importance of skeptical arguments with a charge of epistemic self-refutation. The skeptic often appeals to premises which we *believe* and reasoning we trust, and if that reasoning and those premises lead to a skeptical claim we can hardly think that all is well. Consider a realistic and somewhat depressing example. As we get older, many of us will experience various forms of dementia. And one of the many faculties that often deteriorates is memory. At the early stages of such deterioration we might seem to remember often misremembering. To our horror, we might begin to suspect on the basis of such apparent memory, that we can't trust our memory any more. Again, it would presumably do no good to reassure people in such a predicament that if, indeed, their apparent memory is not to be trusted, they don't actually have any good reason to believe (on the basis of apparent memory) that their memory is untrustworthy. Once memory has turned on itself in this way one cannot continue to think that all is well with reliance on apparent memory.

So even if skeptical arguments for global skepticism concerning knowledge or justification are epistemically self-refuting, it doesn't follow that they lose their interest or importance. Still, the vast majority of historically important skeptics have not embraced global skepticism. Most have thought that they could know, or at least justifiably believe, both the premises of their skeptical argument and the proposition that the premises support its conclusion. In what follows, I shall focus on the skeptic's arguments for various forms of local skepticism.

I'll begin by considering skeptical arguments for local skepticism concerning justified belief. On classical accounts of knowledge, knowledge requires at least epistemically justified belief. If those accounts are correct, any successful skeptical attack on justified belief will, ipso facto, constitute a successful attack on knowledge. But knowledge almost certainly involves satisfying conditions stronger than mere justified true belief, and there may be skeptical arguments that work against the possibility of knowledge even if they are not effective in attacking the possibility of justified belief.

Local skepticism directed at justified belief

A. J. Ayer once argued (1956) that traditional skeptical arguments against the possibility of justified belief in a given domain seem to follow a common pattern. The first step in the skeptic's argument is to drive a logical wedge between the best available justification for the belief under skeptical attack, and the truth of that belief. The next step is to argue that one cannot bridge the gap through any non-question begging, legitimate *inference*. So consider, for example, the much discussed, and still fascinating skeptical arguments against the possibility of justifiably believing propositions asserting the existence of physical objects. Most of the modern philosophers presupposed some version of foundationalism and took it to be almost obvious that we have no foundational (noninferential) justification for believing that physical objects exist. Although this is to some extent speculative, it seems to me that they thought this, in part, because they understood noninferential justification as something that requires direct awareness of the truthmaker for the proposition believed, where the awareness in question is a real relation that requires relata. On such a supposition the argument rejecting propositions about the external world for inclusion in the epistemic foundations proceeds straightforwardly, they thought. Consider the best possible justification for believing that a given physical object exists— for example, experiences you have of the tree in front of you under optimal conditions of perception. Now ask yourself whether you could have precisely that kind of justification even though what you believe isn't true. You should, they thought, answer the question affirmatively. The possibility of dreams and vivid hallucination makes clear that you could have the same sort of experiential justification for believing that there is a tree in front of you when there isn't. But the justification you have in the case of dreams or hallucinations is obviously not direct awareness of the truthmaker for what you believe—there is no truthmaker. So the justification in veridical experience (justification that is of the same kind) cannot consist in direct awareness of the truthmaker for the belief either.

Let's call the alleged experiential common denominator of both veridical visual experience of a tree and its phenomenologically indistinguishable hallucinatory counterpart, *seeming to see* a tree. One can introduce similar expressions (seeming to hear, seeming to feel, seeming to smell, seeming to taste) to describe the experiences associated with the other sense modalities. The skeptic thinks that to be justified in believing that the tree exists one must find some way of justifiably *inferring* the existence of the tree from what we know about the occurrence of fleeting, subjective sense experience. Furthermore, the traditional skeptic brings to the debate certain controversial assumptions concerning the conditions required for legitimate inference. Specifically, the traditional skeptic accepts what I have called the principle of inferential justification (PIJ):

> One has justification for believing P on the basis of E only if (1) one has justification for believing E, and (2) one has justification for believing that E makes probable P.

I call philosophers who accept the second clause of the principle, *inferential internalists*. The skeptic who accepts inferential internalism wants to know how one could justify a belief that subjective sense experiences makes likely the truth of some claim about the physical world. The argument from the possibility of nonveridical experience is supposed to establish that we cannot discover a relation of entailment between subjective experience and external reality. Moreover, it seems hopeless to attempt an inductive justification for supposing that there subjective experience indicates the existence of external reality. An inductive argument would require one to have established a past correlation between the occurrence of certain kinds of experiences and the existence of certain kinds of physical objects. But if one must always ultimately rely on what one knows about subjective sense experience to reach conclusions about the external world, then there is no *independent* way of establishing the existence of physical objects, and thus no independent way of certifying the relevant correlations. One can correlate sensations with sensations, but one can't correlate sensations with something other than sensations. Convinced that the only plausible candidate for nondeductive reasoning is enumerative induction, skeptics like David Hume (1888) saw no way to avoid a radical skepticism concerning the possibility of justifying belief in the existence of an external world.

Similar skeptical arguments can be run against the possibility of justifiably believing propositions describing other minds, theoretical entities in physics, or propositions about the past. Consider the last. No one needs much convincing to realize that one can seem to remember having done something that one hasn't done. So just as with the problem of perception, the inferential internalist will argue that one needs a reason to think that apparent memory is a reliable indicator of past events. Furthermore, the skeptic will insist that you not presuppose the legitimacy of relying on memory in justifying your belief that memory is reliable. It is an understatement to suggest that the philosopher trying to meet this skeptic's challenge faces an uphill battle. Whatever reasoning is employed, it had better be employed quickly, for the premises of any argument justifying the legitimacy of relying on memory will be lost to the past in a moment. Certainly, any inductive justification for relying on memory would seem to be hopeless. How could one justify one's belief in the premises of an argument describing *past* correlations if one is not permitted to rely on apparent memory? Our reliance on apparent memory is so pervasive throughout our reasoning (both a posteriori and even a priori—deductively valid reasoning takes time) that one might worry that a successful skeptical attack of this sort will morph into something approaching global justification skepticism.

Responses to the arguments for local justification skepticism

Reduction

Responses to the skeptic have taken many forms. One sort of response turns to controversial views in metaphysics. Inspired by different versions of verificationism and positivism, some philosophers attempted to bridge the problematic epistemic gaps through reductive analysis. George Berkeley, John Stuart Mill, and a number of early-twentieth-century philosophers thought that we could analyze the *meaning* of claims about the physical world so that they make only complicated assertions about what Mill called the permanent possibility of sensations. If one could successfully defend the view that our thought about the external world is just thought about what sensations a subject would have were one to have others, one would be in a better position to avoid skepticism even granting the skeptic's claim that one can never correlate anything but subjective states. A full discussion of phenomenalism (as the view was called) would take us far beyond the limits of this chapter. While positivists were heroic in their efforts to defend the view, most concluded that the attempt was Quixotic. Still, there may be defensible variations on the view that would minimize, if not eliminate, the relevant epistemological problems.[1] Even if imaginative analysis might conceivably help narrow *some* epistemological gaps, the approach seems hopeless in blunting skeptical attacks directed at other local justification. Logical behaviorists tried to reduce the epistemic distance between observations of behavior and conclusions about the mental states of others by attempting to reduce talk about mental states to talk about complex dispositions to behave. But anyone who has experienced stabbing pain knows that such analyses are almost comically implausible. For some reason, functionalism— the view that we can understand mental states in terms of the input/output causal role they play—is still seen as respectable in contemporary philosophy of mind. While pain undoubtedly has a function (in some sense of that term), a functionalist account of what pain *is* has always seemed to me just as implausible as the older reductive behaviorism. And, however implausible it is to identify mental states with dispositions to behave, or states playing functional roles, it seems even more obviously madness to attempt to reduce talk about the past to talk about the present. It is more than outrageous to argue that we can reduce the meaning of claims about past experience to complex claims about disposition to have apparent memory experience.

Internalist responses

The traditional skeptical arguments for local skepticism rest on two controversial premises. One asserts that we have no noninferential justification for believing the propositions under skeptical attack. The other asserts that there is no way to legitimately bridge the gap that exists between available evidence and the truth of what one believes. As we shall see in the following section, classical externalists attempt to resist one or the other of these premises through an analysis of epistemic justification—one that positions the externalist to reject either or both of these premises by refusing to accept the rules by which the skeptic plays the game. But there are also versions of internalism that also reject the claims in question.

While I have introduced earlier the concept of inferential internalism, we haven't said much about what makes an analysis of epistemic justification internalist. There are other chapters in this volume that address the issue, so I'll be brief. There are at least two importantly different internalist camps. One focuses on the "internal" of internalism and subscribes to the slogan—same internal states, same epistemic status. Less cryptically, this internalist (sometimes called a mentalist[2]), claims that necessarily, if you and I are in precisely the same internal states, then whatever you are justified in believing I am justified in believing, and vice versa. As evidence for their view, consider two people one of whom is the victim of massive, demonic deception, the other of whom has experiences with the causes we take them to have. Doesn't it seem obvious, the internal state internalist argues, that both subjects would have precisely the same sort of justification for believing what they do about their external environment? If that is correct, then we had better not let justification depend on factors other than the internal states of the subject.

The other view associated with contemporary internalism focuses on *access* to justification. The strongest version of the view seems to assert that one can have justification J for believing P only if one has access to (justified belief in, knowledge of) the fact that J obtains and is a justifier for believing P. The view is a potential trap, for however seductive it might seem initially, the threat of problematic regress looms.[3] It is important to emphasize that inferential internalism is *not* a form of access internalism. Despite the fact that the inferential internalist insists that inferential justification requires access to inferential connections, that internalist does not insist that when one is justified in believing P one must have access (actual or potential) to the fact that one has such inferential justification.

a) "Permissive" internalisms

How might an internal state internalist respond to the skeptic's arguments for local skepticism? Obviously, a great deal depends on the epistemic principles one endorses. So, for example, a view tailor-made to defeat skepticism is Huemer's (2001) phenomenal conservatism. Huemer claims that there is a familiar state— it's seeming to one as if P—that gives one prima facie (defeasible) justification for believing P. Seeming is different from belief. Think about the fact that in the Muller-Lyer illusion, the lines continue to seem to be of unequal length, even after you become fully convinced that it is an illusion. So when you have visual experiences of a certain sort, it might seem to you that there is a tree before you. When you have certain apparent memories (however those are understood), it might seem to you that you did certain things. When you observe the grimaces and groans of another, it might seem to you that the person is in pain. Huemer claims that the state of seeming, by itself, gives you prima facie noninferential justification for believing what seems to you to be the case.

Alternatively, one might argue that one must infer the truth of what seems to you to be true from the fact that it seemed to you to be true. Either way, one needs to give a satisfying account of why seeming states justify beliefs with the same content. And the response the skeptic will find maddening is that they just do. It is a synthetic necessary truth that epistemic justification supervenes on evidential seeming. The truth is knowable a priori, though, again, on Huemer's view, one needn't employ that a priori knowledge to get the relevant justification provided by seemings. I won't have much to say about phenomenal conservatism here other than that it will strike many as a case of theft over honest toil.[4] Many of us aren't sure that there is a state of seeming that is anything other than a leaning to believe, albeit one that can be resisted, and we aren't sure that the fact that we lean toward a given conclusion (without any sort of argument or truth maker for what we believe in the picture) gives any intellectually satisfying reason for trusting the inclination. There is no reason to treat belief (or seeming, if this is different) as innocent (or guilty, for that matter) until proven otherwise.

Chisholm (1989) defends a version of internal state internalism, and is also sympathetic to the claim that possessing justification carries with it the possibility of accessing that positive epistemic status. Like Huemer, he will simply offer as necessary truths epistemic principles designed to short circuit the skeptic attack. And methodologically, he makes no bones about the fact that this is just what he is doing. In his famous discussion of the problem of the criterion, Chisholm observes that a number of philosophers argue for skepticism by beginning with an assumption about what counts as legitimate inference (he calls these philosophers Methodists). But, Chisholm makes clear, that if one can't get done what one wants (justify the conclusions of commonsense) with the tools provided by the skeptic, you should get yourselves some additional tools. Chisholm suggests a number of principles, each tailor-made, to avoid local skepticism.

Chisholm sometimes describes his approach as particularism. Methodologically, one simply starts with the presupposition that one does have justification for believing most of what one takes oneself to be paradigmatically justified in believing. Such a presupposition is one way of construing the import of Moore's (1925 and 1939) famous defense of commonsense. Infamously, Moore would reject the skeptic's argument by holding out a hand and claiming to know that it exists (and thus that there are truths about the external world). In the same vein, he would claim to know what he had for breakfast and thus that it is possible to know truths about the past. Moore is often ridiculed for these "refutations" of skepticism. The "argument" seems nothing more than a pathetic question-begging refusal to take the skeptic seriously. But that may be the best way to understand the underlying point Moore was trying to make. It is a *metaphilosophical* point. The most common form of argument in all of philosophy is the reductio. We reject our opponent's position by drawing from that position an obviously absurd consequence. But we can't get anywhere employing this method without having a healthy sense of what is and is not absurd. The problem with skeptics is that they have no sense of the absurd. Without it, there is no way of reaching them through argument. Like Chisholm, Moore is drawing a line in the sand which he will not cross. That line is both the rejection of global skepticism and most radical versions of local skepticism.

It is interesting to note that Moore is often quick to admit that he may not know precisely where the skeptic has gone wrong. But, he would argue, you don't need to know where an argument goes wrong to know that it has gone wrong. I don't need a solution to Zeno's paradox—an argument that purports to establish that we cannot move from one place to another—to know that Zeno made some sort of error in his reasoning. But we are philosophers after all. And if we harbor the suspicion that the skeptic has a flawed argument, we do need to uncover the flaw in the argument or admit failure in the refutation of skepticism. Those are the rules by which we judge winning and losing the game of argument. If I can't find anything wrong with the skeptic's premises or the skeptic's reasoning, the skeptic wins the philosophical debate.

Jim Pryor's "dogmatism" (2000) is a view Moorean in character. It is also similar in general approach to both Huemer's and Chisholm's. Pryor takes sensory states to be intentional states. Like beliefs (desires, fears, hopes) they represent the world as being a certain way. A sensation and a belief can share the same content (can be about the same state of affairs). Pryor thinks that at least some sensory states are such that one's being in that state gives one noninferential justification for holding a belief with the same content. His *philosophical* justification of such a view, if appreciated, would also presumably allow one to legitimately infer the existence of certain physical objects from one's noticing that one is in a certain sensory state, but (like Huemer) his view is that the availability of such sophisticated reasoning is not necessary for one to get oneself prima facie justification for certain ordinary commonsense beliefs about one's surroundings. Insofar as sensory states give one prima facie justification for believing that one is surrounded by various commonplace objects, those sensory states also give one prima facie reason for rejecting various skeptical scenarios that are either incompatible with the truth of commonplace beliefs, or very unlikely given their truth. Everything I said about Huemer would apply mutatis mutandis to Pryor. The view is obviously dialectically attractive to the philosopher trying to avoid skepticism, but if sensory states are intentional in the same way that beliefs are intentional, we know (as Pryor would admit) that they can misrepresent the way the world is. And the intellectually curious skeptic is going to wonder why we should trust these representations as accurate. If we are going to place that much trust in our instinctual representations, why not take the mere fact that we believe a proposition to be prima facie reason to have the belief and let it go at that (a view known as epistemic conservatism).

Coherence theories of justification

On one sort of coherence theory of justification, the justification for each of S's beliefs is a function of the way in which that belief coheres with the rest of what S believes. On the assumption that beliefs are paradigmatic internal states (an assumption rejected by certain content externalists), the coherence theory of justification will count as a version of internal state internalism. Like phenomenal conservatism and Pryor's dogmatism, the view might seem to be ideally situated when it comes to the refutation of skepticism. After all, even the skeptic will typically concede that we *believe* that propositions under skeptical attack. If we also believe a complex story about the reliability of various faculties, then we may have a story, the pieces of which fit together in a coherent way—a way that gives us justified beliefs according to the coherence theorist.

Much depends on the details of the nature of coherence to which the coherence theorist appeals, but it may not be all that easy to argue that our commonsense beliefs do fit together. Russell once famously argued that common sense leads to science and science leads to the rejection of common sense. Berkeley's Philonous tormented Hylas by getting him to concede that his "obvious" beliefs about direct perception of a mind-independent external world are inconsistent. And Hume (1888) also argued that the "view of the vulgar" leads to contradiction. But if we combine a coherence theory of justification with a commitment to particularlism, it wouldn't seem to be that difficult to come up with a body of beliefs that fit together so as to guarantee justification understood in terms of coherence.

There are, however, technical problems with the central idea behind coherence theories of justification. Lottery and preface puzzles might suggest that even logical coherence among one's beliefs isn't even a necessary condition for epistemic justification. I can justifiably believe of each ticket in a fair lottery that it is a loser while also justifiably believing that one of the tickets will win. I can justifiably believe of each paragraph in my book that it contains no typographical errors while I also justifiably believe that somewhere in my book there is such an error. Furthermore, if I let into my belief system a proposition that turns out to be necessarily false (an occupational hazard for philosophers) there is an obvious sense in which the conjunction of each proposition believed with the rest is a contradiction. But it seems absurd to suppose that this should impact the justification I have right now for believing that I have a backache. But perhaps these problems can be overcome. There are still more fundamental difficulties with the coherence theory.

The coherence theory of justification comes in two importantly different forms. One embraces inferential internalism; the other does not. The inferential internalist who is a coherence theorist concedes that coherence among one's beliefs will not by itself generate epistemic justification. One must in addition be aware of the fact that one's beliefs cohere. The coherence theorist who is an inferential externalist will argue that coherence by itself is sufficient. The latter view is inherently implausible. One need only imagine a person who whimsically comes to believe highly complex propositions which do cohere wonderfully, but when the person in question couldn't for his or her life discover the relevant connections. But the coherence theorist embracing inferential internalism is caught in a trap. One can't discover relations of coherence among one's beliefs without discovering what one believes. But how can one discover what one believes without discovering a coherence between one's metabelief that one has certain beliefs and the rest of what one believes. But again that discovery will itself require already knowing what one believes. The task seems hopeless.

Argument to the best explanation

Jonathan Vogel (1990, 2005) attempts to respond to the skeptic's challenge by employing reasoning to the best explanation. Hume, you will recall, thought there was no hope of bridging the problematic epistemic gaps through inductive reasoning. But C. S. Pierce famously distinguished abductive reasoning or reasoning to the best explanation from inductive reasoning. As Pierce described abduction, one proceeds by noting some phenomenon that seems to cry out for explanation and one moves to a conclusion that, if true, would explain the relevant phenomenon. Formally, Pierce's abductions look just like arguments that commit the fallacy of affirming the consequent. One sees fossilized remains of fish in the rock and one realizes that if the sea once covered the land, then one would expect to find the remains of fish. One then tentatively concludes that the sea once covered the land. Thus characterized the argument form is clearly problematic. I see footprints on the sand and know that if cows wearing boots had walked the beach recently, there would be just such footprints. Should I then tentatively conclude that cows wearing boots walked the beach recently?

An affirmative answer is absurd. And one diagnosis of what goes wrong is that I have independent reason for thinking that footprints are usually produced by people. But, of course, if I rely on that as background evidence I wouldn't need anything other than induction to reach the relevant conclusion. If it is true that in general reasoning to the best explanation collapses into inductive reasoning we are making no progress in our attempt to respond to skepticism.[5]

The proponent of reasoning to the best explanation might well complain that it is hardly fair to focus on Pierce's casual characterization of abduction in an evaluation of what is involved in reasoning to the best explanation. It is, after all, reasoning to the *best* explanation. A more perspicuous rendering of the reasoning involved is the following:

1. O (some observed phenomenon).
2. Of competing possible explanations of O, E is the best. Therefore (in all probability).
3. E.

On this understanding of reasoning to the best explanation, we obviously will need specific criteria for choosing among alternative possible explanations. And there has been considerable literature on this topic. Other things begin equal, for example, it is often argued that the simpler of alternative explanations should be preferred. Additionally, if one has a choice between two explanations, one of which would explain many more observations, that is the preferable of the two. Some also suggest that one should employ, indirectly, a kind of inductive reasoning by preferring explanations that are similar to those that have already been confirmed. So, for example, if the reception on my TV has been bad in the past when the air-conditioner has been running in the room, it might be prima facie plausible to suppose that the running of another electrical appliance is the culprit this time.

It is important to realize that it is a presupposition of reasoning to the best explanation that there is a causal explanation of some phenomenon. To be sure, this does seem to be a methodological presupposition of science (at least it did until theoretical physics became strangely sanguine about radical indeterminacy at the quantum level). Skeptic's won't give you the time of day, however, and will demand an argument for the proposition that the phenomenon we are interested in explaining does, indeed, have a causal explanation. It is equally important to stress that even if one of a number of competing explanation is the most plausible, it does not follow that it is plausible. If a possible explanation has an epistemic probability of 0.2 it might still be more plausible than each of the others that have an epistemic probability of 0.1. To defeat the skeptic, then, one must have good reason to believe that the phenomenon in question does have an explanation and that the explanation for which we are arguing is more likely to be true than the disjunction of all alternative explanations. That task is more than a little formidable given that there will always be indefinitely many explanations that satisfy the formal constraints on explanations (that it will be perfectly acceptable explanations provided that the propositions that constitute the explanations are true).

With that as background how might one proceed in refuting local skepticism through reasoning to the best explanation? Consider the problem of perception and let's suppose that the skeptic concedes that we have justified belief in the occurrence of our own sensations, and even that we can discover patterns among the occurrence of those sensations—when I have certain visual sensations there almost always seems to be the possibility of having a certain tactile sensation. Now when I seem to see something red and round I do find myself inclined to think that that sensation has a cause. In fact I believe that it is the effect of many internal and external causes acting together. I seem to see something red and round. I then have the experience as of closing my eyes followed by the experiences of opening my eyes, and there is that familiar red round appearance again. Isn't it plausible to suppose that there is a common cause of these two qualitatively similar sensations? If the sensations I have are genuinely random then it would be highly unlikely that their patterns remain as stable as they do. One could try to construe antecedent sensations as the cause of later sensations, but there the regularities seem to be too frail. Dreams, hallucinations, and illusions teach us that no sensation invariably precedes any other—we will still need to posit external conditions that explain when the order is and is not broken.

If all we needed to refute skepticism was the justified positing of some external cause or other, we might seem to be making progress. The difficulty, of course, is that our conception of ordinary objects seems to add flesh to the bare bone conception of external cause. On the most extreme views, we want the external cause to be accurately represented by the sensation. We want features of the sensation to correspond, more or less accurately, to features of the object. And we want those features of the object to be mind-independent. To be sure, we may be willing to give up some of these presuppositions. It doesn't take much prodding from the philosopher for the ordinary person to wonder which of the many color appearances presented by an object represents the "real" external color of the object. And after such prodding, one might begin to wonder whether there is anything "in" the object that is the slightest bit like the color of which we are directly aware. Science appears to have given us the once shocking news that the solid table top is really a mass of whirring spatially separated parts. Indeed, it isn't too much of an understatement to suggest that if objects are as we now take them to be, appearance turned out to be a rather unreliable guide to the underlying nature of such objects.

Berkeley was no skeptic. He thought that his view was compatible with common sense. But virtually everyone else thought that it was an extreme form of local skepticism. Berkeley (1954) argued that all of our sensations are produced by a God in accordance with a complex plan. Our interest in Berkeley here is to focus on at least one alternative and competing explanation for the occurrence and pattern of sensations. Hylas (like Locke and Russell after him), toyed with the idea of construing matter as the cause of sensations, unknowable in terms of its intrinsic character but conceived and known by us in terms of its causal role. Although Berkeley (through Philonous) first tries to make something of the terminological agreement to construe "matter" as a term that picks out something causally inert, he realizes that he is not going to get very far with this contractual complaint. Interestingly enough, he then turns to argument to the best explanation. He argues that positing a divine mind causally responsible for the sensations we experience is not only a simpler explanation, but it also is a kind of causation with which we are already familiar. It is simpler, because our metaphysical commitments are restricted to minds and ideas/sensations (properties of minds). The philosopher who posits material things, has minds, sensations, and this third sort of entity, matter. Furthermore, we all have firsthand experience, Berkeley says, of our own minds causing ideas. We conjure up all sorts of vivid imagery in imagination, for example. So the kind of causal connection we posit (broadly enough understood) is already familiar to us. Now if a Berkeleyean ontology is a skeptical ontology, philosophers like Vogel need to explain why it is inferior to the commonsense hypothesis of physical objects.

One might be tempted to suppose an explanation that posits a mind that is so different from our own in effect builds all of the complexity of an external world into the complexity of that mind, replete with its complex plan for connections among sensations. But perhaps the moral to draw is one I hinted at earlier. In one sense the intrinsic nature of the external cause of order among sensations seems utterly irrelevant to the explanatory and predictive power of the theory. And, indeed, the more one can divorce the ordinary conception of physical objects from any commitment as to their intrinsic nature, the easier it will be to avoid skeptical implications of such commitments. As physical objects become mere "powers" to produce sensation, knowledge of their existence becomes no more (though no less) problematic than knowledge that sensations do have an external cause.

If one can bridge a problematic gap between truths about appearance and truths about physical objects employing reasoning to the best explanation, one might also try the same method to bridge other gaps exploited by the skeptic. So, for example, assuming that we have justified beliefs about the physical world, one might try to infer the existence of other minds as the best explanation for observed behavior. As I see you writhe in pain, I might suppose that the obvious explanation for that behavior is that very mental state that I associate in my own case with similar behavior. And one might even try to solve the problem of induction by arguing that necessary connections among universals is the best explanation for constant correlations between observed phenomena. But it is more than a stretch to suppose that one can solve the epistemological problem of memory relying on reasoning to the best explanation. To be sure, I probably do think that my having had a given experience is the correct causal explanation of the fact that I now seem to remember having had that experience, but the reasoning itself seems to take long enough that one loses the critical premises to the past and reliance on memory before one can reach the relevant conclusion.

Externalist responses to justification skepticism

The contemporary epistemological landscape is dominated by the internalism/externalism debate discussed earlier. This is not the occasion on which to evaluate the plausibility of externalist analyses of justification (discussed elsewhere in this volume). The most I can do is sketch the way in which the externalist might respond to the traditional skeptical argument. Even that project is more than a bit difficult given the importantly different versions of externalism that have been offered. But let's look at a sampling of externalist responses that might be made to the controversial premises of the traditional skeptical arguments.

The first gambit in the local skeptic's attack on justified belief, you will recall, is to deny that the propositions under skeptical attack are noninferentially justified. I suggested that in arguing for that conclusion the skeptic typically presupposes that noninferential justification requires something like direct awareness or direct confrontation with the relevant truth makers. That presupposition coupled with the skeptic's claim that we have the same sort of justification in the "skeptical scenarios" (dreams, hallucinations, nonveridical memory, etc.) is supposed to preclude our having noninferential justification for believing the propositions under skeptical attack.

Contemporary externalists will almost all reject the traditional foundationalist's conception of noninferential justification, and depending on the externalist view they offer in its place, they may either reject the claim that we have the same justification in both the veridical and the nonveridical case or they may admit that claim but insist that it is perfectly compatible with the justification being foundational in both cases. Consider the latter first, and let's illustrate the point with a relatively crude process reliabilism. On Goldman's earliest and highly influential version of reliabilism (1979) one has a noninferentially justified belief when one's belief is produced by an unconditionally reliable, belief-independent process. The process is belief-independent just in virtue of the fact that the "input" is something other than a belief (or, more precisely, if it is a belief its epistemic status isn't relevant to the epistemic status of the output belief). Reliability can be spelled out in different ways, but let's suppose for our purposes here that a process is deemed unconditionally reliable when it would produce mostly true beliefs if it were used sufficiently often. (The reliabilist is also likely to relativize the reliability in question to an environment—a problematic task that brings with it a particularly difficult version of the generality problem, the problem of just how to specify the relevant process type.) Now notice that noninferential justification on such a view doesn't need to be very good justification. A noninferentially justified belief might be just barely more likely to be true than not. And the process type that yields mostly true beliefs might occasionally yield false beliefs (as in dreams, or hallucinations).

Alternatively, depending on how one characterizes the relevant process, one can simply deny that the same process is operative in both veridical experience, and its nonveridical counterparts (dreams, hallucinations, nonveridical memory, and the like). If we go back far enough in the causal history leading up to the occurrence of a veridical experience there will obviously be a difference between what happens there and what happens in its hallucinatory counterpart. If that causal difference makes its way into a description of the input that in turn characterizes the process, this reliabilist will be positioned to simply deny that the "same process" is occurring in both the veridical and the nonveridical case.

The externalists need not claim that the beliefs under skeptical attack are noninferentially justified (though often they will). The reliabilist, for example, might concede that the processes that yield beliefs about the external world take as their input at least some other beliefs (perhaps beliefs about conditions of perception). But virtually all externalists will reject the idea that one needs to have justified belief about evidential connections to have inferentially justified beliefs. Again, all the externalist requires for inferential justification is a world that cooperates so as to produce mostly true beliefs when the justified input beliefs are true. The skeptic's demand that we provide non-question begging justification for thinking that the evidential connections hold will fall on deaf ears.

One might suppose that the problem of skepticism for a reliabilist simply reoccurs at the next level. Perhaps we have justified beliefs (if the world cooperates), but how would we ever justify our belief that we have such justified beliefs? But again, this sort of externalist should be unimpressed by the attempt to generate skeptical worries at the metalevel. Consider memory. If memory and induction are reliable, we can use these processes to justify our belief that memory is reliable. Relying on apparent memory we can seem to remember countless occasions on which we did various things while we also seem to remember seeming to have remembered that we did those things. Again, if reliable, those faculties will yield justified belief that apparent memory has been typically reliable and induction will allow us to predict that it will continue to be reliable.

Again, the very ease with which one could in principle get second-level justification might make one nervous (see Fumerton 1995, chapter 6). It strikes many of us that there is something deeply problematic about a view that allows one to use these alleged sources of justification to certify their own legitimacy. Stew Cohen (2002) refers to this as the problem of easy knowledge. He imagines a person wondering whether the apparent color of a shirt is indicative of its real color. The person in question starts worrying about the lighting conditions. Could one really reassure such a person with an argument of the following form: The shirt looks red? That justifies me in believing that it is red. But a red thing wouldn't look red under distorting conditions? Therefore the conditions aren't distorting? Peter Markie (2005) argues that the problem of easy knowledge confuses conditions sufficient for getting higher level justification with conditions that must be met in order to argue without begging the question. He argues that the rules of argument forbid one from using a process that has been questioned to certify its legitimacy, but for all that, if it is legitimate, it can be used to justify a belief that it is so. If getting justification, however, is tied to gaining assurance, I'm not convinced that Markie's interesting suggestion will, or should, satisfy the skeptic.

Timothy Williamson (2000) is another philosopher who will deny the claim that we have the same justification in both veridical cases and their vivid nonveridical counterparts. While much of the tradition has tried to explain knowledge in terms of allegedly more fundamental epistemic concepts like justification and evidence, Williamson suggests a dramatic alternative to this way of thinking. His idea is that we should explain evidence in terms of what he takes to be the more fundamental concept of knowledge. He suggests, in effect, that we should *identify* our evidence with those propositions we know to be true. We can then talk about justified belief that falls short of knowledge in terms of the probability various propositions have for us relative to the evidence we possess. Famously, Williamson refuses to provide a traditional analysis of knowledge (though he is willing to identify various conditions that are necessary for one to know a given proposition). In any event, Williamson will claim that (veridically) remembering that P just is a *species* of knowledge, and that seeing that P is another species of knowledge. In veridical memory and perception our evidence base includes the truths remembered and perceived. There is no corresponding truth in the case of what I have been calling apparent memory and apparent perception, so, trivially, we don't have the same evidence in the veridical and the nonveridical cases. Williamson's view is clearly a version of epistemic externalism. The conditions that constitute one's having a justified belief include the conditions that constitute knowledge. Knowledge requires the truth of what is believed and since he thinks that we know truths about the past and the external world, it is at least sometimes true that the factors that make a given belief justified include facts that lie outside of us.

Williamson thinks that knowledge is a mental state and that its identity conditions include conditions that lie outside of the knower. He is hardly alone these days in embracing content externalism (this view in the philosophy of the mind). The content externalists think that virtually all intentional states (states described in terms of some content or object—believing that, fearing that, hoping that, etc.) are the states they are only, in part, because of their causal origin. Again, a proper discussion of such views takes us too far afield, but the more attractive content externalism is to a philosopher, the less likely it is that philosopher will take the introspective similarity between two states to be a reliable indicator that the states are the *same* intentional states. Since many such philosophers agree with Pryor that sensation is a species of intentional state, their content externalism will apply to criteria for the sameness of sensory states. Such philosophers have, in effect, adopted a philosophy of mind that makes it easier to deny the skeptic's claim that there is an interesting common denominator to veridical and hallucinatory experience.

Ironically, the very externalism that has so many potential advantages in dealing with the skeptic also leads to consequences that many others find strongly counterintuitive. As I indicated, there are many different versions of externalism, but the new evil demon problem faces many externalist accounts of justification. We are asked to compare two internal twins in different possible worlds. One has experiences caused in just the way we think our experiences are caused; the other has experiences caused by a malicious demon bent on inducing false belief. It seems obvious to the traditional internalist that whatever we say about the epistemic status of the one twin's beliefs we should say about the epistemic status of the other twin's beliefs. Though there is, by hypothesis, a different cause of their respective experiences, *they* couldn't through a careful evaluation of the evidence at their disposal discern that difference. And a difference you can't find, the internalist argues, can't make a difference with respect to the rationality of what you believe.

As we saw earlier, content externalists may well deny the claim that the internal twins could have the same experiences or even the same beliefs (given the difference in their external condition and the way in which that is supposed to be relevant to the way in which one represents the world through experience). But they need to do a lot of work to convince us that the thought experiment that *seems* perfectly intelligible is deeply problematic. The hard-core externalist might concede that the experiences and beliefs are the same but deny that they are equally justified. The traditional internalist, however, finds the thought experiment compelling and draws the inference that contrary to the externalist claims, epistemic justification clearly supervenes only on the internal states of a cognizer.

Skepticism concerning knowledge: A postscript

To the extent that knowledge requires justification, any successful skeptical attack on justified belief will be a successful attack on knowledge. But it is tempting to suppose that knowledge requires a particularly high level of justification and that, as a result, knowledge is vulnerable to skeptical argument in ways in which justification is not. For considerations of space I must be brief. But let us begin with the puzzling case of lotteries. No matter how small the chance is that the ticket I purchased is a winner, almost everyone rejects the idea that we can legitimately claim to *know* that the ticket is a loser. Why? The most obvious answer is that we know perfectly well there is at least a chance that the ticket will win, and that existence of that chance is incompatible with knowing that it won't. But that suggests that in order to know some proposition our justification must rule out the possibility of error—the very position that

Descartes famously took. The down side of such an account of knowledge is that the road to local knowledge skepticism is fairly straightforward. Isn't there at least a chance (however slight) that you are dreaming right now, that you are misremembering, that received scientific views about the microworld are false, and so on. Isn't that precisely what the skeptical scenarios establish?

One way of underscoring the looming presence of knowledge skepticism is to appeal to the very plausible principle of knowledge closure. It is surely tempting to think that if you know that P and you know that P entails some other proposition Q then you must at least be in a position to know that Q. So if you know that you put your keys on the kitchen counter then you are in a position to know that you are not misremembering where you put your keys. If you know that your car is in the parking lot then you can know that it hasn't been stolen. If you know that there you are sitting at a table then you can know that you are not in bed dreaming that you are at the table. But it is relatively easy to get most people to admit that they can't really rule out the possibility of any of those "skeptical scenarios" and with the assumption of closure one is in a position to reject the relevant knowledge claims.

There are a host of responses to this pattern of skeptical argument against knowledge claims. Some reject the closure principle. So the contextualist (discussed elsewhere in this volume) argues that context determines when an alternative hypothesis becomes relevant and needs to be ruled out by evidence. On one such view, when skeptical scenarios are raised, they automatically become relevant and one fails to know what one might otherwise have known in a different contexts. Some other epistemologists[6] reject closure by emphasizing what is sometimes called a sensitivity requirement on knowledge. The basic idea is that one knows P only if were not-P to be true one wouldn't believe (in the same way at least) that P. The idea is supposed to be that I could know, for example, that my car is in the parking lot because if it weren't there, I wouldn't believe that it was. That's because, in the language of some philosophers, the close possible worlds in which the car isn't in the parking lot are worlds in which I parked it someplace else, and I would have remembered that. But in the close possible worlds in which the car was stolen, I would still believe that it wasn't stolen—that's why I don't know that it wasn't stolen. There are a host of objections to this sort of view as well, not the least of which is that rejection of closure is an enormous price to pay in the attempt to avoid skepticism.

Though not very popular, one might stick to the first reaction many have to the question about why we don't know that the lottery ticket will lose—the idea that knowledge really does require justification so strong that it eliminates the possibility of error. To be sure, consistently adhering to such a view might require one to admit that most of our knowledge claims are false, but then when pressed many will readily admit in the face of any sort of pressure that they don't really know what they casually say they know.

Notes

1 See Fumerton (1985).
2 See Conee and Feldman (2001).
3 See Fumerton (1995, chapter 3).
4 See Fumerton (2007).
5 See Fumerton (1980).
6 See Nozick (1981, chapter 3).

References

Ayer, A. J. 1956. *The Problem of Knowledge.* Edinburgh: Penguin.

Berkeley, G. 1954. *Three Dialogues Between Hylas and Philonous.* Colin Turbayne, ed., Indianapolis: Bobbs-Merrill.

Chisholm, R. M. 1989. *Theory of Knowledge,* 3rd edn. Englewood Cliffs, NJ: Prentice-Hall.

Cohen, S. 2002. "Basic Knowledge and the Problem of Easy Knowledge." *Philosophy and Phenomenological Research* 65(2): 309–29.

Conee, E. and Feldman, R. 2001. "Internalism Defended." In Hilary Kornblith, ed., *Epistemology: Internalism and Externalism.* Malden, MA: Blackwell, pp. 30–60.

Fumerton, R. 1980. "Induction and Reasoning to the Best Explanation." *Philosophy of Science* December: 589–600.

— 1985. *Metaphysical and Epistemological Problems of Perception.* Lincoln: University of Nebraska Press.

— 1995. *Metaepistemology and Skepticism.* Lanham, MD: Rowman and Littlefield.

— 2007. "Epistemic Conservatism: Theft or Honest Toil?" *Oxford Studies in Epistemology* 2: 64–87.

Goldman, A. 1979. "What is Justified Belief?" In George Pappas, ed., *Justification and Knowledge.* Dordrecht: Reidel, pp. 1–23.

Huemer, M. 2001. *Skepticism and the Veil of Perception.* Lanham, MD: Rowman & Littlefield.

Hume, D. 1888. *A Treatise of Human Nature.* L. A. Selby-Bigge, ed., London: Oxford University Press.

Markie, P. 2005. "Easy Knowledge." *Philosophy and Phenomenological Research* 70: 406–16.

Moore, G. E. 1925. "A Defence of Common Sense." In J. H. Muirhead, ed., *Contemporary British Philosophy*. London: Allen and Unwin, pp. 193–223.

— 1939. "Proof of an External World." *Proceedings of the British Academy* 273–300.

Nozick, R. 1981. *Philosophical Explanations*. Cambridge: Harvard University Press.

Pryor, J. 2000. "The Skeptic and the Dogmatist." *Nous* 34(4): 517–49.

Vogel, J. 1990. "Cartesian Skepticism and Inference to the Best Explanation." *Journal of Philosophy* 87(11): 659–66.

— 2005. "The Refutation of Skepticism." In M. Steup and E. Sosa, eds, *Contemporary Debates in Epistemology*. Oxford: Blackwell.

Williamson, T. 2000. *Knowledge and its Limits*. Oxford: Oxford University Press.

9

Epistemic Relativism

Jonathan Matheson

Relativists claim that there are no absolute facts—facts which don't differ from individual to individual or from community to community—within some domain. Their relativism can be either global or local. Global relativists claim that there are no absolute facts at all, whereas local relativists restrict the domain of relative facts. While ethical relativism is a rather familiar sort of local relativism, epistemic relativism is another type of local relativism, and one which is beginning to receive more attention. Whereas ethical relativism claims that there are no absolute ethical facts, epistemic relativism claims that there are no absolute epistemic facts. So, according to epistemic relativism facts about what an individual is justified in believing or what an individual knows are not absolute, but rather relative to individuals or communities. It is clearly true that not every individual knows or is justified in believing the same propositions, and that what any individual knows or is justified in believing often changes over time, however, epistemic relativism, at least as it is being understood here, is making a more radical claim that this. Epistemic relativism claims that the very standards for knowledge and justification are not absolute, but rather relative to individuals or communities. Since the standards of knowledge and justification are thought to be relative, the truth of epistemic claims are also thought to be relative. So, according to the epistemic relativist, we can fix what information a particular individual has at a particular time, and there are still no absolute facts about what that individual knows or is justified in believing at that time. According to epistemic relativism there may be some standards or rationality by which the individual is epistemically justified in believing some proposition and other standards of rationality by which the individual is not epistemically justified in believing that proposition, and no absolute facts regarding one of these sets of standards being more correct or better than the other. So, the epistemic relativist claims that whether some belief is justified or an item of knowledge is in some sense relative to some set of standards of rationality that can vary from individual to individual or community to community.

Are there good reasons for thinking that epistemic relativism is true? In what follows I will examine the case for epistemic relativism focusing on an argument for epistemic relativism formulated (though not endorsed) by Paul Boghossian. Before examining Boghossian's argument, however, it is worth first examining some preliminary considerations for and against epistemic relativism.

First, if global relativism is correct, then epistemic relativism will also be correct. If all facts are relative, then it follows that the epistemic facts are relative. So, if there was good reason to endorse global relativism, there would be good reason to endorse epistemic relativism. That said, there aren't good reasons to endorse global relativism. In fact, there are powerful reasons to reject global relativism.[1] For one thing, facts about history, mathematics, and geometry are clearly not relative to individuals or communities. So, motivation for epistemic relativism must focus on some feature of *epistemic* facts that is not shared by all the other types of facts and has the consequence that epistemic facts are not absolute.

As with ethical relativism, motivation for epistemic relativism might be thought to come from the widespread and persistent disagreements that we are aware of regarding epistemic claims (claims of the form: S knows p, S is justified in believing p, etc.). We are all very familiar with disputes about who knew what and who should believe what—disagreements that persist even when all parties agree about the relevant descriptive facts. One explanation for these disagreements is that there are no absolute epistemic facts—that the truth-value of epistemic claims is relative to individuals or communities. If this explanation is the best explanation of the existence of these disagreements, then we would have good reason by way of an inference to the best explanation to believe epistemic relativism. That said, it is implausible that epistemic relativism is the best explanation of such disagreements. A more plausible explanation is simply that epistemology is difficult and that it is often quite hard to discover the absolute facts regarding who knows what and who is justified in believing what. In addition, parties to such disagreements typically take themselves to be disputing absolute epistemic facts. This shows that most of us (at least implicitly) take epistemic facts to be absolute facts.

Additional problems for epistemic relativism become apparent once one examines what the truth of that claim would entail. First, it is possible that individuals or communities adopt utterly foolish standards of rationality. So, given epistemic relativism, each of the following epistemic claims could be false (at least to such an individual or community), where S is a normal adult American living in the twenty-first century:

A. S is not justified in believing that the Earth is flat.
B. S is not justified in believing that S does not exist.
C. S is justified in believing that the United States is a country.
D. S is justified in believing that 2 + 2 = 4.

Given the information possessed by a normal adult American living in the twenty-first century A–D are all true. A–D may not be recognized to be true by individuals in other communities, but A–D are nonetheless true—they are absolute epistemic truths. Since epistemic relativism has the consequence that A–D can be false for some individuals[2] or communities, epistemic relativism is false.

Second, if epistemic relativism is correct, then we cannot correctly judge one standard of rationality as being epistemically better or worse than any other standard of rationality. If epistemic standards are relative to individuals or communities and there are no absolute epistemic standards, then no epistemic standard is any better or any worse than any other epistemic standard. But it is clear that some epistemic standards are better or more correct than others. For instance, a standard that requires an individual to proportion her beliefs to the evidence is a better or more correct epistemic standard than one that requires an individual to believe the third proposition they consider every Wednesday and disbelieve the fourth proposition they consider every Friday.[3]

While these seem to be strong reasons to reject epistemic relativism, a more powerful argument for epistemic relativism could cause us to reject these considerations against it. In *Fear of Knowledge,* Paul Boghossian examines one such argument for epistemic relativism. In particular, Boghossian attempts to reconstruct, motivate, and respond to an argument for epistemic relativism coming primarily from Richard Rorty.[4] The argument is as follows:

P1. If there are absolute epistemic facts about what justifies what, then it ought to be possible to arrive at justified beliefs about them (at least in rough approximation).
P2. It is not possible to arrive at justified beliefs about what absolute epistemic facts there are (even in rough approximation).
P3. There are no absolute epistemic facts (epistemic non-absolutism is true). (from P1 and P2).
P4. If there are no absolute epistemic facts, then epistemic relativism is true.
C. Epistemic relativism is true (from P3 and P4).

Boghossian's primary focus in *Fear of Knowledge* is P2, which he ultimately rejects, thus crippling the argument for epistemic relativism. But before looking at the case regarding P2, it is worth briefly examining what Boghossian claims about the other key premises: P1 and P4.

Boghossian doesn't say much regarding P4. He is willing to grant it, while noting that versions of epistemic non-cognitivism would present a challenge to it. Epistemic non-cognitivist views contend that epistemic claims are not true or false at all, but rather are mere expressions of emotion, prescriptions, or expressions of other non-cognitive attitudes. While embracing epistemic non-cognitivism provides a route of escape from the argument for epistemic relativism, the cost of embracing epistemic non-cognitivism is indeed high. It seems clear that there are epistemic facts like those given above (where S is a normal adult American living in the twenty-first century):

A. S is not justified in believing that the Earth is flat.
B. S is not justified in believing that S does not exist.
C. S is justified in believing that the United States is a country.
D. S is justified in believing that 2 + 2 = 4.

The cost of rejecting that A–D are facts is simply too great a cost. So, like Boghossian, I too am willing to grant P4. Since there are epistemic facts, if there are no *absolute* epistemic facts, then there must be *relative* epistemic facts. Epistemic non-cognitivism is not a viable alternative.[5]

Boghossian also accepts P1. In defense of P1, Boghossian claims, "what would be the interest of an absolutism about epistemic truths which combined that absolutism with the affirmation that those truths are necessarily inaccessible to us?"[6] Boghossian tries to further motivate his claim by comparing the oddity of rejecting P1 with the apparent oddity of claiming that there are absolute moral truths, though we cannot be justified in believing what they are (even in rough approximation).

While such a view may be odd in that it posits facts that are inaccessible (at least epistemically) to us, there may be good reasons for endorsing such a view. Boghossian here seems to be ignoring the possibility that there are good reasons for being an absolutist (whether moral or epistemic) even in the absence of good reasons to think that we can be justified in believing what these absolute facts (whether moral or epistemic) are. The appeal of these skeptical positions might end at their truth, but being a true view ought to give each of these absolutisms at least *some* appeal. Further, we have seen some good reasons to think that epistemic relativism is false, so such a move is not without motivation.

Boghossian's remarks here are particularly puzzling since Boghossian himself gives powerful reasons to reject epistemic relativism.[7] In brief, his argument is that the self-aware epistemic relativist will have to adopt epistemic principles which he must take to be false, or at least untrue, prior to his adopting them given his epistemic relativism. Having adopted the (taken to have been untrue) principles, our self-aware relativist should then form and revise his beliefs in accordance with these principles—the very principles he took to be false or at least untrue at the time of adoption. Boghossian's claim is that such a picture is incoherent. We simply shouldn't care about what we should believe according to principles that we can recognize as false or at least untrue.

So, while neither moral skepticism nor skepticism about epistemic facts is appealing, both are more appealing than their alternative relativist theses, at least without further motivation for those relativist claims.[8] If the choice is between epistemic relativism, epistemic non-cognitivism, and skepticism about (absolute) epistemic facts, then given the initial considerations at the outset of this chapter, there seems to be good reason to choose skepticism about (absolute) epistemic facts. At the very least, P1 needs more motivation than simply pointing out that the view which rejects it would "lack interest"—we need reason to think that such a view is false regardless of how interesting one might find it. Nevertheless, Boghossian's primary focus is P2 and following Boghossian that will be my primary focus as well.

The case for P2 comes from thinking about possible encounters, particularly encounters with individuals who have alternative epistemic systems to our own and who disagree with us about the justificatory status of some belief, while at the same time agreeing with us about all the relevant descriptive facts. As Boghossian understands it, an epistemic system is some sort of grid for determining what is evidence for what, and how much each bit of evidence counts. Epistemic systems are comprised of a set of epistemic principles (hereafter EPs), which either claim that some epistemic property obtains whenever some descriptive property obtains (these are generative EPs) or claim when one can transition from one epistemic state to another (these are transmission EPs). A plausible example of a generative EP is the following:

> GEP: If it visually appears to S as if p, then S is *prima facie*[9] justified in believing p.

In contrast, a plausible example of a transmission EP is the following:

> TEP: If S is justified in believing p and justified in believing that p entails q, then S is justified in believing q.

EPs can also be either fundamental or derived. The fundamental EPs of a system need not be derived from any other EPs, and the positive epistemic status they enjoy, if any, does not depend upon other EPs. In contrast, the derived EPs enjoy positive epistemic status, if they do, in virtue of other EPs in the system—at root, in virtue of the fundamental EPs—from which they are ultimately derived. That said, an EP could be fundamental even if according to a derived EP our subject was justified in believing the fundamental EP. The over-determination of its positive epistemic status need not rule out that EP being fundamental. However, if the *sole* epistemic support for any supposed fundamental EP came from a derived EP, then the EP in question is not a fundamental EP, but a derived one.

The EP of phenomenal conservatism is a plausible example of a fundamental EP:

> PC: If it seems to S that p, then S is thereby *prima facie* justified in believing p.[10]

Taking *PC* as the fundamental EP of our epistemic system, the derived EPs of our system would be those EPs (whether generative EPs or transmission EPs) which follow from *PC*—the EPs which seem true to us. With these clarifications in hand, let's turn to the case for P2.

The argument for P2 begins by thinking about the fundamental EPs of any epistemic system. Do fundamental EPs themselves have a positive epistemic status? And, if so, from what do these fundamental EPs get their positive epistemic status? Their positive epistemic status cannot come from other EPs, or at least it cannot *depend* upon other EPs. If it were to, then the principle in question would not be a *fundamental* EP after all. So, what are we to say?

One option is the following:

> Self-Support: A fundamental EP is justified when that fundamental EP has the consequence that it is justified.

According to this option a fundamental EP enjoys (or at least can enjoy) a positive epistemic status, though it is granted this status from itself in some sense. On this picture, the positive epistemic status that any fundamental EP enjoys, it enjoys in virtue of what it itself claims. For instance, S can be justified in believing *PC* in a self-supporting, or norm-circular, way when it seems to S that *PC* is correct. Satisfying the relevant type of descriptive property in *PC* can make it that one is justified in believing *PC*.

Boghossian considers SELF-SUPPORT as a response to P2 and notes that this alternative comes with two worries: (i) that this kind of circularity cannot provide epistemic support, and (ii) that whatever kind of support this kind of circularity can give, it can be had by numerous alternative epistemic systems for their fundamental EPs. If either worry is correct, then SELF-SUPPORT will not be successful in providing a way of rejecting P2.

Regarding the first worry, we have Richard Fumerton:

> "[T]here is no philosophically interesting notion of justification or knowledge that would allow us to use a kind of reasoning to justify the legitimacy of using that reasoning."[11]

Regarding the second worry, we should recognize although *PC* can be justified according to *PC*, *PC* is not unique in this regard—other fundamental EPs can also be self-supporting. For instance we can consider the following competitor fundamental EP:

> TEA LEAF: If S's tea leaf has pattern X, then S is *prima facie* justified in believing p.

Like *PC*, TEA LEAF can also be self-supporting. It may be that S's tea leaf has a pattern that, according to TEA LEAF, renders S justified in believing TEA LEAF. Given this, it may appear that the adherer to *PC* is in no better epistemic position regarding her fundamental EP than the adherent of TEA LEAF is regarding her fundamental EP. Both have a fundamental EP according to which each respective individual is justified in believing their own fundamental EP. Further, everything that the adherer to *PC* can say in justifying her fundamental EP can be mimicked by the adherer to TEA LEAF in justifying her fundamental EP. It seems that if either party were to defend her fundamental EP by referencing the very EP under scrutiny she would be begging the question and doing nothing more. As Boghossian puts it,

> The most that any epistemic practice will be able to say, when confronted by a fundamentally different, genuine alternative, self-supporting epistemic practice, is that it is correct by its own lights, whereas the alternative isn't. But that cannot yield justification of one practice over the other, without begging the question.[12]

If that is the case, then the worry is that neither adherent is justified in believing her fundamental EP.[13] So, we have two powerful worries for SELF-SUPPORT. If either (i) or (ii) is correct, then it looks like SELF-SUPPORT does not provide a way of denying P2.

Indeed, in *Fear of Knowledge* Boghossian rejects SELF-SUPPORT for these reasons and in its place puts forward the following alternative:

> BLIND ENTITLEMENT: We are blindly entitled to the epistemic system we have adopted, at least until we become aware of a better alternative epistemic system.

Initially an appeal to blind entitlement may seem like simply an insistence that P2 is false—an insistence that we can be justified in believing epistemic facts. Boghossian tries to take the sting out of this alternative by noting the unavoidability of adopting an epistemic system before one can even undertake the project of justifying an epistemic system or the EPs contained therein. After all, epistemic systems are justified (if at all) in virtue of fundamental EPs, since those are the things that ultimately prescribe under what conditions beliefs are justified. But which fundamental EPs should one use to determine which epistemic system one is justified in adopting? Alternative epistemic systems have alternative fundamental EPs, so to pick a set of fundamental EPs by which to evaluate various alternative epistemic systems is to *already* have adopted an epistemic system and set of fundamental EPs. Here is Boghossian on the topic:

> [I]f no one is entitled to use an epistemic system without first justifying it, then no one could be entitled to use an epistemic system, for any attempt by the thinker to justify it will depend on his being entitled to use some epistemic system or other.[14]

According to Boghossian, BLIND ENTITLEMENT allows for the falsity of P2 since when we are entitled to an epistemic system we are justified in believing what that system claims that we are justified in believing. Since epistemic claims can be among the propositions which our epistemic system claims we are justified in believing, this alternative is incompatible with P2 and provides a way out of the argument for epistemic relativism. For instance, if I am entitled to adopt *PC* (and the resulting epistemic system which has *PC* as the fundamental EP), then I am justified in believing what *PC* claims that I am justified in believing—the things that seem true to me and do not have this justification defeated. Among the propositions that I may thereby be justified in believing are a number of EPs. So, if I can be entitled to adopt an epistemic system, it is possible to have justified beliefs about epistemic claims. So, BLIND ENTITLEMENT does provide a way out of the argument for epistemic relativism. If BLIND ENTITLEMENT is true, P2 is false.

But even if this is so, is BLIND ENTITLEMENT really acceptable? The problems for it begin by examining how we are to understand the kind of entitlement mentioned therein. Either the entitlement in BLIND ENTITLEMENT is a kind of *epistemic* entitlement or it is not. Let's start by thinking of it as a kind of positive epistemic status. The problem here is that route from unavoidability to *epistemic* entitlement is not a good one. An unavoidable choice might provide pragmatic reasons to take one option over another, but it is hard to see how *epistemic* reasons could be so generated. For instance, coming to a fork in the road and needing to get to the destination may give pragmatic reasons to take one of the forks, but the need to take an option would not itself give any *epistemic* reason to believe that any one fork was the correct path to take. The need to make a choice does not itself give one any *epistemic* reasons in favor of any choice.

Further, entitlement understood this way, simply gives the wrong verdicts in theoretical cases. For instance, according to this understanding of entitlement, even the adherer to TEA LEAF is *initially* epistemically entitled to adopt that epistemic system. So, what is justified for this individual at that time is whatever TEA LEAF claims is justified for her. This is implausible. The adherer to TEA LEAF never has her beliefs enjoy a positive epistemic status simply in virtue of what the EP TEA LEAF claims.[15] So, Boghossian's BLIND ENTITLEMENT is not plausible when the entitlement is understood as epistemic entitlement.

However, if the entitlement in BLIND ENTITLEMENT is not a kind of epistemic entitlement, then Boghossian's alternative faces distinct problems. If the entitlement in is not a kind of *epistemic* entitlement (if it does not give some positive epistemic status to the fundamental EPs), then this alternative gives us no reason to think that one's fundamental EPs have *any* positive epistemic standing. Positive epistemic standing simply does not result from non-epistemic entitlements. If the entitlement is non-epistemic, then one's fundamental EPs do not have a positive epistemic status even if the individual is entitled to them. So, regardless of how we understand the entitlement in Boghoissian's alternative, serious problems ensue.

A third alternative for rejecting P2, one not considered by Boghossian, is the following:

> COHERENCE: EPs are justified when they cohere with one's system of beliefs, and cohere with one's system of beliefs better than alternative EPs.

COHERENCE utilizes a coherentist theory of justification to justify EPs. A coherentist theory of justification claims that beliefs are justified in virtue to their relations to other beliefs, and by coherence relations in particular. Coherentists have a holistic conception of justification rather than the more traditional linear notion. COHERENCE appears to allow for the falsity of P2 since individuals do have systems of beliefs and it is at least possible that some EPs will cohere with these beliefs and cohere with these beliefs better than competitor EPs. So, if COHERENCE is true, then it looks like it is possible to have justified beliefs about what the epistemic facts are.

While COHERENCE has promise, unless SELF-SUPPORT or BLIND ENTITLEMENT is also correct, COHERENCE offers no help in allowing *fundamental* EPs to be justified. While COHERENCE can allow for other EPs to be justified, it does so as a fundamental EP—it is in virtue of COHERENCE that the other EPs are justified. However, for an individual to be justified in believing COHERENCE itself, SELF-SUPPORT or BLIND ENTITLEMENT must also be correct. COHERENCE might be justified for an individual because it coheres with her system of beliefs and does so better than alternative EPs, but if so, then SELF-SUPPORT has been utilized. Alternatively, COHERENCE might be justified for an individual because she has accepted it and has not come across a better fundamental EP or epistemic system, but if so, then BLIND ENTITLEMENT has been utilized. Without affirming either SELF-SUPPORT or BLIND ENTITLEMENT it does not appear that an individual could be justified in believing the fundamental EP COHERENCE.

Further, if it is in principle impossible for an individual to be justified in believing the fundamental EP COHERENCE, then any justification for EPs provided by COHERENCE will disappear once this fact is realized. If an individual recognizes that COHERENCE is the fundamental EP by which she is seeing the other EPs in her epistemic system to be justified and that she *cannot* be justified in believing COHERENCE, then any justification that individual had for believing those other EPs will be defeated or undercut.[16]

In fact, for this very reason, COHERENCE does not provide any advantage in rejecting P2. Like COHERENCE, *PC* too could allow for some EPs to be justified—the EPs that seemed true to the individual in question. But both *PC* and COHERENCE have the problem that without SELF-SUPPORT or ENTITLEMENT the fundamental EP in the epistemic system is in principle unable to be justified. Once this is recognized, any justification provided for the derived EPs by way of the fundamental EP will be defeated or undercut.

So, while *PC* and COHERENCE allow for some EPs to be justified, unless SELF-SUPPORT or BLIND ENTITLEMENT is also correct, they only do so when the individual in question has been unreflective and has not considered the justificatory status of the fundamental EP of her epistemic system. While allowing for some EPs to be justified is sufficient for the falsity P2 (since P2 claimed that it is not possible to come to justified beliefs about what the epistemic facts are), it seems that we have only pushed the epistemic relativist to a slightly revised argument with the following key premise in place of P2:

> P2′ It is not possible to arrive at justified beliefs about what absolute epistemic facts there are (even in rough approximation) once you reflect on how your beliefs are ultimately justified (what fundamental EP you are utilizing).

This premise is no less plausible than P2, and the requisite revisions to P1 do not make it any less plausible either. Since COHERENCE does not provide a way of rejecting P2′ without also embracing SELF-SUPPORT or BLIND ENTITLEMENT, it has not helped in disarming the argument for epistemic relativism.

This should cause us to revisit SELF-SUPPORT. Perhaps Boghossian's dismissal of SELF-SUPPORT was too quick. Recall that SELF-SUPPORT raised two worries:

(i) That this kind of circularity cannot provide *epistemic* support, and
(ii) That whatever kind of support this kind of circularity can give can be had by numerous alternative epistemic systems.

If SELF-SUPPORT is to be accepted and P2 and P2′ rejected, both (i) and (ii) must be shown to be faulty. Let's take these two worries in turn. The first concern was motivated by Fumerton's claim given above. One thing to note here is that we typically *do* think that this kind of norm-circularity can provide *epistemic* support. Deductive defenses of deduction, and inductive defenses of induction both appear to be legitimate ways of justifying their own use.[17] For instance, it appears that I can prove that *Modus Ponens* is a valid argument form as follows:

1. If a *Modus Ponens* argument cannot have all true premises and a false conclusion, then *Modus Ponens* is valid.
2. A *Modus Ponens* argument cannot have all true premises and a false conclusion.
3. *Modus Ponens* is valid.

While this argument is itself a *Modus Ponens* argument, it nonetheless makes it reasonable to believe that *Modus Ponens* is a valid argument form. This kind of norm-circularity can provide positive epistemic support since *Modus Ponens* is in fact a good argument form.[18] Since reasoning according to Modus Ponens is a good way to reason, reasoning in this way, even when the content of the argument concerns Modus Ponens itself, is a good way to reason.[19]

Along these lines, there are theoretical reasons to reject (i). Let's continue to take it that *PC* is a correct fundamental EP. If *PC* is true, then seemings provide *prima facie* justification for the propositions that seem true to those to whom they seem true. If seemings provide *prima facie* justification for such propositions, then they can do so regarding *PC* itself. *PC* can simply be one such proposition that *PC* applies to. If *PC* is correct, then seemings do provide *prima facie* justification for propositions that seem true, and they do so regardless of *which* propositions seems true.[20] To reject this is already to have rejected *PC*, which we are assuming is true. Such a norm-circular justification of *PC* is surely dialectically ineffective, but if *PC* is true, then S can be justified in believing *PC* by it seeming to S that *PC* is correct—this is simply entailed by what we are assuming to be true, namely *PC* itself.[21] No one who was not already convinced of *PC* would become convinced that another individual is justified in believing *PC* by having it pointed out that *PC* seems true to that individual. However, we should recall here the need to keep distinct the *project* of justifying one's beliefs from the *state* of being justified in believing a proposition. Our concern here is the state of being justified, not the project of justifying.[22]

What about the second worry with SELF-SUPPORT? Our response to (i) provides a foundation for a response to it as well. Important to our response to (i) was that *PC* was in fact true, not simply that *PC* was the fundamental EP within our accepted epistemic system. So, while the adherent to *PC* and the adherent to TEA LEAF both have epistemic systems which are justified according to the fundamental EP contained within each respective epistemic system, these alternative epistemic systems do not each have a *true* fundamental EP. Alternative epistemic systems have distinct fundamental EPs, and epistemic relativism is false, so there are objective facts about what the true EPs are.[23]

So, while it might be true that according to TEA LEAF we should believe TEA LEAF, if TEA LEAF is not in fact true, then the adherer to TEA LEAF in fact has no reason to believe TEA LEAF coming simply from the revelations of a tea leaf. If, as we are supposing, *PC* is correct, then seemings do provide *prima facie* justification for what seems true. And if TEA LEAF is incorrect, then the fact that a tea leaf has a pattern which according to which TEA LEAF presented as true, itself gives no reason to believe TEA LEAF. It simply makes no difference what false EPs claim, even when one of the things they claim is that we are justified in believing those very principles. Only true EPs have affect on what we should believe. So, there is an important difference between the adherer of *PC* and the adherer to *Tea Leaf*—only the former has an epistemic system with a true fundamental EP (at least by supposition), and this difference allows for some EPs to be justified and others not.[24]

So, according to Self-Support, P2 and P2′ are false. It *is* possible to arrive at justified beliefs about what absolute epistemic facts there are, even upon reflection about how one is justified in believing the fundamental EP of one's epistemic system. One can do so by believing in accordance with the correct EPs. One thing that it is possible for the correct EPs to claim is that we are justified in believing that some principle is an epistemic fact, and this is so even if the EP in question is taken to be a fundamental EP. So, P2 and P2′ should be rejected, and the argument for epistemic relativism fails.

The endorsement of Self-Support may sound like the type of response to this argument for epistemic relativism offered by Ernest Sosa—a response which embraces a kind of norm-circularity and externalism about epistemic justification.[25] While we have endorsed a form of norm-circularity, we have seen no reason to resort to externalism about epistemic justification here. Everything said here is completely consistent with internalism about epistemic justification. According to externalism about epistemic justification, at least some of the factors that contribute to the justification of a belief are external to the subject's mind. In contrast, internalism about epistemic justification claims that all of the factors which contribute to the justification of a belief are within the subject's mind—that epistemic justification supervenes on the mental.[26]

According to *PC* what justifies a belief are seeming states—its seeming to S that p provides *prima facie* justification for S to believe p. But seemings occur *within* the mind—they are a kind of mental state. Further, this point can easily be divorced from *PC*. Other internalist fundamental EPs about epistemic justification will have a similar result. In general, internalist EPs about epistemic justification will claim that it is some feature(s) internal to the subject's mind that provide(s) *prima facie* justification (and only such feature(s)). Any true fundamental internalist EP will be able to provide *prima facie* justification for itself, and this justification will come from some feature(s) within the subject's mind.

Now, the relevant internalist EP, whether *PC* or something else, is not *itself* within the subject's mind, but internalism was never committed to *this* claim. To claim that the factors which justify a belief are internal to the subject's mind is not to claim that the correct EPs are *themselves* within the subject's mind.[27] No plausible epistemology makes this later claim. For these reasons, internalism about epistemic justification should be kept distinct from a kind of subjectivism about justification which claims that one's beliefs are epistemically justified so long as one is doing one's best by one's own lights.[28]

Nevertheless, this may be enough to make the epistemic internalist worry. After all, according to this story the justification for one's fundamental EPs in some sense depends on *external facts*—facts that are out there in the world—and not simply on one's perspective. Wasn't this the problem that internalists had with externalist account of justification in the first place?[29]

Fortunately for the internalist about epistemic justification, there is still an important distinction to be made. According to internalist theories of epistemic justification, while the (mind independent) epistemic facts matter (and shouldn't we all think that?), the true facts about epistemic justification claim that epistemic justification supervene on features within the subject's mind. While these epistemic facts *themselves* don't depend on the subject's perspective (and who would want that?), the true principles about epistemic justification claim that the descriptive properties upon which epistemic justification supervenes can be (and plausibly are) properties which make a difference from the subject's perspective. The seeming states relevant to *PC* are but one example of this. It is here that internalist and externalist theories of justification differ. Externalist theories claim that the relevant descriptive properties upon which epistemic justification supervenes can include properties outside of the mind of the subject. This is denied by internalist theories of epistemic justification (perhaps because such properties cannot make a difference from the subject's perspective). So, internalists can still maintain that they give the subject's perspective its due—that they make it essential—even while claiming that the epistemic facts themselves don't depend on anyone and that what the epistemic facts are affects who is justified in believing what.

Further all of this is consistent with the internalists supervenience claim: that epistemic justification supervenes on the mental. Epistemic justification will still supervene on the mental even though what an individual is justified in believing will depend in some sense on the epistemic facts. The supervenience relation will still hold since the epistemic facts aren't just absolute facts, they are necessary truths. The epistemic facts do not differ from individual to individual, community to community, or even possible world to possible world. Since epistemic facts are necessary truths, there will be no change in epistemic justification without a change in mental properties. Since the epistemic facts never change, they never get in the way.

While we have seen that epistemic internalism is not committed to the claim that the epistemic principles must themselves be mental, this is not to say that no internalist epistemology requires that the subject be justified in believing the relevant epistemic principles. Strong internalist accounts of justification require just this.[30] But while such theories require that one possess or be aware of the relevant EP, this is still distinct from requiring that the principle *itself* be within the subject's mind. Further, endorsing SELF-SUPPORT does not rule out such strong internalist epistemologies. Suppose instead of *PC* being correct, *SPC* is the truth of the matter:

> *SPC*: S is *prima facie* justified in believing p if and only if it seems to S that p and it seems to S that something's seeming true provides *prima facie* justification for believing it.

The defender of a strong internalist theory like *SPC* still does not claim that *any* principle, including *SPC*, must be within the subject's mind. Rather, the defender of *SPC* claims that there must be several seeming states in the subject's mind. While one of these seeming states is a seeming that a certain EP is true (that seemings provide *prima facie* justification for what seems true), it is the *seeming* which must be in the subject's mind, not the principle itself.

So, the view on offer here is wholly compatible with internalism about epistemic justification (even strong internalism), and its compatibility with internalism does not rest on the epistemic status of seemings. For parallel reasons, alternative internalist epistemologies can also endorse SELF-SUPPORT. Of course, externalist theories of justification can also endorse SELF-SUPPORT. SELF-SUPPORT simply does not affect the internalist/externalist debate in epistemology.

In concluding, I want to consider a further objection to SELF-SUPPORT, one not considered by Boghossian. It might be thought that SELF-SUPPORT does not square well with prevalent views in the epistemology of disagreement. While we saw early on that disagreement itself does not provide support for epistemic relativism, there is a rapidly growing debate on how discovering that another disagrees with you should affect what you believe. SELF-SUPPORT shares some similarity with what has been termed the "right reasons view"[31] in the debate on the epistemic significance of disagreement.[32] SELF-SUPPORT claims that there are true EPs, and so long as you believe in accordance with them, you will be justified in what you believe. Similarly, the "right reasons view" of disagreement claims that the party who reasoned correctly in a case of disagreement remains justified in what she believes (and to the same extent) even after encountering a disagreement with an epistemic peer[33] on the matter. Consider the following case:

> Disagreement: S and S′ each look at a moderately complicated math problem. S concludes that the answer is 17. S knows that S′ is S's epistemic peer. S′ then

tells S that the answer is 15. In fact, S performed the math correctly, and the answer is 17. What should S now believe the answer is?[34]

According to the right reasons view, S has the right reasons to believe the answer is 17, and thus should go on believing (and just as confidently) that the answer is 17 even though S has since learned of S' belief on the matter. Given this, the "right reasons view" is not a very plausible view about the epistemic significance of disagreement.[35] It seems that S should become less confident having discovered this disagreement, so does this spell trouble for the view on offer here? After all, both views seem to say that what matters is simply following the true EPs. So, the worry here is that while SELF-SUPPORT has it that P2 and P2' are false, it only accomplishes this task by making it far too easy to be justified in believing propositions.

I don't think that there is a problem here for SELF-SUPPORT. While what one should believe is entirely a matter of what the true fundamental EPs are, there is no small step from this to the "right reasons view" of disagreement. This is because one of the things that the true fundamental EPs can (and plausibly do) claim (even if indirectly through their endorsement of derived EPs) is that cases of peer disagreement are epistemically significant. Let's continue to consider *PC* as a true fundamental EP. According to *PC*, the justification that S has for believing p can decrease (even dramatically) once S encounters an individual who seems to S to be S's epistemic peer and seems to disagree with S about p. The story about what S is justified in believing about p having encountered the relevant kind of disagreement can be done entirely in terms of how things seem to S. If it seems to S that S' is just as likely to be right about p, and that S' disagrees with S about p, then according to *PC*, S is *prima facie* justified in believing these things. If this justification is not defeated for S, then S is on balance justified in believing these things, and if so, then S will become less justified in believing p (perhaps quite dramatically).[36] Here again though, this is not some special feature of *PC*. Rather many fundamental EPs will give such a verdict. It appears that plausible fundamental EPs will give such a verdict and take the epistemic significance of disagreement seriously. But, we have seen that *PC* can do this, and for similar reasons other internalist fundamental EPs can do the same.

In addition, while *PC* and SELF-SUPPORT made it possible for an individual to be justified in believing epistemic principles, given *PC* this justification is *prima facie*—it can be defeated. Plausibly, cases of peer disagreement are cases where such justification is defeated. The problem for the "right reasons view" of disagreement is that it appears to make reasoning according to correct principles *sufficient* for being on balance justified in believing something. This is why the "right reasons view" gives the wrong verdicts in cases of disagreement. But, *PC* makes no such sufficiency claim, and plausibly the correct fundamental EPs (whether they be *PC* or something else) do not either.

To sum up, we have seen good reason to reject epistemic relativism and no good reason to affirm it. While we have seen a powerful argument for epistemic relativism there are critical problems with both P1 and P2. Further, while epistemic relativism is to be avoided, the best way of avoiding it comes not from endorsing Boghossian's BLIND ENTITLEMENT, but in accepting SELF-SUPPORT and noticing that it entails the falsity of P2 and P2'. We have seen that endorsing this type of response does not require an endorsement of externalism about epistemic justification and does not fail to take seriously the epistemic significance of disagreement.[37]

Notes

1 For theoretical reasons to reject global relativism see Thomas Nagel, *The Last Word* (New York: Oxford University Press, 1997, 15), and Paul Boghossian, *Fear of Knowledge: Against Relativism and Constructivism* (New York: Oxford University Press, 2007, 52–7).

2 This is not to say that there are not individuals (individuals who are not normal adult Americans living in the twenty-first century) who if you substituted them for S in A–D would have the result that A–D would be false.

3 These criticisms of epistemic relativism parallel criticisms of ethical relativism put forward by James Rachels. See James Rachels, "The Challenge of Cultural Relativism," in *The Elements of Moral Philosophy* 3rd edn (New York: Random House, 1999, 20–36).

4 In particular see Richard Rorty, *Philosophy and the Mirror of Nature* (Princeton: Princeton University Press, 1981).

Boghossian understands epistemic relativism slightly differently than I have been understanding it. As Boghossian sees it epistemic relativism consists of the following three claims:

Epistemic non-absolutism: there are no absolute facts about what belief a particular item of information justifies.

Epistemic relationism: If S's epistemic judgment of the form "E justifies belief B" is to be true, it must be seen as expressing "according to the epistemic system C, that I, S, accept, information E justifies B."

Epistemic pluralism: there are many fundamentally different, genuine alternative epistemic systems, but no facts by virtue of which one of these systems is more correct than any other.

Fear of Knowledge. (p. 73)

5   This discussion of epistemic non-cognitivism is admittedly quick. For a more detailed discussion on epistemic non-cognitivism see Michael P. Lynch, "Truth, Value and Epistemic Expressivism," *Philosophy and Phenomenological Research* 79(1) (2009) 76–97; Mathew Chrisman, "From Epistemic Contextualism to Epistemic Expressivism," *Philosophical Studies* (forthcoming); and also Allan Gibbard *Wise Choices, Apt Feelings* and *Thinking How to Live* (Cambridge: Harvard University Press, 1992).

6   *Fear of Knowledge*, p. 76.

7   See *Fear of Knowledge*, chapter 6.

8   In other words, motivation for P1 itself requires motivation for epistemic relativism—at least motivation for it as opposed to an abosolutist skepticism about epistemic facts. Without such motivation, P1 is insufficiently motivated and this argument for epistemic relativism will fail.

9   S is *prima facie* justified in believing p when (i) S has justification to believe p, (ii) that justification to believe p can be defeated or undermined, and (iii) if that justification for believing p is not defeated, then S is on balance justified in believing p.

10   Boghossian does not give *PC* as a fundamental epistemic principle. Rather he offers principles like *Observation:* for any observational proposition p, if it visually seems to S that p and circumstantial conditions D obtain, then S is *prima facie* justified in believing p. *Fear of Knowledge*, p. 64.

However, it seems hat Observation is actually a derived principle, one that is derived from *PC*. For one thing, Observation cannot provide epistemic support for itself since one cannot observe that observation is true. So, in what follows I will be using *PC* as my example of a fundamental epistemic principle. However, which fundamental epistemic principles there are (and what they are) is not central to my argument.

For more on phenomenal conservatism see Michael Huemer's, *Skepticism and the Veil of Perception* (Lanham, MD: Rowman & Littlefield, 2001).

11   Richard Fumerton, *Metaepistemology and Skepticism* (Lanham, MD: Rowman & Littlefield, 1995), p. 180.

12   *Fear of Knowledge*, p. 79.

13   This type of objection has been referred to as "the Great Pumpkin Objection." This name traces back to Alvin Plantinga and an objection he considered to his reformed epistemology. Michael Bergmann has also used this term to refer to such an objection. See Bergmann "Evidentialism and the Great Pumpkin Objection," in

Evidentialism and Its Discontents, Trent Dougherty, ed. (Oxford: Oxford University Press, 2011, 195–209).

14 *Fear of Knowledge,* p. 99.

15 It's worth noting that *PC* allows for the possibility for an individual to be justified in believing *Tea Leaf,* yet it would do so in virtue of it seeming to the subject that *Tea Leaf* is correct—it would be in virtue of *PC* that this is so, not in virtue of *Tea Leaf.* In such a situation, it is the seeming state that is doing real epistemic work, not the mere "indications" of the *Tea Leaf.*

16 Such a situation is a case of higher order defeat. For more on higher order defeat see Matheson "Conciliatory Views of Disagreement and Higher-Order Evidence," *Episteme: A Journal of Social Philosophy* 6(3) (2009) 269–79.

17 This is also why induction and deduction are plausible candidates for fundamental epistemic principles, though by assumption they gain their positive epistemic standing by way of *PC.*

18 For more on this point, see James Van Cleve "Reliability, Justification, and the Problem of Induction," *Midwest Studies in Philosophy* 9(1) (1984) 555–67.

19 Similarly regarding induction, since the past being a certain way does give a reason to believe that the future will be that way, the fact that induction has been a good guide in the past gives us good reason to believe that induction will be a good guide in the future.

20 Parallel points apply to Coherence.

21 This point is made by Earl Conee, "First Things First," in Earl Conee and Richard Feldman, eds, *Evidentialism: Essays in Epistemology* (Oxford: Oxford University Press, 2004).

22 For more on this distinction see James Pryor, "The Skeptic and the Dogmatist," *Nous* 34(4) (2000) 517–49.

23 Here again, this move in the objection to the argument for epistemic relativism will be dialectically ineffective since it is relying on the falsity of epistemic relativism. That said, the project here is to find good reasons to reject the argument, even if those reasons would not convince an epistemic relativist. In this way my project here is like the less ambitious response to the skeptic which does not attempt to convince the skeptic by her own terms, but to provide a satisfactory response to her arguments by our own non-skeptical lights. Additionally, if the epistemic relativist must rely on epistemic relativism to make the case for P2 or P2', then the argument for epistemic relativism here will be question begging.

24 In his reply to Ernest Sosa (see "Replies to Wright, MacFarlane, and Sosa," *Philosophical Studies* 141 (2008) 409–32), Boghossian seems to endorse the view that what the correct fundamental EP(s) are will make a difference as to which epistemic system one is and can be justified in adopting. I take it that this is a departure from Boghossian's view expressed in *Fear of Knowledge.* After all, if one is

adopting an epistemic system because according to the correct fundamental EP(s) one is justified in adopting it, then there does not seem to be any room left for blind entitlement to play—in such a case, one has justification for adopting that system.

25 Ernest Sosa, "Boghossian's Fear of Knowledge," *Philosophical Studies* 141(3) (2008) 407.

26 Conee and Feldman, "Internalism Defended," in Hilary Kornblith, ed., *Epistemology: Internalism and Externalism* (Blackwell, 2001) defend this understanding of internalism as mentalism.

27 Alvin Goldman appears to make a similar mistake when he charges that since the fittingness relation is not itself a mental state, evidentialism (the claim that the doxastic attitude that is justified for an individual at a time is the one which fits the evidence the subject has at that time) is in conflict with internalism (at least as understood as mentalism). See Goldman, "Toward a Synthesis of Reliabilism and Evidentialism," in *Evidentialism and Its Discontents,* Trent Dougherty, ed. (Oxford: Oxford University Press, 2011, 254–80, 269). However, the internalist is simply not committed to this. Just as the internalist is not committed to EPs being mental states, the internalist is not committed to any fittingness relation being internal—only the factors to which the justified doxastic attitude fits need to be internal.

28 For a defender of this type of subjectivism, see Richard Foley's *Intellectual Trust in Oneself and Others* (Cambridge: Cambridge University Press, 2007).

29 This charge is explicitly made by Michael Bergmann in "Evidentalism and the Great Pumpkin Objection" responding to an evidentialist response to worry (ii) like I have outlined here.

30 Though even here, not all internalist epistemologies are strong internalist epistemologies, so from what has already been said there is already a way for an internalist about epistemic justification to accept SELF-SUPPORT. For more on the distinctions between weak and strong internalist theories see Michael Bergmann's *Justification Without Awareness* (Oxford: Oxford University Press, 2009), and Rogers and Matheson, "Bergmann's Dilemma: Exit Strategies for Internalists," *Philosophical Studies* 152(1) (2011) 55–80.

31 This view is often attributed to the view at one time defended by Thomas Kelly, "The Epistemic Significance of Disagreement," in John Hawthorne and Tamar Gendler, eds, *Oxford Studies in Epistemology* (Oxford: Oxford University Press, 2005).

32 For more on the epistemology of disagreement see David Christensen, "Epistemology of Disagreement: The Good News," *Philosophical Review* 116 (2007) 187–218; Richard Feldman, "Reasonable Religious Disagreements," in L. Antony, ed., *Philosophers without Gods: Meditations on Atheism and the Secular Life* (New York: Oxford University Press, 2006); and Thomas Kelly, "The Epistemic Significance of Disagreement," in T. Gendler and J. Hawthorne, eds, *Oxford Studies in Epistemology,* Volume 1 (Oxford: Oxford University Press, 2005).

33 Various formulations of epistemic peers have been given in the literature. What these accounts share, and what is vital to two individuals being epistemic peers is that they are equally likely to be right about the matter. Plausibly this requires that they have the same evidence (or equally good evidence), they have been equally responsible in thinking the matter through, they are equally intelligent, etc.

34 This case parallels one given by David Christensen in "The Epistemology of Disagreement: The Good News," *Philosophical Review* 116(2) (2007) 187–217.

35 See Matheson, "Conciliatory Views of Disagreement and Higher-Order Evidence," *Episteme: A Journal of Social Philosophy* 6(3) (2009) 269–79. Kelly has also since made clear that he never meant to endorse such a view.

36 For more on this kind of defeating effect see my "Conciliatory Views of Disagreement and Higher-Order Evidence," *Episteme: A Journal of Social Philosophy* 6(3) (2009) 269–79.

37 Special thanks to Trent Dougherty, Theodore Locke, Kevin McCain, and Sarah Wright for helpful discussions on this topic.

10

A Priori Knowledge: The Conceptual Approach

Carrie Jenkins

Introduction

A priori knowledge is knowledge that is, in some sense that requires further specification, independent of any evidence gathered through sense experience. A priori justification is justification that is similarly independent. I shall discuss a priori knowledge in this chapter. But I think a priori justification is intimately related to a priori knowledge. Indeed, I adopt the following as a working definition of a priori knowledge: *knowledge which is justificatorily independent of evidence gathered through sense experience.* That is to say, I'll take a priori knowledge to be knowledge whose justification does not consist in or ultimately rest upon[1] empirical evidence.

This is what is sometimes known as a "negative" condition on a prioricity: it refers to the *lack* of justificatory reliance on empirical evidence.[2] Some philosophers believe that a good definition of a priori knowledge should also include either (a) a requirement of empirical indefeasibility, or (b) a positive condition such as that the knowledge in question be secured using a faculty of rational intuition or insight. I explain in section 1 of Jenkins (2008a) why I think such extra conditions are inappropriate; briefly, both these requirements seem to me to make a priori knowledge easily and uninterestingly dismissable by those who think every belief can be defeated by good-enough testimony and that faculties of rational intuition or insight are scientifically unrespectable.

While knowledge and justification are widely accepted as the primary bearers of a prioricity, a *proposition* might also be described as a priori on the grounds that it is one which can be known and/or justified a priori. Truths of mathematics and of logic, and "definitional matters" (propositions such as *all vixens are female*), are widely considered to be leading candidates for propositions meeting these conditions.

Discuss a priori knowledge with a randomly selected analytic philosopher these days, and you can expect one of three reactions. From certain staunch defenders of certain forms of "naturalism" (particularly "Quinean naturalism") and/or of the movement known as "experimental philosophy," you may expect distaste and suspicion of what they perceive to be an outmoded and frankly pernicious notion. From a good number of others, you'll get some degree of bafflement, ranging from a faintly uninterested shrug to a flat-out declaration that philosophy is in a muddle over this topic and hasn't made much progress with it over the last 50 years. The remainder you can expect to find happily *using* the notion of a prioricity, without much willingness to say exactly what they're up to when they do, but lacking the second camp's sense of there being anything very confused or confusing here or any real work that needs to be done.

There are notable exceptions to this tripartite division. Philosophers who work specifically on the a priori themselves are unlikely to fall squarely into the second or third camps. Some fall into the first, but of the others, there are a decent number who believe there is work to do and serious progress is being made, and I'll be talking about some of them in this chapter. However, this chapter is in the first instance addressed to camp number three: those who believe in the a priori (or at least are happy to conduct their philosophical enquiries in other areas *as if* they believe in the a priori), but don't have considered opinions about what it is or how it works. I'll be trying to explain what there is to worry about when one casually signs up for the a priori, and what kinds of options are available by way of solutions to those worries.

I hope also to be providing an overview that may assuage some of the baffled in camp number two. I won't be offering much to sway anybody in camp number one, however. (The most I shall do is gesture toward what I take to be a naturalistically respectable account of how a priori knowledge is possible, which might be of interest to any who are motivated primarily by the thought that the a priori is *not* compatible with naturalistic respectability.) Nonetheless, I invite the members of the first camp to agree with Jeeves that it is as well to know exactly what tunes the devil is playing, and read my chapter anyway.

As I see it, the most serious question facing those who believe in a priori knowledge is to explain *how it could possibly work*. How *can* one secure knowledge without relying on the evidence of one's senses? Maybe knowledge of one's own mind could be secured that way, but classic putative examples of a priori knowable propositions (2 + 2 = 4) seem, prima facie at least, to be about something else altogether. The closest thing to an orthodoxy among believers who are trying to answer this question is that it's got something to do with concepts, conceptual truth, analyticity, or something in the vicinity of those things. According to this semi-orthodoxy, the reason we can know *all vixens are female* a priori has something to do with how our concepts *vixen* and *female* relate to one another, and/or with the fact that *all vixens are female* is an analytic and/or conceptual truth (whatever exactly that might come to). For terminological convenience, I shall use an umbrella term for all forms of the view just described. I shall refer to such views as versions of *the conceptual approach.* Due to its semi-orthodox status, the conceptual approach will be a focal point of this chapter.

Appealing though this kind of (partial) answer may be, any serious defender of it must address the question of exactly *how* it is supposed to help explain how we can have a priori knowledge. This kind of question is being pressed more and more in recent debates about the a priori. Until it is settled, the epistemological value of such appeals is very much in doubt.

After this introduction, in the section "The State of Play," I describe two different ways of categorizing what seem to me to be the most important extant accounts of a priori knowledge. The principal aim of the first is give the reader a sense of why believing in the a priori raises interesting challenges that shouldn't be swept under the carpet, and the principal aim of the second is to indicate how the conceptual approach relates to its competitors, and how its advocates differ from one another.

Then, in section titled "The Problem," I present what I take to be the biggest general challenge to the conceptual approach: the challenge of saying why the way things are with *our concepts* is supposed to be any sort of guide to the way *the world* is. Why, for instance, should the existence of a certain kind of relationship between our concepts of *vixen* and *female* be a source of knowledge of the (prima facie mind-independent, worldly) fact that all vixens are female? I outline two prominent versions of this challenge due to BonJour and Field in "The Problem," then briefly describe my preferred way of answering the challenge in section "The Solution."

In the section "Concluding Remarks," I discuss that answer a little further, moving beyond previously published work. I shall, in particular, address questions concerning the role of *experience* in the proposal (explaining how the proposal is essentially empiricist and not available to a rationalist) and questions about the role of *concepts* in the account (examining whether they could comfortably be dispensed with).

The state of play

In Jenkins (2008a), section 2 (and elsewhere) I describe what I call the "three-step pattern problem," by way of an attempt to explain what I find so puzzling about a priori knowledge. Here (following my 2008a discussion), I shall quickly explain what that problem is, and how theories of the a priori can be categorized by the way in which they seek to address it.

The basic idea is that, when we want to understand how we have knowledge of the mind-independent world, we tend to give accounts that involve three steps:

(1) an input step, wherein information about the world somehow *gets into* our minds,

(2) a processing step, wherein that information is dealt with by our cognitive systems,

(3) a belief-formation step.

For example, any natural account of visual knowledge incorporates an input step when it talks about the impact of the external world on our light-responsive visual receptors, a processing step when it talks about the processing of that input by areas of the brain (in particular, the visual cortex), and a belief-formation step when it is postulated that the upshot of such processing is a belief concerning the visible external world.

The problem with a priori knowledge is that the input step is missing. The senses play no obvious input role, and many philosophers (particularly those who would classify themselves as being of a "naturalistic" bent) are unhappy about postulating other faculties (such as a faculty of "rational intuition") which could provide us with non-empirical input.

Thinking about the three-step pattern problem enables one to categorize classic stances on the a priori by means of the resolution that each attempts to provide. The first classic option is to say that no input step is required for a priori knowledge, because it, or the a priori knowable propositions, is/are either mind-dependent or trivial in some way that obviates the need for an input step. The second is to claim that there is a non-experiential input step, and the third is to deny that there is any a priori knowledge. (I discuss each of these paths, and some of those who walk them, in Jenkins [2008a], section 2.)

Each option involves denying the conjunction of:

(A) there is substantive a priori knowledge of mind-independent truths and

(B) there is no faculty of rational intuition.

Yet each of these two claims has sufficiently widespread and substantial intuitive appeal to keep contemporary philosophers searching for better alternatives to the classic versions of the three classic options. I favor an account according to which there is an empirical input step (see Jenkins 2008b for details).

I think this categorization of views on the a priori in terms of their ways of solving the three-step pattern problem is useful for establishing that a commitment to a priori knowledge raises difficult questions and should not be undertaken lightly. Now, however, I want to describe *another* way of categorizing theories of the a priori, which is in some respects more comprehensive, and also provides a useful way of understanding some of the most significant versions of what I'm calling the conceptual approach, and the relationship between that approach and its rivals. This new categorization is in no sense a competitor to my earlier categorization; it is offered as a complementary way of surveying the field.

Since what I am calling "the conceptual approach" can take many forms, its proponents can (and do) offer many different answers to the key question of how exactly appealing to conceptual truth (or some related notion) is supposed to help us explain the possibility a priori knowledge. I will eventually outline my preferred version of the approach, which allows us to combine a robust mind-independence realism about the subject matter known with a naturalistically motivated epistemological empiricism. As far as I know it is the only extant version which combines these features; other forms of the conceptual approach force us, on reflection, into either anti-realism or some kind of rationalism. That is one reason why an unexamined commitment to a priori knowledge is problematic: the conceptual approach is (as close as we get in philosophy to) an orthodoxy, while it is rather unorthodox to be either a rationalist or an anti-realist about every (putatively) a priori knowable subject matter. There is a tension here that should not be ignored.

With this in mind, let me proceed by locating some of the key philosophical positions with regard to a priori knowledge, including versions of the conceptual approach. I shall do this by means of a series of questions, answers to which distinguish the various parties to the debate from one another. Necessarily, the descriptions of other views in this section will be sketchy; the aim is to give a broad-brush sense of the motivation for a certain version of the conceptual approach, not to do full justice to its many rivals. The flowchart below represents the state of play as described in this section diagrammatically.

First, there is the question of whether or not a priori knowledge is a distinctive epistemological phenomenon at all. Is there something interesting

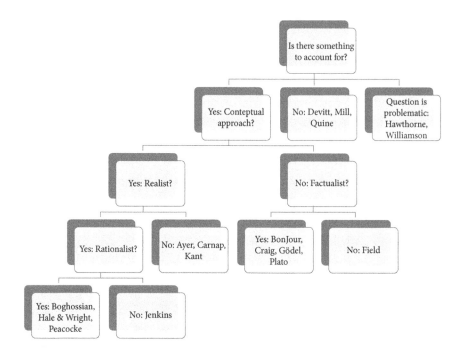

here that we should be trying to account for? Some might say that the question isn't clear enough to answer, or is in other ways problematic. Williamson (2007) and Hawthorne (2007) each argue, in different ways, that there is something suspicious about the very notion of a prioricity. Briefly, Williamson thinks that the notion is "too crude," and Hawthorne doubts whether there is any non-arbitrary way of drawing the distinction between the a priori knowledge and other knowledge. (I discuss and resist these claims in Jenkins [2008a], section 5; I won't rehash my discussion here.)

Those who answer a straightforward "no" to the first question, that of whether there is anything interesting here that we should be trying to explain, include Mill (1843) and Quine (1951). Both of these philosophers argue, in their different ways, that what appear to be cases of a priori knowledge are in fact (extreme) cases of ordinary empirical knowledge. There are also contemporary defenders of this sort of view; Devitt (e.g. 2005) defends the Quinean version extensively.

If it is agreed that a priori knowledge is a distinctive phenomenon, there is the question of whether or not to adopt any version of the conceptual approach. If the answer is no, then we can ask whether or not any form of factualism is correct for claims of a priori knowledge and/or justification: that is, whether there are facts corresponding to acceptable claims of this kind, or whether the acceptability of such claims has some other basis. Field (2000, 2006 and elsewhere) defends a form of non-factualism, at least for basic a priori justification, arguing that claims of (a priori) justification for certain very basic principles are merely expressions of pro-attitude toward these principles. Field here draws on the work of Gibbard (1990), who makes a similar proposal about all epistemically normative talk.

Factualist positions available to those who reject the conceptual approach are various. They include versions of the view that we have direct rational insight into the truth of a priori knowable propositions. Some of the thoughts of Gödel (1947) could be developed in this way: we could posit a priori knowledge of set theory, for instance, via a rational faculty which is "something like a perception" of its objects, without our account appealing to conceptual truth. Contemporary philosophers with views occupying this node of my diagram include BonJour (1998). There are also innatist options (including Plato's view that certain truths are learned through encounters with the Forms prior to birth: see his *Phaedo*). Then there are versions of conventionalism which are not wedded to the conceptual approach (e.g. those which run along the lines suggested in Craig [1975]), and certain positions according to which a priori knowledge is possible without *any* substantive explanation because either it or the propositions known are in some sense trivial (see Jenkins [2008a], section 2 for discussion of how ideas from Lewis and Wittgenstein could be developed in support of such a line.)

For those who favor the conceptual approach, we now ask whether or not mind-independence realism[3] is true for any of the a priori knowable subject matters that are covered by the account. Those who answer "no" here include Carnap (1950), Ayer (1936), and Kant (1781). Those who *do* want to be realists then have to decide whether to be rationalists: that is, whether to accept that some propositions about the independent world can be known in a way which is wholly justificatorily independent of input from the senses. (I take empiricism to be the denial of rationalism: the view that no such proposition can be known without justificatory reliance on the senses). Those who seem to want to answer "yes" to this question include Bealer (e.g. 2000), Boghossian (e.g. 1997), and Peacocke (e.g. 2000). Hale and Wright (see e.g. 2000) also appear to fall into this category.

There is one node left on my diagram. That is the node which I want to occupy. This node represents the view that a priori knowledge is a distinctive phenomenon to be explained by some sort of conceptual approach, that we should be mind-independence realists about (at least some of) the subject matters to be covered by the account, and that rationalism is not true. In what follows I shall try to show that this is an available combination of views, and that it addresses our target question of how appealing to conceptual truth can help us explain a priori knowledge, without committing us to rationalism or anti-realism.[4]

The problem

Two nice, clear presentations of the problem raised by our key question—that of how appealing to conceptual truth or related notions is supposed to help explain a priori knowledge—can be found in the work of BonJour (1998) and, more recently, Field (2006). Chapter 2 of BonJour's (1998) discusses, in particular, *empiricist* theories of the a priori which appeal to various notions of analyticity or conceptual truth. Among the kinds of problems he identifies for such theories are:

1. inadequacies in various of the proffered characterizations of analyticity, conceptual truth, and related notions;
2. inadequacies in the scope of various extant versions of the conceptual approach (i.e. apparent cases of the a priori with which they do not deal); and
3. inadequacies in the explanations (if any are offered at all) of how attributing analyticity or some similar property to a class of a priori knowable propositions is supposed to amount to giving an *account* of how these propositions can be known a priori.

I am focusing on worries of kind 3. The reason is that these worries are general in a way that worries of kinds 1 and 2 are not; skirmishing around the edges of one's theory might rescue versions of the conceptual approach from problems of kinds 1 and 2, but the lack of a good-enough answer to 3 is a serious problem for the whole approach.

As summed up by BonJour (1998, p. 37), the problem is that, even if we are inclined to believe that a priori knowable claims are analytic or conceptually true, "exactly what light is this supposed to shed on the *way* in which such a claim is justified?" If, for example, we say that analytic truths can be known a priori because all that is needed to know them is an understanding of what they mean, we are owed "some articulated account of *how* justification is supposed to result solely from [one's grasp of] meaning" (p. 38).

BonJour argues quite convincingly that what's missing from the versions of the conceptual approach that he considers is an explanation of *why it is epistemically respectable* to hold beliefs just because they are, or seem to be, in some way "integral to," or "the upshot of," or "delivered by," our concepts.

Field (2006, p. 85) presses what I think is essentially this same challenge:

> [W]hy should the fact, if it is one, that certain beliefs or inferences are integral to the meaning of a concept show that these principles are correct? Why should the fact, if it is one, that abandoning those beliefs or inferences would require a change of meaning show that we shouldn't abandon those beliefs or inferences? Maybe the meaning we've attached to these terms is a bad one that is irremediably bound up with error, and truth can only be achieved by abandoning those meanings in favor of different ones (that resemble them in key respects but avoid the irremediable error).

What is to be said in response?

A certain kind of anti-realist could address the challenge by claiming that there *is no way* for meanings or concepts to be "bad" ones that are "irremediably bound up with error." For that to be so, the facts we come to know by examining our concepts would have to be such that those concepts could fail to be decent epistemic guides to it. But, according to the envisaged anti-realist response, the facts we come to know are merely facts *about* our concepts, or at least facts that are determined by how things stand with our concepts. Hence our concepts are *bound* to be decent guides to it.

Rationalists might try to answer that something non-empirical ensures that our concepts are tied to reality in such a way as to be trustworthy guides to how that reality is, rather than "bad" ones. A serious attempt at a rationalist move of this kind is made by Peacocke (2000), who argues in effect that we can trust our concepts as epistemic guides to the world because they are, *by their very natures*, accurate guides. According to Peacocke, for instance, the possession conditions for our concept of conjunction closely reflect the individuation conditions of the conjunction itself. Thus, he claims, possessing the concept *and* puts one in a strong position with respect to knowledge of facts like $A\&B \models A$. Trusting our concepts is a very reliable method of learning the truth. For myself, I fear that for all Peacocke has said, this sort of reliability may not be knowledge-conducive, but rather analogous to the reliability of blindly trusting whatever is written on the subway wall, which luckily for you happens to be a logical truth (see Jenkins [2008b], section 2.5).

One less appealing rationalist answer (not, as far as know, defended by any contemporary philosopher) is that our concepts are linked to the way reality via some non-sensory mechanism of which we have as yet no scientific understanding.

I myself do not find anti-realist or rationalist answers to Field's question appealing. But my aim here has been to indicate that it is fairly clear that answers (of sorts) to that question *are available* if we are prepared to be anti-realists or rationalists. By contrast, it is far from clear what sort of answer, if any, a realist empiricist who favors the conceptual approach might give.

The BonJour/Field challenge is related to the three-step pattern problem insofar as one respectable way to address both challenges is by arguing for an input step (whether empirical or not) for our concept-examining practices, and another is to show that no input step is required in order for concepts to be trustworthy guides to the world. The BonJour/Field challenge is different insofar as it is specific to the conceptual approach, and does not (at least, for all that's been said) need to be addressed by talking about worldly input into the relevant processes of thought.

However, I think my preferred empiricist solution to the three-step pattern problem is also the best response to the BonJour/Field challenge. In the following section, I shall set up the account specifically as a response to the latter challenge.

A solution

I shall be assuming, in describing my version of the conceptual approach, that concepts are sub-propositional mental representations.[5] I shall also assume that we can learn by introspecting at least some of the features of our concepts, and in particular that we can learn how they relate to certain other concepts. For instance, we can learn by introspecting how our concept of *vixen* is related to our concept of *female* (more on the nature of this relationship later). Furthermore, I assume that such conceptual examination is a process which can result in the adoption of certain beliefs, such as the belief that all vixens are female.

I suggest that there are certain conditions on concepts, such that concepts which meet these conditions can and should be trusted as epistemic guides to how the world is. That is to say, I suggest that we will sometimes be able to obtain epistemic grounds sufficient for knowledge through mere conceptual examination, provided the concepts under examination meet the required conditions. The conditions on concepts which I shall discuss are:

1. an accuracy condition: the concepts must be accurate guides to the world and

2. a non-accidentalness condition: the obtaining of 1 must be non-accidental (in a sense analogous to the sense in which knowledge must be non-accidentally true belief).

Concepts which meet those conditions can and should be treated as knowledge-conducive guides to the mind-independent world.[6] We can and should accept the deliverances of an examination of *good* concepts.

The first condition on goodness for concepts is that the concepts in question (or at least the constituent concepts out of which they are built) must *accurately* represent real features of the world, at least in the respects about which we are deriving information from them when we conduct our conceptual examination.[7] Accurate concepts are ones which either stand for something which is really there, or else are built out of concepts which stand for something which is really there.[8] The second condition is that the obtaining of the accuracy condition must be non-accidental, in a sense analogous to the sense in which knowledge must be non-accidentally true belief (see Jenkins [2008b], pp. 59–61 for more on this).

As I am an empiricist, I believe that the way to account for the holding of the relevant accuracy and non-accidentalness conditions is by thinking about how our concepts are epistemologically related to the input we get from the world via our sensory apparatus. I think knowledge through concept examination is possible because, due to our sensory contact with the world, our concepts come to encode trustworthy information about that world, and we can recover this information by examining those concepts.

The idea, then, is that there is an input step into the process of obtaining knowledge through conceptual examination. This input step consists in the impact which sensory contact with the world has upon our concepts. It is what I have elsewhere called the (empirical) *grounding* of the relevant concepts (Jenkins [2008b], chapter 4). As on many versions of the conceptual approach, on the envisaged account there is then a mental processing step, which consists in some kind of examination of our concepts. But now, this examination is not *merely* an examination of ourselves, but rather a way of recovering the information about the world which our concepts have come to encode owing to their sensitivity to sensory input.

Taking a toy example, and speaking rather roughly for the moment, I claim that we can, in some cases, secure a priori knowledge of the proposition *All vixens are female* by noticing that our concept of vixenhood is as of[9] a property that includes[10] the property represented by our concept of femaleness, provided that:

(i) the concepts involved are accurate, in the sense that there are real properties in the world, vixenhood and femaleness, represented by our concepts thereof, and these properties are indeed related in the way suggested by the conceptual examination, and

(ii) the obtaining of (i) is due to the fact that, in forming or selecting those concepts, we were sensitive to our sensory input, and this input guided us to concepts which accurately represent their referents as being related in the way described in (i).

As it stands this is the merest outline. Many different elucidations are possible, and I take this to be one of the appealing features of the research programme which the proposal opens up. But a little more detail on the bare bones given so far will probably help the reader to see what kind of thing I'm after.

Let me first talk a bit about the *accuracy* condition. One might assume at first that this should be the condition that the concepts must be fully accurate representations of real features of the world[11] which are their referents. But in fact what is required is in some ways less and in some ways more than that. It is *less* in two respects. First, I think it is enough if concepts *either* refer themselves *or* are ultimately composed of referring concepts (see Jenkins [2008b], section 4.4). How important this point is will depend on how abundant an ontology one wants to admit.[12] Secondly, some *mis*representation of a concept's referent may be permissible, provided that this does not bear on the accuracy of information being recovered from the concept. So for instance, some versions of the view might have it that a set of geometrical concepts which include some inaccuracy— for example, that would lead us to conclude that all triangles have angles which add up to 180°—can still be safely used as guides to other facts about the world— for example, the fact that all triangles are plane figures with three sides.

What is required is *more* than fully accurate representation of real features of the world in that the way our concepts *relate* to each other must reflect the way that correlating features of the world are related. This was brought out by the vixen example: it is not enough, for the accuracy condition to be met in this case, that our concept *vixen* picks out vixenhood and accurately represents that property, and our concept *female* picks out femaleness and accurately represents that property. The conclusion drawn in this case, that all vixens are female, is driven by the fact that the two concepts are related in a certain way, that is, that the fact the concept *vixen* is a concept as of a property which includes the property represented by our concept *female*. The accuracy condition in this case will therefore also require that the properties represented by these concepts are indeed so related.

Let me now turn to the non-accidentalness condition. In my opinion, the mere accuracy of concepts does not suffice for it to be possible to obtain knowledge by examining them. We might get true beliefs that way, but for knowledge, we need more. Compare: the mere accuracy of Guru's assertions doesn't mean that Gullible can come to know things by listening to Guru. If Gullible has no reason whatever to trust Guru, but does so anyway, then the mere fact that what Guru says is true does not mean that Gullible ends up knowing it. Gullible might get true beliefs that way, but for knowledge, more is needed.[13]

Exactly what more is needed is a matter of debate, and has been since at least Plato's *Meno*. But many—plausibly, all—of the promising stories on offer amount to ways of cashing out the idea that knowledge is *non-accidentally* true belief, in some rather specialized sense of "accidental."[14] If knowledge is indeed non-accidentally true belief, then if our concepts are to count as a source of knowledge, they must be non-accidentally accurate. If they are not, the beliefs we arrive at by examining them will be at best accidentally true.

I believe that our best shot at explaining why our concepts are non-accidentally accurate will have to involve some appeal to the part experience plays in determining which concepts we have and what they are like.[15] There are (at least) two possible avenues to explore here; one is that we acquire concepts in response to sensory input, another is that we have (some of) our concepts innately, and experience determines which ones we keep. (I discuss these options a little in Jenkins [2008b], section 4.5.)

I submit that any knowledge we obtain through the examination of concepts whose pedigree is in this sense empirical will count as empirical knowledge. The mechanisms we are using to secure knowledge of the world, on this type of account, are not purely rational mechanisms like introspection and reflection. It is through the functioning of the senses that our concepts come to encode the information which introspection and reflection enable us to recover. So the senses play a key role in the knowledge-acquisition process, considered in its entirety. Sensory input is not just a precondition of knowledge, but actually *supplies the justification*.

On this view, therefore, to say that knowledge obtained through conceptual examination is non-empirical knowledge is rather like saying that knowledge obtained by observing that p and deducing from p that q is non-empirical knowledge because the *second* step doesn't involve the use of the senses. As with all knowledge of mind-independent subject matters, knowledge obtained through conceptual examination requires an input step, and the input step is empirical.

The accuracy condition and the non-accidentalness condition are conditions which concepts must meet if their examination is to be a way for their possessor to secure a priori knowledge. It is not a further condition that the subject should *know* or *believe* or *have reason to believe* that her concepts are non-accidentally accurate. The proposal is to that extent epistemologically *externalist* in outlook. (For the precise notion of externalism employed here, and discussion, please see Jenkins [2008b], section 2.2.)

The BonJour version of the challenge which motivates this section is that extant empiricist versions of the conceptual approach fail to make clear *how* the status of certain propositions as conceptual truths explains their a priori justification and/ or knowability. The proposal outlined above makes an account of this phenomenon available. Our concepts, because of their sensitivity to experience, have come to encode certain pieces of information about the world. The conceptual truths *are* those pieces of information. That is why those particular truths can be justified and known purely through examination of our conceptual maps.

The Field version of the challenge asks why intimate connections between certain beliefs and certain concepts should be taken to show that those beliefs are true, and raises the concern that our concepts (or, as he puts it in this part of the challenge, the "meanings of our terms") may be "bad" ones that are "irremediably bound up with error." The answer in view is that beliefs that bear the relevant relationship to our concepts are likely to be true because the concepts in question are likely to be non-accidentally accurate (as opposed to "bad"), which in turn is due to the sensitivity of those concepts to experience.

Concluding remarks

Is the account described in the preceding section an account of *a priori* knowledge, properly so called? Obviously, if we define a priori knowledge as knowledge which is non-empirical, that is, justificatorily independent of *all* sense experience, then it is not. But if all that is required for a prioricity is justificatory independence of empirical *evidence* (as many definitions suggest) then it might well be. For the process of securing empirically grounded concepts then recovering information through conceptual examination is sufficiently unlike the process of ordinary empirical evidence-gathering for it to make sense for us to decide not to count it as a form of evidence-gathering.

What we definitely have is an approach which respects the fact that knowledge secured through conceptual examination is independent of all the *familiar* kinds of empirical justification—the fact, that is, that we don't have to do any scientific tests, or look out the window, or check anything other than our concepts, in order to secure this knowledge, and that it could only be undermined if it turned out there was something wrong with our concepts or we had made a mistake in our examination of them. That is why this form of empiricism is significantly different from Mill's or Quine's.

And in fact, it doesn't matter much if we decide that the best use of the terms is one whereby empirical concept grounding counts as empirical "evidence-gathering" and that therefore my account does not rescue "a priori" knowledge properly so called. What is important is that it preserves the idea that the subject matters which have been *called* a priori do indeed have a special epistemological status: they are knowable in a special way, involving conceptual examination, which most things aren't. It is much less important whether we continue to describe that status as "a prioricity." (See Jenkins [2008b], section 9.5 for more on this issue.)

Is it open to a rationalist, especially a rationalist of Peacocke's stripe, to adopt a version of the account proposed in the preceding section? After all, although Peacocke did not impose *non-accidental* accuracy conditions on the concepts we use to secure a priori knowledge (see pp. 187–8 above), he surely *could* have done so. And rationalists in general need not be hostile to the idea that sensory input shapes or filters our concepts, and that this process is important in enabling us to get a priori knowledge. They deny, of course, that such sensory input is used as *evidence* for the propositions so known, but so do I.

What really distinguishes me from a rationalist is that I am willing to count this role that experience plays in securing good concepts as meaning that experience *gives us our justification* for the propositions we know a priori. Although experience is not supplying evidence, it is still supplying justification. Rationalists can allow that experience plays a similar sort of role, but they cannot agree that experience, in playing that role, is *giving us our justification* for the propositions known a priori. To agree to that would be to abandon their rationalism, which says that some propositions about the independent world can be known in a way which is wholly justificatorily independent of input from the senses.[16]

As for Peacocke, it is true that he could have introduced further conditions on the concepts we use to secure a priori knowledge to ensure non-accidental accuracy, rather than merely accuracy. The key question is: what mechanisms could he have appealed to in explaining how we end up with non-accidentally accurate concepts. The account described in the preceding section reaches for sensory input to play this explanatory role: the senses put our concepts in touch with the world, so that it is no accident those concepts end up accurate. But what could Peacocke reach for?

Suppose he too reaches for sensory input. Then he faces the question of why he is not willing to count that input as part of the justification for the a priori knowledge arrived at. (He cannot count it as such, on pain of no longer being a rationalist.) There are certainly things one could say here. Epistemological internalists, for instance, might be unhappy about regarding the sensory input which is responsible for our having good concepts as part of our justification for any proposition because it is not accessible in the right way to the subject. I myself take an externalist approach. But what I'm trying to do here is clarify the lie of the land, and to that end it is important to note that there are close internalist cousins of the proposal of the preceding section which *could* fairly be described as "rationalist."

That said, I do not think that any extant rationalist *has* defended such a proposal. Certain aspects of Peacocke's views are compatible with one, but neither he nor (to my knowledge) any other rationalist has so far taken on the task of making clear how it comes about that our concepts are non-accidentally accurate.

Instead of reaching for sensory input to explain how our concepts are hooked up to the world and hence why it is no accident that they are accurate, Peacocke might reach for some other, non-sensory, mechanism. But this raises the spectre of a "faculty of rational intuition," which haunts rationalisms of a more traditional kind than Peacocke's. It is an option that could be developed by an unrepentantly traditional rationalist, though I doubt whether it would appeal to Peacocke, who describes himself as a "moderate" rationalist precisely because he eschews related elements of traditional rationalism (see, e.g. Peacocke [2000], pp. 261–2).

The role of concepts in the account described in the preceding section is also worth commenting on. According to that account, we acquire a priori knowledge through examination of concepts which are non-accidentally accurate representations of the world. The concepts are useful insofar as they accurately represent reality. So one might wonder whether it is possible to cut out the middleman: why examine concepts which accurately represent reality, when you could be examining reality itself? Instead of saying we examine our concepts of (say) *vixen* and *female*, we could say we acquire a priori knowledge by examining the properties of vixenhood and femaleness.

In a sense, it is my view that examining accurate concepts can *amount* to an examination of reality itself, in the same way that one can examine Scotland by examining a map of it. However, to say merely that would be to miss the point of the question, which is a question about why the proposal needs to involve concepts in the first place. I'm attempting to defend a version of the conceptual approach, so I ought to say something about *why*.

The principal reason for involving concepts is that a priori knowledge seems to be available in the armchair, using only the resources available to one through methods like reflection, introspection, and careful reasoning. The appeal to concepts is supposed to help explain in how, in what sense, and to what extent a priori knowledge is available in the armchair. Concepts are our mental representations—they are things in our minds—and for that reason can be, at least to some degree, examined and learned about in the armchair. It may be that we have to gather all kinds of sensory input in order for those concepts to be reliable as guides to the world, and *that* may not be possible from the armchair, but once the input is in, we carry our concepts around with us like a map of the world, and they are available for examination wherever and wherever.

By contrast, a more direct examination of the things that our concepts are concepts of will not always be possible in the armchair. For instance, I can examine my concept of my brother Nick from the armchair, but unless Nick happens to be in the room with me I can't examine *him* from the armchair. (At least, not directly. I can examine my memories of him, but whatever's going on when we have a priori knowledge seems to be different from any straightforward kind of remembering.)

It might be replied that although I cannot examine Nick directly in any empirical way I can *think* about him and hence learn things about him (e.g. that Nick is self-identical). Indeed, it could well be argued that most people, when they acquire a priori knowledge of (say) *7 + 5 = 12*, are thinking about the numbers and arithmetical relations involved, not about their concepts of those numbers and relations. However, on the view I'm defending, "conceptual examination" can be understood in a fairly lightweight sense, so that it is not in tension with this sort of claim. We can allow that one of the ways — perhaps the most common way—to do "conceptual examination" is not to sit down explicitly to consider one's concepts as such, but merely to think about certain subject matters in a way that is *guided* by the structure of the relevant concepts. So when a child sets out to think hard about whether 7 + 5 is indeed 12, although he does not think of himself as examining his concepts, he is doing so in the relaxed sense that his thoughts are being guided largely or entirely by the nature of the relationships between his concepts of 7, + , 5, = and 12. This kind of unreflective sensitivity to the structure of his conceptual scheme is enough to enable him to recover the information that has been encoded in his concepts through sensory input.

It is an option to deny that concepts playing any significant role here, and propose some other explanation of how the right kind of examination of numbers, people, vixenhood, and so on is possible from the armchair. One reason for being especially interested in a conceptualist view is that it has been so deep-seated a conviction of so many philosophers for so long that concepts and conceptual truth have something crucial to do with a priori knowledge. Another, presumably related to the first, is that it is hard to see what else could be proposed instead. Again, however, with an eye to the lie of the land, it is worth noting that there could be a cousin of my conceptualist proposal which retains some of the key features but is not properly described as a version of the conceptual approach, though I don't know of anyone's having defended such a view to date.[17]

Notes

1 Sensory experience may nonetheless be a *precondition* for possession the relevant justification, as discussed in the Introduction to Kant's *Critique of Pure Reason.*

2 See the introduction to Casullo (2003) for a thorough discussion of positive and negative conditions for a prioricity (of justification).

3 By "realism," I shall mean mind-independence realism as defined in Jenkins (2005).

4   Readers may at this point wonder how I can claim to be an empiricist and to believe in a priori knowledge. The viability of the combination turns on the plausibility of distinguishing between knowledge grounded in empirical *evidence,* which is what a prioricity rules out, and knowledge grounded in empirical *input,* which is what empiricism demands. I return to this point in the section "Concluding Remarks."

5 For other notions of "concept" (such as the view that concepts are bundles of abilities), and their possible relations to a view like the one under development in this paper, see Jenkins (2008b, 260).

6 The idea that our concepts encode information about the *actual* world does not by itself explain how we can secure knowledge of how things *necessarily* are through conceptual examination. In other work (Jenkins [2010]) I argue that such modal knowledge is possible because the structure of the actual world is sufficient as an epistemic guide to the modal facts.

7 Note that this may mean that which concepts count as "good" depends on which conceptual truths we are interested in justifying at the time we are attributing the "goodness."

8 I am inclined to count uninstantiated properties—even necessarily uninstantiated ones—among the things which are "really there." However, many concepts of uninstantiated properties could be counted as accurate by someone who disagreed on this point. For instance, such a person might say that the concept *round square* counts as accurate by virtue of being composed of the instantiated concepts *round* and *square*. Similarly, gruesome concepts might be allowed to count as accurate without out admitting that there is a genuine property of being grue.

9 This "as of" terminology is lifted from the philosophy of perception. I think it is useful here for reasons similar to those which motivate its use in its original context. A concept may be *as of* a property which includes the property of femaleness—that is, may be such that a correctly conducted examination of that concept leads us, in the absence of counterveiling reasons, to believe that it is of a property which includes the property of femaleness—without its actually being *of* such a property. The concept may fail to be of such a property either by failing to have a referent at all, or by referring to a property which does not in fact include the property of femaleness.

10 This talk of property "inclusion" may or may not be best understood as metaphorical. What I require is that there is some substantive metaphysical relation between the properties, the obtaining of which is not the same thing as—though it metaphysically underwrites—the fact that (necessarily) all vixens are female.

11 Which could be properties, objects, or any other kind of thing that exists in the world.

12 See note 8. Unfortunately, I doubt whether the view under discussion will appeal to those who want an ontology *so* sparse that the only concepts which stand for real objects and properties are concepts of microphysical objects and properties. For it isn't very plausible that our concepts of macrophysical objects and properties are composed of concepts of microphysical objects and properties. So most of our concepts will turn out to be inaccurate on such a view, and yet I doubt

whether its advocates will accept what I would take to be a consequence of this: that we cannot know that all tables are artifacts by examining our concepts *table* and *artifact*.

13   If reliabilists are forced to deny this (which the subtler ones are not), so much the worse for reliabilism.

14   Not every kind of accident destroys knowledge; Nozick's glimpse case (1981, 193) establishes that. Exactly which kinds of accident destroy knowledge depends on what the requirements on knowledge are. But various accounts of what the requirements are can be transformed into corresponding accounts of the requirements on good concepts; see Jenkins (2008b, 130–1) for some examples.

15   It is important to note that "experience" here does not mean conceptualized experience; what I'm talking about is the impact of the world upon the brain via the normal functioning of our sensory apparatus.

16   To be more precise, a rationalist could accept the account of the preceding section in its entirety as a story about *some* a priori knowledge without abandoning her rationalism provided she also believed in *other* kinds of a priori knowledge which the account of the preceding section does not cover. What the rationalist cannot do is accept that the account of the preceding section is the correct account of *all* a priori knowledge.

17   I am indebted to Daniel Nolan and J. R. G. Williams for comments and discussions which have considerably improved this chapter.

References

Ayer, A. J. 1936. *Language Truth and Logic.* 1967 edn, London: Gollancz.

Bealer, G. 2000. "A Theory of the A Priori." *Pacific Philosophical Quarterly* 81: 1–30.

Boghossian, P. 1997. "Analyticity." In B. Hale and C. Wright, eds, *Companion to the Philosophy of Language.* Oxford: Blackwell.

BonJour, L. 1998. *In Defence of Pure Reason: A Rationalist Account of A Priori Justification.* Cambridge: Cambridge University Press.

Carnap, R. 1950. "Empiricism, Semantics and Ontology." In *Revue Internationale de Philosophie 4,* pp. 20–40, repr. in H. Feigl, W. Sellars, and K. Lehrer, eds, *New Readings in Philosophical Analysis,* 1972, New York: Appleton-Century-Crofts, pp. 585–96.

Casullo, A. 2003. *A Priori Justification.* Oxford: Oxford University Press.

Craig, E. 1975. "The Problem of Necessary Truth." In S. Blackburn, ed., *Meaning, Reference and Necessity.* Cambridge: Cambridge University Press, pp. 1–31.

Devitt, M. 2005. "There is no *a Priori*." In M. Steup and E. Sosa, eds, *Contemporary Debates in Epistemology.* Oxford: Blackwell, pp. 105–15.

Field, H. 2000. "A Prioricity as an Evaluative Notion." In P. Boghossian and C. Peacocke, eds, *New Essays on the A Priori*. Oxford: Clarendon Press, pp. 117–49.

— 2006. "Recent Debates about the A Priori." In T. Gendler and J. Hawthorne, eds, *Oxford Studies in Epistemology*. Oxford: Oxford University Press, pp. 69–88.

Gibbard, A. 1990. *Wise Choices, Apt Feelings*. Oxford: Clarendon Press.

Godel, K. 1947. "What Is Cantor's Continuum Problem?" In *American Mathematical Monthly 54,* repr. in P. Benacerraf and H. Putnam, eds, *Philosophy of Mathematics,* 1964, Cambridge: Cambridge University Press, pp. 258–73.

Hale, B. and Wright, C. 2000. "Implicit Definition and the A Priori." In P. Boghossian and C. Peacocke, eds, *New Essays on the A Priori*. Oxford: Clarendon Press, pp. 286–319.

Hawthorne, J. (2007). "Externalism and A Priority." In S. Goldberg, ed., *Internalism and Externalism in Semantics and Epistemology*. Oxford: Oxford University Press.

Jenkins, C. S. 2008a. "A Priori Knowledge: Debates and Developments." *Philosophy Compass* 3, 436–50.

— 2008b. "Grounding Concepts: An Empirical Basis for Arithmetical Knowledge." Oxford: Oxford University Press.

— (2010). "Concepts, Experience and Modal Knowledge." *Philosophical Perspectives* 24(1) 255–79.

Kant, I. 1781. *Critique of Pure Reason.* 1929 edn, trans. N. Kemp Smith. Basingstoke: Palgrave.

Mill, J. S. 1843. *A System of Logic.* London: Parker.

Peacocke, C. 2000. "Explaining the A Priori: The Programme of Moderate Rationalism." In P. Boghossian and C. Peacocke, eds, *New Essays on the A Priori*. Oxford: Clarendon Press, pp. 255–85.

Nozick, R. 1981. *Philosophical Explanations*. Oxford: Clarendon Press.

Quine, W. V. O. 1951. "Two Dogmas of Empiricism." In *Philosophical Review,* repr. in his *From a Logical Point of View: Nine Logico-Philosophical Essays,* 1953, edn of 1980, Cambridge, MA: Harvard University Press, pp. 20–46.

Williamson, T. 2007. *The Philosophy of Philosophy*. Oxford: Blackwell.

11

Contextualism and Interest-Relative Invariantism

E. J. Coffman

This chapter surveys the current debate between prominent proponents of **Contextualism** and **Interest-Relative Invariantism (IRI)**.[1] Both camps reject:

Classical Invariantism (CI): The truth value of a given knowledge-ascribing (-denying) sentence is (**a**) *invariant* across conversational contexts and (**b**) *independent* of how important it is to the subject (S) that the relevant proposition (P) be true.

Proponents of IRI (**IRIs**) accept (a) but deny (b), claiming that the truth-value of a knowledge-ascribing sentence (**knowledge-ascription**) depends on how important it is to S that P be true. Contextualists accept (b) but deny (a), claiming that some knowledge-ascriptions have different truth-values relative to different contexts.

In the section "Three Arguments for the Contextualism/IRI Disjunction," I explain three main arguments against CI and for the **Contextualism/IRI Disjunction.** In "Contextualism," I further explain Contextualism and discuss an additional argument for it; I then survey some main objections to Contextualism from prominent IRIs. In "Interest-Relative Invariantism," I further explain IRI and discuss an additional argument for it; I then survey some objections pointing back in Contextualism's direction. In "Conclusion: Tentative Verdicts about Two Important Issues," I conclude by offering tentative answers to two important questions about the Contextualism/IRI debate:

If we've good reason to believe the Contextualism/IRI Disjunction, which view should we prefer?

Do the main anti-CI arguments provide good reason to believe the Contextualism/IRI Disjunction?

Three arguments for the Contextualism/IRI Disjunction

Let's begin with the **Original Argument** against CI, which stems from a pair of cases like these:[2]

> *Low:* Ann and Bob drive past the bank Friday afternoon. Ann mentions that their paychecks needn't be deposited before the middle of next week. Seeing that the bank is busy, Bob suggests they return to deposit their checks in the morning. Ann reminds Bob that some banks are closed on Saturday, then asks: "Do you know the bank will be open tomorrow?" Having visited the bank a week ago last Saturday, Bob believes truly that the bank will be open tomorrow. So Bob answers affirmatively: "Yes, I know the bank will be open tomorrow. I was there a week ago last Saturday."

> *High:* Ann and Bob drive past the bank Friday afternoon. Ann mentions that their paychecks must be deposited before Monday morning. Seeing that the bank is busy, Bob suggests they return to deposit their checks in the morning. Ann reminds Bob that banks sometimes change their hours, then asks: "Do you know the bank will be open tomorrow?" Having visited the bank a week ago last Saturday, Bob believes truly that the bank will be open tomorrow. Yet Bob answers negatively: "Well, no, I don't know the bank will be open tomorrow. I'll go in and make sure."

From here, the Original Argument runs as follows:

> **P1.** Low and High differ only with respect to what's important to Ann and Bob.

> **P2.** In Low, Bob expresses a truth by uttering "I know the bank will be open tomorrow."

> **P3.** In High, Bob expresses a truth by uttering "I don't know the bank will be open tomorrow."

> **C.** "Bob knows the bank will be open tomorrow" has different truth-values across contexts differing only with respect to **practical facts** (i.e. facts about what's important to people in the contexts).

P1 follows from the details of the cases. Two related kinds of evidence support P2 and P3.[3] First, they just seem true. When we consider Low, it seems Bob speaks truly when uttering his knowledge-ascription. And when we consider High, it seems Bob speaks truly when uttering his ignorance-ascription.

Moreover, we can infer P2 and P3 from different, and even stronger, linguistic intuitions. When we consider Low, it seems Bob *asserts properly* when uttering his knowledge-ascription. And when we consider High, it seems Bob asserts properly when uttering his ignorance-ascription. Further, we can understand each case so that Bob holds no false beliefs relevant to his assertion's truth-value.[4] The following principle can now kick in:

> The fact that you asserted P properly, absent relevant false beliefs, is good evidence that your assertion was true.

The driving thought here is that we typically speak truly when we assert properly in the absence of relevant false beliefs.[5] Thus, we can infer P2 and P3 from our intuitions that Bob's assertions are both proper *and* made in the absence of false beliefs relevant to their truth-value.

Anyone endorsing the Original Argument must deny CI. CI holds two implications for knowledge-ascriptions like "Bob knows the bank will be open tomorrow": (i) practical facts are irrelevant to its content and (ii) its content doesn't vary across contexts. So, given CI, "Bob knows the bank will be open tomorrow" expresses the same proposition no matter the context, and the truth of that proposition has nothing to do with practical facts. Because Low and High differ only with respect to practical facts, CI implies there's no difference between the cases that could result in the relevant proposition's[6] having different truth-values across the cases.[7]

Our second anti-CI argument is the **Argument from Variable Assertability Conditions**.[8] Consider variants of Low and High—**Low*** and **High***—identical with their counterparts up to the last line, which is replaced with this:

> So Bob answers affirmatively: "Yes, the bank will be open tomorrow."

The argument now runs as follows:

P1. Whether Bob is positioned to make a conversationally proper assertion of the bank proposition (i.e. [The bank will be open tomorrow][9]) in a given context depends on the practical facts obtaining in that context.

P2. Bob is positioned to make a conversationally proper assertion of the bank proposition in a given context iff "Bob knows the bank will be open tomorrow" is true in that context.

C. Whether "Bob knows the bank will be open tomorrow" is true in a given context depends on the practical facts obtaining in that context (and so, CI is false).

On P1's behalf, DeRose writes (2002: 187–8; cf. 2009: 107):

It is difficult to deny that the matter of how well positioned one must be with respect to a matter to be able to assert it varies with context: What one can flat-out assert in some "easy" contexts can be put forward in only a hedged manner ("I think . . .," "I believe . . .," "Probably . . .," etc.) when more stringent standards hold sway.

DeRose would regard Low* and High* as illustrating P1's truth. Bob's assertion in Low* is conversationally appropriate. But in High*, Bob's assertion is conversationally improper, for it conveys to Ann the falsehood that Bob has different and stronger evidence for the bank proposition than he actually has. Taken together, then, Low* and High* justify P1. On P2's behalf, DeRose cites Williamson's (1996, 2000) influential work on the relation between assertion and knowledge.[10]

Our third and final argument against CI is like unto the second in that it employs cases like Low* and High*. Brown (2008, 2010) formulates this argument in recent work, dubbing it the **Sufficiency Argument**:[11]

P1. If "Bob knows the bank will be open tomorrow" is true in a given context, then there's nothing epistemically wrong with Bob's asserting the bank proposition in that context.

P2. In Low*, "Bob knows the bank will be open tomorrow" is true.

P3. In High*, there's something epistemically wrong with Bob's asserting the bank proposition.

P4. In High*, "Bob knows the bank will be open tomorrow" isn't true. (1, 3)

P5. "Bob knows the bank will be open tomorrow" has different truth-values across Low* and High*. (2, 4)

P6. Low* and High* differ only with respect to practical facts.

C. "Bob knows the bank will be open tomorrow" has different truth-values across contexts differing only with respect to practical facts (and so, CI is false). (5, 6)

P1 is an instance of this prima facie plausible principle: "[I]f one knows that P, then there is nothing epistemically wrong with asserting that P" (Brown 2008, p. 90).[12] Few will seriously consider denying P2; for its denial conflicts with **knowledge fallibilism,** the (nearly) universally accepted view that "someone can know that P, even though their evidence for P is *logically consistent* with the truth of not-P" (Stanley 2005b, p. 127). Turning finally to P3, given that Ann has just reminded Bob how important it is that their checks be deposited before Monday morning, Bob's assertion that the bank will be open tomorrow seems improper. And the impropriety seems due to Bob's grounds for believing the bank proposition: if (e.g.) Bob had earlier today verified the bank proposition via a call to the manager on duty, his assertion would have been (at least closer to) appropriate. So Bob's assertion seems wrong, and for epistemic reasons: there's something epistemically wrong with Bob's assertion in High*.

We now have before us three main arguments against CI and for the Contextualism/IRI Disjunction. In the following section, I'll clarify how Contextualism stands to benefit from those arguments. Then, after explaining an additional argument for Contextualism, I'll discuss some important objections to Contextualism from prominent IRIs.

Contextualism

Exposition

Abstracting from the details of the many specific Contextualist proposals in the literature, the following claims capture the general Contextualist position:

> A variety of "person-involving" facts obtaining in a given context determine which propositions knowledge- (ignorance-) ascriptions express in that context.

Such facts include **practical facts** (i.e. facts about what's important to people in the context) and **salience facts** (i.e. facts about which possible mistakes are salient to people in the context). So the content of a knowledge-ascription can vary across contexts differing only with respect to such person-involving facts. Low and High feature a difference of practical and salience facts yielding a difference in the content of "know" across those contexts.[13]

> The indicated person-involving facts *do not* help determine the truth-values of propositions expressed by knowledge- (ignorance-) ascriptions in context.

The truth-value of the proposition a given knowledge-ascription expresses is fixed completely by "truth-relevant" factors.[14] This traditionally popular view about the kinds of factors that determine the truth-values of propositions expressed by knowledge-ascriptions is often called **Intellectualism** or **Purism**.[15] Recalling Low and High, the typical Contextualist will hold that Bob bears one and the same epistemic relation, call it **ER,** to the bank proposition in these cases. In Low, Bob's bearing ER to the bank proposition suffices for his bearing to that proposition the relation "know" expresses in that context—call this relation **K1.** In High, by contrast, Bob's bearing ER to the bank proposition *doesn't* suffice for his bearing to that proposition the stronger relation, call it **K2,** expressed by "know" in that different ("tougher") context.

We can now see how Contextualists will explain the thesis implied by each of our three anti-CI arguments—viz., that a given knowledge-ascription can have different truth-values relative to contexts differing only with respect to practical facts. This happens because a context's practical and salience facts help determine which proposition a given knowledge-ascription expresses in that context.

An additional pro-contextualist argument

Many Contextualists find support for their position in common reactions to arguments like this **Radical Skeptical Argument (RSA):**[16]

> **P1.** You don't know you're not a handless brain-in-a-vat (**BIV**).
>
> **P2.** If you don't know you're not a handless BIV, then you don't know you have hands.
>
> **C.** You don't know you have hands.

Reflection on common reactions to RSA reveals two data that arguably lend support to Contextualism:

> At least when considering RSA, P1 and P2 seem true.
> RSA's conclusion persistently seems false.

The Contextualist explanation of these data starts with the idea that the relation "know" expresses in contexts where RSA is under consideration—call it **R1**—is stronger than the relation "know" expresses in more ordinary contexts—call it **R2.** Contextualists can claim that **R1** is so strong that we bear it to only a handful of propositions (if any). So, in special, philosophical contexts where RSA is considered, P1 expresses a truth. Further, since (something like) "knowledge is closed under known entailment" is true in *every* context, P2 also expresses a truth. By contrast, R2 is weak enough so that we bear it to numerous "ordinary empirical" propositions (e.g. There are hands). So, in contexts where RSA isn't under consideration—which for most folks will be most of their contexts—RSA's ignorance-ascribing conclusion expresses a falsehood. Finally, even in contexts where RSA is being considered, we remain aware of the fact that RSA's conclusion typically expresses a falsehood.

Contextualism thus enables a promising explanation of the data revealed by reflection on our reactions to RSA-like arguments. Arguably, though, whatever support Contextualism derives from these data depends on arguments like those explained in the section "Three Arguments for the Contextualism/IRI Disjunction."[17] For if "know" never shifted meaning across different ordinary contexts but only across ordinary and philosophical contexts, we wouldn't be so reluctant to accept RSA's conclusion. Contextualists explain this reluctance by appealing to our awareness that such sentences express falsehoods in ordinary contexts. This presupposes we think the meaning "know" has in RSA's conclusion is similar to its meaning in ordinary contexts. But we wouldn't assimilate those contents *if* "know" only shifted meaning across ordinary and philosophical contexts. If *that* were the only semantic shift "know" allowed, Contextualism would be more obvious to us and we wouldn't be so hesitant to accept RSA's conclusion.

Arguably, then, whatever support Contextualism derives from the relevant data depends on arguments like those explained in the section "Three Arguments for the Contextualism/IRI Disjunction"—which, as we've seen, imply that "know" can shift meaning across different ordinary contexts. With this result in hand, Contextualists can then bolster their position by showing how it enables a promising explanation of our reactions to RSA-like arguments.

Let's now consider some influential objections to Contextualism pressed by prominent IRIs.

IRI-motivating objections

Stanley's Dilemma

Here's a summary of our first anti-Contextualist argument, developed by Stanley (2005a, pp. 62–8):

> Distinct occurrences of the same context-sensitive term can have different interpretations within a discourse. We should therefore expect distinct occurrences of the instances of "know that P" to allow for the possibility of distinct interpretations within a discourse. But this opens the contextualist up to a number of objections that she does not otherwise face.

I'll use the following discourse, **Knowledge Downshift (DS),** to reconstruct **Stanley's Dilemma** for Contextualism:[18]

> **A:** Since I can't rule out that animal's being a painted mule, I don't know it's a zebra.

> **B:** Can't rule out its being a painted mule?! We're at the San Diego Zoo, for crying out loud! What's more, today's their annual external review day. They wouldn't even consider putting a mule in the zebra pen on an average day, much less on external review day.

> **A:** You're right—they'd never consider that on an average day, much less today.

> **B:** See, you knew it's a zebra.

> **A:** I didn't know it's a zebra a moment ago, but I do now.

Stanley's Dilemma can be formulated as follows:

> **P1.** *Either* the Contextualist allows that different instances of "know" can express different relations within a discourse *or* he denies this.

> **P2.** If the Contextualist allows this, then he must predict (counterintuitively) that KD's last line could express a truth.

> **P3.** If the Contextualist denies this, then he must hold that "know" has "very different properties from familiar context-sensitive constructions" (Stanley 2005a, p. 72).

> **C.** *Either* the Contextualist predicts (counterintuitively) that KD's last line could be true *or* he holds that "know" is a sui generis context-sensitive term.

On P3's behalf, Stanley (2005a, p. 60) cites a variety of context-sensitive constructions—for example, demonstratives, quantified noun phrases, and context-sensitive determiners—whose instances can have different interpretations within a discourse. We can easily imagine scenarios where sentences like the following are both natural and true:

> That is larger than that.
> Every sailor waved to every sailor.
> There are many serial killers in Atlanta, but not many unemployed men.

So, if the Contextualist denies that different instances of "know" can have different interpretations within a discourse, he'll have to regard "know" as a sui generis context-sensitive term.

This is a formidable anti-Contextualist argument. Fortunately for Contextualists, however, they have a plausible reply available.[19] To begin, P2 is false as it stands. The only claim Contextualists need in order to argue for the persistent falsity of KD's last line is that "our uses of "know(s)"—and its past tense—are governed by the epistemic standards that are in place at the time of a speaker's utterance. . ." (DeRose 2009, p. 206). A utters KD's last line in a relatively "easy" context. Accordingly, its instances of "know" express a relation that A bears to [The animal is a zebra] throughout the exchange. So when A utters "I didn't know it's a zebra a moment ago," A speaks falsely. Contextualists can thus explain the persistent falsity of KD's last line with no more than the claim that what determines the content of an instance of "know" are the epistemic standards in place at the time of utterance. But because different standards can come to govern "know" across an exchange—indeed, this happens in KD—the claim Contextualists need leaves it open that instances of "know" can have different interpretations within a discourse.

Now Stanley's Dilemma can be repaired as follows:

P1´. *Either* the Contextualist allows that different instances of "know" can express different relations within a single clause *or* he denies this.

P2´. If the Contextualist allows that different instances of "know" can express different relations within a single clause, then he must predict (counterintuitively) that KD's last line could express a truth.

To preserve validity, P3 must become

P3´. If the Contextualist denies that different instances of "know" can express different relations within a single clause, then he must hold that "know" has "very different properties from familiar context-sensitive constructions."

This revised argument looks promising. Note, in particular, that the same examples Stanley invokes on P3's behalf also support P3´. Different instances of demonstratives, context-sensitive determiners, and quantified noun phrases can have different interpretations *within a single clause.* If this is true of context-sensitive expressions in general, then Contextualists will after all have to reckon "know" a sui generis context-sensitive term.

But there's a plausible defense available to Contextualists here too. The problem is P3´. Various familiar context-sensitive terms seem as incapable as "know" does of having instances with different interpretations within a single clause.[20] Consider the following exchange, **Possibility Downshift (PD),** involving the clearly context-sensitive term "possible":[21]

A: Since it wasn't possible to fly from New York to London in less than two hours, I had to decline his lunch invitation.

B: Impossible to fly from New York to London in less than two hours?! For a long time now there's been technology that can make that trip in less than *one hour*.

A: Right—in fact, there's technology that can make the trip in 30 minutes.

B: See, it was possible to make the trip in less than two hours.

A: Making the trip that quickly wasn't possible a moment ago, but it is now.

PD's last line seems as persistently false as KD's last line. It seems, then, that the different occurrences of "possible" in PD's last line must get the same interpretation. Contrary to P3', then, denying that different instances of "know" can get different interpretations within a single clause doesn't commit Contextualists to reckoning "know" a sui generis context-sensitive term. With care, Contextualists can successfully defuse Stanley's Dilemma.

Hawthorne's Dilemma

Hawthorne (2004, §2.7) presents the following anti-Contextualist argument, which we'll call **Hawthorne's Dilemma:**

P1. Contextualism entails this is possible: S sincerely asserts "I (= S) know that P," where "S knows that P" is true in S's ("easy") context but false in the Contextualist's ("tough") context.

P2. Competent speakers "take sincere uses of the verb "know" as a straightforward guide to the contents of what people believe" (2004, p. 100).[22]

P3. *Either* the Contextualist sanctions competent speakers' relevant practice *or* she doesn't.

P4. If the Contextualist sanctions that practice, then she's committed to the possibility that a knowledge-ascription be both true and false in a single context.

We can reconstruct Hawthorne's (2004, pp. 101–2) somewhat complex argument for P4 as follows. Suppose the Contextualist sanctions the relevant practice. Then, focusing on the possibility P1 identifies, the Contextualist will judge that S's true utterance of "I (= S) know that P" expresses S's true belief that S knows P. Since the Contextualist thinks S holds a *true* belief that S knows P, she'll think "S knows P" is true in her (i.e. the Contextualist's) context.

But by stipulation, "S knows P" is *false* in the Contextualist's context. So the Contextualist is committed to the possibility that a knowledge-ascription be both true and false in a single context.

> **P5.** If the Contextualist doesn't sanction the relevant practice, then she's committed to competent speakers' being "blind to the semantic working of their language"—in particular, to the view that "[w]hile those speakers are, at least implicitly, well aware of the context-dependence of [e.g.] 'tall' the same is not true for 'know'" (2004, p. 108).

> **C.** *Either* the Contextualist thinks knowledge-ascriptions can be both true and false in a single context *or* she posits "semantic blindness" among competent speakers regarding "know."

Since typical Contextualists deny that a knowledge-ascription could be both true and false in single context, what Hawthorne's Dilemma reveals is that Contextualists must reckon competent speakers confused about the semantics of "know." By Hawthorne's lights, this puts Contextualism at a significant disadvantage to invariantist accounts of "know."[23]

I'll delay assessment of Hawthorne's Dilemma until later ("Contextualism-Motivating Objections").[24] For certain considerations discussed below—ones Contextualists can deploy against IRI—double as an objection to Hawthorne's Dilemma.

Hawthorne's Arguments Concerning Assertion and Practical Reasoning

In §2.4 of his 2004, Hawthorne argues that Contextualism can't honor certain "intuitive connections between knowledge, assertion, and practical reasoning" (85). The following passages together summarize the connections Hawthorne has in mind, along with the problem they allegedly create for Contextualists:

> The practice of assertion is constituted by the rule/requirement that one assert something only if one knows it. Thus if someone asserts P, it is proper to criticize that person if she does not know that P. (23)

> [W]e operate with a conception of deliberation according to which, if the question whether P is practically relevant, it is acceptable to use the premise that P in one's deliberations if one knows it and (at least in very many cases) unacceptable to use the premise that P in one's practical reasoning if one doesn't know it. (30)

> It is natural . . . to think that there is some deep association between facts about knowledge and facts concerning the propriety of assertion and practical

reasoning. What I want to draw attention to here is that, owing to the purported ascriber-dependence of "know," contextualism seems to disconnect facts about knowledge from these normative facts. And this is because the relevant normative facts do *not* seem to be ascriber-dependent. (86)

I'll first explain Hawthorne's argument that Contextualism can't honor an alleged connection between knowledge and assertion. I'll then identify a plausible defense available to Contextualists. Finally, I'll lay out Hawthorne's argument that Contextualism can't preserve an alleged connection between knowledge and practical reasoning, and transition from there into a discussion of IRI. The transition is natural, for (as we'll see) the alleged connection between knowledge and practical reasoning is a main source of support for IRI. I'll delay evaluation of Hawthorne's argument concerning knowledge and practical reasoning until later ("Conclusion").

We begin with Hawthorne's (2004, pp. 86–7) Argument from the Knowledge-Assertion Connection:

> **P1.** Contextualists countenance contexts where these odd-sounding sentences are true:
>
> (5) There are things people know but ought not to assert because their epistemic position is not strong enough with respect to those things.
>
> (6) People [sometimes] flat-out assert things that they do not know to be true but are not thereby subject to criticism [on epistemic grounds].[25]
>
> **P2.** Countenancing such contexts implausibly divorces knowledge from proper assertion.
>
> **C.** Contextualists implausibly divorce knowledge from proper assertion.

To see that P1 is true, recall Low˙ and High˙. The Contextualist claims that, in Low˙, "know" expresses a relation that Bob bears to the bank proposition in both Low˙ *and* High˙. But she'll also claim that, in High˙, there's something epistemically wrong with Bob's asserting the bank proposition. These two claims jointly imply that the following sentence—an instance of the more general (5) above—expresses a truth in Low˙:

> (5˙) In High˙, Bob knows the bank proposition but shouldn't assert it because his epistemic position is too weak.

Moreover, the Contextualist claims that, in High˙, "know" expresses a relation Bob doesn't bear to the bank proposition in either Low˙ *or* High˙. But she'll also claim that, in Low˙, there's nothing epistemically wrong with Bob's asserting the bank proposition. These two claims imply that the following sentence—an instance of the more general (6) above—expresses a truth in High˙:

> (6˙) In Low˙, Bob doesn't know the bank proposition but isn't thereby subject to criticism on epistemic grounds for asserting it.

This case for P1 seems solid. Are the prospects for rejecting P2 any better?

DeRose (2009, pp. 244–51) rejects P2 by showing how Contextualists can explain whatever oddity attaches to the above (by Contextualists' lights) possibly true sentences via the following principle positing a significant connection between knowledge and proper assertion:

> **The Relativized Knowledge Account of Assertion (KAA-R):** A speaker, S, is well enough positioned with respect to P to be able to properly assert that P if and only if S knows that P *according to the standards for knowledge that are in place as S makes her assertion.*[26] (2009, p. 99)

How will KAA-R help Contextualists explain the above sentences' oddity? In brief, such sentences can sound odd because they ascribe incompatible properties to similar relations expressible by "know"—viz., the relation "know" expresses in the context where it's uttered *versus* the relation "know" expresses in the context where the evaluated assertion is made—*without* carefully distinguishing between the different relations in play. The result is that such sentences can sound like contradictions even when they're true. A speaker in Low˙ who wants to clearly express the fact (5˙) only problematically expresses should utter the following:

> In High˙, Bob knows the bank proposition by our current "easy" standards, but shouldn't assert it because his epistemic position relative to it is too weak for him to know it by the "tough" standards governing his context.

And a speaker in High˙ who wants to clearly express the fact (6˙) only problematically expresses should utter the following:

> In Low˙, Bob doesn't know the bank proposition by our current "tough" standards, but there's nothing epistemically wrong with his assertion since he knows the bank proposition by the "easy" standards governing his context.

Endorsing KAA-R thus allows Contextualists to explain why the above sentences can sound odd even if true, all the while maintaining a significant connection between knowledge and proper assertion. This casts doubt on P2 of Hawthorne's Argument from the Knowledge-Assertion Connection.

We turn now to Hawthorne's (2004, pp. 87–91) **Argument from the Knowledge-Practical Reasoning Connection,** and how the considerations it employs point away from Contextualism and toward IRI:

P1. Contextualists countenance contexts where these odd-sounding sentences are true:

(7) People sometimes use things they don't know in their practical reasoning but aren't thereby subject to criticism on epistemic grounds.

(8) There are things people know but shouldn't use in their practical reasoning because their epistemic position relative to those things isn't strong enough.[27]

P2. Countenancing such contexts implausibly divorces knowledge from proper practical reasoning.

C. Contextualists implausibly divorce knowledge from proper practical reasoning.

To see that P1 is true, notice that Contextualists allow that a speaker in High˙ could truly utter this sentence:

(7˙) In Low˙, Bob doesn't know the bank proposition, but he wouldn't be subject to criticism on epistemic grounds for acting on it.

And Contextualists allow that a speaker in Low˙ could truly utter this sentence:

(8˙) In High˙, Bob knows the bank proposition, but shouldn't act on it because his epistemic position is too weak.

As will soon become clear, Hawthorne's worry that Contextualism effects an implausible divorce of knowledge from proper practical reasoning yields an anti-Contextualist reaction to our three arguments against CI ("Three Arguments for the Contextualism/IRI Disjunction"). This reaction—**Interest-Relative Invariantism**—now constitutes Contextualism's main competitor.

Interest-Relative Invariantism

Exposition

The following claims capture the general position taken by IRIs:

The practical facts obtaining in a context help determine the truth-values of propositions expressed by knowledge- (ignorance-) ascriptions in the context.

IRIs maintain that whether a subject, S, knows a proposition, P, depends not only on "truth-relevant" factors but also on how important it is to S that P be true—on how much is at stake for S relative to the question whether P is true, on how much S has riding on P's truth. According to IRIs, S knows that P iff S "meets whatever epistemic standard is relevant to [S's] current practical situation" (DeRose 2009, p. 259). IRI thus implies the following:

> The meaning of "knows" is invariant across contexts (at a time); accordingly, practical facts *do not* help determine which propositions are expressed by knowledge- (ignorance-) ascriptions in context.

Recalling Low and High, Bob bears mutually excluding epistemic relations to the bank proposition across these cases. Let's pause to ensure we clearly see the fundamental disagreement between IRIs and Contextualists on this point.

Contextualism, recall, implies that Bob bears one and the same epistemic relation to the bank proposition across Low and High. According to Contextualists, what differs across the cases is how the one epistemic relation Bob bears to the bank proposition relates to "know." In Low, that relation is strong enough for "know" to apply to it. In High, by contrast, that same relation is too weak for "know" to apply to it. The word "know" expresses a stronger epistemic relation in High than it does in Low.

IRIs tell a different, conflicting story. "S knows that P" has one and the same meaning across Low and High—roughly, *S meets the epistemic standard relevant to S's practical situation with respect to P.* In Low, Bob meets the epistemic standard relevant to his practical situation regarding the bank proposition, and so Bob knows the bank proposition. In High, by contrast, Bob falls short of the epistemic standard relevant to his practical situation regarding the bank proposition, and so he doesn't know the bank proposition. Bob knows the bank proposition in Low but not in High. Here, then, is how IRIs explain the thesis implied by our three anti-CI arguments—viz., that a knowledge-ascription can have different truth-values relative to contexts differing only with respect to practical facts. This happens, IRIs explain, because knowledge itself depends on *practical facts* along with various traditionally popular "truth-relevant" factors (e.g. evidence and reliability).

In addition to the above anti-CI arguments, there are arguments for IRI that threaten to give it a leg up on Contextualism. Here, I'll discuss an influential argument developed by Fantl and McGrath (2002, 2007, 2009a), two prominent long-time proponents of IRI.[28]

An additional pro-IRI argument

Say that S's epistemic position relative to P is as strong as S'''s iff S bears precisely the same truth-relevant (e.g. evidential, reliability, etc.) relations to P as S' does. The **Fantl–McGrath Argument** for IRI goes like this:[29]

> **P1.** If you know P, then you're rational to act as if P.
>
> **P2.** For some P, you know P *but* there's a possible scenario where your epistemic position relative to P is just as strong as it actually is yet you aren't rational to act as if P.
>
> **C.** For some P, you know P *but* there's a possible scenario where your epistemic position relative to P is just as strong as it actually is yet you don't know P.

That's to say: there can be a difference in whether you know *without* a difference in truth-relevant factors. Whether you know P also depends on practical facts, on how important it is to you that P be true.

Fantl and McGrath (2007, pp. 561, 564) offer the following justification for P1:[30]

> We often defend actions by citing knowledge. For example, I might say to my spouse, in defending my driving straight home without stopping off to get yams the night before Thanksgiving, "I know we have them at home." In citing my knowledge, I am trying to convince my spouse that I am rational to act as if we have yams at home—that is, head home rather than stop off and buy some. [. . .] We also criticize actions in an analogous fashion. [. . .] The fact that knowledge-citations play the role they do in defending and criticizing actions is evidence that [P1] is true. Consider again the yams example. When I defend my choice to drive home without stopping to buy yams, I cite my knowledge that we have yams at home as a reason for thinking my act is rational. And presumably, if I do know, my knowing is a *good* reason for thinking my act is rational. But how could the fact that I know that we have yams at home be a good reason for thinking my not stopping at the grocer's is rational? The two claims seem unrelated. [P1] seems required to provide the needed link: "I know we have yams, and so I am rational to act as if we do, and so am rational to just drive home and not stop by the grocer's." [. . .] The truth of [P1] thus seems to be required if in defending and criticizing actions our knowledge-citations can provide good reasons for our judgments about actions.

Low and High can be employed to support P2. In Low, Bob knows the bank proposition. In High, Bob's epistemic position relative to the bank proposition is (by stipulation) exactly as strong as it is in Low. Intuitively, though, while Bob is, in Low, rational to act as if the bank proposition is true (e.g. go on home), in High Bob *isn't* rational to act as if the bank proposition is true.

Once again, it'll be best to delay evaluation of this argument until later ("Conclusion"). It's now time to consider some prominent criticisms of IRI that point back in Contextualism's direction.

Contextualism-motivating objections

Our first objection to IRI comes from DeRose (2004, 2009), and doubles as an objection to Hawthorne's Dilemma for Contextualism (section "Hawthorne's Dilemma").[31] DeRose (2004, pp. 347–8) presents a case that's arguably a counterexample to both IRI *and* P2 of Hawthorne's Dilemma:

> Thelma is talking with the police about whether it might have been John who committed some horrible crime . . . Thelma is admitting that she does not "know" various propositions if she is not in an *extremely* strong epistemic position with respect to them. Thus, even though Thelma has grounds that would usually suffice for claiming to "know" that John was at the office on the day in question (she heard from a very reliable source that he was in, and she herself saw his hat in the hall), she is in her present context admitting that she does "not know" that he was in . . . [. . .]

> [IRI] falls into trouble when we consider how speakers in such a "high standards" context will use third-person attributions (or denials) of knowledge to describe whether other subjects not present at the conversation "know" various propositions. In many such contexts, speakers will apply to such far-away subjects the same high standards that they are applying to themselves. [. . .] Thus, for instance, if the police ask Thelma whether Louise, who is not present, but whom they are considering questioning, might know whether John was in, and Thelma knows Louise is in the same position that she's in with respect to the matter (she too heard the report and saw the hat, but did not herself see John), Thelma will say that Louise too does "not know" that John was in . . .

> Note that Thelma will deny that Louise "knows" even if Thelma knows that Louise happens to be in a "low-standards" conversational context. Suppose Louise is at the local tavern, a place renowned for the low epistemic standards that govern conversations that take place there, and that Louise is discussing the matter of where John was . . . in a light-hearted effort to decide who has to pay up on a mere $2 bet on whether the often-absent John had been to the office more

than five times in the last two weeks. Thus, in Louise's context, having heard a reliable report of John's presence and having seen his hat in the hall is more than enough to claim to "know" he was present on the day in question, and Louise has indeed claimed to "know" on just that basis. And suppose that Thelma is somehow aware of all this about Louise's context. Still, in Thelma's "high-standards context," if Thelma is counting herself as a non-knower, then, when she is considering Louise as a potential informant, she will likewise describe Louise as a non-knower, regardless of Louise's conversational context.

Here's how this case threatens both IRI *and* P2 of Hawthorne's Dilemma. First, because Louise doesn't have much riding on the issue whether John was at work,[32] IRI implies that "Louise knows John was at work" is true in *every* conversational context. But that sentence seems *false* relative to Thelma's context—that is, Thelma's ignorance-ascription regarding Louise seems true.

Moreover, the case defends Contextualism from P2 of Hawthorne's Dilemma:[33]

> **P2.** Competent speakers "take sincere uses of the verb "know" as a straightforward guide to the contents of what people believe" (Hawthorne 2004, p. 100).

Suppose the police tell Thelma that Louise has (at the "low-standards" tavern) sincerely claimed to know John was at work. P2 implies that Thelma will now believe and assert what's expressed in *her* context by "Louise thinks she knows John was at work." But it's far from obvious that Thelma will believe or assert the indicated proposition; indeed, it seems clear Thelma *won't* so believe or assert. Careful reflection on such cases thus yields evidence against IRI as well as P2 of Hawthorne's Dilemma.

A second prominent objection to IRI highlights certain apparently false counterfactuals and conjunctions that IRIs must judge true.[34] Suppose High obtains, but that Low would've obtained had it not been so important to Ann and Bob that their checks be deposited before Monday morning. Given this assumption, IRI entails that this sentence is true:

> (S1) Bob would know the bank will be open tomorrow if it weren't so important to him that his check be deposited before Monday morning.

IRI also entails that the following sentence could be truly uttered by one of Bob's peers who (**a**) has exactly the same evidence for the bank proposition as Bob but (**b**) has nothing at all riding on that proposition:

> (S2) Bob's evidence for the bank proposition is just as strong as mine; but while my evidence positions me to know the bank will be open, Bob's doesn't.

(S1) and (S2) seem persistently false. But supposing High obtains and that Low would've obtained if High hadn't, IRI implies that the above sentences express truths. Contextualists can claim this consequence constitutes a significant strike against IRI.[35]

How big a problem for IRIs is this? Regarding IRI's commitment (under the relevant assumption) to the truth of (S1), Stanley (2005a, pp. 113–14) argues that such an implication isn't a *special* problem for IRI. According to Stanley, any view on which each relation expressed by "know" involves a reliability component—which includes most of the main contemporary approaches to knowledge, invariantist and contextualist alike—implies that there are true readings of sentences just as bad as (S1):

> If one is innocently traveling through Carl Ginet's fake barn country, where there are as many barn facades erected to trick the unwary as there are genuine barns, one's visual experience of a barn façade is not enough to know that one is seeing a barn, even when one is seeing a barn. Reliabilism captures this intuition, because, in Ginet's fake barn country, perception is not a reliable method. Nevertheless, we cannot say, of a person in fake barn country who is looking at a genuine barn:
>
> (5) Poor Bill. He doesn't know that it is a barn. But if there were fewer fake barns around then he would know that is a barn.
>
> We do not take the fact that reliabilism entails the truth of (5) and similar apparently false counterfactuals to show that reliabilism is false. So it would be excessively hasty to take counterfactuals such as [(S1)] as demonstrating the falsity of IRI.

This attempted defense of IRI fails miserably (cf. Blome-Tillman 2009, pp. 320–1). For starters, the targeted reliability-invoking views simply don't entail (5). Recall Stanley's stipulation that, in the case being considered, "there are as many barn facades erected to trick the unwary as there are genuine barns." So the proportion of fake barns is at least 0.5. Supposing the proportion of fake barns is still fairly large (albeit less than 0.5) in cases close to the one under consideration, the targeted reliability-invoking views will entail *the denial of* (5). Granted, those views *do* imply

> (5') Poor Bill. He doesn't know that it is a barn. But if there were no fake barns around then he would know that is a barn.

But (5') seems both natural and true (cf. Blome-Tillman 2009, p. 321). So Stanley can't repair his attempted defense of IRI by replacing (5) with (5').

Finally, on IRI's commitment (under the relevant assumption) to the truth of (S2), it's worth noting that IRIs can't simply reply that the (S2)-based objection "begs the question." For such a reply runs the risk of committing IRIs to the general dialectical impropriety of reductio argumentation. To get anything like the envisaged defense off the ground, IRI's proponent would have to supplement the charge of question-begging with an argument clarifying he's not committing himself to the general impropriety of reductio argumentation. Since it's hard to see how such an argument could go, it's doubtful IRIs can defend themselves from the (S2)-based objection via a charge of question-begging.[36]

Conclusion: Tentative Verdicts about Two Important Issues

It's time to wrap up our (admittedly, but necessarily, selective and incomplete) survey of the Contextualism/IRI debate. I'll do so by offering tentative answers to two important questions:

> *If* we've good reason to believe the Contextualism/IRI Disjunction, which view should we prefer?
>
> Do the main anti-CI arguments provide good reason to believe the Contextualism/ IRI Disjunction?

We'll start with the second question, and an answer to the first will emerge as we proceed.

I believe the main anti-CI arguments *don't* provide good reason to accept the Contextualism/IRI Disjunction. The Argument from Variable Assertability Conditions (**AVAC**) and the Sufficiency Argument (**SA**) can be discussed together. Recall the following premises:

> **AVAC-P2.** Bob is positioned to make a conversationally proper assertion of the bank proposition in a given context iff "Bob knows that the bank will be open tomorrow" is true in that context.
>
> **SA-P1.** If "Bob knows the bank will be open tomorrow" is true in a given context, then there's nothing epistemically wrong with Bob's asserting the bank proposition in that context.

There are apparent counterexamples in the literature to SA-P1 as well as both directions of AVAC-P2. To begin, here's a putative counterexample to the left-to-right direction of AVAC-P2 presented by Lackey (2007, pp. 598–9; cf. Douven 2006, p. 461):

Distraught Doctor: Sebastian is an extremely well-respected pediatrician and researcher who has done extensive work studying childhood vaccines. He recognizes and appreciates that all of the scientific evidence shows that there is absolutely no connection between vaccines and autism. However, shortly after his apparently normal 18-month-old daughter received one of her vaccines, her behavior became increasingly withdrawn and she was soon diagnosed with autism. . . [T]he grief and exhaustion brought on by his daughter's recent diagnosis cause him to abandon his previously deeply-held beliefs regarding vaccines. Today, while performing a well-baby checkup on one of his patients, the child's parents ask him about the legitimacy of the rumors surrounding vaccines and autism. Recognizing . . . that he has an obligation to his patients to present what is most likely to be true, Sebastian asserts, "There is no connection between vaccines and autism." In spite of this, at the time of this assertion, it would not be correct to say that Sebastian himself believes or knows this proposition.

According to Lackey (2007, p. 600), such cases' moral is that

> *it is a mistake to require proper assertion to pass through the doxastic states of the asserter . . .* [In such cases], even though the person in question may be subject to criticism *qua believer,* she is nonetheless subject to praise *qua asserter.*

Distraught Doctor suggests that, even if you don't know P, you may nevertheless be positioned to make a conversationally proper assertion that P—and so, casts doubt on the left-to-right direction of AVAC-P2.[37] Distraught Doctor also impugns a key thought behind Hawthorne's anti-Contextualist Argument from the Knowledge-Practical Reasoning Connection (section "Hawthorne's Arguments Concerning Assertion and Practical Reasoning")[38]—viz., that you're not rational to act as if P *unless* you know P. Sebastian seems rational to act as if there's no connection between vaccines and autism (e.g. assert there's no connection), notwithstanding the fact that he presently fails to believe—and so, to know—there's no connection.

As for both SA-P1 and the right-to-left direction of AVAC-P2, consider the following exchange—**Affair**—described by Brown (2008b, pp. 176–7):[39]

> A husband is berating his friend for not telling him that his wife has been having an affair even though the friend has known of the affair for weeks.
>
> **Husband:** Why didn't you say she was having an affair? You've known for weeks.
>
> **Friend:** Ok, I admit I knew, but it wouldn't have been right for me to say anything before I was absolutely sure. I knew the damage it would cause to your marriage.

Brown (2008b, p. 177) offers this commentary on Affair:

> [T]he friend admits knowing but claims that it would have been inappropriate
> for him to act on that knowledge by telling the husband. Of course, there are a
> variety of non-epistemic reasons why a friend in this situation might not reveal
> the affair... We will stipulate that none of these factors apply to the case in hand.
> Nonetheless, the friend's statement seems perfectly intelligible and plausible: he
> is saying that although he knew of the affair his epistemic position wasn't strong
> enough to act on that knowledge. He needed to be absolutely certain before
> proceeding to inform the husband.

Cases like Affair suggest that, even if you know P, your asserting P might
nevertheless be conversationally improper for epistemic reasons—and so,
cast doubt on both SA-P1 and the right-to-left direction of AVAC-P2. We can
understand Affair so that Friend's making the relevant assertion to Husband
would convey the (misleading relative to conversational purposes) falsehood
that Friend is "absolutely sure" Husband's wife is having an affair. Affair also
impugns a key thought behind Hawthorne's anti-Contextualist Argument from
the Knowledge-Practical Reasoning Connection—viz., that you're rational to act
as if P *provided that* you know P. As Friend makes clear, it wouldn't have been
rational for him to act as if Husband's wife is having an affair (e.g. assert as much),
notwithstanding the fact that he's known the wife is having an affair. Since the
indicated thought also plays a key role in the Fantl–McGrath Argument for IRI
(section "Contextualism-motivating objections")—indeed, it's the argument's
lead premise—Affair impugns that argument as well.[40]

To sum up, cases like Distraught Doctor and Affair pose serious threats to

DeRose's Argument from Variable Assertability Conditions,

Hawthorne's Argument from the Knowledge-Practical Reasoning Connection,
and

the Fantl–McGrath Argument.

Having finally critically assessed those last two arguments, I think we're now
positioned to tentatively answer the first of our two important questions above:
If we've good reason to believe the Contextualism/IRI Disjunction, we should be
Contextualists.[41]

What remains is the Original Argument against CI. I'll close by arguing we
lack good reason to believe

P3. In High, Bob expresses a truth by uttering "I don't know the bank will be
open tomorrow."

Start by considering a version of High where Bob (i) doesn't preface his ignorance-ascription with a discourse marker like "well"[42] *and* (ii) makes his assertion "flat-footedly"—specifically, with no special stress whatsoever on "know." When High is so constructed, I lack a sense that Bob's assertion is true or even proper.[43] Honestly, I'd be surprised if, upon considering this "unembellished" version of High, many people had a strong sense that Bob's assertion is true and/or proper. That High won't engender such senses when unembellished is, I speculate, at least part of the reason why DeRose's most prominent formulations of such cases (1992, 2009) include "well" before Bob utters his ignorance-ascription.

So, provided that Bob's ignorance-ascription isn't embellished with (i) a discourse marker like "well" *and* (ii) at least a bit of stress on "know," we'll lack good reason to believe P3. But *even if* High is so embellished, we'll *still* lack good reason to believe P3. To begin to see this, note that C follows from P1-P3 only if we understand P3 as follows:

> Bob's *literal* utterance of "I don't know the bank will be open tomorrow" expresses a truth.[44]

Crucially, though, once we embellish Bob's ignorance-ascription with a relevant discourse marker and some stress on "know," it's at best unclear whether the senses of truth and/or propriety it engenders support (the required reading of) P3. That's because the relevant discourse marker and stress together constitute reason to think Bob's utterance is *non-literal.*[45]

When "well" is used as a discourse marker, it can perform two complementary functions (cf. Swan 2005, pp. 143–5): "to soften something which might upset other people" and/or "to say that the hearer's expectations were not fulfilled." So, in prefacing his ignorance-ascription with "well," Bob signals that something unexpected and/or upsetting to Ann is upcoming. What might that be, given Bob's suggestion—made in light of Ann's reminder about the stakes—that they wait till tomorrow to deposit their checks? The obvious candidate for unexpected/upsetting fact is that Bob lacks the "better-than-usual" evidence Ann would clearly like him to have for thinking the bank will be open tomorrow. The presence of "well" is thus some reason to think Bob is using the ignorance-ascription non-literally, to say that he lacks the indicated kind of evidence. Moreover, it's well known that special stress or intonation can be used to indicate that an utterance is non-literal.[46] The required stress on "know" in the embellished version of High thus confirms what "well" already signaled: Bob is using the ignorance-ascription non-literally, to say that he lacks the better-than-usual evidence Ann would clearly like him to have for thinking the bank will be open tomorrow.[47]

I submit, then, that the required (to engender strong senses of truth and/or propriety) discourse marker "well" and stress on "know" constitute reason to think Bob's utterance of the ignorance-ascription in High is non-literal. But if Bob's utterance is non-literal, then P3 is false. On balance, then, we lack good reason to think P3 true. Regardless of whether High is embellished in the indicated ways, careful reflection on Bob's ignorance-ascription doesn't provide firm support for P3. Since such reflection is what's supposed to support P3, we should conclude that the Original Argument falters at that step.

Notes

1   The view here called "Interest-Relative Invariantism" (following Stanley 2005a) also goes under the labels "Subject-Sensitive Invariantism" and "Pragmatic Encroachment."

2   For important anti-CI discussions employing such cases, see (e.g.) Cohen (1999); DeRose (1992, 2009); and Stanley (2005a).

3   What follows in the main text summarizes an argument for P2 and P3 that DeRose defends in chapter 3 of his 2009, which updates his 2005. Writes DeRose (2009, 49–50): "The contextualist argument based on such pairs of cases [as Low and High] ultimately rests on the key premises that the positive attribution of knowledge in [Low] is true, and that the denial of knowledge in [High] is true. Why think that both of these claims are true? Well, first, and most directly, where the contextualist's cases are well chosen, those are the fairly strong intuitions about the cases, at least where each case is considered individually. [. . .] To reinforce these intuitions, the contextualist can appeal to the facts that his cases display how speakers in fact, and with propriety, use the claims in question."

4   We can assume, e.g., that Bob isn't mistaken about the strength of his confidence in, or his evidence concerning, the bank's Saturday hours.

5   Writes DeRose (2009, 50–1): "[G]enerally (though there are some exceptions), one cannot properly claim something that from one's own point of view (given one's beliefs about the underlying matters of fact relevant to the claims in question) is false. So, since the contextualist's cases do not involve speakers who are involved in some mistaken belief about a relevant underlying matter of fact, there is good reason to think that their claims, which are made with perfect propriety, are true. . ."

6   That is, the proposition "Bob knows the bank will be open tomorrow" expresses in every context.

7   Skeptical CIs (e.g. Unger 1975) will say that the relevant proposition is false in both contexts. Non-skeptical CIs (e.g. Brown 2005, 2006; Williamson 2005a, 2005b) will say the proposition is true in both contexts.

8   See chapter 3 of DeRose (2009), which updates DeRose (2002).

9   Here and elsewhere, "[P]" is shorthand for "the proposition that P."

10 DeRose reads chapter 9 of Williamson (2000) (which updates Williamson 1996) as developing the standard cumulative case for P2. There, Williamson collects and discusses the following three data (drawing on Moore 1962; Slote 1979; and Unger 1975):

    (1)   You can challenge an assertion by asking a question like: "How do you know?"
    (2)   Your evidence never positions you to make a lottery assertion (e.g. "I won't win the lottery").
    (3)   You can't properly assert a proposition of the form [P and I don't know P].

    On the basis of these data, Williamson argues that "[t]o have the (epistemic) authority to assert P is to know P" (2000, 252). As I said, DeRose understands Williamson as here endorsing P2 of the Argument from Variable Assertability Conditions. But this interpretation of Williamson isn't obviously correct. For good discussion of relevant issues—including a strong argument that DeRose has misinterpreted Williamson—see Brown (2005). For additional criticism of the Argument from Variable Assertability Conditions, see Coffman (2011a).

11 Notably, Brown (2008, 2010) rejects the Sufficiency Argument after formulating it. For a reformulation and defense of the Sufficiency Argument, see Coffman (2011b).

12 Explicit advocates of such principles include Timothy Williamson (2000), Keith DeRose (2002), and Steven Reynolds (2002). Williamson may be better known as a proponent of the view that there's something epistemically wrong with your asserting P *unless* you know P. But see his (2000, 241, 252), where he says that (**a**) "If an assertion satisfies the [C rule, which soon becomes the thesis that epistemically correct assertion requires knowledge], whatever derivative norms it violates, it is correct in a salient sense" and (**b**) "To have the (epistemic) authority to assert *p* is to know *p*."

13 Just to be clear, the focus in this debate is the semantic behavior of "know(s)" in "S knows that P" and similar constructions.

14 For example, the strength of the subject's evidence for the relevant proposition, the subject's reliability on the proposition's subject matter, which cognitive faculties gave rise to the subject's belief, how well those faculties are functioning, and so on.

15 Stanley (2005a, 6) credits Earl Conee with "Intellectualism." Fantl and McGrath (2007, 558) coined "Purism."

16 For influential presentations of such arguments for Contextualism, see Cohen (1988), DeRose (1995), and Lewis (1996).

17 Cf. Brown (2006), DeRose (1999, 2002).

18 KD is modeled on discourses discussed by DeRose (1992, 2000, 2009), Stanley (2005a), and Yourgrau (1983).

19 See chapters 5 and 6 of DeRose (2009), especially sections 5.6 and 6.9–10.

20 Cf. DeRose (2009, 171–4, 206–12).

21 PD is modeled on exchanges discussed by (among others) Hawthorne (2004) and Stanley (2005a).

22 Writes Hawthorne (2004, 100–1): "[I]f Jones says 'I know I have feet' and I reckon that he is being sincere, I will have no hesitation at all in reporting the contents of his mind [by uttering this sentence:] 'Jones believes that he knows that he has feet.'" Hawthorne (2004, 106) notes that competent speakers are not at all tempted by parallel claims about clearly context-sensitive terms like "tall" and "ready."

23 Hawthorne writes (2004, 109): "Obviously, we do not wish to posit semantic blindness when we don't have to. Other things being equal, a semantic theory that didn't claim semantic blindness on the part of competent speakers would be a better theory."

24 Except to note in passing the following simple but (I think) compelling defense of Contextualism offered by DeRose (2009, 159–60): ". . . I suppose there must be something to the charge that if contextualism is true, we suffer from some degree of 'semantic blindness': Speakers are to some extent blind to the context-sensitivity of 'know(s)'. But this is not a consideration that favors invariantism over contextualism, for speakers seem about equally afflicted by semantic blindness whether contextualism or invariantism is correct. [. . .] Look, when [High] and [Low] are constructed right, whether [the knowledge ascription in High] contradicts [the ignorance ascription in Low] is just a tough question, about which there is no intuitively clear answer. So there *simply is* a good deal of 'semantic blindness' afflicting speakers here, whichever answer is correct."

25 I'm following Hawthorne's numbering here.

26 Notably, P2 of the Argument from Variable Assertability Conditions against CI ("Three Arguments for the Contextualism/IRI Disjunction") is an instance of the more general KAA-R.

27 As before, I'm following Hawthorne's numbering.

28 For a different and equally interesting argument for IRI, see Fantl and McGrath (2009b).

29 I'm here focusing on the version of the argument Fantl and McGrath develop and defend in their (2007).

30 For an additional subargument for P1 (which Fantl and McGrath label "KA"), see their (2007, 564–8).

31   Recall that we earlier saved assessment of Hawthorne's Dilemma for this section.

32   Plus other assumptions we can safely make about the case—e.g., John was indeed at work on the relevant day, Louise believes John was at work on the basis of relevant grounds, Louise isn't "gettiered."

33   Cf. DeRose (2009, 161–6).

34   See, e.g., Blome-Tillman (2009), DeRose (2007), and Stanley (2005a).

35   For other apparently persistently false sentences that IRI countenances true readings of, see Blome-Tillman (2009). While it may go without saying, it's worth explicitly noting that, unlike IRI, Contextualism doesn't entail that (S1) and (S2) are true under the relevant assumption. Contextualists can hold that, in High, "know" expresses a relatively strong epistemic relation that Bob and his peer don't bear to the bank proposition in either High *or* Low. On this view, (S1) and (S2) both come out false.

36   Cf. Blome-Tillman (2009, 330).

37   But won't Sebastian's assertion convey to his audience the falsehood that he believes (knows) there's no connection between vaccines and autism? Perhaps so; but, as Lackey correctly points out (2007, 617), this doesn't (all by itself) entail that Sebastian's assertion is conversationally improper. What *would* make Sebastian's assertion conversationally improper is a false implicature that's misleading relative to the purpose of the conversation in which the assertion is made. The purpose of the conversation in Distraught Doctor is for Sebastian's audience to form the right belief as to whether there's a connection between vaccines and autism. His audience's mistakenly thinking Sebastian currently believes there's no relevant connection clearly doesn't frustrate their forming the right belief as to whether such a connection exists—indeed, it will help achieve that aim.

38   Recall that we earlier saved assessment of Hawthorne's argument for this section.

39   For relevantly similar cases, see Brown (2010), Levin (2008), and Lackey (2011).

40   Recall that we earlier saved assessment of this argument for this section.

41   For a prominent dissenting voice, see chapter 6 of Stanley (2005a).

42   Discourse markers are "words and expressions . . . used to show how discourse is constructed. They can show the connection between what a speaker is saying and what has already been said or what is going to be said; they can help to make clear the structure of what is being said; they can indicate what speakers think about what they are saying or what others have said" (Swan 2005, 138).

43   That's not to say I have a strong sense, when considering such a version of High, that Bob's ignorance-ascription is improper or false. I don't have strong such senses. I *do* often have a weak sense, when considering such a version of High, that Bob's ignorance-ascription is at least somewhat improper (it can seem "too strong" to me).

44 If P2 and P3 aren't about *literal* utterances of the relevant sentence-tokens, we won't be justified in drawing a conclusion about the semantics of the relevant sentence-types in that context.

45 That is, doing something other than expressing the sentence-type's content in that context.

46 Cf. DeRose (2009, 15–16). DeRose himself provides the following nice example (15): "The situation seemed hopeless. Mary *knew* that she wasn't going to survive. Fortunately, she was wrong: The rescue party found her just in time."

47 Cf. Brown (2005, 2006) and Rysiew (2001, 2005, 2007).

References

Blome-Tillman, M. 2009. "Contextualism, Subject-Sensitive Invariantism, and the Interaction of 'Knowledge'-Ascriptions with Modal and Temporal Operators." *Philosophy and Phenomenological Research* 79: 315–31.

Brown, J. 2005. "Adapt or Die: The Death of Invariantism?" *Philosophical Quarterly* 55: 263–85.

— 2006. "Contextualism and Warranted Assertability Manoeuvres." *Philosophical Studies* 130: 407–35.

— 2008a. "The Knowledge Norm for Assertion." *Philosophical Issues* 18: 89–103.

— 2008b. "Subject-Sensitive Invariantism and the Knowledge Norn for Practical Reasoning." *Nous* 42: 167–89.

— (2010). "Knowledge and Assertion." *Philosophy and Phenomenological Research* 81(3): 549–66.

Coffman, E. J. 2011a. "Two Claims about Epistemic Propriety." *Synthese* 181: 471–88.

— 2011b. "Does Knowledge Secure Warrant to Assert?" *Philosophical Studies* 154: 285–300.

Cohen, S. 1988. "How to be a Fallibilist." *Philosophical Perspectives* 2: 91–123.

— 1999. "Contextualism, Skepticism, and the Structure of Reasons." *Philosophical Perspectives* 13: 57–89.

DeRose, K. 1992. "Contextualism and Knowledge Attributions." *Philosophy and Phenomenological Research* 52: 913–29.

— 1995. "Solving the Skeptical Problem." *Philosophical Review* 104(1): 1–52.

— 1999. "Contextualism: An Explanation and Defense." In J. Greco and E. Sosa, eds, *The Blackwell Guide to Epistemology*. Malden, MA: Blackwell Publishers, pp. 187–205.

— 2000. "Now You Know It, Now You Don't." In *Proceedings of the Twentieth World Congress of Philosophy, v: Epistemology*. Bowling Green, OH: Philosophy Documentation Center, pp. 91–106.

— 2002. "Assertion, Knowledge, and Context." *Philosophical Review* 111: 167–203.

— 2004. "The Problem with Subject-Sensitive Invariantism." *Philosophy and Phenomenological Research* 68: 346–50.

— 2005. "The Ordinary Language Basis for Contextualism and the New Invariantism." *Philosophical Quarterly* 55: 172–98.

— 2007. "Review of Stanley (2005a)." *Mind* 116: 486–9.

— 2009. *The Case for Contextualism*. Oxford: Oxford University Press.

Douven, I. 2006. "Assertion, Knowledge, and Rational Credibility." *Philosophical Review* 115: 449–85.

Fantl, J. and McGrath, M. 2002. "Evidence, Pragmatics, and Justification." *Philosophical Review* 111: 67–94.

— 2007. "On Pragmatic Encroachment in Epistemology." *Philosophy and Phenomenological Research* 75: 558–89.

— 2009a. *Knowledge in an Uncertain World*. Oxford: Oxford University Press.

— 2009b. "Advice for Fallibilists: Put Knowledge to Work." *Philosophical Studies* 142: 55–66.

Hawthorne, J. 2004. *Knowledge and Lotteries*. Oxford: Oxford University Press.

Lackey, J. 2007. "Norms of Assertion." *Nous* 41: 594–626.

— 2011. "Assertion and Isolated Secondhand Knowledge." In J. Brown and H. Cappelen, eds, *Assertion: New Philosophical Essays*. Oxford: Oxford University Press, pp. 251–75.

Levin, J. 2008. "Assertion, Practical Reason, and Pragmatic Theories of Knowledge." *Philosophy and Phenomenological Research* 76(2): 359–84.

Lewis, D. 1996. "Elusive Knowledge." *Australasian Journal of Philosophy* 74: 549–67.

Moore, G. E. 1962. *Commonplace Book 1919–1953*. Bristol: Thoemmes Press.

Reynolds, S. 2002. "Testimony, Knowledge, and Epistemic Goals." *Philosophical Studies* 110: 139–61.

Rysiew, P. 2001. "The Context–Sensitivity of Knowledge Attributions." *Nous* 35: 477–514.

— 2005. "Contesting Contextualism." *Grazer Philosophische Studien* 69: 51–69.

— 2007. "Speaking of Knowing." *Nous* 41: 627–62.

Slote, M. 1979. "Assertion and Belief." In J. Dancy, ed., *Papers on Language and Logic*. Keele: Keele University Library.

Stanley, J. 2005a. *Knowledge and Practical Interests*. Oxford: Oxford University Press.

— 2005b. "Fallibilism and Concessive Knowledge Attributions." *Analysis* 65: 126–31.

Swan, M. 2005. *Practical English Usage*. Oxford: Oxford University Press.

Unger, P. 1975. *Ignorance: A Case for Skepticism*. Oxford: Oxford University Press.

Williamson, T. 1996. "Knowing and Asserting." *Philosophical Review* 105: 489–523.

— 2000. *Knowledge and Its Limits*. Oxford: Oxford University Press.

— 2005a. "Contextualism, Subject-Sensitive Invariantism, and Knowledge of Knowledge." *Philosophical Quarterly* 55: 213–35.

— 2005b. "Knowledge, Context, and the Agent's Point of View." In G. Preyer and G. Peter, eds, *Contextualism in Philosophy: Knowledge, Meaning, and Truth*. Oxford: Oxford University Press.

Yourgrau, P. 1983. "Knowledge and Relevant Alternatives." *Synthese* 55: 175–90.

12

Formal Epistemology

Gregory Wheeler

Dedicated in memory of Horacio Arló-Costa

Narrowly construed, formal epistemology is a methodological approach to traditional analytic epistemology. According to this view, the aim of formal epistemology is to harness the power of formal methods to bring rigor and clarity to traditional philosophical concerns.

Yet, in broader terms, formal epistemology is not merely a methodological tool for epistemologists, but a discipline in its own right. On this programmatic view, formal epistemology is an interdisciplinary research program that includes work by philosophers, mathematicians, computer scientists, statisticians, psychologists, operations researchers, and economists which aims to give mathematical and sometimes computational representations of, along with sound strategies for reasoning about, knowledge, belief, judgment and decision making.

This essay presents a two-pronged argument for viewing formal epistemology in programmatic terms. The first part addresses the general question of why anyone should bother with formal methods by illustrating, through a historical example, the role that formal models can play in inquiry. The second part describes two specific examples of recent work within formal epistemology, one that addresses a longstanding issue within traditional epistemology—namely, what to make of coherentist justification—and another addressing a fallacy of probabilistic reasoning which has implications across a wide range of disciplines, thereby making a case for a broader, programmatic view. Finally, we close with a methodological proposal for epistemology that incorporates formal, experimental, and traditional approaches into one.

Why be formal?

When you fiddle with the controls of your computer to select a color, either by typing a triplet of numbers to specify how much red, green, and blue to include, or by selecting a point within a color wheel, you are making use of a model that dates back to 1802. It was that year, in a London lecture hall, that Thomas Young first speculated that human color perception involves three different receptors in the eye, and a half-century later Hermann Helmholtz, that nineteenth century colossus, reckoned that each receptor was sensitive to three distinct frequencies of light, corresponding roughly to our perceptions of red, green, and blue (Helmholtz 1860). Helmholtz went on to propose a mathematical model whereby a good portion of the visible color spectrum can be represented by an additive mixture of those three basic frequencies. Although it took another century to confirm the physiological claims behind the Young-Helmholtz's theory of color vision, in that span of time the RBG additive color model spurred the development of color photography, halftone color printing, and color television, among other things.

The story of the RBG color model offers an allegory for how to think about formal models. For the story illustrates the impact a formal model can have on inquiry, and it also highlights how to assess the merits of a formal model. But one may reasonable ask whether the analogy holds for epistemology. There is, after all, plenty of epistemology that is not informed by formal methods, and plenty of epistemologists seem determined to keep it that way. Giants have made their mark with little more than commonsense and a smidgeon of logic. Why, they ask, bother being so formal?

The best short answer is one given years ago by Rich Thomason.[1] Thomason, commenting on philosophers who view formal methods as a distraction to real philosophical advancement, observed that the only real advantage that we have over the great philosophers of the past are the new methods that we have at our disposal. Probability. First-order logic. Calculus. The number zero. It is hard to imagine improving on Aristotle without resorting to methods that were simply unavailable to him. Knowing just this much about history, a better question is this: why limit your options?

To begin a longer answer, return to the Young-Helmholtz theory and notice three important stages in its development. First, there was Young's idea that people with normal color perception rely on three receptors in their eyes. This was a great insight, but there was neither a model nor much empirical evidence for it, so the idea languished for 50 years. At that time common wisdom held that those three receptors would surely be sensitive to red, *yellow,* and blue, since Newton's color wheel designated those three as the primary colors, and painters for centuries had mixed their paints from red, yellow, and blue bases. But intuition and tradition notwithstanding, Young's insight went nowhere until Helmholtz came along. His ingenious contribution was to run experiments in which subjects were instructed to match the color of a swatch to a color of their choice, which they selected by mixing three wavelengths of light. He also observed that the subjects could not make a match with only two of those three basic light sources. Helmholtz's experiments contributed important empirical evidence for the trichromatic account, mainly by offering grounds for replacing yellow with green, but it was his introduction of a *mathematical model* to represent visible color as an additive mixture of three basic colors that really set things in motion. Helmholtz's mathematical model marked the beginning of the second stage of the theory, one which unleashed a number of innovations. James Maxwell introduced the first trichromatic color photograph within a decade of Helmholtz's work. Halftone printing presses came along soon after. Color television and color motion pictures followed several decades later. And yet, all of these developments occurred well before the last stage, when the physiological mechanism that underpins the Young-Helmholtz trichromatic theory of color vision was finally confirmed.

What is striking about this schematic history of the Young-Helmholtz theory of color vision is not simply the outsized impact of the RGB color model had on the theory and on other developments far afield, but the timing and sequence of events. I wish to draw out two of those features and consider what lessons they hold for epistemology.

Experimental evidence is important but far from sufficient

Some philosophers have attacked a practice within traditional analytic epistemology of justifying normative claims by appeals to intuition—a methodology that Weinberg, Nichols, and Stich have dubbed 'Intuition Driven Romanticism (Weinberg *et. al.* 2001). For these critics, the first part of the Young-Hemlhotz history will resonate, for Young's insight was stalled because people at that time were mislead by their intuitions about the three basic 'colors' necessary for the trichromatic theory. It was Helmholtz's experiments that set the program on the right track by identifying the correct set of frequency ranges to base the theory on.

Even so, the second half of this history complicates matters for advocates of experimental philosophy. For although Helmholtz's experiments were crucial for pointing to the right set of basic 'colors', the experimental evidence was far from conclusive for establishing the central physiological thesis about the photoreceptors in the human eye. The role these initial experiments played was to shift the focus from an unworkable RYB model to a *plausible* RGB additive color model, not to nail down the RGB model before any other progress could be made.

But look closely at Weinberg, Nichols, and Stich's attack on traditional analytic epistemology and you will see, oddly enough, a refashioning of a longstanding criticism of experimental psychology over *convenience sampling* (Carlson 1971, Sears 1986, Henrich *et. al.* 2010). The problem with convenience sampling in social psychological research in particular is the problem of basing general conclusions about human nature on results garnered from studies of undergraduate psychology students, subjects who are overwhelmingly WEIRD (Henrich *et. al.* 2010): that is, members of Western, Educated, Industrialized, Rich, and Democratic societies. In a comparative review of the literature, Henrich, Heine, and Norenzayan found that WEIRD people are often the *least* representative populations in studies of visual perception, fairness, cooperation, spatial reasoning, categorization and inferential induction, moral reasoning, reasoning styles, self-concepts, and the heritability of IQ. They remark that

> there are no obvious *a priori* grounds for claiming that a particular behavioral phenomenon is universal based on sampling from a single subpopulation. Overall, these empirical patterns suggest that we need to be less cavalier in addressing questions of *human* nature on the basis of data drawn from this particularly thin, and rather unusual, slice of humanity (Henrich et. al. 2010, p. 61).

So, while the knock against traditional analytic epistemology is that experimental evidence of differences in epistemic intuitions among different groups undermines claims that epistemic intuitions are universal (Weinberg et. al. 2001), the knock against experimental psychology is that differences between the subpopulation used for the lion's share of studies and the general population undermines 'species-level' generalizations (Henrich et. al. 2010).

Weinberg, Nichols and Stich would have us believe that different epistemic intuitions about Gettier cases (Gettier 1963) they have observed among students from East Asian or the Indian sub-continent, on the one hand, and WEIRD people on the other, undermines the appeal to epistemic intuitions to justify universal philosophical claims. (NB: It is unclear what they make of dual process theories within cognitive and social psychology,[2] which distinguish between intuitive and deliberative judgments and are susceptible to an analogous WEIRD critique of Henrich *et. al.* Criticism of the dual-process theories within psychology does not involve explaining away intuitive judgments; the dispute is instead over how to provide a psychological explanation for intuitive judgments (Kruglanski and Gigerenzer 2011).)

But the problem with this line of attack on epistemic intuition is that it cloaks the fact that experimental philosophy is liable to the same criticism. Aimed at traditional philosophy, it is the intuitions of self-selected, highly trained, high socioeconomic status professors of philosophy that are called into question. Aimed at psychology, it is an overreliance on college sophomores. The shared methodological problem is how to avoid making cavalier claims of generality from non-representative samples of a population. No experimental philosopher denies there are universal epistemic norms. No experimental philosopher denies there are general facts about human nature. Yet, without a solution to this methodological problem, experimental philosophy cannot hope to evolve from an insurgency campaign to a governing philosophy with a positive program.

The introduction of formal models can help on this front, but before considering how, let us turn to another feature of the Young-Helmholtz history.

Counterexamples are not always decisive

Traditional epistemology, in addition to its commitment to epistemic intuitions, also tends to rely on counterexamples to assess theories, meaning that for traditional epistemologists, a miss is as good as a mile. But it does not have to be this way.

Look again at the Young-Helmholtz history, for the RGB additive color model is by no means comprehensive: there are visible colors which cannot be represented within the model. Yet this limitation has never been seriously considered to be a 'counterexample' to the RGB model, nor has it been viewed as a threat to the physiological theory of vision that the model was originally designed to serve. Rather, the exceptions to the theory were weighed against the power of the model, and a recognition that the empirical basis for the theory— which remained without confirmation through the last half of the 19th century and the first half of the 20th—was likely to be in the neighborhood of the truth. A successful formal model can make it sensible to view one theory as standing closer to the truth than another.

If experimental philosophers' complaint about epistemic intuition boils down to a complaint about philosophers putting their intuitions about empirical claims before experimental evidence to the contrary, and then having the nerve to offer an *a priori* argument to justify the practice, then the complaint about unchecked counterexamples boils down to a complaint against constructing theories to resist objections—no matter how contrived—above all other considerations.

The problem with aspiring to counterexample-proof philosophy without taking into account either formal or empirical constraints is that the exercise can quickly devolve into a battle of wits rather than a battle of ideas. And the problem is only compounded by pseudo-formal philosophy—the unfortunate practice of using formal logic informally—because this encourages philosophers to describe rather than define the fundamental operations of their theories. Memories are 'accessed in the right way'; justified beliefs are 'based' on one's 'evidence'; coherent beliefs 'hang together'. But, like a bump in a rug carefully pushed from one corner of a crowded room to another, this reliance on pseudo-formalisms to avoid any and all counterexamples inevitably means that the hard, unsolved philosophical problems are artfully avoided rather than addressed. At its worst, rampant counterexample avoidance turns philosophy into little more than a performance art.

But, one way to arrest this slide is by constraining epistemological theories by a combination of empirical evidence and formal models. For if you replace those fudged terms with a formal model, or a provably correct algorithm, and hem in imagination by known empirical constraints, then if a theory is successful in explaining a range of cases, that hard won success can be weighed against the theory's failings. In other words, if we set aspirations for epistemology higher than conceptual analysis, that will open more room to judge success and failure than the all-or-nothing stakes of counterexample avoidance. That is one lesson of the RGB model. Prior to the introduction of the RGB model, people only had a vague idea how to 'combine' colors and it was not recognized that there was a crucial difference between a *subtractive* color model, which models how paints mix to create new colors, and an *additive* color model, which is appropriate for modeling color perception. That insight far outweighed the limitations of the model, and it is an important reason why exceptions to the theory did not undermine it.

What formal models can do

So far we have been discussing the merits of formal methods by drawing lessons from a historical example, and by pointing to similar shortcomings in traditional analytic epistemology and experimental philosophy. There is one last piece of stage setting, which returns to a distinction we introduced at the very beginning, between formal epistemology as a methodological approach within analytic epistemology and formal epistemology as an interdisciplinary research program. I've discussed this programmatic approach elsewhere—in terms that may lead to confusion—as a type of *methodological naturalism* (Wheeler and Pereira 2008). Here I want to simply point out the advantages to epistemologists from embracing this broader, programmatic view—whatever one may wish to call it.

Sometimes a formal technique is used in several fields to model a family of problems, and in these cases there is often an opportunity for a formal epistemologist to build a rich repertoire of similarly structured problems and a library of techniques for working with them. Probabilistic methods offer one example (Haenni *et. al.* 2011). But in addition to fixing the method and varying the problems, one may also focus on a single problem, which can appear in different guises in various disciplines, and vary the methods. An advantage of viewing the same problem through different models is that we can often identify which features of the problem are enduring and which are merely artifacts of our particular methods. Because abstraction is a license for us to ignore information, looking at several approaches to modeling a problem can give you insight into what is important to keep and what is noise to ignore. Moreover, discovering robust features of a problem can reshape your intuitions. In precisely this way formal epistemology can be used to train philosophical intuitions rather than simply serve as a tool for rigorous exposition of prior philosophical commitments. Here then is a partial reply to the problem which besets traditional epistemology, with its reliance on epistemic intuitions, and experimental philosophy, with its similar difficulties from relying on too many WEIRD people. The entire load of a theory does not need to rest on the grounds for its claims if the theory includes a reasonable model that gives us new abilities to predict and to explain. A good formal model is one that can be put to such uses.

While this essay presents a case for formal epistemology, it should be clear that this is hardly a manifesto. There is a place for experimental work in philosophy, and there is a place for intuitions, too. Moreover, formal methods are not the only route to precision, and it may well be that understanding the most important human undertakings—love, friendship, political compromise— is hampered rather than helped by placing too high a stock in precision. Live long enough and you'll discover that not everything yields to hard thought.

Coherence and dilation

So far we have discussed formal epistemology from a bird's-eye point of view. In this section we shift focus to consider two recent examples of work within formal epistemology. The first example reports a breakthrough in figuring out some of the fundamentals for a theory of coherence, which remains an open problem for the coherence theory of justification. Here is a classic example of formal methods being applied to a problem within traditional analytic epistemology. The second example examines principles of sound probabilistic reasoning and the role that independence assumptions play. This is an example of formal epistemology pursued as a stand-alone discipline, for the ramifications from this example affect the application of Bayesian methods within philosophy and beyond.

Toward a theory of coherence

In 1985, Laurence BonJour provided some structure to the coherence theory of justification,[3] and his postulates for coherentism (1985, pp. 95–9) describe a role for probability along the lines of C. I. Lewis's probabilistic model of 'congruent', self-justifying memories (Lewis 1946). Since then several authors working within the framework of Bayesian epistemology have explored the prospects of developing a probabilistic model of coherence along this basic Lewis-BonJour outline.[4]

Much of the work in Bayesian epistemology concerns coherence among a set of propositions and whether a probabilistic measure of coherence can be adduced which is 'truth-conducive'—that is, whether a higher degree of coherence among a set of propositions ensures that those propositions are more likely to be true, *ceteris paribus*. The general consensus among Bayesian epistemologists is that no probabilistic measure of coherence fully succeeds in being truth-conducive, and this pessimistic consensus is based largely on results by Luc Bovens and Stephan Hartmann (2003a) and Erik Olsson (2005) that show in effect how any probabilistic measure of coherence will fail to ensure a corresponding 'boost' in their likelihood of truth.

The general question is whether there are logical relationships between probabilistically correlated evidence (thought to model 'coherence') and incremental confirmation[5] (thought to model 'justification'), and Bayesian epistemology has investigated this relationship in terms of *models for witness testimony* (Olsson 2002, 2005, Bovens and Hartmann 2003a, 2003b). Think of a witness model as composed of two sets of things, a group of messengers, each with a message to deliver, and the contents of those messages, which we may gather together to form an *information set*. Olsson's model differs from Bovens and Hartmann's model in important ways, but both share two key assumptions about the structure of a *Bayesian witness model*, namely

(bw1) a messenger *i* who reports that A is true is positive evidence for A, that is, $Pr(A \mid Reporti(A)) > Pr(A)$, and

(bw2) that each messenger is an independent reporter, that is, whether A or ¬A *screens off*[5] whether messenger *i* reports A or reports ¬A from all other contingent facts and all other messenger reports.

The idea is to ensure that a messenger considering whether to report A or its negation is only influenced by whether in fact A or its negation is true, and not on other facts of the matter nor what other messengers might be saying.

According to Olsson, these two assumptions—the twin pillars of Bayesian witness models—offer not only the most favorable circumstance in which to see if there is any hope of showing that some probabilistic measure of coherence can possibly be truth-conducive, but necessary conditions as well:

> ... coherence cannot be truth conducive in the comparative sense in the absence of independence and individual credibility (Olsson 2005, p. 3).
>
> While these assumptions may seem restrictive from a formal perspective, they should ... in fact be seen as describing fortunate circumstances ... [and what Olsson's impossibility] theorem says is that not even under fortunate circumstances can there be any interesting measure of coherence or agreement that is truth conducive in the comparative sense (Olsson 2005, p. 135).

And yet, while (bw1) and (bw2) may seem intuitively both favorable and necessary, it turns out that neither is the case. The witness testimony models are among the least favorable models for exploring the relationship between coherence and likelihood of truth (Wheeler 2009, Wheeler and Scheines forthcoming, propositions 3 and 4). The problem is the Bayesian witness model, not the general features of measures of coherence and confirmation.

Indeed, if you drop the conditional independence condition that is built into Bayesian witness models—assumption (bw2) above—there is a measure of association, called *focused correlation* (Myrvold 1996, Wheeler 2009), which robustly tracks incremental confirmation (Wheeler and Scheines 2011, Schlosshauer and Wheeler 2011, Wheeler and Scheines, forthcoming).

Briefly, focused correlation is the ratio of two quantities, the degree of association among evidence given a hypothesis, over the degree of association in the evidence alone. This relationship is clearest in the rightmost expansion of the measure, *For*, which is defined here for two evidence statements, E1 and E2, and a single hypothesis, *H*.

$$For_H\left(E_1, E_2\right) =_{df} \frac{\Pr\left(H \mid E_1, E_2\right)}{\Pr\left(H \mid E_1\right)\Pr\left(H \mid E_2\right)} = \frac{\dfrac{\Pr\left(E_1, E_2 \mid H\right)}{\Pr\left(E_1 \mid H\right)\Pr\left(E_2 \mid H\right)}}{\dfrac{\Pr\left(E_1, E_2\right)}{\Pr\left(E_1\right)\Pr\left(E_2\right)}}.$$

Given some provisos,[7] it turns out that comparing one evidence set (e.g., $\{E_1, E_2\}$) to another (e.g., $\{E_1, E_3\}$) by their degree of focused correlation (with respect to a designated hypothesis *H*), more focused correlation entails more incremental confirmation, *ceteris paribus* (Wheeler and Scheines forthcoming, Schlosshauer and Wheeler, 2011). What's more, making even weaker assumptions, when focused correlation of an evidence set (with respect to a hypothesis, *H*) is greater than 1, then the incremental confirmation of *H* given that evidence is positive (Wheeler 2009, Wheeler and Scheines, forthcoming).

Our point is not that the Bayesian impossibility results fail to be theorems, but rather that they are only representative of a narrow class of models. What we see is that while the tracking condition for focused correlation doesn't hold within witness models—because *ceteris* is not *paribus*—it works fine in many cases outside of the constraints imposed by the witness models. Why? The reason boils down to an insight from focused correlation, which is that there is a parameter missing from previous attempts to give a probabilistic theory of coherence. For it is not enough to look at the association of evidence (e.g., the event of messengers all telling a similar story); instead, we must account for the *reason* for that association. After all, witnesses might agree to agree without any regard for the truth of the matter. This is the possibility that (bw2) was designed to prevent. But, in so doing, the witness models also inadvertently scupper the possibility of connecting a higher measure of association to higher likelihood of truth. That is the surprising and important insight from the Bayesian impossibility results.

Given this observation that one must account for the cause of the association ('coherence'), Scheines and I have proposed a general model—called the CCC framework—that takes account of the causal structure regulating the relationships between the evidence (or messenger reports, if you prefer) and hypothesis (the truth of the reports, if you prefer). This requires rethinking the commitment to Lewis-BonJour witness models, and moving away from defining coherence solely in terms of information sets, but BonJour himself seems to have already had this idea in mind:

> The fact that a belief was caused in this way rather than some other can play a crucial role in a special kind of coherentist justification. The idea is that the justification of these perceptual or observational beliefs, rather than merely appealing to the coherence of their propositional contents with the contents of other beliefs (so that the way that the belief was produced would be justificationally irrelevant), appeals instead to a general belief that beliefs caused in this special way (and perhaps satisfying further conditions as well) are generally true (2002, p. 206–7).

In summary, taking the cause of coherence into account is crucial for making progress on a formal, probabilistic theory of coherence, and the CCC framework follows up on this idea by combing into one model focused correlation, for cases in which there are no independence conditions to foul up the probabilistic machinery, and causal structure to help identify how associated evidence will affect incremental confirmation. The CCC framework is hardly comprehensive, and there are intriguing irregularities which the impossibility results allude to (Wheeler, 2012); indeed, we present a more general version of Olsson's impossibility result in Wheeler and Scheines forthcoming). But, CCC is a concrete step in the right direction for solving the riddle of coherence.

Dilating sets of probabilities

Open an introductory textbook on probability and within the first few pages you will invariably find a definition of stochastic independence. Defined with respect to a classical probability function, Pr, we say that event E is *stochastically independent* of event F just in case the joint probability distribution of both E and F is equal to the product of the marginal distribution for E and the marginal distribution for F, that is:

$$(\text{IND}) \ \Pr(E,F) = \Pr(E) \times \Pr(F).$$

For example, suppose that E is the event of a fairly flipped 1 Euro coin landing 'tails' and F is the event of a fairly flipped American quarter landing 'tails'. The two tosses are stochastically independent just when the probability of both coins landing 'tails' is ¼.

Those textbooks often will give an alternative definition, too. So long as Pr(F) is non-zero, we may also say that E is stochastically independent of F just when F is *epistemically irrelevant* to the probability of E:

$$\text{(IR) } \Pr(E \mid F) = \Pr(E), \text{ when } \Pr(F) > 0.$$

Event F is epistemically irrelevant to E when there is no difference between the probability of E conditional on F and the probability of E alone. Returning to our coins, the probability that a fairly tossed American quarter landing 'tails' given that a fairly tossed 1 Euro coin has landed 'tails' is ½, which is the same as the probability that a fairly tossed American quarter lands 'tails'. In other words, knowing how the experiment with the Euro turns out is irrelevant to estimating the outcome of a fairly tossed quarter.

Finally, we may just as well switch the places of F and E—so long as we make the appropriate accommodations to avoid conditioning on zero-probability events. Let us say then that E is *epistemically independent* of F just when each is epistemically irrelevant to the other, that is:

$$\text{(EI) } \Pr(E \mid F) = \Pr(E), \text{ when } \Pr(F) > 0 \text{ and } \Pr(F \mid E) = \Pr(F), \text{ when } \Pr(E) > 0.$$

When working with a single probability distribution, Pr, these three independence notions are equivalent when $\Pr(F) > 0$ and $\Pr(E) > 0$: that is, (IND) iff (IR) iff (EI). Indeed, you are unlikely to see names for each of these notions in your text-book, since they are generally thought to be expressions of one and the same concept: *probabilistic independence.*[8]

However, there are differences between each of these three notions. If Pr is given a behavioral interpretation and viewed to represent an agent's degrees of belief, then arguably that agent learns that two events are stochastically independent (IND) by observing that one event is epistemically irrelevant to the other (IR). In other words, on a behavioral interpretation of Pr, the way for an agent to justify that two events are stochastically independent is from observing that one event is epistemically irrelevant to the other. Furthermore, since we know that (IR) if and only if (EI), the notion of epistemic independence seems an unnecessary, intermediary step. Finally, knowing that a joint distribution satisfies (IND) licenses us to factorize that joint distribution by the marginal distributions, which gives probability some semblance of acting like a logic since the probability of (E and F) is determined by taking the product of the probability of E and the probability of F. The ability to factorize a joint distribution into a product of marginal probabilities and conditional probabilities is a tremendous advantage to computing probabilities.

So, one way to look at the equivalence of (IND), (IR), and (IND), is that it licenses learning about stochastic independence through observing when one event is irrelevant to the probability estimate of another, and then allows us to leverage what we learn about those independence conditions to yield tractable methods for probabilistic reasoning. The theory of causal Bayes nets illustrates this strategy perfectly (Pearl 2000, Spirtes *et. al.* 2000). Our own approach—the PROGICNET approach—to probabilistic logic is another example (Haenni et. al. 2011).

Yet, there is a question of how sound a foundation this strategy rests on. It turns out, surprisingly, that these three independence concepts are distinct mathematical notions after all. They only appear to be three equivalent ways of expressing the same concept when viewed through the lens of a single probability measure, Pr. What this means, philosophically, is that sound probabilistic reasoning from independence and conditional independence assumptions which glide freely between (IND), (IR), and (EI), will turn out to depend on reasoning with a single probability distribution. So, those sounds principles of probabilistic reasoning depend on the grounds that you have for assuming a numerically precise probability distribution.

Assuming that agents *always* have numerically determinate degrees of belief, however, is a stretch, and several authors have argued that probability models should accommodate approximate or interval values.[9] Take for example that coin in your pocket: it is an idealization to assume that the probability of a single, fair toss of that coin landing 'tails' is precisely ½. Instead, the argument for imprecision goes, it is more reasonable to assume that the chance of 'tails' is ½ plus or minus some small ε. Yet opening the door to interval-valued probabilities even just a crack introductions a number of difficult issues, some of which go to the heart of probabilistic reasoning. The question of whether there is one concept of probabilistic independence or several independence concepts is an example.

Suppose that the probability of E is the interval $[l,u]$, where l is understood to be the lower bound of the probability that E, and u is the upper bound of the probability that E. There are several distinct ways to flesh this idea out,[10] but a common one is to interpret an interval probability assignment $[l,u]$ to an event E by a set of probability functions, $\mathbf{Pr} = \{Pr_1, Pr_2, \ldots, Pr_n\}$, where the *lower probability* of E is the *infimum* of $\mathbf{Pr}(E)$, and the *upper probability* of E is the *supremum* of **Pr**(*E*). Define lower and upper probability, with respect to a set of probabilities **Pr,** as:

$$\underline{Pr}(E) = l = \inf_{Pre\,Pr} Pr(E) \,(\text{lower probability})$$

$$\overline{Pr}(E) = u = \sup_{Pre\,PT} Pr(E) \,(\text{upper probability})$$

As it stands, the set **Pr** could represent a set of classical Bayes agents who express different judgments about *E*; **Pr** could also be interpreted as a model for studying sensitivity and robustness in classical Bayesian statistical inference; and **Pr** can also be viewed as a model of imprecise credal probabilities for a single agent. This is the interpretation which has drawn fire from epistemologists, but it is worth pointing out that the underlying mechanics of the example we're about to consider are not tied to this interpretation.

Although imprecise probability theory is sometimes described as 'exotic', in reality classical Bayesianism drops out as a special case: when the set **Pr** contains just one measure. From what we've said, the set **Pr** may contain a single measure or two or several different measures. If classical Bayesianism marks one end of set-based Bayesianism, then *convex Bayesianism* (Levi 1980) marks another important endpoint. For we can think of convexity as a closure condition on the set **Pr:**

(CVX)   **Pr** is *a closed convex set* when, for any two probability measures Pr_1, Pr_2 in **Pr,** then for all $0 \leq r \leq 1$, the measure $Pr^{\cdot} = r\,Pr_1 + (1 - r)Pr_2$ is also in **Pr.**

Condition (CVX) says that, for any two measures in **Pr,** the measure $Pr^{\cdot}$ defined by the convex mixture of those two measures is also in **Pr.** Informally, we say that a set satisfying (Cx) is closed under convex mixtures, and adding (Cx) as a condition is common when a set of probabilities is interpreted to represent imprecise credences. In what follows, we will assume (Cx) holds. With these preliminaries in place, let's turn to dilation.

We say that an event *F dilates* the event *E* just in case

$$\underline{Pr}(E / F) < \underline{Pr}(E) < \overline{Pr}(E) < \overline{Pr}(E / F)$$

In words, outcome *F* dilates *E* just in case the range of unconditional probability assignments to *E* is a proper subset of the range of probability assignments to

E given *F*. Now suppose that **B** is a measurable partition of possible outcomes. Then, the partition of outcomes **B** *strictly dilates E* just in case:

$$\Pr(E/F) < \underline{\Pr}(E) \le \overline{\Pr}(E) < \overline{\Pr}(E/F), \quad \text{For all } F \in B$$

The remarkable thing about strict dilation is the specter of turning a more precise estimate of *E* into a less precise estimate, *no matter the outcome.*

To illustrate strict dilation, we recount Peter Walley's canonical coin tossing example.

Example. Suppose that a fair coin is tossed twice. The first toss of the coin is a fair toss, but the second toss is performed in such a way that the outcome may depend on the outcome of the first toss. Nothing is known about the type or degree of the possible dependence. Let H_1, T_1, H_2, T_2 denote the possible outcomes for the pair of tosses. We know the coin is fair and that the first toss is a fair toss, so the Agent's ($\Pr_A$) estimate for the first toss is precise. The interaction between the tosses is unknown, but in the extreme the first toss may determine the outcome of the second. This likewise puts a precise constraint on A's estimate of the second toss prior to the experiment. Hence,

$$(a) \quad \underline{\Pr}_A(H_1) = \overline{\Pr}_A(H_1) = \Pr_A(H_1) = \frac{1}{2} = \underline{\Pr}_A(H_2) = \overline{\Pr}_A(H_2) = \Pr_A(H_2)$$

However, little is known about the direction or degree of dependence between the pair of tosses. Model A's ignorance by

$$(b) \quad \underline{\Pr}_A(H_1, H_2) = 0, \text{ and } \overline{\Pr}_A(H_1, H_2) = \Pr_A(H_1) = \frac{1}{2}$$

Suppose now that A learns that the outcome of the first toss is *heads*. The extremal points from (b), namely 0 and ½, can be conditioned by Bayes' rule yielding

$$(c) \quad (i) \quad \underline{\Pr}_A(H_2 \setminus H_1) = \underline{\Pr}_A(H_2, H_1) / \underline{\Pr}_A(H_1) = 0 \text{ and}$$

$$(ii) \quad \overline{\Pr}_A(H_2 \setminus H_1) = \overline{\Pr}_A(H_2, H_1) / \overline{\Pr}_A(H_1) = 1$$

So, although initially $\Pr_A(H_2) = \frac{1}{2}$, learning that the first toss lands heads dilates A's estimate of the second toss to any value within the interval [0,1]. An analogous argument holds if instead A learns that the outcome of the first toss is tails. Since these two outcomes partition the outcome space, i.e., there are no other ways the first toss can turn out, A's precise probability about the second toss strictly dilates to the vacuous unit interval, no matter which way the first coin toss lands (Walley 1991, pp. 298–9).

One way to interpret the two extreme points is that they stand for two opposing hypotheses about the mechanism controlling the second toss. Each hypothesis specifies a deterministic mechanism: case (*i*) says that the second coin is certain to match the outcome of the first, whereas case (*ii*) says that the second coin is certain to not match the outcome of the first. So, on this interpretation, the agent knows that the outcome of the first toss may provide relevant information about the outcome of the second toss, and possibly definitive information about the second toss, but merely observing the outcome of the first toss is insufficient to determine in what way the information is relevant. Arguably, then, the outcome of the first toss gives the agent information—or, better, signals a potentially important gap in her information—which warrants the change in belief. This is by no means universally accepted, but it is a more plausible position than the next example, which seems to reproduce the same result while assuming that there is no connection between the first toss and the second toss.

Suppose that instead of tossing a single coin twice and hiding from the agent the manner in which the second toss is performed, we instead flip two different coins, one which is known to be normal and the other of unknown bias. Whereas in the first coin example the methods used for performing the tosses varied but the constitution of the coin remained fixed, in this example the mechanism for tossing the coins is normal—that is, the coin tosses are independent—but the constitution of the coins are different.[11] What we are doing is replacing (a) in the example above by

$$(d) \quad \underline{\mathrm{Pr}}_A(H_2) = \overline{\mathrm{Pr}}_A(H_2) = \mathrm{Pr}_A(H_2) = \frac{1}{2}$$

$$\underline{\mathrm{Pr}}_A(H_1) = 0, \overline{\mathrm{Pr}}_A(H_1) = 1,$$

which appears to dilate the second toss as well. But the explanation we provided for the first example is not available to explain this second example, since we have stipulated that the tosses are independent. Yet, even though the two events are independent, it appears that the imprecision of one event can dilate the sharp probability estimate of another, independent event. How can this be?!

What is interesting is that 'independent event' in this setting is ambiguous between analogues of *stochastic independence, epistemic independence,* and *epistemic irrelevance* which are defined for sets of probabilities. A necessary condition for dilation is for E and F to not be stochastically independent (Seidenfeld and Wasserman 1993, Theorems 2.1–2.3), which is a bulwark against the paradoxical conclusions critics have drawn. What Seindenfeld and Wasserman's theorems tell us is that where there is dilation, there is dependence. So, it would appear, the flips in the second coin toss are dependent after all. How could this be?

The answer returns us to our earlier discussion of independence: there are several independence concepts rather than a single, unified independence concept (Kyburg and Pittarelli 1996, Cozman 2012, Wheeler, forthcoming). Within the imprecise probability setting, and assuming (CVX), stochastic independence entails epistemic independence, and epistemic independence entails epistemic irrelevance, but it is not the case that epistemic irrelevance entails epistemic independence nor, shockingly, does epistemic independence entail stochastic independence! The reasons for this are technical, and will have to be dealt with in another essay.[12] But the larger, philosophical point is that recent discussions about dilation have foundered on a real (if understandable) fallacy in probabilistic reasoning which hinge on assuming, falsely, that probabilistic independence is a unitary notion, and that the principles of sound probabilistic reasoning which hold for a single measure extend to settings in which there are sets of measures.

This observation suggests the controversy over dilation is a side issue, and that really the issue is that there are a plurality of independence concepts. This points to a dilemma for Bayesianism, with orthodox Bayesians on one horn, and set-based Bayesians on the other:

- *For orthodox Bayesians*: Imprecise probability theory reveals a fact about (IND), (EI), and (IR), namely that they are distinct properties which are collapsed when working with a single probability distribution, Pr. Orthodox Bayesianism hides this fact from view. However, even if you reject set-based approaches, are you confident that your elicitation procedure for determining numerically precise degrees of belief warrants collapsing these distinctions?
- *For set-based Bayesians*: In so far as you rely on a behavior interpretation of your convex set of distributions, how do you provide a *behavioral* justification for treating two events as completely stochastically independent given that (IND) does not follow from (EI)?[13]

In short, the discovery that there are many independence concepts rather than a single concept is an example of research within formal epistemology—which in this case includes statistics, operations research, and computer science—that has far reaching consequences. Although we have illustrated this discovery through diagnosing a common misstep in the recent literature on dilation, the underlying point concerns the very foundations of sound probabilistic reasoning.

The FIE-Model of inquiry[14]

C.P. Snow observed long ago that universities are made up of two broad types of people, literary intellectuals and hard scientists, yet a typical individual of one type is barely able, if able at all, to communicate with a counterpart from the other. Snow's observation, popularized in his 1959 lecture *Two Cultures and the Scientific Revolution* (reissued by Cambridge 1993), goes some way to explaining the two distinct cultures one hears referred to as 'the humanities' and 'the sciences'.

Certainly there is some basis for grouping academic subjects the way we do. Physics, chemistry, and biology are the pillars of experimental science. Although the skills and methods differ from each, all aim to reconcile theory about some part of the natural world with experimental evidence. However, the subjects studied by the humanities typically don't yield to experimental data; there are no experimental branches of history, no laboratories of literature. It is tempting to view the importance placed on experimental data as an indication of how scientific a subject is. (Some experimental philosophers seem to think so.) The hard sciences put experimental evidence front and center, this thinking goes, whereas the humanities either do not or cannot. The quarrels over experimental philosophy, and to some extent, the debate over formal epistemology, are very often viewed as pitched battles about whether philosophy is part of the humanities or part of the sciences. Heaped on top of that fight is another about where philosophy should be housed.

Although familiar, this is a misleading picture. Mathematics has no more to do with experimental data than poetry, and professional cooking is as concerned with experimentation as any of the social sciences. But cooking is clearly a trade, not an academic subject, much less a science.

In closing, I want to suggest that we should instead think of academic disciplines as dividing into three categories rather than into two. There are *formal* disciplines, *experimental* disciplines, and *interpretive* disciplines. This three-way distinction was proposed by Henry Kyburg in *Science and Reason* (1990, 16) to better represent the activities that make up a university, but there is much to recommend this way of thinking about academic disciplines, particular those— like philosophy—which are restlessly interdisciplinary in nature. Call this the FIE-model of inquiry.

Mathematics is essentially a formal discipline, the empirical sciences are largely empirical disciplines, and the traditional fine arts and letters are the leading exemplars of the interpretive disciplines. But nearly all fields draw upon skills from each mode of inquiry. Biology and literature are often concerned with formal structures, mathematics and psychology are sometimes concerned with interpretation, and psychology and literature are at various times interested in the facts about the society or groups that produced an observed behavior, or whose members wrote a series of plays.

It is unclear whether this FIE-model would help in organizing a university, as Kyburg suggested when he proposed it. The idea would need an administrative Helmholtz to sort that question out—or, perhaps, a Clausewitz. But, the categories are helpful for a scholar to have in mind when working on a topic like epistemology. It is not so much that epistemology calls upon results from the cognitive, computational, and decision sciences, and insights from philosophy, mathematics, psychology, statistics, and linguistics—although it certainly does. Rather, the point is that epistemology calls upon the full range of inquiry, even if truly harnessing together formal, experimental, and interpretive *skills* do not readily match the way we have happened to organize our universities and most of our philosophy departments. That Snow was right is surely no reason to believe that he must go on being right.

Notes

1 Krister Segerberg recounts Thomason's remarks in (Segerberg 2005, p. 166).
2 For overview of dual process theories, see Kruglanski and Orehek (2007), Evans (2008) and Kruglanski and Gigerenzer (2011).
3 He later despaired of meeting those demands and quit the theory altogether, but that is another story.
4 See, for example, Huemer 1997, Cross 1999, Shogenji 1999, Bovens & Hartmann 2003a, 2003b, 2006, Olsson 2002, 2005, Fitelson 2003, Meijs, 2004, Douven and Meijs 2004, Glass 2006.

5 See Carnap 1962, Cohen 1977, Earman 1992, Milne 1996, Kulpers 2000, and Crupi et al. 2007; See Kyburg 1983 for a historical review, and Eells and Fitelson 2002 for recent overview.

6 See Pearl 2000 and Spirtes *et. al.* 2000 for a thorough treatment.

7 Conditions (A1, A2) in (Wheeler and Scheines forthcoming) which is generalized in (Schlosshauer and Wheeler 2011).

8 Or if there is a distinction draw, it is simply between conditional independence (IR) and independence (IND).

9 Pioneers of imprecise probability theory includes B. O. Koopman (1940), Alfred Horn and Alfred Tarski (1948), Paul Halmos (1950), I. J. Good (1952), C. A. B. Smith (1961), Daniel Ellsberg (1961), and Henry Kyburg, Jr. (1961). Notable contemporary advocates include Isaac Levi (1980), Peter Walley (1991), Teddy Seidenfeld (2010), James Joyce (2010), Fabio Cozman (2000), Gert de Cooman and Enrique Miranda (2007, 2009). See also Haenni et. al. (2011).

10 Recent textbook treatments include Paris 1994, Halpern 2003, Haenni et. al. 2011.

11 A version of this is discussed by Walley (1991), Seidenfeld (1994), White (2010), Sturgeon (2010), and Joyce (2010).

12 However, if you drop (CVX), then Stochastic independence does not entail Epistemic independence (Wheeler, forthcoming). See also (Williamson 2010).

13 Seidenfeld et al. 2010's axiomatization of choice functions do allow for a behavioral justification of stochastic independence, but this construction depends on a difference between epistemic and stochastic independence appearing in the underlying set of probabilities. But consider, for example, a set of extremal points which is not convex and may be indistinguishable under epistemic independence and stochastic independence. Even so, the agent may know something about the uncertain mechanism which induces that set to select one notion of independence and rule out the other without that evidence appearing as a property of the (non-convex) set of extremal probabilities.

14 This section is adapted from Wheeler 2007.

References

BonJour, Laurence 1985: *The Structure of Empirical Knowledge*. Cambridge, MA, Harvard University Press.

BonJour, Laurence 1999: 'The Dialectics of Foundationalism and Coherentism'. In Greco and Sosa 1999, pp. 117–42.

BonJour, Laurence 2002: *Epistemology*. Oxford: Rowman and Littlefield.

Bovens, Luc and Stephan Hartmann 2003a: *Bayesian Epistemology*. Oxford: Oxford University Press

Bovens, Luc and Stephan Hartmann 2003b: 'Solving the Riddle of Coherence'. *Mind,* 112, pp. 601–33.

Bovens, Luc and Stephan Hartmann 2006: 'An Impossibility Result for Coherence Rankings'. *Philosophical Studies,* 128, pp. 77–91.

Bovens, Luc and Erik Olsson 2000: 'Coherentism, Reliability, and Bayesian Networks'. *Mind,* 109: 685–719.

Carlson, Rae: 1971: 'Where is the person in personality research?' *Psychological Bulletin,* 75, p. 212.

Carnap, Rudolf 1962: *The Logical Foundations of Probability.* Chicago: University of Chicago Press.

Cohen, L. J. 1977: *The Probable and the Provable.* Oxford: Clarendon Press.

Cozman, Fabio 2012: 'Sets of Probability Distributions, Independence, and Convexity'. *Synthese,* in press.

Cross, Charles B. 1999: 'Coherence and Truth Conducive Justification'. *Analysis,* 59(3), pp. 186–93.

Crupi, V., K. Tentori, and M. Gonzalez 2007: 'On Bayesian Measures of Evidential Support: Theoretical and empirical issues'. *Philosophy of Science,* 74(2), pp. 229–52.

de Cooman, Gert and Enrique Miranda 2007: 'Symmetry of models versus models of symmetry'. In Harper and Wheeler 2007, pp. 67–149.

de Cooman, Gert and Enrique Miranda 2009: 'Forward Irrelevance'. *Journal of Statistical Planning,* 139, pp. 256–76.

Douven, Igor and Wouter Meijs 2007: 'Measuring Coherence'. *Synthese,* 156(3), pp. 405–25.

Earman, John 1992: *Bayes or Bust: A Critical Examination of Bayesian Confirmation Theory.* Cambridge, MA: MIT Press.

Eells, Ellery and Branden Fitelson 2002: 'Symmetries and Asymmetries in Evidential Support'. *Philosophical Studies,* 107(2), pp. 129–42.

Ellsberg, Daniel 1961: 'Risk, Ambiguity, and the Savage Axioms'. Quarterly Journal of Economics, 75: pp. 643–69.

Evans, J. St. B. T. 2008: 'Dual-processing Accounts of Reasoning, Judgement, and Social Cognition'. *Annual Review of Psychology,* 59, pp. 255–78.

Ewing, Alfred C. 1934: *Idealism: A Critical Survey.* London: Methuen.

Fitelson, Branden 2003: 'A Probabilistic Theory of Coherence'. *Analysis,* 63, pp. 194–99.

Gendler, Tamar and John Hawthorne (eds) 2010: *Oxford Studies in Epistemology, volume 3.* Oxford: Oxford University Press.

Gettier, Edmund 1963: 'Is Justified True Belief Knowledge?' *Analysis,* 23, pp. 121–23.

Glass, D. H. 2006: 'Coherence Measures and their Relations to Fuzzy Similarity and Inconsistency in Knowledge Bases'. *Artificial Intelligence Review.* 26, pp. 227–49.

Good, I. J. 1952: 'Rational Decisions'. *Journal of the Royal Statistics Society, Series B.* 14(1), pp. 107–14.

Greco, John and Ernest Sosa (eds) 1999: *The Blackwell Guide to Epistemology.* Malden, MA: Blackwell.

Haenni, R. J.W. Romeyn, G. Wheeler, and J. Williamson 2011: *Probabilistic Logic and Probabilistic Networks,* Dordrecht: The Synthese Library, Springer.

Halmos, Paul 1950: *Measure Theory.* New York: Van Nostrand Reinhold Company.

Halpern, Joseph 2003: *Reasoning about Uncertainty.* Cambridge, MA: MIT Press.

Harper, William and Gregory Wheeler (eds) 2007: *Probability and Inference: Essays in Honour of Henry E. Kyburg, Jr.* London: College Publications.

Hartmann, Stephan, Marcel Weber, Wenceslao J. Gonzalez, Dennis Dieks, Thomas Uebe (eds) 2011: *Explanation, Prediction, and Confirmation: New Trends and Old Ones Reconsidered.* Dordrecht: Springer.

Helmholtz, Hermann 1860: 'The Young-Helmholtz Theory of Color Vision', in Dennis, Wayne 1948, pp. 199–205.

Henrich, Joseph, Steven Heine and Ara Norenzayan 2010: The Weirdest People in the World? *Behavioral and Brain Sciences.* 33(2–3), pp. 61–83.

Horn, Alfred and Alfred Tarsk 1948: 'Measures in Boolean Algebras'. *Transactions of the AMS.* 64(1): 467–97.

Huemer, Michael 1997: 'Probability and Coherence Justification'. *The Southern Journal of Philosophy,* 35, pp. 463–72.

Joyce, James 2010: 'In Defense of Imprecise Credences in Inference and Decision Making'. *Philosophical Perspectives,* 21(1): 281–323.

Koopman, B. O. 1940: 'The axioms and algebra of intuitive probability'. *Annals of Mathematics,* 41(2): 269–92.

Kruglanski, Arie and Gerd Gigerenzer 2011: 'Intuitive and Deliberate Judgments Are Based on Common Principles'. *Psychological Review,* 118(1): 97–109.

Kruglanski, Arie and Edward Orehek 2007: 'Partitioning the Domain of Human Inference: Dual mode and system models and their alternatives'. *Annual Review of Psychology,* 8, 291–316.

Kuipers, Theo 2000: *From Instrumentalism to Constructive Realism.* Dordrecht: The Synthese Library, Springer.

Kyburg, Jr., H. E. 1961: *Probability and the Logic of Rational Belief.* Middletown, CT: Wesleyan University Press.

Kyburg, Jr., H. E. 1983: 'Recent Work in Inductive Logic'. In Lucey and Machan, 1983, pp. 87–150.

Kyburg, Jr., H. E. 1990: *Science and Reason.* Oxford: Oxford University Press.

Kyburg, Jr., H. E. and M. Pittarelli 1996: 'Set-based Bayesianism'. *IEEE Transactions on Systems, Man, and Cybernetics A.* 26(3): 324–39.

Levi, Isaac 1980: *Enterprise of Knowledge.* Cambridge, MA: MIT Press.

Lewis, C. I. 1946: *An Analysis of Knowledge and Valuation.* La Salle: Open Court.

Lucey, Kenneth and Tibor Machan 1983: Recent Work in Philosophy, Totowa, N.J.: Rowman and Allanheld.

Meijs, Wouter 2004: 'A Corrective to Bovens and Hartmann's Measure of Coherence'. *Philosophical Studies.* 133(2), pp. 151–80.

Milne, Peter 1996: 'Log[P(h/eb)/(P(h/e)] Is the One True Measure of Confirmation'. *Philosophy of Science* 63(1): 21–6.

Myrvold, Wayne 1996: 'Bayesianism and Diverse Evidence: A Reply to Andrew Wayne'. *Philosophy of Science*. 63, pp. 661–5.

Olsson, Erik J. 2002: 'What is the Problem of Coherence and Truth?' *Journal of Philosophy*. 94, pp. 246–72.

Olsson, Erik J. 2005: *Against Coherence: Truth, Probability and Justification*. Oxford: Oxford University Press.

Paris, Jeff 1994: *The Uncertain Reasoner's Companion: A Mathematical Companion*. Cambridge: Cambridge University Press.

Pearl, Judea 2000: *Causality*. Cambridge: Cambridge University Press.

Prawitz, Dag., Brian Skyrms, and Dag Westertahl, (eds.) *Logic, Methodology and Philosophy of Science*. North Holland: Elsevier Science, B. V.

Schlosshauer, Maximillian and Gregory Wheeler 2011: 'Focused Correlation, Confirmation, and the Jigsaw Puzzle of Variable Evidence'. *Philosophy of Science*, 78(3), pp. 276–92.

Sears, D. O. 1986: 'College Sophomores in the laboratory: influences of a narrow data base on social psychology's view of human nature'. *Journal of Personality and Social Psychology*, 51, pp. 515–30.

Segerberg, Krister 2005: 'Krister Segerberg', in Hendricks and Symons 2005, pp. 159–67.

Seidenfeld, Teddy 1994: 'When Normal and Extensive Form Decisions Differ'. In Prawitz, D., Skyrms, G., and Westertahl, D. (eds.), 1994.

Seidenfeld, Teddy, Mark J. Schervish and Joseph B. Kadane 2010: 'Coherent Choice Functions under Uncertainty'. Synthese, 172(1), pp. 157–76.

Seidenfeld, Teddy and Larry Wassermann 1993: 'Dilation for sets of probabilities'. *The Annals of Statistics*, 21: 1139–54.

Shogenji, Tomoji 1999: 'Is Coherence Truth Conducive?' *Analysis*, 59, 1999, 338–45.

Snow, C. P. 1959 (1998): *The Two Cultures*. 9th *Printing*. Cambridge: Cambridge University Press.

Spirtes, P., C. Glymour, and R. Scheines 2000: *Causation, Prediction, and Search*. 2nd edition. Cambridge, MA: MIT Press.

Sturgeon, S. 2010: 'Confidence and Coarse-grain Attitudes'. In Gendler and Hawthorne 2010, pp. 126–49.

Walley, Peter 1991: *Statistical Reasoning with Imprecise Probabilities*. London: Chapman and Hall.

Weinberg, J., S. Nichols and S. Stich 2001: 'Normativity and Epistemic Intutions'. *Philosophical Topics*, 29, pp. 429–60.

Wheeler, Gregory 2007: 'Humanists and Scientists'. *The Reasoner*. 1(1): 3–4.

Wheeler, Gregory 2009: 'Focused Correlation and Confirmation'. *The British Journal for the Philosophy of Science*. 60(1), pp. 79–100.

Wheeler, Gregory 2012: 'Explaining the Limits of Olsson's Impossibility Result'. *The Southern Journal of Philosophy*. 50(1): 136–50.

Wheeler, Gregory: 'Objective Bayesian Calibration and the Problem of Non-convex Evidence'. *The British Journal for the Philosophy of Science*, to appear.

Wheeler, Gregory and Luís Moniz Pereira 2008: 'Methodological Naturalism and Epistemic Internalism'. Synthese, 163(3): 315–28.

Wheeler, Gregory and Richard Scheines 2011: 'Coherence, Association, and Causation'. In Hartmann, Weber, Gonzalez, Dieks, and Uebe, pp. 37–51.

Wheeler, Gregory and Richard Scheines: 'Coherence and Confirmation through Causation'. under review.

White, Roger 2010: 'Evidential symmetry and mushy credence'. In Gendler and Hawthorne 2010, pp. 161–81.

Williamson, Jon 2010: *In Defence of Objective Bayesianism*. Oxford: Oxford University Press.

13

Experimental Epistemology

James R. Beebe

Experimental epistemology is the use of the experimental methods of the cognitive sciences to shed light on debates within epistemology, the philosophical study of knowledge and rationally justified belief. Some skeptics contend that "experimental epistemology" (or "experimental philosophy" more generally) is an oxymoron. If you are doing experiments, they say, you are not doing philosophy. You are doing psychology or some other scientific activity. It is true that the part of experimental philosophy that is devoted to carrying out experiments and performing statistical analyses on the data obtained is primarily a scientific rather than a philosophical activity. However, because the experiments are designed to shed light on debates within philosophy, the experiments themselves grow out of mainstream philosophical debate and their results are injected back into the debate, with an eye to moving the debate forward. This part of experimental philosophy is indeed philosophy—not philosophy as usual perhaps, but philosophy nonetheless.

A variety of other misconceptions about experimental philosophy contribute to making it far more controversial than it should be. For example, no experimental philosopher has ever claimed that experimentation should completely replace philosophical theorizing. Yet experimental philosophers are continually faced with the following challenge from would-be critics: "If we surveyed everyone and discovered that they believe that skepticism is false (or that it's rational to believe in the existence of God, the external world, etc.), how is this fact supposed to put an end to the centuries-old philosophical debate?" The simple answer is "It is not." The empirical data gathered by experimental philosophers is supposed to *inform* rather than *replace* philosophical debate. Furthermore, experimental philosophers do not claim that their methods and results will necessarily be relevant to every area of philosophy. Again, however, it is common for critics to try to think of areas of philosophical debate where experimentation would not seem to be relevant and present them as evidence for the lack of worth of experimental philosophy. Yet consider the fact that no philosopher would dream of offering the following argument: "Insights from modal logic are not relevant to every area of philosophy; therefore, modal logic has no philosophical value and should not be practiced." It turns out that the experiments being performed by experimental philosophers can shed light on surprisingly wide swaths of philosophical debate, but there is no claim that they must somehow be relevant to every dispute. What follows is an overview of the main areas of epistemological debate to which experimental philosophers have been contributing and the larger, philosophical challenges these contributions have raised.

Gettier and Truetemp

Most of the major movements and innovations of the last 50 years of contemporary epistemological debate have relied heavily upon intuitions elicited by key thought experiments. Edmund Gettier (1963), for example, appeared to successfully undermine the analysis of knowledge as justified true belief with two simple thought experiments in which the protagonists seemed to have justified true beliefs but lacked knowledge. The externalist theories of epistemic justification that appeared in the 1970s and 1980s were attacked primarily on the grounds that they seemed to conflict with widely shared intuitions about cases such as Norman the clairvoyant,[1] Truetemp the amazingly accurate temperature perceiver,[2] and victims of evil demon deception.[3] More recently, epistemic contextualism has been both defended and attacked on the grounds that it comports well or poorly with common intuitions about key cases.[4]

All of these uses of philosophical thought experiments are based on the assumption that the intuitions they elicit will be widely shared—indeed, that they *ought* to be shared by anyone who possesses the concepts of knowledge and justified belief and who exercises at least minimal capacities for reflection upon the correct application of those concepts. Recently, some work in experimental epistemology has put this simple assumption to the test. More precisely, experimental epistemologists have gathered data about people's intuitive responses to philosophically influential thought experiments in a controlled fashion, and the results have often been surprising.

Gettier cases

Having a justified true belief usually means having knowledge. However, Gettier (1963) famously introduced a class of cases in which cognitive agents have justified true beliefs that do not seem to count as knowledge. In what is usually considered to be the founding document of experimental epistemology, Weinberg et al. (2001) discovered that, while most American college students of European ancestry (i.e. "Westerners") gave the "correct" or typical philosophical response to Gettier cases, many American college students of East Asian (i.e. Korean, Japanese, and Chinese) and South Asian (i.e. Indian, Pakistani, Bangladeshi) descent did not. Weinberg et al. (2001) presented participants with the following version of one of Gettier's original cases:

> Bob has a friend, Jill, who has driven a Buick for many years. Bob therefore thinks that Jill drives an American car. He is not aware, however, that her Buick has recently been stolen, and he is also not aware that Jill has replaced it with a Pontiac, which is a different kind of American car. Does Bob really know that Jill drives an American car, or does he only believe it?

Bob's belief is justified because of his past familiarity with Jill's driving habits, and his belief is true because Jill really does drive an American car. However, according to the overwhelming majority of epistemologists, the fact that makes Bob's belief justified and the fact that makes it true are not related in an epistemically proper fashion. Seventy-four percent of Western participants surveyed seemed to agree, as they indicated that Bob only believed but did not really know that Jill drives an American car. Fifty-three percent of East Asians and 61 percent of South Asians, however, indicated that Bob really knows this fact (cf. Table 13.1).

When intuitive responses are found to diverge in cases where it had been previously assumed that they would be unanimous, a challenge is posed to the evidential and argumentative force of these cases. If everyone who possessed the concept of knowledge agreed that the protagonists in Gettier cases lacked knowledge, the cases could be persuasively used to impugn the "justified true belief" account of knowledge. But if there is significant disagreement, matters become more complicated. It could be that some respondents are simply confused or have made some kind of performance error that prevents their responses from adequately reflecting their conceptual competence. Or it may be that some participants (e.g. from one culture) are operating with one concept of knowledge, whereas other participants (e.g. from another culture)

Table 13.1 Propsortion of participants who thought that Bill 'really knows' vs' only believes' that Jill drives an American car

Gettier Case	Really Knows (%)	Only Believes (%)
Westerners	26	74
East Asians	53	47
South Asians	61	39

are operating with a different one. Some have suggested that in cases of disagreement greater weight should be given to the intuitions of experts than to those of the philosophically untrained. Several experimental epistemologists have suggested that the diversity and instability of epistemic intuitions point to a more radical conclusion, viz., that intuitions should not be used as evidence in philosophical theorizing at all.

Not everyone is convinced that the results cited above pose a significant philosophical challenge. Simon Cullen (2010), for example, replicated the Gettier studies of Weinberg et al. (2001) but instructed participants to choose between saying that Bob *knows* or *does not know* that Jill drives an American car instead of offering them the choices *really knows* and *only believes*. Cullen correctly notes that "really knows" seems to express a distinct concept from "knows" and is perhaps more akin to "knows with certainty." When Western participants were offered the dichotomous choice between knowing and not knowing, 42 percent chose "knows"—sigsnificantly more than chose "really knows" in the Weinberg et al. study. Cullen's replication shows that conclusions drawn about participants' concept of "knowledge" should not be drawn from participant responses to questions about "really knowing," but it should be kept in mind that this does not undermine conclusions one might want to draw about participants' concept of "really knowing."

Citing an array of evidence from cognitive, developmental, and cross-cultural psychology that seems to show that the cognitive processes underlying epistemic evaluation should be universal and relatively independent of culture, Jennifer Nagel (2007, forthcoming) predicted that further empirical investigation would overturn the claim that there is philosophically significant variation in epistemic intuitions about Gettier cases across demographic groups. Indeed, when Nagel, San Juan, and Mar (in prep.) presented participants with eight different Gettier cases, eight ordinary knowledge cases, eight justified false belief cases, and eight cases in which skeptical possibilities were raised, they found no ethnicity- or gender-based differences.

While further investigation of Gettier case intuitions and the psychological processes underlying them is required, epistemologists should at the very least heed the following cautionary message offered by Nagel (2007, p. 802): "reactions to sketchy cases can involve a complex array of factors, and one should not be hasty to assume that one's own initial reactions are always definitive."

Truetemp cases

One of the more prominent areas of debate within contemporary epistemology has been the dispute between epistemic internalism and externalism. Describing the distinction between internalism and externalism about epistemic justification, Laurence BonJour (1992, p. 132) writes:

> The most generally accepted account of this distinction is that a theory of justification is *internalist* if and only if it requires that all of the factors needed for a belief to be epistemically justified for a given person be *cognitively accessible* to that person, internal to his cognitive perspective; and *externalist,* if it allows that at least some of the justifying factors need not be thus accessible, so that they can be *external* to the believer's cognitive perspective, beyond his ken.

The most common form of epistemic externalism is reliabilism, which claims that beliefs are justified just when they are produced by cognitive processes that are highly reliable or truth-conducive.[5] Reliabilism does not require that subjects know or be able to recognize that their cognitive processes are reliable. They must simply be reliable. This feature of reliabilism makes it a form of epistemic externalism, and it has been the target of most of the objections lodged against the theory.

Critics of reliabilism (and externalism more generally) have used thought experiments in which a hypothetical cognitive agent satisfies the reliabilist (or otherwise externalist) conditions for knowledge or justified belief, yet intuitively seems to lack knowledge or justification. One of the most widely discussed such thought experiments is Keith Lehrer's (1990) story of Mr. Truetemp. Weinberg et al. (2001) employed the following version of the story in one of their experiments:

> One day Charles is suddenly knocked out by a falling rock, and his brain becomes re-wired so that he is always absolutely right whenever he estimates the temperature where he is. Charles is completely unaware that his brain has been altered in this way. A few weeks later, this brain re-wiring leads him to believe that it is 71 degrees in his room. Apart from his estimation, he has no other reasons to think that it is 71 degrees. In fact, it is at that time 71 degrees in his room. Does Charles really know that it was 71 degrees in the room, or does he only believe it?

Almost all epistemologists have maintained that Truetemp-style subjects like Charles lack justification for their beliefs and, since justification is necessary for knowledge, they take him to lack knowledge as well. Among Western participants surveyed by Weinberg et al. (2001) 68 percent of them seem to agree. But an even greater proportion of East Asians agree (cf. Table 13.2). The difference between Eastern and Western responses is statistically significant.

A key feature of Charles' epistemic situation—and the original Truetemp story it was patterned after—is that Charles has a belief-forming process that is not shared by anyone else in his community. Drawing upon work in social psychology that suggests that people from East Asian cultures tend to be more collectivist in their thinking and less inclined toward understanding objects and individuals in detachment from their contexts than Westerners, Weinberg et al. (2001) constructed some other Truetemp-style cases that were less individualistic. In one version, the rock that gave Charles his new perceptual ability was replaced by a team of well-meaning scientists that are sent by the elders in his community. In another version, the entire community shares the new perceptual process in question. In both cases where some kind of community-based sanction is introduced, the statistically significant difference between Westerners and East Asians disappears. Seventy-five percent of East Asians responded that the protagonist whose brain has been rewired with elder approval only believed the proposition in question, and 68 percent of East Asians said that the protagonist who shared his new perceptual process with others in his community only believed and did not really know (cf. Tables 13.3 and 13.4).

Swain et al. (2008) found that intuitions given in response to the basic Truetemp case are also subject to an ordering effect. If participants are first presented with a clear case of knowledge before considering the Truetemp case, they are less willing to attribute knowledge to the protagonist in the Truetemp case. But if they are first presented with a clear case of non-knowledge, they are more willing to attribute knowledge in the Truetemp case. Because Truetemp intuitions are thus unstable, Swain et al. (2008) suggest that they are unsuitable for use in philosophical argumentation.

Table 13.2 Proportion of participants who thought that Charles 'really knows' vs' only believes' that it was 71 degrees in the Individualistic Truetemp Case

	Really Knows (%)	Only Believes (%)
Westerners	32	68
East Asians	12	88

Table 13.3 Proportion of participants who thought that Charles 'really knows' vs' only believes' that it was 71 degrees in the Elders Truetemp Case

	Really Knows (%)	Only Believes (%)
Westerners	35	65
East Asians	25	75

Table 13.4 Proportion of participants who thought that Charles 'really knows' vs' only believes' that it was 71 degrees in the Community Wide Truetemp Case

	Really Knows (%)	Only Believes (%)
Westerners	20	80
East Asians	32	68

Jennifer Cole Wright (2010), however, highlights the fact that not all of the intuitive responses gathered by Swain et al. (2008) are unstable. The clear cases of knowledge and non-knowledge were consistently recognized as knowledge and non-knowledge, respectively, regardless of the order in which they were presented. Building upon this observation, Wright replicated the findings of Swain et al. (2008) but asked participants to rate how confident they were in their judgments about the various cases. She found that participants were significantly more confident in their judgments about the clear cases than they were about Truetemp. Wright claims that her findings provide an answer to the question raised by many experimental philosophers about whether there is any way to calibrate intuitions and distinguish the reliable ones from the unreliable. Wright argues that because high degrees of confidence track stability and low degrees of confidence track instability, participants have introspective access to features that be used to distinguish those intuitions that are less subject to biasing influences from those that are not.

Cullen (2010) also replicated Swain et al.'s (2008) study but instructed participants to evaluate each vignette separately. When this was done, the order effect found by Swain et al. (2008) disappeared. Cullen argues that when participants are asked a question and the point of the question is not terribly clear to them, they will look around in the context surrounding the question (where this may include other vignettes previously encountered in a questionnaire) in search of clues that can guide them in how to answer. Cullen hypothesizes that participants who are not specifically instructed to consider each vignette separately will tend to think that being shown the Truetemp case immediately after an apparently obvious case of non-knowledge is a clue that they should compare the two cases. Cullen contends that participants who compare the Truetemp case to a clear case of knowledge are in effect answering a different question from participants who are comparing the Truetemp case to a clear case of non-knowledge. When participants are given the explicit instruction to evaluate vignettes separately, however, Cullen maintains they come closer to answering the question researchers want them to answer.

In a replication of the original Charles experiment above, Cullen had Western participants choose between "Charles knows" and "Charles does not know" rather than "Charles really knows" and "Charles merely believes." Cullen found that 57 percent of participants answered that Charles knows—almost twice as many as those who claimed that Charles *really* knows in Weinberg et al.'s (2001) original experiment.

An often unremarked feature of the empirical findings on Truetemp cases is that before experimental epistemology came onto the scene, epistemologists almost unanimously agreed that the intuition that Truetemp does not know is obviously correct and is one that would be universally shared. Even Alvin Goldman (1994) and William Alston (1989)—two of the foremost defenders of reliabilism—shared this opinion and agreed that the Truetemp case presented a deep and significant challenge to their theory. However, it seems that a substantial portion of ordinary subjects view the case differently. One of the basic contributions experimental epistemology has made has been to test a variety of empirical assumptions made by contemporary epistemologists and show how the empirical data can often surprise us.

Error possibilities and stakes

The versions of epistemic contextualism developed by Keith DeRose (1992, 1995, 2005), Stewart Cohen (1988, 1999), and David Lewis (1996) have been at the forefront of epistemological debate for the last two decades. Contextualists and their contrastivist (e.g. Schaffer 2004) or subject-sensitive invariantist critics[6] maintain that it can be true to assert "Bob knows that Jill drives an American car" or "Mike knows that the animal is a zebra" in some conversational contexts but false to assert them in other contexts. Although these various theorists disagree about the semantics of knowledge attributions, they generally agree that when error possibilities are made sufficiently salient in conversational contexts of certain kinds, it may no longer be true to say that someone knows, even if it would have been true before those possibilities were raised. They also claim that when the stakes are raised—that is, when the cost of someone's belief being wrong increases—it may be false to say that someone knows certain propositions, even though it will be true to say that someone knows those propositions in contexts where the stakes are low.

Perhaps more than any other recent position in epistemology, contextualism has made clear its aim to be grounded firmly on the epistemic intuitions of the average person. DeRose (2005, p. 172), for example, claims:

> The best grounds for accepting contextualism concerning knowledge attributions come from how knowledge-attributing (and knowledge-denying) sentences are used in ordinary, non-philosophical talk: what ordinary speakers will count as "knowledge" in some non-philosophical contexts they will deny is such in others.

Jason Stanley (2004, p. 11) contends that his invariantist alternative to contextualism can be shown to be superior to contextualism in part because intuitive responses to his favored thought experiments will "provide powerful intuitive evidence for [the] antecedently plausible principle concerning the relation between knowledge and action" that he wishes to defend. These claims are obviously ripe for empirical testing.

Because several leading epistemological theories predict that getting subjects to think about possibilities in which their beliefs are mistaken should make them less willing to attribute knowledge to themselves or others, Weinberg et al. (2001) presented participants with the following cases in which error possibilities have been raised:

> It's clear that smoking cigarettes increases the likelihood of getting cancer. However, there is now a great deal of evidence that just using nicotine by itself without smoking (for instance, by taking a nicotine pill) does not increase the likelihood of getting cancer. Jim knows about this evidence and as a result, he believes that using nicotine does not increase the likelihood of getting cancer. It is possible that the tobacco companies dishonestly made up and publicized this evidence that using nicotine does not increase the likelihood of cancer, and that the evidence is really false and misleading. Now, the tobacco companies did not actually make up this evidence, but Jim is not aware of this fact. Does Jim really know that using nicotine doesn't increase the likelihood of getting cancer, or does he only believe it?

Mike is a young man visiting the zoo with his son, and when they come to the zebra cage, Mike points to the animal and says, "that's a zebra." Mike is right—it is a zebra. However, as the older people in his community know, there are lots of ways that people can be tricked into believing things that aren't true. Indeed, the older people in the community know that it's possible that zoo authorities could cleverly disguise mules to look just like zebras, and people viewing the animals would not be able to tell the difference. If the animal that Mike called a zebra had really been such a cleverly painted mule, Mike still would have thought that it was a zebra. Does Mike really know that the animal is a zebra, or does he only believe that it is?

In both cases, a purely hypothetical scenario involving deception is made salient to the reader, even though the reader is told that the scenario is not actual. Contrary to the widely shared assumption in epistemology that all participants should be equally disinclined to attribute knowledge in such cases, Weinberg et al. (2001) found that South Asians appear to be much less likely than their Western counterparts to deny that the protagonists really know (cf. Tables 13.5 and 13.6).

Weinberg et al. (2001) initially reported that high socioeconomic status participants were significantly more likely than low socioeconomic status participants to deny that the cognitive agents in the Cancer Conspiracy Case and a variation of the zebra-in-the-zoo case really knew the propositions in question. However, Weinberg et al. (2001) no longer think this finding is robust.)

Nichols et al. (2003) also found that a significant majority of American college students who had taken three or more philosophy courses thought that the protagonist in a typical brain-in-a-vat case only believed and did not know

Table 13.5 Proportion of participants who thought that Jim 'really knows' vs' only believes' that using nicotine doesn't increase the likelihood of getting cancer

	Really Knows (%)	Only Believes (%)
Westerners	11	89
South Asians	30	70

Table 13.6 Proportion of participants who thought that Mike 'really knows' vs' only believes' that the animal is a zebra

	Really Knows (%)	Only Believes (%)
Westerners	31	69
South Asians	50	50

that he was not a virtual-reality brain, while a narrow majority of students who had taken two or less thought that he really knew this fact. Buckwalter and Stich (forthcoming) presented participants with a scenario in which two protagonists are discussing the possibility that they might be bodiless brains in vats that have been deceived into believing their perceptual experiences are veridical. They found that female participants were significantly more likely than male participants to agree that the protagonists know they are not bodiless brains in vats (mean for females = 6.72 on a 7-point scale; males = 5.62).

After reviewing findings concerning the variability of epistemic intuitions about skeptical scenarios, Nichols et al. (2003, p. 243) conclude:

> Our predicament is in some ways analogous to the predicament of a person who is raised in a homogeneous and deeply religious culture and finds the truth of certain religious claims to be obvious or compelling. When such a person discovers that other people do not share his intuitions, he may well come to wonder why his intuitions are any more likely to be true than theirs.

In addition to casting doubt upon the reliability of our intuitions, Nichols et al. (2003, p. 243) also think that the foregoing data should make us question the central place that debates about skepticism have occupied in western philosophy:

> For if people in different cultural and SES [socioeconomic status] groups and people who have had little or no philosophical training do not share *"our"* intuitions (that is, the intuitions of the typical analytic philosopher who is white, western, high SES and has had *lots* of philosophical training) then they are unlikely to be as convinced or distressed as *"we"* are by arguments [in support of skepticism] whose premises seem plausible only if one has the intuitions common in our very small cultural and intellectual tribe. *Pace* McGinn's "anthropological conjecture," skepticism is neither primitive nor inevitable. And *pace* Stroud there is no reason to think that skepticism "appeals to something deep in our nature." Rather, it seems, its appeal is very much a product of our culture, our social status and our education!

Wesley Buckwalter (2010) tested for the effects of error possibilities and high stakes by presenting participants with three versions of DeRose's "bank" cases, one of which is the following:

> **Bank.** Sylvie and Bruno are driving home from work on a Friday afternoon. They plan to stop at the bank to deposit their paychecks, but as they drive past the bank they notice that the lines inside are very long. Although they generally

like to deposit their paychecks as soon as possible, it is not especially important in this case that they be deposited right away. Bruno tells Sylvie, "I was just here last week and I know that the bank will be open on Saturday." Instead, Bruno suggests that they drive straight home and return to deposit their paychecks on Saturday. When they return to the bank on Saturday, it is open for business.

In the "High Stakes" variant of this case, instead of being told that "it is not especially important in this case that [their paychecks] be deposited right away," participants were told "Bruno has written a very large check, and if the money from his pay is not deposited by Monday, it will bounce, leaving Bruno in a very bad situation with his creditors." In the "High Standards" variant, participants were given the following, additional piece of information: "Sylvie says, 'Banks are typically closed on Saturday. Maybe this bank won't be open tomorrow either. Banks can always change their hours, I remember that this bank used to have different hours.'" Thus, the costs of being wrong are high for Bruno only in High Stakes, and an error possibility is raised only in High Standards.

Buckwalter found that while 74 percent of participants agreed that Bruno's assertion "I know that the bank will be open on Saturday" was true in Bank, 69 percent of participants in High Stakes and 66 percent in High Standards also thought that Bruno's assertion was true. Statistical analysis reveals that the mean responses in each case are significantly above the midpoint—that is, most people agree that Bruno's knowledge attribution is true in all three cases—but that there is no significant difference between the means of the three sets of responses. At least in the cases studied by Buckwalter, raising error possibilities and stakes had no appreciable effect on participants' willingness to attribute knowledge.

May et al. (2010) ran a similar experiment, which included an additional case that combined both error possibilities and stakes, and came up with comparable results. May et al. (2010) found that "neither raising the possibility of error nor raising stakes moves most people from attributing knowledge to denying it." However, even though participants generally attributed knowledge in both high and low stakes cases, they were more strongly inclined to attribute knowledge in low stakes cases. May et al. (2010) found no such effect for error possibilities.

One important difference between Buckwalter's study and that of May et al. (2010) is that Buckwalter had participants evaluate the correctness of a knowledge attribution made by a character within the vignette, whereas May et al. asked participants whether they thought the character had knowledge.

Because one of the most important lines of difference between contextualists and many of their critics concerns the question of whether the epistemic standards of putative knowers or the standards of attributors and deniers of knowledge should determine the truth values of knowledge attributions, the bearing that empirical results from experimental epistemology are taken to have upon extant theories of knowledge or justification can be greatly affected by which kind of probe question was asked. Subject-sensitive invariantists, for example, maintain that there should be no significant difference between the "correct" participant response to the question of whether a vignette's protagonist knows and the "correct" response to the question of whether an attribution of knowledge to the protagonist made by another character in the vignette is correct. This is because the truth conditions for knowledge attributions, according to subject-sensitive invariantism, are not affected by how much is at stake or whether error possibilities are salient for those who are merely reading and commenting on the vignettes.

However, according to contextualism, the truth conditions for knowledge attributions are tied to the circumstances of those who are attributing or denying knowledge. If a character in a vignette is attributing knowledge, the epistemic standards in place at that character's conversational context determine the truth value of the knowledge attribution. But if the reader of a vignette is asked to attribute or deny knowledge, it will be the standards of the reader's context that determine the attribution's truth value. Furthermore, DeRose (2010) contends that it is not as clear as many epistemologists think about what predictions extant versions of contextualism will make regarding participant responses when they are simply asked whether a vignette character knows or does not know. In fact, DeRose thinks that no version of contextualism is sufficiently developed and detailed to make any clear prediction.

In other research, Adam Feltz and Chris Zarpentine (2010) ran a set of experiments that tested for the effect of high stakes upon knowledge attributions but found no effect in their studies. Mark Phelan (forthcoming) ran a related set of experiments that looked at how strong participants thought the evidence of protagonists was and again found that raising stakes did not affect folk attributions, as long as the cases were presented individually. However, he did find an effect when high and low stakes cases were presented in a juxtaposed fashion. Phelan takes the fact that no effect was found in individual cases to indicate that stakes do not in general factor into people's assessments of strength of evidence.

Researchers in any area of scientific inquiry need to be careful about the conclusions they draw from null results—that is, results that fail to pass tests of statistical significance. If, for example, I look very carefully at my hands but fail to see any microbes, obviously I am not entitled to conclude that there are no microbes on my hands. Similarly, experimental epistemologists need to be careful about the conclusions they draw from studies in which no statistical differences were found between participants' responses to sets of cases. One reason why no such differences were found may be that the tools researchers used to probe for such differences were not sufficiently fine-grained or otherwise attuned to the phenomena under investigation.

In contrast to the foregoing studies that failed to find that making error possibilities salient had any effect on knowledge attributions, a study by Jonathan Schaffer and Joshua Knobe (forthcoming) did reveal such an effect when possibilities of error were presented in what they claim was "a concrete and vivid fashion." Instead of having one character in a Bank case simply mention the abstract possibility that banks might change their hours and thus be closed on one Saturday after having been open on another, Schaffer and Knobe had one of the characters in their vignettes make the following statements:

> Well, banks do change their hours sometimes. My brother Leon once got into trouble when the bank changed hours on him and closed on Saturday. How frustrating! Just imagine driving here tomorrow and finding the door locked.

Even though all participants were told that the cognitive agent whose belief was in question remained "just as confident" as he or she was that the bank will be open on Saturday, participants were less inclined to think that the character knew the bank would be open when the possibility of error was presented in this concrete fashion (mean rating: 3.05 out of 7) than when the possibility of error was presented more abstractly (mean rating: 5.54 out of 7). DeRose (2010), however, claims that the extra information provided about Leon above may well have the (unintended) effect of raising the stakes in the vignette. He writes:

> It seems it could just as easily be thought that what [Schaffer and Knobe] are pounding home to the survey takers is thoughts about the practical consequences or stakes of being wrong. Sarah tells Hannah about poor Leon and the frustration he had to endure when he was wrong about the bank's hours, and then, turning to Hannah's and her own situation, adds, "Just imagine driving here tomorrow and finding the doors locked." Is this not at least hinting that the stakes may be quite high and/or encouraging respondents to focus on the matter of the practical consequences or stakes of being wrong? . . . [T]hat Sarah would carry on as she does in [Schaffer and Knobe's] beefed up HIGH case might well indicate to the survey takers that the stakes are high somehow.

Further empirical investigation of DeRose's suggestion is obviously required.

In order to investigate whether folk attributions of knowledge are sensitive to stakes, Ángel Pinillos (forthcoming) presented participants with two versions of a vignette about a college student who has a term paper due the following day. In a low-stakes condition nothing of significance hangs upon whether there are any typos in the paper. In a contrasting high stakes condition, the student needs to get an A in order to keep his scholarship. Instead of simply asking whether the student knows that there are no typos in the paper, Pinillos chose to ask participants "How many times do you think [the student] has to proofread his paper before he knows that there are no typos?" The median answer in the low-stakes condition was 2, and the median answer in the high-stakes condition was 5. Pinillos found similar results using high- and low-stakes versions of a vignette in which a protagonist must correctly count the pennies in a medium size jar in order to win a prize.

Experimental epistemologists, then, seem to have found modest evidence in support of the claim that salient error possibilities and high stakes can affect folk knowledge attributions. However, much more data need to be obtained before we can know whether patterns of folk attributions will tend to favor contextualism, contrastivism, classical invariantism, subject-sensitive invariantism, or some other mainstream epistemological perspective.

Knowledge and action

If stakes do in fact affect knowledge attributions, it represents one kind of connection between knowledge and action, since the practical costs of failing to know are costs associated with the actions one is undertaking. Another kind of connection between knowledge and action has been found by James Beebe and Wesley Buckwalter (2010) and James Beebe and Mark Jensen (forthcoming). Beebe and Buckwalter initially presented participants with either the help or the harm versions of the following vignette (based upon Knobe 2003a's original study):

> The vice-president of a company went to the chairman of the board and said, "We are thinking of starting a new program. We are sure that it will help us increase profits, and it will also *help/harm* the environment." The chairman of the board answered, "I don't care at all about *helping/harming* the environment. I just want to make as much profit as I can. Let's start the new

program." They started the new program. Sure enough, the environment was *helped/harmed*. Did the chairman know that the new program would *help/harm* the environment?

Participants were asked to indicate their response to the question "Did the chairman know that the new program would *help/harm* the environment?" on a seven-point Likert scale, ranging from − 3 (labeled as "the chairman didn't know") to 3 (labeled as "the chairman knew'). Almost twice as many participants chose the strongest possible affirmation of the chairman's knowledge (viz., response "3") in the harm condition (67.5%) as in the help condition (35.5%), and the percentage of participants who chose responses 1, 2, or 3 in the harm condition (90%) was significantly greater than the number of participants who chose 1, 2, or 3 in the help condition (61%).

Buckwalter (forthcoming) found a significant gender difference in how participants responded to the chairman case. Women were significantly less likely than men to attribute knowledge to the chairman in the help condition, which means that the difference between helping and harming had more of an overall effect on how women responded than men. Beebe and Jensen also found that subjects were more likely to attribute knowledge when the side-effect in question involved aesthetic or prudential (as opposed to moral) harm.

These findings suggest that the practice of making epistemic evaluations may be more closely related—at least psychologically—to other practices of normative assessment than epistemologists have thought. According to the traditional epistemological view of the relationship between knowledge and action, whether a subject knows a proposition is completely independent of whatever actions that subject may undertake in light of believing that proposition. Recent proponents of "pragmatic encroachment" in epistemology (e.g. Fantl and McGrath 2002, 2007; Hawthorne 2004; Stanley 2005), however, have challenged this view and argued that whether a true belief counts as knowledge can depend in part upon non-epistemic facts about how much is at stake for a subject concerning the truth of the belief. Yet it is unlikely that any of these scholars would embrace the view that the goodness or badness of actions performed in light of a belief can affect that belief's status of knowledge. However, many defenders of pragmatic encroachment (e.g. Hawthorne and Stanley) place a premium on making their own epistemological theories square with the epistemic intuitions of ordinary people. By demonstrating another respect in which folk epistemic intuitions diverge from *a priori* expectations concerning them, the foregoing results place pressure on anyone wishing to maintain this combination of views.

Larger methodological issues

Although the findings of experimental epistemologists obviously raise challenges to the use of this or that thought experiment for this or that purpose in epistemology, experimental philosophy is most often associated with more global methodological challenges. Consider the following, widely endorsed theses:

(i) Whether a true belief counts as knowledge depends only upon epistemic factors such as evidence or reliability.

(ii) Because the target of philosophical analyses of knowledge is the ordinary person's concept of knowledge, such analyses should be answerable to data about "what the ordinary person would say" in response to various epistemological thought experiments.

Many experimental epistemologists believe that the variability, instability, and seeming irrationality of folk responses to thought experiments makes the conjunction of (i) and (ii) increasingly difficult to maintain. While it may be possible to dismiss a small class of the surprising patterns of variation as due to performance errors or noise, if more and more experimental data are gathered that shows that ordinary peoples' knowledge attributions are influenced by a variety of non-epistemic factors such as culture, education, socioeconomic status, and the moral properties of actions, this line will become ever more difficult to hold.

The strongest form of the "experimentalist's challenge" to standard philosophical practice has been dubbed the "restrictionist view," according to which "the results of experimental philosophy should figure into a radical restriction of the deployment of intuitions as evidence."[7] Restrictionists maintain that "the problem with standard philosophical practice is that experimental evidence seems to point to the unsuitability of intuitions to serve as evidence at all."[8] Weinberg et al. (2001) claim, "a sizeable group of epistemological projects—a group which includes much of what has been done in epistemology in the analytic tradition—would be seriously undermined if one or more of a cluster of empirical hypotheses about epistemic intuitions turns out to be true." Critics of experimental philosophy have responded to these challenges in a variety of ways.

Surface intuitions vs robust intuitions

Antti Kauppinen (2007, p. 105) questions whether the intuitive responses gathered by experimental philosophical research are sufficiently robust to underwrite the experimentalist's challenge:

> There is no support to be had from responses of those non-philosophers who only appear to understand the question, who may have an imperfect grasp of the concept in question, who may or may not think hard about the application of the concept in circumstances that may or may not be conducive to avoiding conceptual mistakes, who may or may not rush in their judgements, and who may or may not be influenced by various pragmatic factors . . . [T]he *actual studies* conducted so far have failed to rule out competence failures, performance failures, and the potential influence of pragmatic factors, and as such do not yield the sort of results that could support or raise doubts about philosophical appeals to conceptual intuitions.

Kauppinen is correct that experimental philosophers have sometimes been too quick to draw conclusions about the conceptual competence and narrative comprehension of their participants. However, when Kauppinen goes on to express grave doubts about whether it is possible for experimental epistemologists to deal with the worries he raises, his case becomes much less convincing. Kauppinen does not think that the methods used by experimentalists allow for the possibility of (i) testing for how well participants grasp key concepts, (ii) providing sufficient motivation for participants to display a high level of performance, or (iii) testing for the effects of pragmatic factors in research materials. However, many experimental philosophers have already been testing these factors. For example, Weinberg et al. (2001) and Swain et al. (2008) include the following vignette to test the conceptual competence of their participants:

> Dave likes to play a game with flipping a coin. He sometimes gets a "special feeling" that the next flip will come out heads. When he gets this "special feeling," he is right about half the time, and wrong about half the time. Just before the next flip, Dave gets that "special feeling," and the feeling leads him to believe that the coin will land heads. He flips the coin, and it does land heads.

When participants were asked whether Dave knew that the coin was going to land heads, Swain et al. (2008) excluded from further analysis any participant who answered in the affirmative, on the presumption that the participants either did not understand the question or were operating with alternative conceptions of knowledge. Comprehension checks are standard fare in social psychology and can be deployed any time concerns about participant comprehension are germane.

Regarding the effects that pragmatic factors may have on participant responses, Knobe (2003b) and Nadelhoffer (2004) have already run experiments that have tested for and apparently ruled out various pragmatic effects. If researchers suspect that one kind of vignette used in experimental philosophical research has a certain pragmatic implicature and that participants may be responding to that implicature rather than to the semantic content alone (as perhaps intended by the original researchers), modified versions of the vignette that uncontroversially lack such an implicature can be used to test this suspicion. Thus, the difficulties raised by Kauppinen seem to be practical rather than principled.

The different concepts response

Ernest Sosa (2007, pp. 102–3) offers the following reply to the experimentalist's challenge:

> The bearing of these surveys on traditional philosophical issues is questionable, however, because the experimental results really concern in the first instance only people's responses to certain words. But verbal disagreement *need* not reveal any substantive, real disagreement, if ambiguity and context might account for the verbal divergence. . . . The experimentalists have not yet done enough to show that they have crossed the gaps created by such potential differences in meaning and context, so as to show that supposedly commonsense intuitive belief is really not as widely shared as philosophers have assumed it to be.

Sosa is certainly correct that too often experimental philosophers have tried to support far-reaching conclusions on the basis of too few studies and should do more to rule out alternative, less radical explanations of their experimental data. However, it is also important to note that pointing to the bare possibility that participants who offer different responses to survey questions may be parties to a merely verbal dispute does nothing to show that this is indeed the correct explanation of the surprising data.

Sosa (2005) also raises the following, related objection:

> When we read fiction we import a great deal that is not explicit in the text. We import a lot that is normally presupposed about the physical and social structure of the situation as we follow the author's lead in our own imaginative construction. . . . Given that these subjects are sufficiently different culturally and socio-economically, they may because of this import different assumptions

as they follow in their own imaginative construction the lead of the author of the examples, and this may result in their filling the crucial [description of a protagonist's epistemic condition] differently. But if [this description] varies across the divide, then the subjects may not after all disagree about the very same content.

Sosa's objections here are versions of the "different concepts" response to the experimentalist's challenge. According to this response, if it can be shown that people from different demographic groups (e.g. East Asians vs Westerners, male vs female) repeatedly respond to philosophical thought experiments in systematically different ways, then the two groups may be deploying non-equivalent concepts. If they are using non-equivalent concepts, the attempt by some experimental philosophers to use cross-demographic variation to challenge current ways of thinking in epistemology will come to naught, since the different groups will not even be talking about the same thing. Again, however, the "two concepts" response merely points to a hypothetical possibility without providing any reason for believing the possibility is real. If this possibility were realized, the experimentalist's challenge would indeed be neutralized. But in the absence of reasons to think that it is, the experimentalist's challenge stands.

The expert response

A more common response to the experimentalist's challenge is to try to find some reason to privilege the intuitions of those who are experts concerning the application of the concepts in the relevant domain. Michael Devitt (2006, p. 103) takes up this line of response and argues that intuitions are "empirical theory-laden central-processor responses to phenomena, differing from many other such responses only in being fairly immediate and unreflective, based on little if any conscious reasoning." He argues that we should trust a person's intuitions to the degree that we should trust the theory and experience underwriting those intuitions:

> Sometimes the folk may be as expert as anyone: intuitions laden with "folk theory" are the best we have to go on. Perhaps this is the case for a range of psychological kinds. For most kinds, it clearly is not: we should trust intuitions laden with established scientific theories. Consider, for example, a paleontologist in the field searching for fossils. She sees a bit of white stone sticking through grey rock, and thinks "a pig's jawbone." This intuitive judgment is quick and unreflective. She may be quite sure but unable to explain just how she knows.

We trust her judgment in a way that we would not trust folk judgments because we know that it is the result of years of study and experience of old bones; she has become a reliable indicator of the properties of fossils. Similarly we trust the intuitions of the physicist over those of the folk about many aspects of the physical world where the folk have proved notoriously unreliable.[9]

One can grant that Devitt's proposal sounds plausible for disciplines like paleontology and physics and yet wonder whether there is anyone who has comparable expertise in matters philosophical. The mere fact that philosophers spend more time thinking about philosophical concepts does not guarantee that time spent translates into expertise. Alexander and Weinberg (2007) note that extended reflection might simply reinforce intuitive judgments philosophers already made before engaging in reflection—that is, that philosophical reflection might not be what produces the intuitions of philosophers at all.

Another possibility is that long hours of participating in philosophical debate may have an effect more akin to enculturation or socialization than enlightenment. Extended practice in philosophy may simply enable one to participate successively in the culture of philosophy, where giving certain kinds of recognized responses to philosophical thought experiments is part of what makes one a full member of the culture. Experimental philosophers are not committed to the view that this is all there is to being a professional philosopher, but the experimentalist's challenge calls upon proponents of the expert response to provide non-question-begging reasons to rule out these alternatives. It is widely agreed that reasons of this sort have not been forthcoming. Moreover, Thomas Nadelhoffer and Eddy Nahmias (2007, p. 129) note that "to establish that pre-philosophical folk intuitions should *not* be trusted and that philosophically informed intuitions *should* be trusted would require more, not less, experimental research" because it is only through rigorous empirical investigation that we could establish the putative unreliability of folk intuitions.

Conclusion

Experimental epistemologists have begun to gather a variety of interesting data about epistemic cognition—that is, about how ordinary people think about knowledge, evidence, and related epistemic notions. Sometimes their experiments confirm established philosophical opinion, while at other times they surprise us. Contrary to what some philosophers may think, it is not the case that experimental epistemology can be deemed profitable only if it succeeds in radically overturning traditional philosophical methodology. To the degree that mainstream epistemologists engage with the ordinary person's notions of knowledge, evidence, and justified belief, we need to understand what those notions are—in all of their (perhaps messy) details. Experimental epistemology is one attempt to provide us with this important kind of understanding.

Notes

1 See BonJour (1980).
2 See Lehrer (1990).
3 See Cohen (1984).
4 See DeRose (1992, 1995, 2005); Hawthorne (2004); Stanley (2005).
5 Cf. Goldman (1986).
6 For example Hawthorne (2004); Stanley (2005).
7 See Alexander and Weinberg (2007, p. 61).
8 Ibid., p. 63.
9 See Devitt (2006, pp. 104–5).

References

Alston, W. P. 1989. "An Internalist Externalism." In *Epistemic Justification: Essays in the Theory of Knowledge.* Ithaca, NY: Cornell University Press, pp. 227–45.

Alexander, J. and Weinberg, J. M. 2007. "Analytic Epistemology and Experimental Philosophy." *Philosophy Compass* 2: 56–80.

Beebe, J. and Wesley, B. 2010. "The Epistemic Side-Effect Effect." *Mind & Language* 25: 474–98.

Beebe, J. and Mark, J. (forthcoming). "Surprising Connections Between Knowledge and Intentional Action: The Robustness of the Epistemic Side–Effect Effect." *Philosophical Psychology.*

Bishop, M. A. and Trout, J. D. 2005. *Epistemology and the Psychology of Human Judgment.* Oxford and New York: Oxford University Press.

BonJour, L. 1980. "Externalist Theories of Empirical Knowledge." In P. French, T. Uehling and H. Wettstein, eds, *Midwest Studies in Philosophy,* Vol. 5: Epistemology, University of Minnesota Press, Minneapolis, pp. 53–73.

— 1992. "Externalism/Internalism." In J. Dancy and E. Sosa, eds, *A Companion to Epistemology,* Blackwell, Oxford, pp. 132–6.

Buckwalter, W. 2010. "Knowledge Isn't Closed on Saturday: A Study in
Ordinary Language." *Review of Philosophy and Psychology* 1: 395–406.

— (forthcoming). Gender and epistemic intuition.

Buckwalter, W. and Stephen, S. (forthcoming) Gender and Philosophical
Intuition. In J. Knobe and S. Nichols eds, *Experimental Philosophy*, Vol. 2.
Oxford University Press.

Cohen, S. 1984. "Justification and Truth." *Philosophical Studies* 46: 279–96.

— 1988. "How to be a Fallibilist." *Philosophical Perspectives* 2: 91–123.

— 1999. "Contextualism, Skepticism, and the Structure of Reasons." *Philosophical
Perspectives* 13: 57–89.

Cullen, S. 2010. "Survey-Driven Romanticism." *Review of Philosophy and Psychology* 1.

DeRose, K. 1992. "Contextualism and Knowledge Attributions." *Philosophy and
Phenomenological Research* 52(4): 913–29.

— 1995 "Solving the Skeptical Problem." *Philosophical Review* 104(1): 1–52.

— 2005. "The Ordinary Language Basis for Contextualism and the New Invariantism."
The Philosophical Quarterly 55: 172–98.

— 2010. "Contextualism, Contrastivism, and X-PhiSurveys." Presented at the
39th Oberlin College Colloquium in Philosophy. 9 May 2010.

Devitt, M. 2006. *Ignorance of Language.* Oxford: Clarendon Press.

Fantl, J. and McGrath, M. 2002. "Evidence, Pragmatics, and Justification." *Philosophical
Review* 111: 67–94.

Fantl, J. and McGrath, M. 2007. "On Pragmatic Encroachment in Epistemology."
Philosophy and Phenomenological Research 75: 558–89.

Feltz, A. and Zarpentine, C. 2010. "Do You Know More When It Matters Less?"
Philosophical Psychology 23: 683–706.

Gettier, E. L. 1963. "Is Justified True Belief Knowledge?" *Analysis* 23: 121–3.

Goldman, A. 1986. *Epistemology and Cognition.* Cambridge, MA:
Harvard University Press.

Goldman, A. I.1994. "Naturalistic Epistemology and Reliabilism." In P. French,
T. Uehling and H. Wettstein, eds eds, *Midwest Studies in Philosophy*, Vol. 19.
Minneapolis: University of Minnesota Press, pp. 301–20.

Hawthorne, J. 2004. *Knowledge and Lotteries.* Oxford: Oxford University Press.

Kauppinen, A. 2007. "The Rise and Fall of Experimental Philosophy." *Philosophical
Explorations* 10: 95–118.

Knobe, J. 2003a. "Intentional Action and Side Effects in Ordinary Language." *Analysis*
63: 190–3.

— 2003b. "Intentional Action in Folk Psychology: An Experimental Investigation."
Philosophical Psychology 16(2): 309–23.

Lehrer, K. 1990. *Theory of Knowledge.* Boulder and London: Westview Press.

Lewis, D. 1996. "Elusive Knowledge." *Australasian Journal of Philosophy* 74: 549–67.

Liao, M. 2008. "A Defense of Intuitions." *Philosophical Studies* 140: 247–62.

May, J., Sinnott-Armstrong, W., Hull, J. G. and Zimmerman, A. 2010. "Practical Interests, Relevant Alternatives, and Knowledge Attributions: An Empirical Study." *Review of Philosophy and Psychology* 1: 265–73.

Nadelhoffer, T. 2004. "The Butler Problem Revisited." *Analysis* 64(3): 277–84.

Nadelhoffer, T. and Nahmias, E. 2007. "The Past and Future of Experimental Philosophy." *Philosophical Explorations* 10: 123–49.

Nagel, J. 2007. "Epistemic Intuitions." *Philosophy Compass* 2: 792–819.

— (forthcoming). "Intuitions and Experiments: A Defense of the Case Method." *Philosophy and Phenomenological Research.*

Nagel, J., San Juan, V. and Mar, R. (in prep). Gettier Case Recognition.

Nichols, S., Stich, S. and Weinberg, J. M. 2003. "Metaskepticism: Meditations in Ethno-Epistemology." In S. Luper, eds ed., *The Skeptics.* Burlington, VT: Ashgate Press, pp. 227–47.

Phelan, M. (manuscript). "Evidence that Stakes Don't Matter for Evidence."

Pinillos, N.Á. (forthcoming). "Knowledge, Experiments and Practical Interests." In J. Brown and M. Gerken, eds eds, *Knowledge Ascriptions.* Oxford: Oxford University Press.

Schaffer, J. 2004. "From Contextualism to Contrastivism." *Philosophical Studies* 119: 73–103.

Schaffer, J. and Joshua, K. (manuscript). "Contrastive Knowledge Surveyed." *Nous.*

Sosa, E. 2005. "A Defense of the Use of Intuitions in Philosophy." In D. Murphy and M. Bishop, eds eds, *Stich and his Critics.* Oxford: Blackwell, pp. 101–12.

— 2007. "Experimental Philosophy and Philosophical Intuition." *Philosophical Studies* 132: 99–107.

Stanley, J. 2005. *Knowledge and Practical Interests.* Oxford: Oxford University Press.

Swain, S., Alexander, J. and Weinberg, J. M. 2008. "The Instability of Philosophical Intuitions: Running Hot and Cold on Truetemp." *Philosophy and Phenomenological Research* 76: 138–55.

Weinberg, J. M., Nichols, S. and Stich, S. 2001. "Normativity and Epistemic Intuitions." *Philosophical Topics* 29: 429–60.

Wright, J. C. 2010. "On Intuitional Stability: The Clear, the Strong, and the Paradigmatic." *Cognition* 115: 491–503.

14

Epistemic Value

Dennis Whitcomb

Introduction

Epistemology is normative. This normativity has been widely recognized for a long time, but it has recently come into direct focus as a central topic of discussion. The result is a recent and large turn toward focusing on epistemic value.

I'll start by describing some of the history and motivations of this recent value turn.[1] Then I'll categorize the work within the value turn into three strands, and I'll discuss the main writings in those strands.[2] Finally, I'll explore some themes that are ripe for further development.

Motivations

The value turn has numerous motivations; I'll discuss three of them. The first of these motivations consists in the ancient roots of the idea that epistemology is in some important way value-theoretic. Plato and Aristotle both took epistemic states such as knowledge and understanding to have particular and distinctive value. So too did their immediate and medieval followers (Zagzebski 2001). These historical foci on value in epistemology have played a role in motivating some current writers to develop similar foci (Roberts and Wood 2007; Zagzebski 1996).

A second motivation for the value turn consists in certain recent debates about the nature of knowledge and justification: debates about the Pyrrhonian problematic, the Gettier problem, naturalism, contextualism, epistemic goals, and eliminativism about justification.

As for the Pyrrhonian problematic, early forms of virtue epistemology were designed (in part) to resolve it by giving virtuously produced beliefs as special role in blocking the epistemic regress (Sosa 1980).

As for the Gettier problem, certain later forms of virtue epistemology were designed (in part) to resolve it. The central idea here is that in some cases one's belief is true *because* it was formed via one's epistemic virtues. It is said that in these sorts of cases the truth of one's belief is to one's *credit,* and moreover that the credit at work here is precisely what we lack in Gettier cases but have when we know (Greco 2003, 2010; Riggs 2002; Sosa 1988, 2003; Zagzebski 1996).

As for contextualism, some theorists have entertained the thought that there might well be different values, or at least different degrees of value, attaching the referents of "knows" in different contexts. This thought naturally suggests questions about what kind of values knowledge has in the first place, and (if there are several such values) about which of those values are more important than which others (Sosa 2000).[3]

As for naturalism, some epistemologists have pursued value-focused themes in part as a reaction against epistemological naturalism, which they think renders humans and their mental states too much like machines and mere objects, and too little like agents and their genuine achievements, to have the sort of value we associate with knowledge, understanding, and other epistemic goods (Zagzebski 1996).

As for epistemic goals, many theorists hold that belief and justification have goals or aims. Debates about what these aims are (truth, avoidance of falsehood, knowledge, justification, etc.), and what their relative weights are, amount to debates about what has epistemic value and what has more epistemic value than what else (DePaul 2001; David 2001; Feldman 1988, 2002; Kvanvig 2005).

As for eliminativism about justification, Alston (1993, 2005) has argued with some persuasiveness that the notion of epistemic justification should be abandoned because it has no unique referent, and because this lack of a unique referent regularly leads theorists to talk past one another. Now, suppose we follow Alston in eliminating the notion of justification in our theorizing. What do we do next? With what do we *replace* debates about justification? Here Alston's answer is that in the place of justification we should theorize about a full range of "epistemic desiderata"—things that are good epistemically, such as true belief and belief in accordance with one's evidence. This replacement project squarely deals with epistemic value, and it is motivated by eliminativism about justification.

A third motivation for theorizing about epistemic value consists in the idea that epistemology should evaluate various "applied" phenomena like reasoning and research design. Early partisans of this idea (Goldman 1978, 1986; Kitcher 1992) developed it far before the value turn began in earnest. In doing so they explored many of the themes the current trend is now beginning to explore again. For instance, they expanded the so-called epistemic goals to include, not only truth and the avoidance of falsehood, but also significant as opposed to trivial belief and even such higher states as understanding. These themes naturally arose in the course of trying to apply epistemology to evaluate reasoning, research design, and other similar phenomena. More recent attempts to apply epistemology to such phenomena can by found in work by Bishop and Trout (2005), Laudan (2007), Roberts and Wood (2007), and others.

Now that I've outlined some of the main motivations for the value turn, I'll go on to discuss the main branches of theorizing within that turn.[4]

Main branches of work

There are three main branches of writings within the value turn. The first branch—"value-driven epistemology"—addresses the *nature* of states like knowledge, justified belief, and understanding, and in doing so it places a particular focus on the idea that these states have epistemic value.[5] The second branch—"epistemic value theory"—focuses on epistemic value directly, and for its own theoretical sake, as opposed to focusing on it for the purpose of theorizing about the nature of states (like knowledge and justified belief) that exemplify it.[6] The third branch—"applied epistemic value theory"—stands to epistemic value theory as applied ethics stands to normative ethics. Applied ethicists focus on the ethical status of particular types of acts (e.g. abortion), whereas normative ethicists focus on the normative status of acts *in general.* Similarly, applied epistemic value theorists focus on the epistemic status of particular phenomena (e.g. the instructions judges give juries), whereas epistemic value theorists focus on the epistemic status of phenomena in general. So, to repeat, *value-driven epistemology* addresses epistemic value in an attempt to illuminate the nature of epistemic states instantiating it, *epistemic value theory* addresses epistemic value for its own theoretical sake, and *applied epistemic value theory* addresses the epistemic value of particular types of phenomena.

Value-driven epistemology

Value-driven epistemology addresses many epistemic states, but most of it focuses on knowledge. In the *Meno*, Plato claims that knowledge is better than true belief. There are three important questions about this claim: the questions of whether it is true, why it is true, and what follows from the putative fact that it is true. These three questions are complicated in four important ways.

First, they are complicated by the fact that theorists sometimes replace "true belief" with a term like "proper parts of knowledge," the idea being (roughly) that the questions should be asked not only about true belief, but about every state that, like true belief and justified belief, features some of the necessary conditions on knowledge but not others. Other times, theorists replace "true belief" with some very general term like "everything in the ballpark of knowledge," the idea being that we should ask if (and why, and what follows from the putative fact that) knowledge is better than every other epistemic state.

The second and third complications have to do with the notion of betterness. Different theorists can mean to invoke different *dimensions* of betterness by the term "better than": they can mean to invoke prudential betterness, moral betterness, epistemic betterness, or all-things-considered betterness. Also, different theorists can mean to invoke different *kinds* of betterness: betterness as a means, and betterness as an end (as well as more exotic kinds of betterness such as contributory betterness—see Whitcomb 2007 and Pritchard 2010). The second and third complications, then, are that different theorists invoke different dimensions and kinds of value.

The fourth complication arises from the issue of which items of knowledge are supposed to be better than which items of true belief (or whatever true belief has been replaced by). In some cases, theorists seem to be comparing every item of knowledge to every item of true belief (etc.). In other cases, they just try to compare items of knowledge and true belief (etc.) of a certain class, for instance the class of pairs of these items across which *other things are equal*. And in other cases still, the authors just take the relevant betterness to hold generically, as for example, it holds generically that grizzlies are bigger than black bears.

In summary, the *Meno* drives theorists to ask numerous questions about the value of knowledge. Those questions focus on whether knowledge is better than true belief, and why, and what follows from that fact; and they are complicated because different theorists fill in the details differently: the notion of true belief is sometimes replaced by other notions, the notion of betterness is sometimes replaced by other (more specific) notions, and class of the items compared to one another is sometimes wider and other times narrower.

For each exhaustive way of specifying (and/or refraining from specifying) these niceties, there is a particular question about the value of knowledge. Each such question is its own Meno problem; these problems form an interesting domain of inquiry centered on the idea that knowledge is somehow better than states like true belief. We can get a reflective understanding of this domain by classifying its constituent questions in accordance with Figure 14.1:

For instance, suppose that we set the variables such that

a = Why is it true that
b = epistemically
c = as an end
d = true belief
e = <removed>

This leaves us with the following question:

Why is it true that knowledge is better epistemically as an end than true belief?

This figure encodes hundreds of distinct Meno problems—540 of them, to be exact. Some of these problems are very specific and others are rather unspecific. Each Meno problem amounts to the question formed by substituting phrases from the boxes for their corresponding variables, or simply removing those variables. The more variables we replace instead of removing, the more specific the resulting Meno problem. To solve a given Meno problem is to answer the given question.

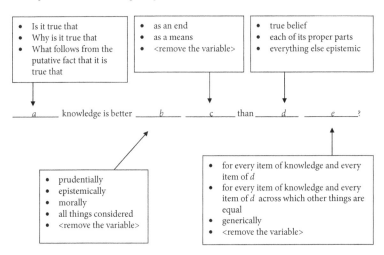

Figure 14.1 A Smorgasbord of Meno Problems.

Or to pose the same question more concisely by semantically descending from the truth predicate,

Why is knowledge better epistemically as an end than true belief?

The recent literature on epistemic value features numerous attempts to answer this question, and to answer the many other questions we get by setting the variables differently.[7] In some cases, theorists are quite clear about which question or questions they are addressing. In other cases they are unclear on the matter, and as a result there is a significant literature trying to get straight on what the Meno problem really is, or on what the various Meno problems really are (Baehr 2009; Greco 2010, 2011; Kvanvig 2010; Pritchard 2010, 2011; Riggs 2009). The best way to get straight on this issue, I think, is to appreciate that there are at least 540 distinct Meno problems, and to keep in mind the distinctions among them.

Among the attempts to solve these problems, the three most prominent themes are what I'll call denial, credit theory, and anti-reliabilism. Deniers focus on the *is it true that* questions. They conclude that knowledge is in fact not better than true belief (or one or more of its other parts), or at least that there are one or more significant ways in which knowledge fails to be better than true belief (or one or more of its other parts). Credit theorists focus on the *why is it true that* questions. They argue for a certain theory of the nature of knowledge, namely the credit theory, on the grounds that it answers some or all of these why-questions. Anti-reliabilists focus on the *what follows from the putative fact that* questions. They argue that a certain important conclusion follows, that conclusion being that reliabilism is false.

Each of these three themes—denial, credit theory, and anti-reliabilism—comes in many flavors, as do numerous other themes. The differences across these themes and their flavors are often determined by the (often implicit) choice to focus on one (or more) of the 540 Meno problems as opposed to others. It seems safe to say that these themes will continue to work out for a good while, and that advancements can be made by paying greater attention to precisely which Meno problems are at issue.

All of the work on the Meno problems focuses on the value of knowledge. But other work in value-driven epistemology focuses on lesser-theorized states. These states include true belief, significant (as opposed to trivial) knowledge and true belief, curiosity, understanding, and wisdom.

Taking these states one at a time, let us start with true belief. Many theorists take it that true belief is good epistemically. The most common arguments for that view are teleological. Many theorists hold that belief has a telos or "aim," much like knives have the aim of cutting things. These theorists often identify truth with that aim, and in doing so they take truth to be particularly good epistemically (Shah and Velleman 2005; Wedgwood 2002). Other theorists identify the aim of belief with, not truth, but *knowledge* (Sutton 2005; Williamson 2000). At least one theorist identifies the aim of belief with *justification* (Feldman 2002).[8] There are numerous theoretical difficulties with all of these views, perhaps most importantly the difficulties of unpacking the idea of an "aim" in such a way that beliefs, as well as knives, can turn out to have one. Other theorists in a similar vein focus not on the notion of belief but on the notion of *inquiry*. For these theorists, inquiry has a telos or aim, for example, truth (Hookway 2003) or knowledge (Whitcomb 2010). Like the aim-of-belief theorists, these aim-of-inquiry theorists have as a central theoretical difficulty explaining the notion of inquiry's "aim."

Knowledge and true belief, then, are often taken to be epistemic goods. To the extent that it is plausible that these things *are* epistemic goods, something else is plausible as well, to wit that it is better epistemically to have more rather than less of them. It is possible to know more rather than less, and to have more rather than less true belief (and for that matter, more rather than less of any epistemically valuable state including justified belief, understanding, and others). It is occasionally remarked that we do better epistemically by having more rather than less of these things (Goldman 1986; Levi 1980). Such remarks are ripe for further development. In developing them we need, among other things, to make sense of the "measure" involved—the units or quantities of knowledge and belief (Treanor forthcoming).

Another epistemically valuable state, closely related to large (as opposed to small) amounts of knowledge and belief, is significant (as opposed to trivial) knowledge and belief. It is better epistemically to know deep theoretical truths about, for example, metaphysics or physics, than it is to know trivial truths such as truths about the number of grains of sand on the nearest beach. Indeed, even if one were to know a lot of trivial truths, and thereby fulfill the epistemic value of having more rather than less knowledge, one's epistemic states would still be deficient owing to their triviality. Just as theorists inquire into the measure of knowledge, then, they also inquire into the nature of significance—the property that makes significant knowledge significant as opposed to trivial. Some approaches to significance make it a wholly objective mind-independent matter, for instance by making knowledge significant to the extent that it encodes laws of nature and classifies objects into natural kinds (Kitcher 1993). Other approaches make significance more subjective or mind-dependent, for instance by taking one's knowledge to be significant to the extent that it answers whatever questions one happens to be curious about (Goldman 1999).

Curiosity is thus sometimes taken to be the determiner of epistemic significance. It is also sometimes given other roles, for instance the role of explaining (or at least partly explaining) why true belief or knowledge is valuable epistemically (Alston 2005; Goldman 1999; Miscevic 2007). Here the idea is not (a) that certain items of knowledge or true belief are significant in virtue of satisfying our curiosity, but instead (b) that true belief (or knowledge) *per se* is epistemically valuable because of its relationship to curiosity. There is considerable controversy over whether either (a) or (b) is correct (Brady 2009; Grimm 2008). There is also controversy over what curiosity *is*. Some claim that it is a desire for true belief (Foley 1987; Goldman 1991); others claim that it is a desire for knowledge (Schmitt and Lahroodi 2008; Williamson 2000; Whitcomb 2010a); and others still have views more complicated than either of these (Kvanvig 2003).

We see, then, that there are epistemically valuable states other than knowledge, and that these states include true belief, bigger as opposed to smaller amounts of knowledge and true belief, and significant as opposed to trivial knowledge and true belief. In many cases, *curiosity* is taken to be particularly relevant to these states and their epistemic values. In recent years though, a different state entirely—*understanding*—has seen more focus than any of these.

In several cases, philosophers exploring the various Meno problems have concluded with some sort of denial, that is to say, some version of that view that knowledge actually isn't better than true belief. It is common among such philosophers to conjecture that a different state has what knowledge here lacks, and that this different state is understanding (Kvanvig 2003; Pritchard 2010). Unsurprisingly, though, there are numerous disagreements about what understanding *is*. These disagreements are complicated by the fact that understanding comes in several forms: understanding *why* ("I understand why the litmus paper just turned pink") and understanding *that* ("I understand that the meeting is on Wednesday"), as well as the understanding of domains ("She understands physics").[9] Some of these forms of understanding may be reducible to others; there are active debates on the matter (Grimm 2010). There are also active debates on several related matters, including the matters of whether understanding is a species of knowledge (Grimm 2006), whether it somehow requires truth (Elgin 2009; Kvanvig 2003), and whether we can always reflectively access the facts about whether we have it (Zagzebski 2001).

In any case, understanding is widely taken to be a "higher" epistemic good: a state that is like knowledge and true belief, but even better, epistemically speaking. Another such state is *wisdom*. Aristotle identified two sorts of wisdom, the practical (roughly: a capacity for good judgment) and the theoretical (roughly: deep understanding). He took both of these sorts of wisdom, and particularly the theoretical sort, to be especially important epistemic goods. Contemporary epistemologists who theorize about wisdom most often take it to come in only the practical variety (Garrett 1996; Nozick 1989; Ryan 1996, 1999, 2007), although some of them argue that there is a *theoretical* form of wisdom as well (Whitcomb 2010b).

Now that I have surveyed some of the main work in value-driven epistemology, I'll move on to a more radical branch of the value turn. This more radical branch, *epistemic value theory*, is aimed directly at the epistemic value of various states, and inquires into that value for its own theoretical sake as opposed to the sake of identifying the natures of those states.

Epistemic value theory

Most contemporary epistemologists organize their theorizing around two standard questions: "What is knowledge?" and "How much of it do we have?" Subsidiary questions arise in the course of trying to answer and clarify these. But these organizing questions themselves, the questions from which all the subsidiary questions get their significance, are the questions of what knowledge is and how much of it we have.

Now imagine epistemology as organized by different questions, these focused on epistemic value. What *is* epistemic value? How is it related to other sorts of value, for instance moral and prudential value? What is the best structural vocabulary for describing it—deontological talk of duties and rights, consequentialist talk of ends and means, virtue-theoretic talk of character traits and persons, some combination of these, or something else entirely?

Epistemologists are beginning to sometimes take *these* questions as theoretically central. When they do so, they are engaged in *epistemic value theory*. This branch of the value turn is a more radical break from recent tradition than is value-driven epistemology; it focuses on epistemic value for its own theoretical sake, whereas value-driven epistemology focuses on epistemic value for the sake of uncovering the nature and extent of knowledge and similar states like justified belief. The published work in epistemic value theory can be roughly categorized into three branches: truth-consequentialism, thick virtue theory, and credit theory.

Several theorists take epistemic value to have consequentialist structure, theorizing that all of epistemic value can be described in terms of epistemically good ends and the means toward those ends. The most prominent partisans of this approach are Alvin Goldman and William Alston, both of whom take true belief, or some combination of true belief and the avoidance of false belief, to be the sole epistemic ends. Goldman and Alston try to use this identification of the epistemic ends, along with the idea epistemic value has a consequentialist structure, to explain the epistemic value of various states other than true belief—for example, consistent belief, belief based on evidence, reliably produced belief, and knowledge (Alston 2005; Goldman 2001; Goldman and Olsson 2009). Goldman brings degrees of belief into the picture as well, constructing a system for evaluating them in terms of truth (and the avoidance of falsehood) and evaluating numerous phenomena as means to these things (Goldman 1999).

Truth-consequentialists sometimes use virtue-theoretic talk to describe their views. But the second branch of epistemic value theory, namely thick virtue epistemology, uses that talk in a much more full-blown manner (Baehr 2011; Code 1987; Roberts and Wood 2007; Zagzebski 1996). Whereas truth-consequentialists in epistemology are comparable to utilitarians, thick virtue epistemologists are comparable to virtue ethicists. Just as virtue ethicists focus on moral character traits instead of means and ends, thick virtue epistemologists focus on intellectual character traits instead of means and ends. Such character traits include inquisitiveness, attentiveness, open-mindedness, love of knowledge, intellectual humility, impartiality, sensitivity to detail, perceptiveness, insightfulness, and perspicacity. Thick virtue epistemologists focus on such questions as what makes these traits intellectual virtues, what distinguishes them from other things in the ballpark such as intellectual skills, how intellectual virtues relate to moral virtues, and how they relate to epistemic states like knowledge and true belief.

The third branch of epistemic value theory is something of a middle ground between thick virtue epistemology and the truth-consequentialism. We'll call this third branch of epistemic value theory as the *credit approach*. Partisans of this approach include Greco (2003, 2010), Riggs (2002), and Sosa (1988, 2003,

2007). Each of these theorists engages in value-driven epistemology as well as epistemic value theory, and each of them wields themes about credit in both projects. But as for the credit approach in epistemic value theory, its basic idea is as follows.

Sometimes it is good in a certain way for a certain performance to be a certain way: for instance, good aesthetically for a dance to be graceful, or good athletically for an arrow-shooting to hit its target. Moreover, it is better in these ways (aesthetically, athletically) for these things (dances, arrow-shootings) to *be creditably* beautiful and target-hitting, than to *be merely* beautiful and target-hitting. To see the difference between creditably being these ways and merely being these ways, compare two cases. In the first case, a skilled shooter releases his arrow; seemingly out of nowhere, a gust of wind blows it off course; and seemingly out of nowhere again, another gust blows it back on course to finally hit the target. In the second case, the same skilled shooter shoots as usual, and there are no unexpected gusts of wind or any other funny business; the arrow hits the target cleanly. In this second case—but not the first—there is a sense in which the shooter deserves credit for hitting the target. We might even say: in the first case the shooter hit the target *because* of the wind, but in the second case he hit the target *because* of his archery virtues. Credit theorists *do* say as much. They believe that the in second case (but not the first), the arrow hits its target because of the archer's athletic virtues, and therefore that in the second case (but not the first) the target-hitting is to the archer's credit. Moreover, they believe that the creditability featured in the second case is to the good athletically. They believe that, when it is good in some way (e.g. athletically) for some performance (e.g. an arrow-shooting) to *merely be* some way (e.g. target-hitting), then it is *even better* in that way for that performance to *creditably be* that way.

Now, credit theorists have it that beliefs stand to truth as arrow-shootings stand to target-hits. They therefore take creditably true belief to better epistemically than merely true belief, just as arrow-shootings that creditably hit their targets are better athletically than arrow-shootings that merely hit their targets. In holding this combination of views, credit theorists hold an epistemic value theory; they hold a theory about what is better than what else epistemically. That theory takes truth to be a good end epistemically, and it evaluates true belief and creditably true belief accordingly.[10] But the notion of creditability at work in the theory is not, or at least not obviously, a consequentialist notion, that is, a notion fully explicable in terms of ends and means. As a result of this, the credit theory is something of a half-way point between truth-consequentialism and thick virtue epistemology.

Credit theorists (or at least all of the credit theorists to have published on the matter so far) also adopt an additional view: namely that knowledge is identical to creditably true belief. Given this additional view, their theory takes knowledge to be superior to true belief. Moreover, it *explains why* that superiority holds, or at least purports to do as much. The credit theory thus proposes solutions to many of the Meno problems we identified earlier. These proposed solutions have been widely discussed in recent work within the value turn (Lackey 2009; Pritchard 2010; Greco 2010).

Applied epistemic value theory

Now to the final branch of work within the value turn: applied epistemic value theory, the branch of thought that standing to epistemic value theory as applied ethics stands to normative ethics. Applied ethicists inquire into the moral status of particular kinds of acts (e.g. abortion) or institutions (e.g. systems of rules about who can become president of a country). Similarly, applied epistemic value theorists inquire into the epistemic value of particular kinds of belief-forming methods (e.g. trusting the testimony of others) or institutions (e.g. systems of rules about the admissibility of evidence in court).

The most extensive work within applied epistemic value theory is Alvin Goldman's (1999) book *Knowledge in a Social World*. That book analyzes markets, schools, legal systems, science, and several other domains, and in each case it argues that the domain ought, from an epistemic point of view, to be structured in some particular way. Bishop and Trout (2005) also epistemically analyze numerous domains, including job interviews and medical diagnosis. Borrowing from the work of Gigerenzer et al. (2000) and other psychologists, Bishop and Trout make numerous recommendations about how we should go about forming our beliefs, given the particular psychological makeup with which we are endowed.

Laudan (2007) gives an extensive treatment of the contemporary American system of trial by jury, arguing among other things that this system has epistemically suboptimal rules about the conditions under which a given piece of evidence is admissible in court. Kitcher (1993) explores the division of cognitive labor among scientists; he argues among other things that it is good epistemically for scientific communities to include a few maverick dissenters from orthodoxy, since these people can help keep the community from getting stuck in a rut. In similar work, Zollman (2007) explores the extent to which scientists ought, epistemically, to share their research results with one another. He argues that in an interesting set of cases, the epistemically optimal outcomes are produced by *restricting* information sharing among researchers. Fallis and Whitcomb (2009) apply epistemic value theory to library management, offering up a decision-theoretic approach for librarians to use in constructing policies about, for example, book acquisition so as to balance various epistemic goods such as knowledge and understanding. Quite a bit of applied epistemic value theory goes on, as well, in recent literatures on testimony and disagreement among peers. Those literatures feature attempts to tell us when we should trust the testimony of others, and how (if at all) we should change our beliefs upon finding out that equally informed and equally intelligent people disagree with us (Feldman and Warfield 2010; Lackey and Sosa 2006).

All of this work evaluates particular kinds of things epistemically, just as applied ethics evaluates particular kinds of things ethically. Work of this sort has been rapidly expanding in recent years, as has work in the other branches of the value turn. I've distinguished those branches from one another and given several examples of work in those branches. Figure 14.2 summarizes this classificatory overview.

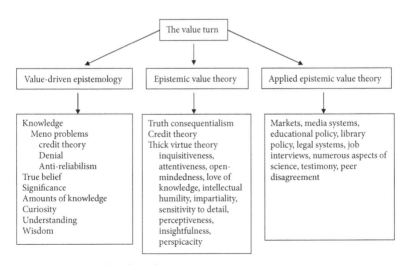

Figure 14.2 Work within the value turn.

New directions

There are many new directions ripe for development in the value turn. For instance, it is worth making the point that several paradigmatic writings in the value turn are also paradigmatic writings in naturalized epistemology (Kitcher 1993, Goldman 1999, Bishop and Trout 2005, Neta 2006, Laudan 2007). This point conflicts with the widespread belief that normativity and naturalism are at odds with one another. Perhaps, then, that widespread belief should be revised. In any case, the issue is ripe for development (Whitcomb 2008). Another such issue consists in the possibility of importing themes from "knowledge first" epistemology into the value turn literature. In recent years, several epistemologists have experimented with taking the knowledge first, and using it to illuminate other epistemic notions, such as the notions of evidence and justified belief (Williamson 2000, Sutton 2005, Bird 2007, Hossack 2007). This sort of epistemology is a theoretical inversion of recent tradition, as that tradition tends to take the other notions first and define knowledge in terms of *them*. Perhaps the knowledge-first approach would pay dividends if it were applied to the issues at play in the value turn. We might, for instance, take knowledge (as opposed to truth) to be the aim of belief. Given this identification of knowledge with the aim of belief, we could try to solve some of the Meno problems. For instance, we might try to explain why knowledge is better epistemically as an end than true belief by pointing out that merely true beliefs do not reach the epistemic goal, whereas beliefs constituting knowledge do. (Whitcomb [2007] advocates a version of this explanation; Pritchard 2010 explores the explanation without advocating it).

In summary, both the possibility of taking knowledge first, and the possibility of revising certain widespread beliefs about the relationship between naturalism and normativity, are issues ripe for development within the value turn. I'd like to explore a third such issue as well, this one in slightly more detail. This third issue consists in expanding the theme that credit matters to epistemic value.

Epistemologists who have thus far advocated the idea that credit matters to epistemic value have, as we saw earlier, added two more specific claims to that idea: first, that creditably true belief is better epistemically than noncreditably true belief, and second, that creditably true belief is identical to knowledge. Now, it is possible to coherently advocate one of these two claims without advocating the other. For example, we can coherently advocate the claim that creditably true belief is better epistemically than noncreditably true belief, without identifying the former state with knowledge. This is all to the good, since the identification of creditably true belief with knowledge is quite controversial. The first way we can expand the credit theme, then, is by liberating the idea that creditably true belief is better than noncreditably true belief, breaking it free from the more controversial claim that creditably true belief is identical to knowledge.

Once liberated, the idea naturally suggests several questions. To see them, notice that truth is not the only epistemically goodmaking property beliefs can instantiate. They can also be supported by one's evidence, coherent with one's other beliefs, virtuously produced, reflectively defensible, constitutive of understanding, or even knowledge. If it is better epistemically for beliefs to be creditably true than noncreditably true, then is it *also* better epistemically for beliefs to creditably instantiate these *other* epistemically goodmaking properties, than to noncreditably instantiate them? For example, compare two cases in which one's belief coheres with one's other beliefs. In the first case, Joe forms his beliefs just as we all do, namely by some more or less reasonable combination of perception, testimony, reflection, and so on. Most of us have incoherent beliefs as a result of this process (with most of us, the incoherence can be rapidly demonstrated by a modicum of clever Socratic questioning). Joe, however, is different: unlikely as it may be, his beliefs happen to be maximally coherent with one another.

Contrast Joe with John, who also forms his beliefs in the ways the rest of us do. One day, John engages in some philosophical reflection and finds that his beliefs are incoherent. In response to the incoherence he adds and subtracts beliefs so as to render the whole corpus coherent after all. When John's beliefs are (here at the end of the story) coherent after all, is it *creditable* to him that they are coherent, just as in our archery cases above without the wind gusts, it is creditable to the archers that their shots hit their targets. But the coherence of Joe's beliefs is *not* creditable to him; *that* coherence is more like the target-hitting of an unskilled shooter whose arrow hits the target through improbable lucky wind gusts.

What we have here, then, is a pair of cases one of which features *creditably coherent* beliefs, and the other of which features *noncreditably coherent* beliefs. If we are to say that creditably true beliefs are better epistemically than noncreditably true beliefs, then should we also say that creditably coherent beliefs are better epistemically than noncreditably coherent beliefs? More generally, should we say of *every* epistemically goodmaking property of beliefs, that beliefs instantiating that property creditably are better epistemically than beliefs instantiating it noncreditably?

And just as there are epistemically goodmaking properties such as truth and coherence, there are also epistemically *badmaking* properties. It is bad epistemically for beliefs to be false, unsupported by one's evidence, incoherent with one's other beliefs, viciously produced, reflectively indefensible, not aspects of understanding, or even for them to fail to be knowledge. For instance, compare two cases of false belief. In both cases, you know a coin to be fair; that is to say, you know that the coin has a 50 percent chance of landing heads, and a 50 percent chance of landing tails, given that it is flipped. The coin is flipped, and you predict that it will land tails. Unfortunately for you, it lands heads instead. Then it is flipped again. Reasoning via the gambler's fallacy (which fallacy has been explained to you several times), you predict and come to believe that the coin will land tails on this second flip. It lands heads instead; your belief turns out to be false.

All of that happens in both cases. But in one case the coin lands heads due to chance, and in the other case it lands heads because a powerful demon has manipulated the speed at which the coin falls through the air, altering that speed so as to make the coin land on whatever side makes your belief false: tails if you believe it will land heads, and heads if you believe it will land tails.

In the first case, where the coin lands heads due to chance, your belief is false because you engaged in bad reasoning; and so plausibly, the falsity of that belief is attributable to you, that is, to your credit.[11] But in the second case, where the coin lands heads due to the manipulations of the demon, your belief is false because of the demon's manipulations. And so, plausibly, the falsity of your belief in this second case is not attributable to you, not to you credit.

Perhaps the creditably false belief here is *worse* epistemically than the non-creditably false belief here—just as a given creditably true belief might be *better* epistemically than a noncreditably true one. More generally, if we are to say that epistemic goods are *even better* when held creditably, then perhaps we should also say that epistemic bads are *even worse* when held creditably. We might say that creditably false belief is worse epistemically than noncreditably false belief, and creditably incoherent belief is worse epistemically than noncreditably incoherent belief—just as we might say that creditably true belief is better epistemically than noncreditably true belief, and creditably coherent belief is better epistemically than noncreditably true belief. These considerations suggest a general principle about credit and epistemic value, to wit:

The credit amplification principle

For every belief and every property of epistemic value or disvalue:

it is epistemically *better* for that belief to have that property creditably than noncreditably, if that property is of epistemic *value*

and

it is epistemically *worse* for that belief to have that property creditably than noncreditably, if that property is of epistemic *disvalue.*

This principle tells us that, in general, credit *amplifies* epistemic value by making epistemic goods even better and epistemic bads even worse. Now this principle may be true, and it may be false. It certainly seems plausible in the cases we discussed earlier. But perhaps there are other cases where it is implausible. If there are such cases, then perhaps the principle does not hold in general—which would suggest that it does not hold in the special case of truth either, that special case already advocated by credit theorists writing about epistemic value. On the other hand, if the principle *does* hold in general, then it provides an interesting expansion of the themes already on offer from credit theorists. Either way, the credit amplification principle is a conjecture that is ripe for development, as are the conjectures that naturalism and normativity are not conflicting but coherent, and that we can make theoretical progress by taking knowledge first.[12]

Notes

1   The phrase "value turn" comes from Riggs (2006), and it echoes back to the "linguistic turn" of the 1950s through the 1970s. Sometimes, the term "value" is used in a restricted way so that it refers only to the subject matter of axiology—the "good" as opposed to the "right." Other times, the term "value" is used more broadly to refer to everything normative—the good, the right, virtues, and so on. It is in this latter, broader sense that I will use the term in this chapter.

2   Alternative overviews of work within the value turn include Pritchard (2007a, 2007b) and Greco 2011.

3   This connection between the value turn and contextualism has been underappreciated in the literatures on both of those topics. Another such connection, also underappreciated in both literatures, can be found in recent work by John Greco. In that work Greco develops a version of contextualism which takes the referent of "knows" to shift via facts about credit, as opposed to shifting via facts about required amounts of sensitivity or safety or evidential support. See Greco (2003, 2010).

4   Pritchard (2007b) further discusses the motivations behind the value turn.

5   The label "value driven epistemology" is often used with a less restricted meaning than I am stipulating here, a meaning that counts as "value driven epistemology" each of the three branches of what I am calling the value turn.

6   Thanks to Don Fallis for suggesting the term "epistemic value theory" for this branch of thought.

7   As John Greco pointed out to me, it is worth highlighting the fact that the questions encoded by Figure 14.1 aren't as independent from one another as they might at first seem. In many cases, answering one of them puts us in a position to very quickly answer some of the others. For instance, if we answer "yes" to the question "Is (it true that) knowledge is epistemically better as an end than true belief for every item of knowledge and every item of true belief?," then we are in a position to quickly also answer "yes" to the question "Is (it true that) knowledge is epistemically better as an end than true belief for every item of knowledge and every item of true belief across which other things are equal?" If every item of knowledge is in that way better than *every* item of true belief, then *ipso facto,* every item of knowledge is in that way better than every item of true belief *for which other things are equal.*

8   Thanks to Kristoffer Ahlstrom for helpful discussion here.

9   Notice that knowledge also comes in these forms; we can know why the litmus paper just turned pink, know that the meeting is on Wednesday, and know physics.

10   Sosa (2003) is especially helpful in developing this theme.

11   Would it be better to say "your *discredit*"?

12   Thanks to Kristoffer Ahlstrom, Selim Berker, Don Fallis, John Greco, Clayton Littlejohn, Dan Howard-Snyder, Duncan Pritchard, Ernest Sosa, and John Turri for helpful comments on this material.

References

Alston, W. 1993. "Epistemic Desiderata." *PPR* (53/3): 527–51.

— 2005. *Beyond "Justification": Dimensions of Epistemic Evaluation.* Ithaca, NY: Cornell University Press.

Baehr, J. 2009. "Is there a Value Problem?" In A. Haddock, A. Millar and
  D. H. Pritchard, eds, *Epistemic Value*. Oxford: Oxford University Press.
— (forthcoming). *The Inquiring Mind: On Intellectual Virtues and Virtue Epistemology*.
  Oxford: Oxford University Press.
Bird, A. 2007. "Justified Judging." *PPR* 74: 81–110.
Bishop, M. and Trout, J. D. 2005. *Epistemology and the Psychology of Human Judgment*.
  Oxford: Oxford University Press.
Brady, M. 2009. "Curiosity and the Value of Truth." In A. Haddock, A. Millar and
  D. H. Pritchard, eds, Epistemic Value. Oxford: Oxford University Press.
Code, L. 1987. *Epistemic Responsibility*. Hanover, NH: Brown University Press.
David, M. 2001. "Truth as the Epistemic Goal." In Steup (2001).
DePaul, M. 2001. "Value Monism in Epistemology." In Steup (2001).
DePaul, M. and Zagzebski, L. eds, 2003. *Intellectual Virtue*. Oxford: Oxford University
  Press.
Elgin, C. 2009. "Is Understanding Factive." In A. Haddock, A. Millar and
  D. H. Pritchard, eds, Epistemic Value. Oxford: Oxford University Press.
Fairweather, A. and Zagzebski, L. eds, 2001. *Virtue Epistemology*. Oxford: Oxford
  University Press.
Fallis, D. and Whitcomb, D. 2009. "Epistemic Values and Information Management."
  The Information Society 25/3: 175–89.
Feldman, R. 1988. "Epistemic Obligations." *Philosophical Perspectives* 2: 235–56.
— 2002. "Epistemological Duties." In Moser 2002, pp. 361–84.
Feldman, R. and Warfield, T. eds, 2010. *Disagreement*. Oxford: Oxford University Press.
Foley, R. 1987. *The Theory of Epistemic Rationality*. Harvard: Harvard University Press.
Garrett, R. 1996. "Three Definitions of Wisdom." In Lehrer et al. 1996.
Greco, J. 2003. "Knowledge As Credit For True Belief." In DePaul and Zagzebski, eds,
  Intellectual Virtue. Oxford University Press.
— 2011. "The Value Problem." In Bernecker and Pritchard, eds, *The Routledge
  Companion to Epistemology*. Routledge.
Gigerenzer, G., Todd, P. and The ABC Research Group. 2000. *Simple Heuristics that
  Make us Smart*. Oxford: Oxford University Press.
Goldman, A. I. 1978. "Epistemics: the Regulative Theory of Cognition." *Journal of
  Philosophy* 75/10: 509–23.
— 1986. *Epistemology and Cognition*. Harvard: Harvard University Press.
— 1991. "Stephen P. Stich: *The Fragmentation of Reason*." *PPR* 51/1: 189–93.
— 1999. *Knowledge in a Social World*. Oxford: Oxford University Press.
— 2001. "The Unity of Epistemic Virtues." In Fairweather and Zagzebski 2001.
Goldman, A. I. and Olsson, E. J. 2009. "Reliabilism and the Value of Knowledge." In
  A. Haddock, A. Millar and D. H. Pritchard, eds, Epistemic Value. Oxford: Oxford
  University Press.
— 2003. "Knowledge as Credit for True Belief." In DePaul and Zagzebski 2003.
— 2010. *Achieving Knowledge*. Cambridge: Cambridge University Press.

— (2010). "Epistemic Value." In D. Pritchard and S. Bernecker, eds, *The Routledge Companion to Epistemology*. New York, NY: Routledge.

Grimm, S. 2006. "Is Understanding a Species of Knowledge." *BJPS* 57: 3.

— 2008. "Epistemic Goals and Epistemic Values." *PPR* 77: 3.

— 2010. "Understanding." In D. Bernecker and S. Pritchard, eds, *The Routledge Companion to Epistemology*. New York: Routledge.

Hendricks, V. and Pritchard, D. eds, 2006. *New Waves in Epistemology*. New York, NY: Palgrave Macmillan.

Hookway, C. 2003. "How to be a Virtue Epistemologist." In DePaul and Zagzebski 2003.

Hossack, K. 2007. *The Metaphysics of Knowledge*. Oxford: Oxford University Press.

Kitcher, P. 1992. "The Naturalists Return." *Philosophical Review* (101/1): 53–114.

— 1993. *The Advancement of Science*. New York: Oxford University Press.

Kvanvig, J. 2003. *The Value of Knowledge and the Pursuit of Understanding*. Cambridge: Cambridge University Press.

— 2005. "Truth is not the Primary Epistemic Goal." In Steup and Sosa (2005).

— (2010). "The Swamping Problem Redux: Pith and Gist." In Haddock, Millar, and Pritchard eds, *Social Epistemology*. Oxford University Press.

Lackey, J. 2009. "Knowledge and Credit." *Philosophical Studies* 142: 27–42.

Lackey, J. and Sosa, E. eds, 2006. *The Epistemology of Testimony*. Oxford: Oxford University Press.

Laudan, L. 2007. *Truth, Error, and Criminal Law*. Cambridge: Cambridge University Press.

Levi, I. 1980. *The Enterprise of Knowledge*. Cambridge MA: MIT Press.

Miscevic, N. 2007. "Virtue-Based Epistemology and the Centrality of Truth." *Acta Analytica* 22/3: 239–66.

Moser, P. ed., 2002. *The Oxford Handbook of Epistemology*. Oxford: Oxford University Press.

Neta, R. 2006. "How to Naturalize Epistemology." In Hendricks and Pritchard (2006).

Nozick, R. 1989. *The Examined Life*. New York, NY: Touchstone Press.

Pritchard, D. 2007a. "The Value of Knowledge." In E. Zalta, ed., *Stanford Encyclopedia of Philosophy*.

— 2007b. "Recent Work on Epistemic Value." *American Philosophical Quarterly* 44: 85–110.

— (2010). "Knowledge and Understanding." In A. Miller and A. Haddock, co-writers. *The Nature and Value of Knowledge: Three Investigations*. Oxford: Oxford University Press.

— (2011). "What is the Swamping Problem?" In A. Reisner and A. Steglich-Petersen, eds, Reasons for Belief. Cambridge, UK: Cambridge University Press.

Riggs, W. 2002. "Reliability and the Value of Knowledge." *PPR* (64): 79–96.

— 2006. "The Value Turn in Epistemology." In Hendricks and Pritchard (2006).

— 2009. "Understanding, Knowledge, and the Meno Requirement." In A. Haddock, A. Millar and D. H. Pritchard, eds, Epistemic Value. Oxford: Oxford University Press.

Roberts, R. and Wood, J. 2007. *Intellectual Virtues: An Essay in Regulative Epistemology.* Oxford: Oxford University Press.

Ryan, S. 1996. "Wisdom." In Lehrer et al. 1996.

— 1999. "What Is Wisdom?" *Philosophical Studies* (93): 119–39.

— 2007. "Wisdom." *Stanford Encyclopedia of Philosophy.* (ed.) E. Zalta, available at http://plato.stanford.edu/entries/wisdom.

Shah, N. and Velleman, D. 2005. "Doxastic Deliberation." *Philosophical Review* 114/4: 497–534.

Sosa, E. 1980. "The Raft and the Pyramid: Coherence versus Foundations in the Theory of Knowledge." *Midwest Studies in Philosophy* 5(1): 3–26.

Sosa, E. 1988. "Beyond Skepticism, to the Best of Our Knowledge." *Mind* (97): 153–88.

— 2000. "Skepticism and Contextualism." *Philosophical Issues* 10: 1–18

— 2003. "The Place of Truth in Epistemology." In DePaul and Zagzebski 2003, pp. 155–80.

— 2007. *A Virtue Epistemology.* Oxford: Oxford University Press.

Schmitt, F. and Lahroodi, R. 2008. "The Epistemic Value of Curiosity." *Educational Theory* 58/2: 125–48.

Sutton, J. 2005. *Without Justification.* Cambridge MA: MIT Press.

Treanor, N. (forthcoming). "The Measure of Knowledge." *Nous.*

Wedgwood, R. 2002. "The Aim of Belief." *Philosophical Perspectives* 16: 267–97.

Whitcomb, D. 2007. *An Epistemic Value Theory.* PhD Diss, Rutgers University. Available at: http://hdl.rutgers.edu/1782.2/rucore10001600001.ETD.16794

— 2008. "Review of *New Waves in Epistemology,* In Hendricks and Pritchard, eds, *Notre Dame Philosophical Reviews.*

— 2010a. "Curiosity was Framed." *Philosophy and Phenomenological Research.* 81(3): 95–106.

— 2010b. "Wisdom." In Bernecker and Pritchard, eds, *The Routledge Companion to Epistemology.* Routledge, pp. 95–106.

Williamson, T. 2000. *The Routledge Companion to Epistemology. Knowledge and its Limits.* Oxford: Oxford University Press.

Zagzebski, L. 1996. *Virtues of the Mind.* Cambridge: Cambridge University Press.

Zagzebski, L. 2001. "Recovering Understanding." In M. Steup ed., *Knowledge, Truth, and Duty.* Oxford: Oxford University Press.

Zollman, K. 2007. "The Communication Structure of Epistemic Communities." *Philosophy of Science* 74(5): 574–87.

15

The Deep Rationality Theory of Wisdom

Sharon Ryan

When I have ceased to beat my wings
Against the faultiness of things,
And learned that compromises wait
Behind each partly opened gate,
When I can look life in the eyes,
Grown, calm and very coldly wise,
Life will have given me the truth,
And taken in exchange my youth.[1]

Introduction

What is wisdom? Philosophers, psychologists, poets, playwrights, spiritual leaders, and a wide variety of other serious thinkers have tried to understand and define "wisdom." Psychologists tend to think of wisdom as the highest developmental state or as an especially valuable type of intelligence.[2] Nearly everyone agrees that being wise is among the highest virtues, and many reflective and morally ambitious human beings spend their lives trying to achieve wisdom. Some contemporary philosophers and psychologists working on this topic advocate a revolution in education and society. They argue that we should be teaching not with the aim of merely imparting information, but for the development of wisdom.[3] Despite our love for and pursuit of wisdom, I believe we have fallen short of providing a fully adequate account of wisdom. In this chapter, I will present some interesting ideas about wisdom, including some of my former ideas on this topic. I will explain why I think those ideas, although interesting and helpful, are ultimately inadequate. I will also defend a new theory of wisdom. I think my current theory of wisdom is at least *more adequate* than any of the other theories I have considered. The theory I will propose here, characterizes wisdom as a deep state of rationality.

As I see it, many theories of wisdom can be put into at least one of three categories.[4] One category focuses on epistemic humility, or appreciating all that one does not really know, being scrupulous when forming beliefs, and possessing a healthy dose of skepticism. A second main category focuses on possessing extensive knowledge, or understanding, about reality. A third category focuses on the ability to successfully navigate through life's practical and moral challenges.

Wisdom as epistemic humility

Epistemic humility theories are theories that characterize wisdom as a humble attitude toward what we really know. Socrates' view about wisdom, as described in Plato's *Apology,* can be understood as an epistemic humility account of wisdom.[5,6] In *The Apology,* Socrates learns from the oracle at Delphi, that he is the wisest person of all. Plato leads us to believe that this is puzzling to Socrates because Socrates claims ignorance on so many issues. In all of his conversations, Socrates is fully equipped with the most probing questions, but he very seldom puts forth any direct answers of his own. In an attempt to figure out the oracle's puzzling proclamation, Socrates contrasts himself with some other thinkers that he and his peers find to be the most impressive candidates for wisdom. They are poets, politicians, and craftsmen. After interviewing an assortment of poets, Socrates appreciates their deep insights, but since Socrates believes the poets are basically taking dictation from the gods, they really do not deserve much credit for their revelations. Thus, they are not worthy of the honor of being counted among the truly wise. Socrates interviews some politicians and he acknowledges that some of the most impressive among them are capable of moving people with their powerful rhetoric. What matters for Socrates, however, is not whether speech *actually* moves people, but whether it *ought* to move people. And, as it turns out, he is not at all impressed with the quality of their ideas. The craftsmen turn out to be Socrates' favorite candidates for the honor of wisdom. They at least know something useful, and, unlike the poets, they deserve credit for what they know. They have practical knowledge and they apply that knowledge to make chairs and other useful objects. Unfortunately, the craftsmen suffer from a fatal flaw that they share with all of the poets and politicians. Every one of them proclaims to know all sorts of things that they have no right to claim to know. The poets, for example, make unsupported and fully confident assertions about politics, the politicians make unsupported generalizations about nearly everything, and the craftsmen, for example, make unsupported assertions about love and justice. Socrates is driven absolutely crazy by epistemic arrogance, and that flaw, Socrates concludes, is sufficient to rule a person out as wise. Socrates' hypothesis for why he is wise, and why the others are not wise, is that he does not (or so he claims) suffer from epistemic arrogance. Socrates fully acknowledges his own ignorance.

This idea that wisdom is some sort of epistemic humility is a common theme in the contemporary wisdom literature in psychology. Patricia Kennedy Arlin, a contemporary psychologist, finds wisdom not in the answers one reaches, but in the questions one poses.[7] Although many people who have thought seriously about this topic, such as Sara Teasdale in her poem, "Wisdom," included above, take for granted that wisdom typically increases with age and experience, John Meacham, a contemporary psychologist, challenges this assumption. He contends that for many people, wisdom actually *decreases* with age.[8] According to Meacham, this is because as we age, many of us become more epistemically arrogant and less intellectually cautious. Wise people, according to Meacham, appreciate their own fallibility. The idea that wisdom is epistemic humility shows up in great works of literature as well. For example, in William Shakespeare's comic play, *As You Like It,* Touchstone, the clown, says, "The fool doth think he is wise, but the wise man knows himself to be a fool."[9] There is widespread agreement among many intelligent people who have pondered the nature of wisdom, that epistemic humility is, *at least,* an important aspect of wisdom.

There are many different ways to formulate epistemic humility theories. The theory could be cashed out as an endorsement for some healthy form of skepticism. It could be developed as a viewpoint falling short of skepticism, but nevertheless restricting the virtue of wisdom to people who do not extend their beliefs, their confidence, or their claims to know, beyond what they really do know. And, certainly, there are also several more complicated formulations of the theory. In some of my previous work on wisdom, I presented and carefully analyzed several distinct formulations of epistemic humility theories.[10] I will refrain from going over that again, here. Instead, I will simply explain why I think all epistemic humility theories fail to provide a satisfactory understanding of wisdom. Being wise is not just being careful about what you believe. It is not just about asking good questions. It is not just about realizing one's epistemic limits. Being wise requires much more. A person could be perfectly epistemically humble, in any interesting sense of "humble," and yet be very uninformed about most subjects, live a miserably self-destructive and unsatisfying life, and be definitively unwise. Epistemic humility, no matter how it is precisely understood, is just not enough for wisdom. Before moving on to other approaches to understanding the nature of wisdom, let me point out that while I will avoid the pitfalls of epistemic humility theories, the theory I will ultimately defend in this chapter will utilize what is attractive about some sort of epistemic humility being a requirement for being wise. Thus, my theory should satisfy all those who appreciate the importance of epistemic humility.

Wisdom as knowledge

After appreciating the insufficiency of epistemic humility theories, it is natural to explore the hopes for theories of wisdom that focus, not on appreciating fallibility, uncertainty, or ignorance, but on the possession of knowledge or understanding. There are a wide variety of knowledge theories of wisdom. They vary, for the most part, on the basis of what, and how much, the wise person must know. Some theories, such as Aristotle's account of theoretical wisdom, or *sophia*, focus on knowing fundamental, scientific laws or general truths.[11] Aristotle's theory of practical wisdom, or *phronesis*, in part, focuses on knowing how to live well.[12] Robert Nozick develops a similar line of thought.[13] According to Ned Markosian, wisdom is earned through the acquisition of intrinsically valuable knowledge.[14] Markosian would count a deep understanding of philosophical concepts such as truth, justice, wisdom, etc. as the most intrinsically valuable.[15] William James said, "The art of being wise is the art of knowing what to overlook."[16] Paul Baltes and Jacqui Smith, leading wisdom researchers on the psychological literature on wisdom, outlined five criteria for wisdom. All five focus on knowledge. They are:

1. Rich factual knowledge about matters of life.
2. Rich procedural knowledge about life problems.
3. Knowledge about the contexts of life and their relationships.
4. Knowledge about differences in values and priorities.
5. Knowledge about the relative indeterminacy and unpredictability of life.[17]

Almost every reasonably plausible theory of wisdom has knowledge built in as a necessary condition for wisdom. I say *almost* because the theory I will ultimately defend actually lacks a knowledge condition. Although it would be interesting to outline and carefully analyze all of the best knowledge theories of wisdom, I am unable to take on that project in this short chapter. Instead, I will simply note that all knowledge theories suffer from some devastating problems. One problem is that knowledge is not enough. Wisdom requires a successful navigation through the challenges of life. Weakness of will, lack of courage, and a failure to appreciate the value of living well, for example, can leave an extremely knowledgeable person without wisdom. Later in this chapter, I will take my criticism of knowledge theories a step further. I will argue that knowledge is not even necessary for wisdom.

Wisdom as living well

Many theories of wisdom focus on how we apply what we know and how we actually live out our lives. When we do it well, by taking the long view on things, knowing what is worth worrying about and what we should just shrug off and move on from, knowing how best to spend our time and effort, etc., we achieve wisdom. I defended a version of this sort of theory in an earlier essay.[18] Theories developed by John Kekes,[19] Nicholas Maxwell,[20] Copthorne MacDonald,[21] Richard Garrett,[22] Keith Lehrer,[23] Aristotle,[24] and Robert Nozick[25] include, among various other requirements, the idea that the way a person applies their knowledge in real-life situations, is part of what determines whether or not one is wise. I agree that how we live our lives is essential to the achievement of wisdom. However, a theory such as one I defended at one point, that focuses *exclusively* on how one lives and the knowledge required for living well (living rationally and morally, having sound judgment, etc.), leaves something crucial out of a satisfactory account of wisdom. I believe that knowing how to live well and actually living well are not enough for wisdom. There is an intellectual and educational component to wisdom that is missing from all such theories. Wisdom is more than practical knowledge than living well. Although I rejected this idea in my earlier discussion of Ned Markosian's view, I now believe my rejection was too hasty.[26] *I* now believe that "book smarts" *is* an important part of wisdom. It is not, as Markosian thinks, the whole story, but it is an important part of the story. An understanding of basic subjects such as philosophy, science, literature, history, etc., is one requirement for wisdom. Someone who has not had the privilege of a well-rounded education[27] may be living well, and may be a person to admire and consult on relationship problems and moral dilemmas, but he or she is not informed enough to count as wise.

Hybrid theory

I closed my 2007 *Stanford Encyclopaedia of Philosophy* entry on "wisdom" holding out the promise for the development of a hybrid theory along the following lines:[28]

Sharon Ryan's SEP HYBRID:

S is wise iff (1) S has extensive factual and theoretical knowledge.

(2) S knows how to live well.

(3) S is successful at living well.

(4) S has very few unjustified beliefs.

I liked the basic idea of this theory because it utilizes the idea that wise people are people we can go to for reliable information, understanding, and insights. I felt that the theories that I had defended in my earlier work on wisdom were too narrowly focused on knowing how to live well, and did not give enough attention to "book smarts." I had not given due respect to Ned Markosian's views on wisdom. The SEP hybrid theory rectifies that mistake. Moreover, the SEP hybrid theory also requires that the wise person have successful strategies for navigating through life's practical and moral challenges. And, I liked that some epistemic humility is preserved in the fourth condition of this theory. By knowing a lot, and by not having many unjustified beliefs, one is a trustworthy source of information. Such a person would avoid the fatal flaw suffered by all of the poets, politicians, and craftsmen who were interviewed by Socrates. I am extremely sympathetic to Socrates' intolerance of epistemic arrogance. I agree with Socrates' judgment that a person with a lot of unjustified beliefs has a character flaw that disqualifies him as wise. Such a person does not have trustworthy opinions, and having trustworthy opinions is essential to wisdom. I also liked the vagueness built into the theory. Any acceptable theory of wisdom must respect the fact that wisdom comes in degrees. Some people are wiser than others. And, a wiser person can increase (or decrease) his or her level of wisdom. Wisdom is definitely a vague concept, and this hybrid theory gets that right.

After an interesting conversation that took place during one of my philosophy classes at West Virginia University, I realized that this theory is not as promising as it once seemed to me. My student asked us to imagine a "wise" elder from an ancient tribe, or society, with little contact with the rest of the world. Imagine that she is radically mistaken in her beliefs about science, math, geography, history, etc. Suppose she, like the other people in her society, bases her beliefs on superstition, the Ouija board, and similar methods. Suppose further, that she and her compatriots are intellectually satisfied with her opinions, and they are not interested in seeking out alternative ideas from the rest of the world. The student claimed that such a person could be regarded, in her remote society, as a deeply wise person. But, it seems that the hybrid theory would exclude her as a wise person. It seems that she would violate conditions 1 and 4, and it seems that it would be exceedingly difficult for her to satisfy conditions 2 and 3. If she lives according to what the Ouija board says, it seems safe to predict that she will very likely encounter a lot of failure and unhappiness. Thus, if this "wise" elder is actually wise, it appears that this hybrid theory is in serious trouble.

One might argue that this objection could be avoided by interpreting the SEP hybrid theory in a way that counts the "wise" elder as wise. One might say that wisdom is not only a vague concept, but a relative, or subjective, concept as well. That is, wisdom not only comes in degrees, but it is also something to be measured against a relative, as opposed to an absolute, standard. "Tall" is a concept that one might reasonably think is both vague and relative. Consider a man who is 6′5″ tall. Is he tall? It seems obvious that he is. How about a male who is 5′5″ in height? Is he tall? It seems obvious that he is definitely not tall. But what should we say about a man who is 6′ tall? That seems to be a borderline case that falls somewhere between tall and average. "Tall" is a vague concept without sharp boundaries between what counts and what does not count. "Tall" is not only vague, but it is also relative, or subjective. In America, 6′ may well count as a borderline case for being tall. However, in Japan, a 6′ tall man would be considered tall. And, in America, even a 6′5″ man would not count as tall in all contexts. He would not be tall relative to NBA players, for example. One might insist that all of the conditions of the hybrid theory should be interpreted relativistically. That is, as long as the elder has a lot of knowledge *relative to her society and time period,* she lives successfully *relative to her society and time period,* and she has few unjustified beliefs *compared to others in her society and time period,* then she is wise *for her society and time period.*

There is reason to have serious reservations about this attempt to salvage the SEP hybrid theory of wisdom. What is a society? How do we determine what society a person belongs to? Probably, we all belong to many societies, but which ones are relevant when determining if one is wise? What is a time period? These are deeply perplexing questions, and without satisfactory answers to these questions, we cannot really understand and evaluate this interpretation of the theory.[29] Moreover, even if we could give answers to all of these questions, any person who joins a very unwise society of people will turn out to be wise, as long as that person is relatively "wiser" than the others. That is an unacceptable consequence of this line of thought. Fortunately, there is a better response to this objection to the hybrid theory.

It would be better to accept the consequence that the "wise" elder, in the circumstances described, is not actually wise. That is, the SEP hybrid theory gives the correct assessment of the so-called "wise" elder. Although her tribe may have regarded her as wise, and members of her tribe may have been justified in making that assessment about her, the tribe was mistaken. The Ouija board and superstition are not reliable guides to the truth. If we are willing to accept this consequence, then the example, although interesting and instructive, does not refute the SEP hybrid theory.

Although I do not think the previous example refutes the SEP hybrid theory, it does open the door to big problems. A modification of the example will show that the SEP hybrid theory needs to be abandoned. In discussion of the previous example about the person who is regarded as wise, but who lacks justified beliefs and knowledge about a wide variety of subjects, I argued that it would be best to accept the consequence that the "wise" elder is not really wise. She may be interesting, inspirational, and in high demand for her thoughts, but she is not wise. This is an example where a society simply gets it wrong. If the "wise" elder is irrational, and her beliefs are radically unjustified, then she's not really wise. Although the SEP hybrid theory does successfully avoid this criticism, the SEP hybrid theory ultimately fails because knowledge is not an essential component of wisdom. Imagine a wise and rational elder who forms her beliefs based on extremely credible and reliable evidence (not Ouija boards and superstition), but fails, through no epistemic fault of her own, to be right. Suppose, that is, that she has a lot of very highly justified, but false, beliefs. A nice example of this is Ptolemy. Ptolemy had justified beliefs about a geocentric solar system. I will assume that given how intelligent he was, that he had a lot of epistemically justified beliefs about a wide variety of subjects. He discussed his ideas and experiments with the best scientists of his time. As it turned out, many of Ptolemy's justified beliefs about the solar system were false. Ptolemy did not *know* that the earth is the center of our solar system. If he had a lot of false, but highly justified beliefs about a wide variety of subjects, he should not, on that basis alone, be excluded from the honor of being a genuinely wise person. Since so much of what was considered knowledge has been abandoned, or has evolved over time, a theory that requires truth (through a knowledge condition) would exclude almost all people who are now long dead, including Hypatia, Socrates,

Aristotle, Homer, Lao Tzu, etc. from the list of the wise. Bad epistemic luck should not count against being wise. But, since truth is a necessary condition for knowledge, bad epistemic luck is sufficient to undermine a claim to knowledge. What matters, as far as being wise goes, is not that a wise person has knowledge, but that she has highly justified and rational beliefs about a wide variety of subjects, including how to live well, science, philosophy, mathematics, history, geography, art, literature, psychology, and so on. The wider the variety of interesting topics, the better. Another way of developing this same point is to imagine a person with highly justified beliefs about a wide variety of subjects, but who is unaware that she is trapped in the Matrix or some other skeptical scenario. Such a person could be wise even if she is sorely lacking knowledge. A theory of wisdom that focuses on having rational, or epistemically justified beliefs, rather than the higher standard of actually having knowledge, would be more promising.

Matthew Robinson noted another shortcoming of the SEP hybrid theory.[30] It seems that the theory neglects an attitude that all wise people have. Truly wise people value learning, and they look out for new evidence and critically examine and re-examine their opinions. Wise people are continually pursuing a deeper and wider understanding of various aspects of reality, and they follow through by putting that understanding into practice. In the original attempt to refute the SEP hybrid theory, the unwise elder suffers from this flaw. She is intellectually satisfied with her irrational set of beliefs. A truly wise person would be more intellectually open and curious, seeking out alternative opinions on the many matters that are complex, uncertain, and controversial. Any acceptable theory of wisdom needs to include this intellectual virtue.

Wisdom as Deep Rationality

Appreciating the many strengths and weaknesses of alternative theories has led me to embrace a theory of wisdom that focuses on rationality. I will call my current theory "The Deep Rationality Theory of Wisdom." More specifically, I endorse the following theory:

Deep Rationality Theory

Person S is wise at time *t* iff at time *t*:

(1) S has a wide variety of epistemically justified beliefs on a wide variety of valuable subjects such as: philosophy, science, literature, mathematics, art,

history, geography, psychology, etc., and living rationally (epistemically, practically, emotionally, and morally).

(2) S has very few unjustified beliefs.

(3) S is deeply committed to both:

> (a) the intellectual pursuit of acquiring a wider variety of epistemically justified beliefs on a wide variety of valuable subjects such as: philosophy, science, literature, mathematics, art, history, geography, psychology, etc., and living rationally (practically, emotionally, and morally) and
>
> (b) living rationally (practically, emotionally, and morally).

In condition (1), The Deep Rationality Theory takes account of what is attractive about knowledge theories and, to some extent, the various living well theories, by requiring epistemically justified beliefs about a wide variety of standard academic subjects, as well as epistemically justified beliefs about how to live in a practically, emotionally, and morally rational way. Some of those beliefs about how to live rationally would include the basic ideas (sans knowledge) from Baltes and Smith's theory that were noted earlier in this chapter. That is:

1. Epistemically justified beliefs about matters of life.
2. Epistemically justified beliefs about life problems.
3. Epistemically justified beliefs about the contexts of life and their relationships.
4. Epistemically justified beliefs about differences in values and priorities.
5. Epistemically justified beliefs about the relative indeterminacy and unpredictability of life.

Having justified beliefs about what really matters, what ought to be ignored, when one should just laugh, how to treat others, how to best spend one's time, what would be the best course of action in various situations, and so on, would be captured in the first condition of the Deep Rationality Theory. For example, having justified beliefs about how to live in a *practically* rational way would include having a well-reasoned strategy for dealing with the practical aspects of life. Having a rational plan does not require perfect success. It requires having good reasons behind one's actions, responding appropriately to, and learning from, one's mistakes, and it requires having a rational plan for all sorts of practical situations and problems. Having justified beliefs about how to live in a morally rational way would not involve being a moral saint, but it would require that one has good reasons backing his or her beliefs about what is morally right and wrong, and about what one morally ought and ought not do in a wide variety of circumstances. Having justified beliefs about living in an emotionally rational way would involve, not dispassion, but having justified beliefs about what is, and what is not, an emotionally rational response to a situation. For example, it is appropriate to feel deeply sad when dealing with the loss of a loved one. But, ordinarily, feeling deeply sad or extremely angry is not an appropriate emotion to spilled milk. A wise person should have a good understanding of emotions.

The Deep Rationality Theory respects epistemic humility. Condition (2) requires that a wise person not believe things without epistemic justification. The Deep Rationality Theory rules out all of the unwise poets, politicians, and craftsmen that were ruled out by Socrates.[31] Wise people do not think they know when they lack sufficient evidence. Wise people are not epistemically arrogant.

The Deep Rationality Theory requires that one be deeply committed to seeking out new ideas, becoming more educated, and testing one's own theories against all of the best evidence available.[32] It requires the wise person to put his or her justified beliefs into practice. The theory requires the wise to be deeply committed to having appropriate emotions, treating others morally, and having successful strategies for getting through the trials and tribulations of life, etc. Surely, being rational would include asking the right questions, having strong and creative problem-solving skills, possessing good judgment about what to overlook, and treating others kindly, fairly, and justly. The Deep Rationality Theory does not require knowledge or perfection. But it does require rationality, and it accommodates degrees of wisdom.

Thus far, I have left many interesting issues unanswered. For example, what makes a belief epistemically justified for a person? The theory would be best if it accommodated any of the leading accounts of epistemic justification. It is a virtue of the Deep Rationality Theory that this question is left somewhat open. As far as I can see, the theory is compelling, whether one takes a coherentist, or foundationalist, or evidentialist, or reliabilist, interpretation of epistemic justification.[33] However, it is important to acknowledge that my theory is definitely meant to have an exclusively objectivist interpretation of epistemic justification. All I mean by "objectivist" is that what matters is whether one's beliefs are *actually supported* by evidence or reliably formed, rather than that one *merely thinks that* his or her beliefs are supported by evidence or reliably formed. The theory also leaves imprecise what being "deeply committed" and "being rational" mean. Like "wisdom," these concepts are intended to be vague concepts that come in degrees. In this short chapter, I cannot do full justice to developing those ideas. The basic idea of being "deeply committed" is that a wise person is a seeker of truth and understanding. Again, the idea of epistemic humility is at work. A wise person appreciates the complexity of things and she is interested in keeping eye out for more information and evidence. A wise person is devoted to living an examined life, and she works at intellectual, moral, and practical improvement.

It is inevitable that there will be occasions in which it is impossible to be rational in all senses. Thus, being deeply committed to being rational will involve making hard decisions. For example, being morally rational might require patience working through a problem, while being practically rational, in the exact same situation, might involve dealing swiftly with the problem. Being epistemically rational might not always be practically rational. Surely, there will be conflicts. This theory does not rank the various kinds of rationality. That is another virtue of the theory. In such a situation, all the theory would require is that the wise person have justified beliefs about what is more important to focus on in various different situations, and that she be committed to doing what's best.

Although the Deep Rationality Theory leaves us with a lot of interesting issues to ponder and discuss, I think it very nicely captures the essence of wisdom. I also believe the Deep Rationality Theory accommodates and respects all of the best ideas from leading philosophers and psychologists working on this topic.[34]

Notes

1   Sara Teasdale, "Wisdom," 1917.
2   As a stage of development, Jean Piaget's and Erik Erickson's work are good examples. As a kind of intelligence, Robert Sternberg's work is a good example.
3   For example, see Nicholas Maxwell, *From Knowledge to Wisdom* (Oxford: Blackwell, 1984) and Copthorne MacDonald, "Wisdom: The Highest Aim of Life and Higher Education," on The Wisdom Page http://www.wisdompage, and Robert Sternberg's, "Why Schools Should Teach for Wisdom: The Balance Theory of Wisdom in Educational Settings," *Educational Psychologist* 36(4) (2001) 227–45.
4   This is overly simplified. Of course, many theories, including those I have defended in my own writing, fit into several of these categories. And, some theories do not neatly fit into any of these categories. This categorization is not intended to be exhaustive, but merely helpful for the purposes of this short chapter.

5   Plato, *The Apology* 20e–23c.

6   For a more thorough presentation of this interpretation of Socrates's view, see my "Wisdom," in *Knowledge, Teaching, and Wisdom,* eds, Keith Lehrer, B. Jeannie Lum, Beverly A.Slichta and Nicholas Smith (Dordrecht: Kluwer Academic Publishers, 1996, 233–42).

7   Patricia Kennedy Arlin, "Wisdom: The Art of Problem Finding," in Robert J. Sternberg, ed., *Wisdom: Its Nature, Origins and Development* (Cambridge: Cambridge University Press, 1992, 230–43).

8   John A. Meacham, "The Loss of Wisdom," in Sternberg (1992, 181–211).

9   William Shakespeare, *As You Like It,* Act V, Scene I, 1623.

10   Sharon Ryan, "Wisdom," in *Knowledge, Teaching, and Wisdom* ed., Lehrer et al. (1996).

11   Aristotle, *Nicomachean Ethics,* book 6.

12   Aristotle, *Nicomachean Ethics,* book 6. Aristotle's theory of practical wisdom goes far beyond mere knowledge, however. He thinks how one actually lives also matters. In particular, Aristotle insists that the wise person is morally virtuous.

13   Robert Nozick, "What Is Wisdom and Why Do Philosophers Love it So," in *The Examined Life* (New York: Touchstone Press, 1989, 267–78).

14   Defended in discussion and developed in Sharon Ryan, "What Is Wisdom?," *Philosophical Studies* 93 (1999, 119–39).

15   A refreshing consequence of Markosian's theory is that philosophers have a nice advantage in the quest for wisdom.

16   William James, *The Principles of Psychology* (New York, NY: Henry and Holt, 1890).

17   Paul B. Baltes and Jacqui Smith, "Toward a Psychology of Wisdom and Its Ontogenesis," in Sternberg (1992, 87–120).

18   Sharon Ryan, "What Is Wisdom?" 122–3.

19   John Kekes, "Wisdom," *American Philosophical Quarterly* 20:3 (July 1983) 277–86.

20   Nicholas Maxwell, *From Knowledge to Wisdom* (Oxford: Blackwell, 1984).

21   Copthorne MacDonald, "Wisdom: The Highest Aim of Life and Higher Education," on The Wisdom Page http://www.wisdompage

22   Garrett, in Lehrer et al. (1996, 221–32).

23   Keith Lehrer, "Introductory Essay," in Lehrer et al. (1996).

24   As phronesis, in *Nichomachean Ethics.*

25   Nozick, "What is Wisdom and Why Do Philosophers Love it So," in 267–78.

26   Ryan, "What Is Wisdom?" 122–3.

27   I am not suggesting that one must learn in a traditional school environment, but one must be exposed to, and understand, the big ideas and questions.

28   Sharon Ryan, "Wisdom," *Stanford Encyclopedia of Philosophy* http://plato.stanford. edu/entries/wisdom/

29 Fred Feldman makes this point in his chapter about moral relativism in his *Introductory Ethics* (Englewood Cliffs, NJ: Prentice-Hall, 1978, 160–72).

30 In discussion in my Theory of Knowledge class at West Virginia University in May 2010.

31 Of course, I am not claiming that *all* poets, politicians, and craftsmen are unwise. I am only claiming that those poets, politicians, craftsmen, . . . philosophers, astronauts, and anyone else who lacks epistemic humility, because they have a lot of unjustified beliefs, is unwise.

32 By "available" I mean to include both evidence one explicitly has "in his head" and also evidence that a person is personally unaware of but could become aware of it with a diligent investigation.

33 For the record, I endorse an internalist evidentialism, as defended by Richard Feldman and Earl Conee in *Evidentialism: Essays in Epistemology* (New York: Oxford University Press, 2004) and a very modest version of foundationalism.

34 I am grateful to Michael Blumenthal, Andrew Cullison, and the students in my 2010 Theory of Knowledge class at West Virginia University for helpful discussions about the ideas in this chapter.

Glossary

This glossary is intended to be a very quick reference to understand the meaning of some core terminology in epistemology. I have tried to keep these definitions brief. In some cases that required that I simplify some things and ignore subtle ways in which some of the terms below are sometimes fleshed out in the literature.

a priori. A proposition is known (or justifiably believed) *a priori* just in case it is known (or justifiably believed) independent from experience.

a posteriori. The opposite of *a priori.* Something is known (or justifiably believed) *a posteriori* just in case it is known (or justifiably believed) on the basis of experience.

abduction. See **inference to the best explanation.**

basic belief. A belief that is not based on an inference from some other belief.

basing relation. Some epistemologists believe that a belief must be appropriately based on the features that justify the proposition believed. This relation is called the basing relation. This relation is introduced by some epistemologists to distinguish between propositional justification and doxastic justification. The basic idea is that a belief is doxastically justified just in case the proposition believed is propositionally justified by one's evidence, and the belief is based on that evidence. One of the main debates concerning the basing relation is whether it is causal or not.

bootstrapping. See **epistemic circularity.**

cartesian foundationalism/skepticism. This is the most classic formulation of foundationalism, and it is characterized by three theses. First, there are epistemically basic beliefs that serve as the foundation for all other knowledge. Second, epistemically basic beliefs are justified because they are certain/indubitable. Third, all justified/known non-basic beliefs are justified by deduction.

causal theory of knowledge. The most basic causal theory of knowledge is roughly that S knows P iff S's true belief that P is caused by the fact that P. It's one of the first *externalist* theories of knowledge to appear in the literature.

closure. *Closure* refers to the principle that people know (or are in a position to know) the known consequences of propositions that they know. There is significant debate about how best to articulate the principle precisely, but a rough way to state a closure principle is as follows: If S knows P and S knows that P entails Q, then S is in a position to know Q.

coherentism. Coherentism is a view about the structure of justification (or epistemic reasons). Classically, coherentists held that beliefs are justified soley in virtue of standing in some kind of epistemic support relation to other beliefs. There are no justified basic beliefs. All justified beliefs are in some sense, inferentially justified. Justified beliefs are also, in some sense, mutually self-supporting. This distinguishes coherentism from both foundationalism and infinitism.

contextualism. Contextualism is the view that the word "knows" and its cognates are context sensitive. A standard way to state this more precisely is to say that the word "knows" denotes one property in some contexts, but in other conversational contexts it denotes a different property. Standardly, the context is shifted when speakers are thinking about the possibility of being wrong with respect to a given proposition. For example, when thinking about skeptical scenarios, the word "knows" might pick out a property or relation that the speaker does not have or stand in, but when that speaker is not thinking about skeptical scenarios the word might shift in meaning to a property or relation that the person *does* have or stand in.

contrastivism. The view that some epistemic concepts are relative to a contrast class. A prominent form of contrastivism holds that *knowledge,* for example, is not a two-place relation between a person and a proposition (as is traditionally assumed). Instead, it is a three-place relation between a person, a proposition, and a relevant contrast class. According to this version of contrastivism, you don't know that there is a sheep in the field *simpliciter.* You know that there is a sheep in the field *rather than a car.*

deduction. Perhaps the most familiar method of reasoning. Deductive reasoning is a method of reasoning that involves inferring a proposition on the basis of premises that logically entail the proposition. Inferring that *Socrates is mortal* from (a) All men are mortal and (b) Socrates is a man is an example of deductive reasoning.

defeater. The word *defeater* is used in a few different ways. One notion of defeat is evidential. If a person has a perception of a tiger, but then becomes aware of conflicting evidence, they have what is called a *rebutting defeater.* If they acquire evidence that they should not trust their perceptions (e.g. that they have been slipped a hallucinogenic drug), then they have what is called an *undercutting* defeater. However, there are also notions of *defeater* that have little to do with conflicting evidence. Some philosophers hold that a belief (whether rational or not) can serve as rebutting or undercutting defeaters for another belief. For example, on this view, if I merely *believe* the proposition that what I'm looking at is a dog disguised as a tiger, then I have a rebutting defeater for the proposition that I'm looking at a tiger. There are also *external* notions of defeat. For example, some philosophers appeal to a notion called a *knowledge defeater* that is clearly external. These philosophers hold that there are sometimes true propositions (beyond the ken of the subject) that can defeat knowledge (or justification) even if they are not aware of the truth of that proposition. Some diagnoses of what goes wrong in *Gettier cases* make use of this external notion of defeater.

deontologism. The view that epistemic justification is a matter of satisfying epistemic duties or obligations.

doxastic attitude. A blanket term for three different attitudes one could have toward a proposition related to belief. Belief, disbelief, and suspension of judgment are the three main kinds of doxastic attitudes that one could have toward a proposition.

doxastic justification. See **epistemic justification.**

doxastic voluntarism. The view that beliefs are under a person's direct, voluntary control.

empiricism. The view that all knowledge or justification is evidentially based on empirical input.

epistemic circularity (rule circularity, premise circularity). There are, at least, two kinds of epistemic circularity. The first is sometimes called premise circularity. Premise circularity occurs when the conclusion of an argument appears as a premise in the argument or when justification for a premise in the argument requires antecedent justification for the conclusion. This is also sometimes called *begging the question.* The other kind of epistemic circularity is called *bootstrapping,* also sometimes called *rule circular reasoning* bootstrapping is a method of reasoning where a subject reasons that a belief-forming process or method is reliable by using premises that rely on that method. Discussions of bootstrapping come up in connection with reliabilist theories of epistemic justification (and more recently all foundationalist theories of epistemic justification). The basic charge is that these theories have no way to prohibit bootstrapping.

epistemic justification. Epistemologists also talk about two different kinds of justification worth mentioning here; propositional justification and doxastic justification. According to most theories of justification there are circumstances under which a person *would be* justified in believing a proposition whether they in fact believe it or not. In those circumstances the person has propositional justification. Propositional justification is fundamentally a relation between a person and a proposition. Doxastic justification is a property of a belief state.

Some epistemologists maintain that someone's belief state is doxastically justified just in case it stands in an appropriate relationship to the features that make a person propositionally justified. What that appropriate relationship is may well depend on other views one might have about the nature of epistemic justification. See **basing relation** for an example of how a view might articulate the relationship between these two concepts.

epistemic relativism. The view that there are no objective epistemic facts about what is rational to believe on the basis of a given body of evidence.

epistemology. An area of philosophy concerned with questions related to knowledge, justification, and reasonable belief.

evidentialism. A view about epistemic justification that holds that justification depends soley on your evidence.

externalism. A view about epistemic justification that holds that factors other than the internal mental states that a person is aware of are relevant to justification (or knowledge). Common externalist views are *reliabilism* and *proper functionalism*.

fallibilism. See **infallibilism.**

foundationalism. A view about the structure of epistemic justification that responds to the *infinite regress argument* by maintaining that the regress of justification can terminate in a special class of *basic beliefs,* beliefs that do not depend for their justification on other beliefs. See **Cartesian foundationalism** and **modest foundationalism.**

Gettier cases. Possible cases that are designed to show that knowledge is not justified true belief. Sometimes the label is broadened to apply to cases that are designed to be counterexamples to minor modifications of the justified true belief analysis of knowledge.

induction. Induction is a method of reasoning that involves making an inference about members of a certain kind from propositions about *other* members of that kind. A common kind of inductive reasoning is when someone comes to believe a general proposition like *All swans are white* based on limited experience with a small class swans and observing that they are all white.

infallibilism. Infallibilism is used in (at least) two senses in epistemology. Sometimes it is used to label the thesis that knowledge requires impossibility of error. If you know that P, then you couldn't be wrong about P. Sometimes it's used to label the thesis that *warrant* entails truth.

inference to the best explanation. A method of inferring a conclusion on the grounds that it is best explained by the data. There are a number of features that might count in favor of an explanation. One feature is the number of entities involved in the explanation. If one explanation posits more entities without explaining any additional data, that tends to count against the explanation. If an explanation is more complex (e.g. postulates that the entities involved are engaged in more complicated processes) than another explanation, that counts against it. There is, however, little agreement about how competing virtues of explanations should be weighed to determine which explanation is best. This is a particularly difficult issue when two competing explanations fare very well compared to the other on *one* of the theoretical virtues but not another.

inferential beliefs. Beliefs that are based on inferences from other beliefs.

infinite regress argument. An argument that raises one of the core puzzles about the structure of knowledge and justification. It seems that in order to be justified in believing something, you'll need to be justified on the basis of another justified belief. This looks like it will require an infinite (vicious) regress of justified beliefs. The alternatives are to permit the chain to go in a circle or allow beliefs to be mutually self-supporting, or permit the chain to stop at some special class of justified beliefs. Some skeptics argue that all of the above options are unsatisfactory. *Foundationalism, Coherentism, and Infinitism* are all views that are designed to respond to the Infinite Regress Argument.

infinitism. A view about the structure of epistemic justification that responds to the *infinite regress argument* by maintaining that the infinite regress is not vicious and that justification can (in a qualified sense) depend on an infinite number of beliefs.

interest-relative invariantism. See **subject-sensitive invariantism.**

internalism. Internalism (in epistemology) typically refers to a view about the nature of epistemic justification that holds that justification depends entirely on internal mental states. It is also common among internalists to hold that subjects must be aware of these mental states. Evidentialism is a classic kind of internalist view.

intuition. An (alleged) kind of evidence distinct from perceptual input. A common view among philosophers is that there are propositions that are not justified by perceptual experience that can and often are justified on the basis of intuitions. Mathematical propositions are examples of propositions that might be justified on the basis of intuition.

invariantism. The view that the word "knows" and its cognates are semantically invariant across conversational contexts. They pick out the same relation in any context. This view is often contrasted with *Contextualism*.

justification. (see epistemic justification).

knowledge. The concept that is one of the primary concerns of epistemology. How best to define it in epistemology is, of course, a major point of contention. While it is common to think that knowing a proposition requires that one have a justified true belief in that proposition, there is very little agreement about what if anything must be added in order to have a full account of what knowledge is.

naturalized epistemology. The word *naturalized epistemology* is used in two different ways. Some argue that epistemlogy should be *naturalized* in the sense that we should abandon traditional arm-chair epistemology and only engage in those projects that can be conducted empirically. Quine argued that epistemology ought to become a branch of emprical psychology. Sometimes when people talk about naturalized epistemology, they have something like what Quine has in mind. However, some have a different idea in mind when they talk about naturalized epistemology. Some argue that all epistemic concepts like knowledge and justification should be reducible to naturalistically respectable properties, properties that our best physics would recognize. Some have used this idea to motivate paradigmatic externalist theories of knowledge and justification.

non-inferential belief. See **basic belief**.

pragmatic encroachment. A term used to describe the phenomenon that some epistemologists hold happens when the practical stakes of being wrong about a proposition are (or become) very high. Some epistemologists hold that non-epistemic facts (such as practical stakes) can affect whether or not a person knows something. See **subject sensitive invariantism**.

pragmatism. There are two theses that one might call *pragmatism*. The first is the view that whether or not something is true depends on what the practical consequences of accepting it are. The second view is that whether or not you're justified in believing something depends on what the practical consequences of accepting it are.

proper functionalism. The view that a belief is justified if, and only if, it was formed by properly functioning cognitive faculties that are appropriately aimed at truth.

propositional justification. See **epistemic justification**.

rationalism. The view that some knowledge is *a priori* or not evidentially based on empirical input.

rebutting defeater. See **defeaters**.

reliabilism. The core idea behind reliabilism is that a belief is justified if, and only if, it was formed by a reliable process or mechanism.

safety. Several recent theories of knowledge add a *safety* requirement. There are many different ways of articulating what it is for a belief to be safe. One simple formulation of a safety principle is that a belief that P is safe for some person just in case that person believes P in most nearby worlds where it is true. Safety theories are thought to be an improvement on Nozick's sensitivity principle. Safety theories are also thought to be a way to articulate reliabilism.

sensitivity. Several recent theories of knowledge have a sensitivity requirement, most notably Robert Nozick. Roughly the idea is that knowing P requires that you be *sensitive* to the truth that P. A believer is sensitive to the truth that P just in case in the nearest world where P is not true the person does not believe P.

skeptical scenario. A scenario that is used to to motivate a skeptical conclusion. The recipe for presenting a skeptical scenario is to imagine a possible way that things could be where everything appears exactly as it does right now, but much of what appears to be true is actually false. One commonly discussed skeptical scenario is the The Brain-in-a-Vat Hypothesis. For all you know, you could be a bodiless brain-in-a-vat hooked up to a super computer being tricked into thinking you have a human body. Imagined scenarios like this have been used in a variety of arguments to motivate skeptical conclusions.

skepticism. Skepticism in the broadest sense of the term is the view that we have no knowledge. This view is also sometimes called *Global Skepticism*. There are few proponents of Global Skepticism, but there are more limited worrisome kinds of skepticism. External world skepticism for example holds that we have no knowledge about the world external to our minds.

subject-sensitive invariantism. This is a species of *invariantism* that tries to preserve some of the benefits of contextualism. According to subject-sensitive invariantism, the relation that "knows" and its cognates might invariantly pick out the same relation in all contexts, but whether or not subjects stand in that relation could vary on certain non-epistemic facts about the situation (e.g. how high the practical stakes are in a given context).

undercutting defeaters. See **defeaters**.

virtue epistemology. The view that knowledge (or justification) depends on the exercise of various epistemic virtues.

warrant. Warrant whatever it is that needs to be added to true belief to yield knowledge. Before Gettier argued that knowledge is not justified true belief, many would have thought that warrant and justification were the same thing.

Research Resources

The following is a list of journals, websites, and centers that will be of interest to epistemologists.

Journals

Episteme
Synthese
Logos and Episteme
The Reasoner

Phil Papers

Epistemology Category
http://philpapers.org/browse/epistemology

Blogs and Websites

Certain Doubts
http://el-prod.baylor.edu/certain_doubts/

Epistemic Value
http://epistemicvaluestirling.blogspot.com/

Internet encyclopedia of philosophy
(select epistemology articles)

Epistemology
http://www.iep.utm.edu/epistemo/

Circularity
http://www.iep.utm.edu/ep-circ/

Closure Principles
http://www.iep.utm.edu/epis-clo/

Coherentism
http://www.iep.utm.edu/coherent/

Defeaters
http://www.iep.utm.edu/ep-defea/

Entitlement
http://www.iep.utm.edu/ep-en/

Epistemic Luck
http://www.iep.utm.edu/epi-luck/

Fallibilism
http://www.iep.utm.edu/fallibil/

Feminist Epistemology
http://www.iep.utm.edu/fem-epis/

Internalism and Externalism
http://www.iep.utm.edu/int-ext/

Moral Epistemology
http://www.iep.utm.edu/mor-epis/

Naturalistic Epistemology
http://www.iep.utm.edu/nat-epis/

Perception
http://www.iep.utm.edu/epis-per/

Religious Epistemology
http://www.iep.utm.edu/relig-ep/

Testimony
http://www.iep.utm.edu/ep-testi/

Transmission and Transmission Failure
http://www.iep.utm.edu/transmis/

Virtue Epistemology
http://www.iep.utm.edu/virtueep/

Stanford encyclopedia of philosophy articles
(select epistemology articles)

Evolutionary Epistemology
http://plato.stanford.edu/entries/epistemology-evolutionary/

Social Epistemology
http://plato.stanford.edu/entries/epistemology-social/

The Epistemology of Religion
http://plato.stanford.edu/entries/religion-epistemology/

Feminist Social Epistemology
http://plato.stanford.edu/entries/feminist-social-epistemology/

Naturalized Epistemology
http://plato.stanford.edu/entries/epistemology-naturalized/

Virtue Epistemology
http://plato.stanford.edu/entries/epistemology-virtue/

Bayesian Epistemology
http://plato.stanford.edu/entries/epistemology-bayesian/

The Epistemology of Modality
http://plato.stanford.edu/entries/modality-epistemology/

Moral Epistemology
http://plato.stanford.edu/entries/moral-epistemology/

Epistemology
http://plato.stanford.edu/entries/epistemology/

The Value of Knowledge
http://plato.stanford.edu/entries/knowledge-value/

The Analysis of Knowledge
http://plato.stanford.edu/entries/knowledge-analysis/

A Priori Justification and Knowledge
http://plato.stanford.edu/entries/apriori/

Reliabilism
http://plato.stanford.edu/entries/apriori/

Epistemological Problems of Testimony
http://plato.stanford.edu/entries/testimony-episprob/

Epistemic Contextualism
http://plato.stanford.edu/entries/contextualism-epistemology/

The Ethics of Belief
http://plato.stanford.edu/entries/ethics-belief/

Epistemological Problems of Memory
http://plato.stanford.edu/entries/memory-episprob/

Evidence
http://plato.stanford.edu/entries/evidence/

The Epistemic Basing Relation
http://plato.stanford.edu/entries/basing-epistemic/

Foundationalist Theories of Epistemic Justification
http://plato.stanford.edu/entries/justep-foundational/

Coherentist Theories of Epistemic Justification
http://plato.stanford.edu/entries/justep-coherence/

The Epistemic Closure Principle
http://plato.stanford.edu/entries/closure-epistemic/

Internalist vs Externalist Conceptions of Epistemic Justification
http://plato.stanford.edu/entries/justep-intext/

Skepticism
http://plato.stanford.edu/entries/skepticism/

Wisdom
http://plato.stanford.edu/entries/wisdom/

Centers, societies, and annual conferences

Carnegie Mellon Center for Formal Epistemology
Experimental Epistemology Research Group
Arche Research Center for Logic, Language, Metaphysics, and Epistemology
Midwest Epistemology Workshop
Rutgers Epistemology Conference
Canadian Society for Epistemology
Society for Skeptical Studies

Bibliography

Alcoff, L. and Potter, E. 1993. *Feminist Epistemologies*. New York, NY: Routledge.

Alexander, J. and Weinberg, J. 2007. "Analytic Epistemology and Experimental Philosophy." *Philosophy Compass* 2: 56–80.

Alston, W. 1976. "Two Types of Foundationalism." *The Journal of Philosophy* 73(7): 165–85.

— 1980. "Level-Confusions in Epistemology." *Midwest Studies in Philosophy* 5(1): 135–50.

— 1989a. *Epistemic Justification: Essays in the Theory of Knowledge*. Ithaca, NY: Cornell University Press.

— 1989b. "Has Foundationalism Been Refuted?" In Alston 1989a, pp. 39–56.

— 1989c. "What's Wrong with Immediate Knowledge?" In Alston 1989a, pp. 57–78.

— 1989d. "Epistemic Circularity." In Alston 1989a, pp. 319–49.

— 1989e. "An Internalist Externalism." In Alston 1989a, pp. 227–45.

— 1993. "Epistemic Desiderata." *Philosophy and Phenomenological Research* 53(3): 527–51.

— 1994. "Belief-Forming Practices and the Social." In F. Schmitt, ed., *Socializing Epistemology*. Maryland: Rowman & Littlefield, pp. 29–52.

— 1999. "Back to the Theory of Appearing." *Philosophical Perspectives* 13: 181–203.

— 2005. *Beyond "Justification": Dimensions of Epistemic Evaluation*. Ithaca, NY: Cornell University Press.

Alston, W. P. 1985 (1989). "Concepts of Epistemic Justification," The Monist 68. Reprinted in "Epistemic Justification: Essays in the Theory of Knowledge." Ithaca, NY: Cornell University Press.

Anderson, E. 1995. "Feminist Epistemology: An Interpretation and a Defense." *Hypatia* 10(3): 50–84.

Armstrong, D. M. 1973. *Belief, Truth and Knowledge*. CUP Archive.

Audi, R. 1993. "The Foundationalism-Coherentism Controversy: Hardened Stereotypes and Overlapping Theories." In R. Audi, ed., *The Structure of Justification*. New York: Cambridge University Press, pp. 117–64.

— 1994. "Dispositional Beliefs and Dispositions to Believe." *Noûs* 28(4): 419–34.

Ayer, A. J. 1936. *Language Truth and Logic*. 1967 edn. London: Gollancz.

— 1956. *The Problem of Knowledge*. Edinburgh: Penguin.

Baehr, J. (2011). *The Inquiring Mind: On Intellectual Virtues and Virtue Epistemology*. Oxford: Oxford University Press.

— 2009. "Is there a Value Problem?" In A. Haddock, A. Millar and D. H. Pritchard, eds, *Epistemic Value*. Oxford: Oxford University Press.

Bealer, G. 1999. "A Theory of the A Priori." *Noûs* 33: 29–55.

— 2000. "A Theory of the A Priori." *Pacific Philosophical Quarterly* 81: 1–30.

Beebe, J. R. 2004. "The Generality Problem, Statistical Relevance and the Tri-Level Hypothesis." *Noûs* 38(1): 177–95.

Beebe, J. and Buckwalter, W. 2010. "The Epistemic Side-Effect Effect." *Mind and Language* 25: 474–98.

Beebe, J. and Jensen, M. (forthcoming). "Surprising Connections between Knowledge and Intentional Action: The Robustness of the Epistemic Side-Effect Effect." *Philosophical Psychology.*

Bergmann, M. 2006. *Justification without Awareness: A Defense of Epistemic Externalism.* NewYork, NY: Oxford University Press.

— 2007. "Is Klein an Infinitist about Doxastic Justification?" *Philosophical Studies* 134(1): 19–24.

— 2011. "Evidentialism and the Great Pumpkin Objection." In T. Dordherty, ed., *Evidentialism and its Discontents.* Oxford: Oxford University Press, pp. 195–209.

Berkeley, G. 1954. *Three Dialogues Between Hylas and Philonous.* Colin Turbayne, ed., Indianapolis: Bobbs-Merrill.

Bird, A. 2007. "Justified Judging." *Philosophy and Phenomenological Research* 74: 81–110.

Bishop, M. and Trout, J. D. 2005. *Epistemology and the Psychology of Human Judgment.* Oxford: Oxford University Press.

Blome-Tillman, M. 2009. "Contextualism, Subject-Sensitive Invariantism, and the Interaction of 'Knowledge'-Ascriptions with Modal and Temporal Operators." *Philosophy and Phenomenological Research* 79: 315–31.

Boghossian, P. 1997. "Analyticity." In B. Hale and C. Wright, eds, *Companion to the Philosophy of Language,* Oxford: Blackwell.

— 2007. *Fear of Knowledge: Against Relativism and Constructivism.* New York, NY: Oxford University Press.

Boghossian, P. and Peacocke, C. 2001. *New Essays on the A Priori.* New York, NY: Oxford University Press.

BonJour, L. 1980a. "Externalist Theories of Empirical Knowledge." In P. French, T. Uehling and H. Wettstein, eds, *Midwest Studies in Philosophy,* Vol. 5: *Epistemology.* Minneapolis: University of Minnesota Press, pp. 53–73.

— 1980b. "Externalist Theories of Empirical Knowledge." *Midwest Studies in Philosophy* 5: 53–73.

— 1985. *The Structure of Empirical Knowledge.* Cambridge, MA: Harvard University Press.

— 1992. "Externalism/Internalism." In J. Dancy and E. Sosa, eds, *A Companion to Epistemology.* Oxford: Blackwell, pp. 132–6.

— 1998. *In Defense of Pure Reason: A Rationalist Account of A Priori Justification.* Cambridge: Cambridge University Press.

— 1999. "The Dialectics of Foundationalism and Coherentism." In Greco and Sosa, eds, 1999, pp. 117–42.

— 2002a. "Internalism and Externalism." In P. K. Moser, ed., *The Oxford Handbook of Epistemology*. Oxford: Oxford University Press, pp. 234–63.

— 2002b. *Epistemology*. Oxford: Rowman & Littlefield.

Botham, T. 2003. "Plantinga and Favorable Mini-Environments." *Synthese* 135: 431–41.

Bovens, L. and Hartmann, S. 2003a. *Bayesian Epistemology*. Oxford: Oxford University Press.

— 2003b. "Solving the Riddle of Coherence." *Mind* 112: 601–33.

— 2004. *Bayesian Epistemology*. New York: Oxford University Press.

— 2006. "An Impossibility Result for Coherence Rankings." *Philosophical Studies* 128: 77–91.

Bovens, L. and Olsson, E. 2000. "Coherentism, Reliability, and Bayesian Networks." *Mind* 109: 685–719.

Brady, M. 2009. "Curiosity and the Value of Truth." In A. Haddock, A. Millar and D. H. Pritchard, eds, *Epistemic Value*. Oxford: Oxford University Press.

Braun, D. 2006. "Names and Natural Kind Terms." In E. Lepore and B. Smith, eds, *The Oxford Handbook of Philosophy of Language*. Oxford: Oxford University Press, pp. 490–515.

— 2007. "Externalism in Mind and Epistemology." In S. Goldberg, ed., *Internalism and Externalism in Semantics and Epistemology*. Oxford: Oxford University Press, pp. 13–34.

Brown, J. 2005. "Adapt or Die: The Death of Invariantism?" *Philosophical Quarterly* 55: 263–85.

— 2006. "Contextualism and Warranted Assertability Manoeuvres." *Philosophical Studies* 130: 407–35.

— 2008a. "The Knowledge Norm for Assertion." *Philosophical Issues* 18: 89–103.

— 2008b. "Subject-Sensitive Invariantism and the Knowledge Norm for Practical Reasoning." *Nous* 42: 167–89.

— (forthcoming). "Knowledge and Assertion." *Philosophy and Phenomenological Research*.

Buckwalter, W. 2010. "Knowledge Isn't Closed on Saturday: A Study in Ordinary Language." *Review of Philosophy and Psychology* 1: 395–406.

— (forthcoming). Gender and Epistemic Intuition.

Buckwalter, W. and Stich, S. (forthcoming). Gender and Philosophical Intuition.

Burge, T. 2003. "Perceptual Entitlement." *Philosophy and Phenomenological Research* 67(3): 503–48.

Carlson, R. 1971. "Where is the Person in Personality Research?" *Psychological Bulletin* 75: 212.

Carnap, R. 1950. "Empiricism, Semantics and Ontology." *Revue Internationale de Philosophie* 4: 20–40, repr. in H. Feigl, W. Sellars and K. Lehrer, eds, *New Readings in Philosophical Analysis,* 1972, New York: Appleton-Century-Crofts, pp. 585–96.

— 1962. *The Logical Foundations of Probability.* Chicago: University of Chicago Press.

Casullo, A. 2003. *A Priori Justification.* New York: Oxford University Press.

Chalmers, D. (forthcoming). "Two-Dimensional Semantics." In LePore and Smith, eds, *Oxford Handbook for Philosophy of Language.* Oxford: Oxford University Press.

Chisholm, R. M. 1977. *The Theory of Knowledge,* 2nd edn. Englewood Cliffs, NJ: Prentice Hall.

— 1989. *Theory of Knowledge,* 3rd edn. Englewood Cliffs, NJ: Prentice-Hall.

Chrisman, M. (2007). "From Epistemic Contextualism to Epistemic Expressivism." *Philosophical Studies* 135(2): 225–54.

Christensen, D. 2007. "Epistemology of Disagreement: The Good News." *Philosophical Review* 116(2): 187–218.

Code, L. 1987. *Epistemic Responsibility.* Hanover, NH: Brown University Press.

Cohen, L. J. 1977. *The Probable and the Provable.* Oxford: Clarendon Press.

Cohen, S. 1984. "Justification and Truth." *Philosophical Studies* 46(3): 279–95.

— 1988. "How to be a Fallibilist." *Philosophical Perspectives* 2: 91–123.

— 1999. "Contextualism, Skepticism, and the Structure of Reasons." *Noûs* 33: 57–89.

— 2002. "Basic Knowledge and the Problem of Easy Knowledge." *Philosophy and Phenomenological Research* 65(2): 309–29.

— 2003. "Greco's Agent Reliabilism." *Philosophy and Phenomenological Research* 66(2): 437–43.

Comesana, J. 2002. "The Diagonal and the Demon." *Philosophical Studies* 110(3): 249–66.

— 2006. "A Well-Founded Solution to the Generality Problem." *Philosophical Studies* 129(1): 27–47.

Conee, E. 1992. "The Truth Connection." *Philosophy and Phenomenological Research* 52(3): 657–69.

— 2007. "Externally Enhanced Internalism." *Internalism and Externalism in Semantics and Epistemology.* New York: Oxford University Press, pp. 51–67.

Conee, E. and Feldman, R. 1998. "The Generality Problem for Reliabilism." *Philosophical Studies* 89(1): 1–29.

— 2001. "Internalism Defended." In H. Kornblith, ed., *Epistemology: Internalism and Externalism.* Malden, MA: Blackwell, pp. 30–60.

Cortens, A. 2002. "Foundationalism and the Regress Argument." *Disputatio* 12: 22–37.

Craig, E. 1975. "The Problem of Necessary Truth." In S. Blackburn, ed., *Meaning, Reference and Necessity.* Cambridge: Cambridge University Press, pp. 1–31.

Cross, C. 1999. "Coherence and Truth Conducive Justification." *Analysis* 59(3): 186–93.

Crupi, V., Tentori, K., and Gonzalez, M. 2007. "On Bayesian Measures of Evidential Support: Theoretical and Empirical Issues." *Philosophy of Science* 74(2): 229–52.

Cullen, S. 2010. "Survey-Driven Romanticism." *Review of Philosophy and Psychology* 1(2): 275–96.

Danks, D. and Glymour, C. 2001. "Linearity Properties of Bayes Nets with Binary Variables." In Breese and Koller 2001, pp. 98–104.

David, M. 2001. "Truth as the Epistemic Goal." In Steup (2001).

Davidson, D. 1986a. "A Coherence Theory of Truth and Knowledge." In
Ernest LePore, ed., *Truth and Interpretation: Perspectives on the Philosophy of
Donald Davidson*. Oxford: Blackwell Publishing: 307–19.

— 1986b. "Empirical Content." In Ernest L. Putnam, ed., *Truth and Interpretation:
Perspectives on the Philosophy of Donald Davidson*. Oxford: Blackwell Publishing.

de Cooman, G. and Miranda, E. 2007. "Symmetry of Models Versus Models of
Symmetry." In Harper and Wheeler 2007, pp. 67–149.

— 2009. "Forward Irrelevance." *Journal of Statistical Planning* 139: 256–76.

DePaul, M. 2001. "Value Monism in Epistemology." In Steup (2001).

DePaul, M. and Zagzebski, L. 2003. *Intellectual Virtue*. Oxford: Oxford University Press.

DeRose, K. 1992. "Contextualism and Knowledge Attributions." *Philosophy and
Phenomenological Research* 52: 913–29.

— 1995. "Solving the Skeptical Problem." *Philosophical Review* 104(1): 1–52.

— 1999. "Contextualism: An Explanation and Defense." In J. Greco and E. Sosa,
eds, *The Blackwell Guide to Epistemology*. Malden, MA: Blackwell Publishers,
pp. 187–205.

— 2000. "Now You Know It, Now You Don't." In *Proceedings of the Twentieth
World Congress of Philosophy*, v: *Epistemology*. Bowling Green, OH: Philosophy
Documentation Center, pp. 91–106.

— 2002. "Assertion, Knowledge, and Context." *Philosophical Review* 111: 167–203.

— 2004. "The Problem with Subject-Sensitive Invariantism." *Philosophy and
Phenomenological Research* 68: 346–50.

— 2005. "The Ordinary Language Basis for Contextualism and the New Invariantism."
Philosophical Quarterly 55: 172–98.

— 2007. "Review of Stanley (2005a)." *Mind* 116: 486–9.

— 2009. *The Case for Contextualism*. Oxford: Oxford University Press.

— 2010. "Contextualism, Contrastivism, and X-Phi Surveys." Presented at the
39th Oberlin College Colloquium in Philosophy. May 9, 2010.

Devitt, M. 2005. "There Is no *A Priori*." In M. Steup and E. Sosa, eds, *Contemporary
Debates in Epistemology*, Oxford: Blackwell, pp. 105–15.

— 2006. *Ignorance of Language*. Oxford: Clarendon Press.

Dietrich, F. and Moretti, L. 2005. "On Coherent Sets and the Transmission of
Confirmation." *Philosophy of Science* 72(3): 403–24.

Douven, I. 2006. "Assertion, Knowledge, and Rational Credibility." *Philosophical Review*
115: 449–85.

Douven, I. and Wouter, M. 2007. "Measuring Coherence." *Synthese* 156(3): 405–25.

Dretske, F. 1981. *Knowledge and the Flow of Information*. Cambridge, MA: MIT Press.

Earman, J. 1992. *Bayes or Bust: A Critical Examination of Bayesian Confirmation Theory*.
Cambridge, MA: MIT Press.

Eells, E. and Fitelson, B. 2002. "Symmetries and Asymmetries in Evidential Support."
Philosophical Studies 107(2): 129–42.

Elgin, C. 2009. "Is Understanding Factive." In A. Haddock, A. Millar and
    D. H. Pritchard, eds, *Epistemic Value*. Oxford: Oxford University Press.
Ellsberg, D. 1961. "Risk, Ambiguity, and the Savage Axioms." *Quarterly Journal of
    Economics* 75: 643–69.
Empiricus, S. 1976. *Outlines of Pyrrhonism*. Cambridge, MA: Harvard University Press.
Evans, J. St, B. T. 2008. "Dual-Processing Accounts of Reasoning, Judgement, and Social
    Cognition." *Annual Review of Psychology* 59: 255–78.
Everitt, N. and Fisher, E. 1995. *Modern Epistemology*. New York: McGraw Hill.
Ewing, A. 1934. *Idealism: A Critical Survey*. London: Methuen.
Fairweather, A. and Zagzebski, L. 2001. *Virtue Epistemology*. Oxford: Oxford University
    Press.
Fallis, D. 2011. "Wikipistemology." In A. Goldman and D. Whitcomb, eds, *Social
    Epistemology: An Anthology*. NewYork, NY: Oxford University Press, pp. 297–313.
Fallis, D. and Whitcomb, D. 2009. "Epistemic Values and Information Management."
    The Information Society 25(3): 175–89.
Fantl, J. and McGrath, M. 2002. "Evidence, Pragmatics, and Justification." *Philosophical
    Review* 111: 67–94.
— 2007. "On Pragmatic Encroachment in Epistemology." *Philosophy and
    Phenomenological Research* 75: 558–89.
— 2009a. *Knowledge in an Uncertain World*. Oxford: Oxford University Press.
— 2009b. "Advice for Fallibilists: Put Knowledge to Work." *Philosophical Studies* 142:
    55–66.
Feldman, R. 1993. "Proper Functionalism." *Nous* 27: 34–50.
— 1995. "In Defence of Closure." *The Philosophical Quarterly* 45: 487–94.
— 1999. "Contextualism and Skepticism." *Noûs* 33: 91–114.
— 2001. "Naturalized Epistemology." *Stanford Encyclopedia of Philosophy*.
— 2004. *Evidentialism: Essays in Epistemology*. New York: Oxford University Press.
— 2006. "Reasonable Religious Disagreements." In L. Antony, ed., *Philosophers without
    Gods: Meditations on Atheism and the Secular Life*. New York: Oxford University
    Press.
Feldman, R. and Conee, E. 1985. "Evidentialism." *Philosophical Studies* 48(1): 15–34.
— 2001. "Internalism Defended." *American Philosophical Quarterly* 38(1): 1–18.
Feldman, R. and Warfield, T. 2010. *Disagreement*. New York: Oxford University Press.
Feltz, A. and Zarpentine, C. 2010. "Do You Know More When It Matters Less?"
    Philosophical Psychology 23: 683–706.
Field, H. 2000. "A Prioricity as an Evaluative Notion." In P. Boghossian and C. Peacocke,
    eds, *New Essays on the A Priori*. Oxford: Clarendon Press, pp. 117–49.
— 2006. "Recent Debates about the A Priori." *Oxford Studies in Epistemology* 1: 69.
Firth, R. 1978. "Are Epistemic Concepts Reducible to Ethical Concepts?" In Goldman,
    Alvin and Kim, Jaegwon, eds, *Values and Morals,* Dordrecht: Reidel.
Fitelson, B. 2003. "A Probabilistic Theory of Coherence." *Analysis* 63: 194–99.
— 2005. "Review: Bayesian Epistemology." *Mind* 114(454): 394.

Foley, R. 1987. *The Theory of Epistemic Rationality*. Cambridge, MA: Harvard University Press.

— 2007. *Intellectual Trust in Oneself and Others*. Cambridge: Cambridge University Press.

Fumerton, R. 1980. "Induction and Reasoning to the Best Explanation." *Philosophy of Science* December: 589–600.

— 1985. *Metaphysical and Epistemological Problems of Perception*. Lincoln: University of Nebraska Press.

— 1995. *Metaepistemology and Skepticism*. Lanham, MD: Rowman & Littlefield.

— 2007a. "What and About What is Internalism?" In S. Goldberg, ed., *Internalism and Externalism in Semantics and Epistemology*. Oxford: Oxford University Press, pp. 35–50.

— 2007b. "Epistemic Conservatism: Theft or Honest Toil?" *Oxford Studies in Epistemology* 2: 64–87.

Gendler, T. and Hawthorne, J. 2005. "The Real Guide to Fake Barns: A Catalogue of Gifts for Your Epistemic Enemies." *Philosophical Studies* 124: 331–52.

— 2010. *Oxford Studies in Epistemology, Volume 3*. Oxford: Oxford University Press.

Gettier, E. L. 1963. "Is Justified True Belief Knowledge?" *Analysis* 23: 121–3.

Gibbard, A. 1990. *Wise Choices, Apt Feelings*. Oxford: Clarendon Press.

Gigerenzer, G., Todd, P., and The ABC Research Group. 2000. *Simple Heuristics That Make Us Smart*. New York: Oxford University Press.

Ginet, C. 2005. "Infinitism is not the Solution to the Regress Problem." In M. Steup and E. Sosa, eds, *Contemporary Debates in Epistemology*. Oxford: Blackwell Publishing, pp. 140–9.

Glass, D. H. 2006. "Coherence Measures and their Relations to Fuzzy Similarity and Inconsistency in Knowledge Bases." *Artificial Intelligence Review* 26: 227–49.

Glymour, C. 1998. "What Went Wrong: Reflections on Science by Observation and The Bell Curve." *Philosophy of Science* 65(1): 1–32.

Glymour, C., Scheines, R., Spirtes P., and Kelly, K. 1987. *Discovering Causal Structure*. London: Academic Press.

Godel, K. 1947. "What Is Cantor's Continuum Problem?" *American Mathematical Monthly* 54(9): 515–25, repr. in P. Benacerraf and H. Putnam, eds, *Philosophy of Mathematics,* 1964, Cambridge: Cambridge University Press, pp. 258–73.

Goldberg, S. 2010. *Relying on Others: An Essay in Epistemology*. Oxford: Oxford University Press.

— 2007. *Internalism and Externalism in Semantics and Epistemology*. New York: Oxford University Press.

Goldman, A. 1967. "A Causal Theory of Knowing." *The Journal of Philosophy* 64(12): 357–72.

— 1978. "Epistemics: The Regulative Theory of Cognition." *Journal of Philosophy* 75(10): 509–23.

— 1979. "What is Justified Belief?" In G. Pappas, ed., *Justification and Knowledge*. Dordrecht: D. Reidel, pp. 1–23.

— 1986. *Epistemology and Cognition.* Cambridge: Harvard University Press.

— 1988. "Strong and Weak Justification." *Philosophical Perspectives* 2: *Epistemology,*
    pp. 51–69.

— 1991. "Stephen P. Stich: The Fragmentation of Reason." *Philosophy and
    Phenomenological Research* 51(1): 189–93.

— 1994. "Naturalistic Epistemology and Reliabilism." In P. French, T. Uehling and
    H. Wettstein, eds, *Midwest Studies in Philosophy,* Vol. 19. Minneapolis: University of
    Minnesota Press, pp. 301–20.

— 1999a. *Knowledge in a Social World.* New York: Oxford University Press.

— 1999b. "Internalism Exposed." *The Journal of Philosophy* 96(6): 271–93.

— 2001. "The Unity of Epistemic Virtues." In Fairweather and Zagzebski 2001.

— 2008. "Immediate Justification and Process Reliabilism." In Q. Smith, ed.,
    Epistemology: New Essays. New York: Oxford University Press.

— 2011. "Toward a Synthesis of Reliabilism and Evidentialism." In T. Dougherty, ed.,
    Evidentialism and its Discontents. Oxford: Oxford University Press, pp. 393–426.

Good, I. J. 1952. "Rational Decisions." *Journal of the Royal Statistics Society, Series B,*
    14(1): 107–14.

Grasswick, H. 2011. *Feminist Epistemology and Philosophy of Science: Power in
    Knowledge.* Dordrecht: Springer Verlag.

Greco, J. 1993. "Virtues and Vices of Virtue Epistemology." *Canadian Journal of
    Philosophy* 23: 413–32.

— 1999. "Agent Reliabilism." *Noûs* 33: 273–96.

— 2000. *Putting Skeptics in their Place.* Cambridge: Cambridge University Press.

— 2002. "Virtues in Epistemology." In P. Moser, ed., *The Oxford Handbook of
    Epistemology.* Oxford University Press.

— 2003. "Knowledge as Credit for True Belief." In DePaul and Zagzebski 2003.

— 2004. "Knowledge as Credit for True Belief." In Michael DePaul and Linda Zagzebski,
    eds, *Intellectual Virtue: Perspectives from Ethics and Epistemology.* pp. 111–34.

— 2010. *Achieving Knowledge.* Cambridge: Cambridge University Press.

— (forthcoming). "Epistemic Value." In D. Pritchard and S. Bernecker, eds,
    The Routledge Companion to Epistemology. New York, NY: Routledge.

Greco, J. and Sosa, E. eds, 1999. *The Blackwell Guide to Epistemology.* Malden, MA:
    Blackwell.

Greco, J. and Turri, J. 2009. "Virtue Epistemology." In Edward N. Zalta, ed.,
    The Stanford Encyclopedia of Philosophy. Available at: http://plato.stanford.edu/
    entries/epistemology-virtue/

Grimm, S. 2006. "Is Understanding a Species of Knowledge." *The British Journal for the
    Philosophy of Science* 57(3): 515–35.

— 2008. "Epistemic Goals and Epistemic Values." *Philosophy And Phenomenological
    Research* 77(3): 725–44.

— 2010. "Understanding." In S. Bernecker and D. Pritchard, eds, *The Routledge
    Companion to Epistemology.* New York, NY: Routledge.

Haack, S. 1993. *Evidence and Inquiry*. Oxford: Blackwell Publishing.

Haenni, R., Romeyn, J., Wheeler, G., and Williamson, J. 2011. *Probabilistic Logic and Probabilistic Networks*. Dordrecht: The Synthese Library.

Hale, B. and Wright, C. 2000. "Implicit Definition and the A Priori." In P. Boghossian and C. Peacocke, eds, *New Essays on the A Priori*. Oxford: Clarendon Press, pp. 286–319.

Halmos, P. 1950. *Measure Theory*. New York: Van Nostrand Reinhold.

Halpern, J. 2003. *Reasoning about Uncertainty*. Cambridge, MA: MIT Press.

Harper, W. and Wheeler, G. 2007. *Probability and Inference: Essays in Honour of Henry E. Kyburg, Jr*. London: College.

Hartmann, S., Weber, M., Gonzalez, W., and Dieks, D. 2011. *Explanation, Prediction, and Confirmation: New Trends and Old Ones Reconsidered*. Dordrecht: Springer.

Hawthorne, J. 2005. *Knowledge and Lotteries*. New York: Oxford University Press.

— 2007. "Externalism and A Priority." In S. Goldberg, ed., *Internalism and Externalism in Semantics and Epistemology*. Oxford: Oxford University Press.

Heller, M. 1995. "The Simple Solution to the Problem of Generality." *Noûs* 29(4): 501–15.

Helmholtz, H. 1860. "The Young-Helmholtz Theory of Color Vision." In Wayne 1948, pp. 199–205.

Henderson, D. and Horgan, T. 2007. "The Ins and Outs of Transglobal Reliabilism." In S. Goldberg, ed., *Internalism and Externalism in Semantics and Epistemology*. Oxford: Oxford University Press, pp. 100–30.

Hendricks, V. and Pritchard, D. 2006. *New Waves in Epistemology*. New York, NY: Palgrave Macmillan.

Hendricks, V. and Symons, J. 2005. *Formal Philosophy*. Rolskilde: Automatic Press.

Henrich, J., Heine, S., and Norenzayan, A. 2010. "The Weirdest People in the World?" *Behavioral and Brain Sciences* 33(2–3): 61–83.

Hookway, C. 2003. "How to Be a Virtue Epistemologist." In DePaul and Zagzebski.

Horn, A. and Tarski, A. 1948. "Measures in Boolean Algebras." *Transactions of the AMS* 64(1): 467–97.

Hossack, K. 2007. *The Metaphysics of Knowledge*. Oxford: Oxford University Press.

Howard-Snyder, D. 1998. "BonJour's 'Basic Antifoundationalist Argument' and the Doctrine of the Given." *Southern Journal of Philosophy* 36: 163–77.

— 2002. "On an 'Unintelligible Idea': Donald Davidson's Case against Experiential Foundationalism." *Southern Journal of Philosophy* 40: 523–55.

— 2004. "Lehrer's Case against Foundationalism." *Erkenntnis* 60: 51–73.

Howard-Snyder, D. and Coffman, E. J. 2005. "Foundationalism and Arbitrariness." *Pacific Philosophical Quarterly* 86(1): 18–24.

— 2006. "Three Arguments against Foundationalism: Arbitrariness, Epistemic Regress, and Existential Support." *Canadian Journal of Philosophy* 36: 535–64.

Howard-Snyder, D., Howard-Snyder, F., and Feit, N. 2003. "Infallibilism and Gettier's Legacy." *Philosophy and Phenomenological Research* 66(2): 304–27.

Huemer, M. 1997. "Probability and Coherence Justification." *The Southern Journal of Philosophy* 35: 463–72.

— 2001. *Skepticism and the Veil of Perception.* Rowman & Littlefield Publishers.

Hume, D. 1888. *A Treatise of Human Nature.* L. A. Selby-Bigge, ed., London: Oxford University Press.

Jeffrey, R. 1965. *The Logic of Decision.* New York: McGraw-Hill.

Jenkins, C. S. 2008a. "A Priori Knowledge: Debates and Developments." *Philosophy Compass* 3: 436–50.

— 2008b. *Grounding Concepts: An Empirical Basis for Arithmetic Knowledge.* New York: Oxford University Press.

— (forthcoming). "Concepts, Experience and Modal Knowledge." *Philosophical Perspectives* 24.

Jones, W. 1997. "Why Do We Value Knowledge?" *APQ* (34): 423–39.

Joyce, J. 2010. "In Defense of Imprecise Credences in Inference and Decision Making." *Philosophical Perspectives* 21(1): 281–323.

Junker, B. W. and Ellis, J. L. 1997. "A Characterization of Monotone Unidimensional Latent Variable Models." *The Annals of Statistics* 25: 1327–43.

Kalderon, M. 2009. "Epistemic Relativism." *Philosophical Review* 118(2): 225–40.

Kant, I. 1781. *Critique of Pure Reason.* 1929 edn, trans. N. Kemp Smith. Basingstoke: Palgrave.

Kauppinen, A. 2007. "The Rise and Fall of Experimental Philosophy." *Philosophical Explorations* 10: 95–118.

Kelly, T. 2005. "The Epistemic Significance of Disagreement." In J. Hawthorne and T. Gendler, eds, *Oxford Studies in Epistemology.* Oxford: Oxford University Press.

Kim, J. 1988. "What is Naturalized Epistemology." *Philosophical Perspectives* 2: 381–405.

Kitcher, P. 1992. "The Naturalists Return." *Philosophical Review* 101(1): 53–114.

— 1993. *The Advancement of Science.* Oxford: Oxford University Press.

— 2001. *Science, Truth, and Democracy.* Oxford: Oxford University Press.

Klein, P. 1985. "The Virtues of Inconsistency." *Monist* 68(1): 105–35.

— 1998. "Foundationalism and the Infinite Regress of Reasons." *Philosophy and Phenomenological Research* 58(4): 919–25.

— 1999. "Human Knowledge and the Infinite Regress of Reasons." *Philosophical Perspectives* 13: 297–325.

— 2003. "Skepticism." In Edward N. Zalta, ed., *The Stanford Encyclopedia of Philosophy.* Available at: http://plato.stanford.edu/archives/fall2003/entries/skepticism.

— 2004. "What *IS* Wrong with Foundationalism is that it Cannot Solve the Epistemic Regress Problem." *Philosophy and Phenomenological Research* 65: 166–71.

— 2005. "Infinitism is the Solution to the Regress Problem." In Steup and Sosa 2005: 131–40.

— 2007. "How to be an Infinitist about Doxastic Justification." *Philosophical Studies* 134(1): 25–9.

Klein, P. and Warfield, T. A. 1996. "No Help for the Coherentist." *Analysis* 56(2): 118–21.

— 1994. "What Price Coherence?" *Analysis* 54(3): 129.

Knobe, J. 2003a. "Intentional Action and Side Effects in Ordinary Language." *Analysis* 63: 190–3.

— 2003b. "Intentional Action in Folk Psychology: An Experimental Investigation." *Philosophical Psychology* 16(2): 309–23.

Koopman, B. O. 1940. "The Axioms and Algebra of Intuitive Probability." *Annals of Mathematics* 41(2): 269–92.

Kornblith, H. 1983. "Justified Belief and Epistemically Responsible Action." *The Philosophical Review* 92(1): 33–48.

— 1999. "Knowledge in Humans and Other Animals." *Noûs* 33: 327–46.

— 2001. *Epistemology: Internalism and Externalism.* Wiley-Blackwell.

— 2003. "Roderick Chisholm and the Shaping of American Epistemology." *Metaphilosophy* 34(5): 582–602.

Kruglanski, A. and Gigerenzer, G. 2011. "Intuitive and Deliberate Judgments Are Based on Common Principles." *Psychological Review* 118(1): 97–109.

Kruglanski, A. and Orehek, E. 2007. "Partitioning the Domain of Human Inference: Dual Mode and System Models and their Alternatives." *Annual Review of Psychology* 8: 291–316.

Kvanvig, J. 1996. *Warrant in Contemporary Epistemology.* New York: Rowman and Littlefield.

— 2003. *The Value of Knowledge and the Pursuit of Understanding.* Cambridge: Cambridge University Press.

— 2005. "Truth is not the Primary Epistemic Goal." In Steup and Sosa.

— 2007. "Coherentist Theories of Justification." In Edward N. Zalta, ed., Available at: http://plato.stanford.edu/entries/justep-coherence/

— 2010. "The Swamping Problem Redux: Pith and Gist." In Adrian Haddock, Alan Miller and Duncan Pritchard, eds, *Social Epistemology.* Oxford: Oxford University Press, pp. 89–111.

Kyburg, Jr, H. E. 1961. *Probability and the Logic of Rational Belief.* Middletown, CT: Wesleyan University Press.

Kyburg, Jr, H. E., and Pittarelli, M. 1996. "Set-based Bayesianism." *IEEE Transactions on Systems, Man, and Cybernetics A* 26(3): 324–39.

Lackey, J. 2007. "Norms of Assertion." *Nous* 41: 594–626.

— 2008. *Learning from Words: Testimony as a Source of Knowledge.* New York: Oxford University Press.

— 2009. "Knowledge and Credit." *Philosophical Studies* 142: 27–42.

— (forthcoming). "Assertion and Isolated Secondhand Knowledge." In J. Brown and H. Cappelen, eds, *What Is Assertion?* Oxford: Oxford University Press.

Lackey, J. and Sosa, E. 2006. *The Epistemology of Testimony.* New York: Oxford University Press.

Laudan, L. 2007. *Truth, Error, and Criminal Law: An Essay in Legal Epistemology.* Cambridge: Cambridge University Press.

Le Morvan, P. 2008. "Sensory Experience and Intentionalism." *Philosophy Compass* 3(4): 685–702.

Lehrer, K. 1974. *Knowledge.* Oxford: Clarendon Press.

— 1986. "The Coherence Theory of Knowledge." *Philosophical Topics* 14(1): 5–25.

— 1990. *Theory of Knowledge.* Boulder, Colorado: Westview Press.

Lehrer, K. and Cohen, S. 1983. "Justification, Truth, and Coherence." *Synthese* 55: 191–207.

Lehrer, Keith, Jeannie Lum, B., Slichta, Beverly A., and Smith, Nicholas D. (eds), 1996, *Knowledge, Teaching, and Wisdom,* Dordrecht: Kluwer Academic Publishers.

Leite, A. 2004. "On Justifying and Being Justified." *Philosophical Issues* 14: 219–53.

Levi, I. 1980. *Enterprise of Knowledge.* Cambridge, MA: MIT Press.

Levin, J. 2008. "Assertion, Practical Reason, and Pragmatic Theories of Knowledge." *Philosophy and Phenomenological Research* 76(2): 359–84.

Lewis, C. I. 1946. *An Analysis on Knowledge and Valuation.* LaSalle, IN: Open Court.

Lewis, D. 1996. "Elusive Knowledge." *Australasian Journal of Philosophy* 74: 549–67.

Liao, M. 2008. "A Defense of Intuitions." *Philosophical Studies* 140: 247–62.

List, C. 2005. "Group Knowledge and Group Rationality: A Judgment Aggregation Perspective." *Episteme* 2(1): 25–38.

Lycan, W. 1988. *Judgement and Justification.* Cambridge: Cambridge University Press.

Lynch, M. (forthcoming). "Truth, Value and Epistemic Expressivism." *Philosophy and Phenomenological Research.*

Lyons, J. 2008. *Perception and Basic Beliefs.* Oxford: Oxford University Press.

Markie, P. J. 2005. "Easy Knowledge." *Philosophy and Phenomenological Research* 70(2): 406–16.

Matheson, J. 2009. "Conciliatory Views of Disagreement and Higher-Order Evidence." *Episteme: A Journal of Social Philosophy* 6(3): 269–79.

Matheson, J. and Rogers, J. 2011. "Bergmann's Dilemma: Exit Strategies for Internalists." *Philosophical Studies* 152(1): 55–80.

May, J., Sinnott-Armstrong, W., Hull, J. G., and Zimmerman, A. 2010. "Practical Interests, Relevant Alternatives, and Knowledge Attributions: An Empirical Study." *Review of Philosophy and Psychology* 1: 265–73.

McDowell, J. 1994. *Mind and World.* Cambridge, MA: Harvard University Press.

McGinn, C. 1984. "The Concept of Knowledge." *Midwest Studies in Philosophy* 9: 529–54.

Meijs, W. 2004. "A Corrective to Bovens and Hartmann's Measure of Coherence." *Philosophical Studies* 133(2): 151–80.

Merricks, T. 1995. "Warrant Entails Truth." *Philosophy and Phenomenological Research* 55: 841–55.

Mill, J. S. 1843. *A System of Logic.* London: Parker.

Miscevic, N. 2007. "Virtue-Based Epistemology and the Centrality of Truth."
Acta Analytica 22(3): 239–66.

Moore, G. E. 1925. "A Defence of Common Sense." In J. H. Muirhead, ed.,
Contemporary British Philosophy. London: Allen and Unwin, pp. 193–223.

— 1939. "Proof of an External World." *Proceedings of the British Academy,* 273–300.

— 1962. *Commonplace Book 1919–1953.* Bristol: Thoemmes Press.

Moretti, L. 2007. "Ways in which Coherence is Confirmation Conducive." *Synthese*
157(3): 309–19.

Myrvold, W. 1996. "Bayesianism and Diverse Evidence: A Reply to Andrew Wayne."
Philosophy of Science 63: 661–5.

Nadelhoffer, T. 2004. "The Butler Problem Revisited." *Analysis* 64(3): 277–84.

Nadelhoffer, T. and Nahmias, E. 2007. "The Past and Future of Experimental
Philosophy." *Philosophical Explorations* 10: 123–49.

Nagel, J. 2007. "Epistemic Intuitions." *Philosophy Compass* 2: 792–819.

— (forthcoming). "Intuitions and Experiments: A Defense of the Case Method."
Philosophy and Phenomenological Research.

Nagel, J., San Juan, V., and Mar, R. (forthcoming). Gettier Case Recognition.

Nelson, L. H. 1993. "Epistemological Communities." *Feminist Epistemologies.* 121–60.

Neta, R. 2006. "How to Naturalize Epistemology." In Hendricks and Pritchard 2006.

— 2008. "In Defense of Epistemic Relativism." *Episteme* 4(1): 30–48.

Nichols, S., Stich, S., and Weinberg, J. 2003. "Metaskepticism: Meditations in
Ethno-Epistemology." In Stephen Luper, ed., *The Skeptics.* Burlington, VT: Ashgate
Press, pp. 227–47.

Nozick, R. 1981. *Philosophical Explanations.* Cambridge, MA: Belknap Press.

— 1989. *The Examined Life.* NewYork, NY: Touchstone Press.

Olsson, E. J. 2002. "What is the Problem of Coherence and Truth?" *Journal of
Philosophy* 94: 246–72.

— 2005. *Against Coherence: Truth, Probability, and Justification.* New York: Oxford
University Press.

Pappas, G. 1979. *Justification and Knowledge: New Studies in Epistemology.*
Kluwer Academic Publisher.

Paris, J. 1994. *The Uncertain Reasoner's Companion: A Mathematical Companion.*
Cambridge: Cambridge University Press.

Peacocke, C. 2000. "Explaining the A Priori: The Programme of Moderate Rationalism."
In P. Boghossian and C. Peacocke, eds, *New Essays on the A Priori.* Oxford:
Clarendon Press, pp. 255–85.

Pearl, J. 2000. *Causality.* Cambridge: Cambridge University Press.

Phelan, M. (manuscript). "Evidence that Stakes Don't Matter for Evidence."

Pinillos, N. (forthcoming). "Knowledge, Experiments and Practical Interests." In
J. Brown and M. Gerken, eds, *Knowledge Ascriptions.* New York: Oxford University
Press.

Pinnick, C., Koertge, N., and Almeder, R. 2003. *Scrutinizing Feminist Epistemology: An Examination of Gender in Science.* New Brunswick: Rutgers University Press.

Plantinga, A. 1993a. *Warrant and Proper Function.* New York: Oxford University Press.

— 1993b. *Warrant: The Current Debate.* New York: Oxford University Press.

— 1993c. "Why We Need Proper Function." *Nous,* 27: 66–82.

— 2000. *Warranted Christian Belief.* New York: Oxford University Press.

Pollock, J. 1985. *Contemporary Theories of Knowledge.* Totowa, NJ: Rowman & Littlefield.

Pritchard, D. 2005. *Epistemic Luck.* New York: Oxford University Press.

— 2007. "Recent Work on Epistemic Value." *American Philosophical Quarterly* 44(2): 85.

— 2011. "What is the Swamping Problem?" In A. Reisner and A. Steglich-Petersen, eds, *Reasons for Belief.* Cambridge, UK: Cambridge University Press.

— (forthcoming). "Knowledge and Understanding." In A. Miller and A. Haddock, co-writers. *The Nature and Value of Knowledge: Three Investigations.* New York: Oxford University Press.

Pryor, J. 2000. "The Skeptic and the Dogmatist." *Nous* 34(4): 517–49.

— 2001. "Highlights of Recent Epistemology." *The British Journal for the Philosophy of Science* 52(1): 95–124.

— 2005. "There is Immediate Justification." In M. Steup and E. Sosa, eds, *Contemporary Debates in Epistemology.* Oxford: Blackwell Publishing, pp. 181–202.

Putnam, H. 1973. "Meaning and Reference." *The Journal of Philosophy* 70(19): 699–711.

— 1996. "The Meaning of Meaning." In H. Geirsson and L. Michael, eds, *Readings in Language and Mind,* LePore. Oxford: Blackwell Publishing, pp. 157–98.

Quine, W. V. 1969. "Epistemology Naturalized" in Ontological Relativity and Other Essays. New York: Columbia.

Quine, W. V. O. 1951. "Two Dogmas of Empiricism." In *Philosophical Review,* repr. in *From a Logical Point of View: Nine Logico-Philosophical Essays,* 1953, edn. of 1980, Cambridge, MA: Harvard University Press, pp. 20–46.

Rachels, J. 1999. "The Challenge of Cultural Relativism." *The Elements of Moral Philosophy* 3rd edn. New York, NY: Random House, pp. 20–36.

Reynolds, S. 2002. "Testimony, Knowledge, and Epistemic Goals." *Philosophical Studies* 110: 139–61.

Riggs, W. 2002. "Reliability and the Value of Knowledge." *Philosophy And Phenomenological Research* (64): 79–96.

— 2006. "The Value Turn in Epistemology." In Hendricks and Pritchard 2006.

— 2008. (2003a). "Understanding 'virtue' and the Virtue of Understanding." In De Paul and Zagzebski 2003.

— 2009. "Understanding, Knowledge, and the Meno Requirement." In A. Haddock and D. Pritchard, eds, *Epistemic Value.* Oxford: Oxford University Press.

Roberts, R. and Wood, J. 2007. *Intellectual Virtues: An Essay in Regulative Epistemology.* Oxford: Oxford University Press.

Rorty, R. 1981. *Philosophy and the Mirror of Nature.* Princeton: Princeton University Press.

Russell, B. 1948. *Human Knowledge: Its Scope and its Limits.* New York, NY: Simon & Schuster.

Ryan, S. 1996. "Wisdom." In Lehrer et. al. 1996.

— 1999. "What is Wisdom?" *Philosophical Studies* (93): 119–39.

— 2007. "Wisdom." *Stanford Encyclopedia of Philosophy.*

Rysiew, P. 2001. "The Context-Sensitivity of Knowledge Attributions." *Nous* 35: 477–514.

— 2005. "Contesting Contextualism." *Grazer Philosophische Studien* 69: 51–69.

— 2007. "Speaking of Knowing." *Nous* 41: 627–62.

Salmon, N. 1986. *Frege's puzzle.* Massachusetts, MA: MIT Press.

Schaffer, J. 2004. "From Contextualism to Contrastivism." *Philosophical Studies* 119: 73–103.

Schaffer, J. and Knobe, J. (manuscript). Contrastive Knowledge Surveyed. *Nous.*

Schlosshauer, M. and Wheeler, G. 2011. "Focused Correlation, Confirmation, and the Jigsaw Puzzle of Variable Evidence." *Philosophy of Science* 78(3): 276–92.

Schmitt, F. and Lahroodi, R. 2008. "The Epistemic Value of Curiosity." *Educational Theory* 58(2): 125–48.

Sears, D. 1986. "College Sophomores in the Laboratory: Influences of a Narrow Data Base on Social Psychology's View of Human Nature." *Journal of Personality and Social Psychology* 51: 515–30.

Segerberg, K. 2005. "Krister Segerberg." In Hendricks and Symons 2005, pp. 159–67.

Seidenfeld, T. and Wassermann, L. 1993. "Dilation for Sets of Probabilities." *The Annals of Statistics* 21: 1139–54.

Seidenfeld, T., Schervish, M. and Kadane, K. 2010. "Coherent Choice Functions under Uncertainty." *Synthese* 172(1): 157–76.

Sellars, W. 1956. "Empiricism and the Philosophy of Mind." In H. Feigl and M. Scriven, eds, *Minnesota Studies in the Philosophy of Science, Volume I: The Foundations of Science and the Concepts of Psychology and Psychoanalysis.* Minneapolis: University of Minnesota Press, pp. 253–329.

Shah, N. and Velleman, D. 2005. "Doxastic Deliberation." *Philosophical Review* 114(4): 497–534.

Shogenji, T. 1999. "Is Coherence Truth Conducive?" *Analysis* 59: 338–45.

Silva, R., Glymour, C., Scheines, R., and Spirtes, P. 2006. "Learning the Structure of Latent Linear Structure Models." *Journal of Machine Learning Research* 7: 191–246.

Slote, M. 1979. "Assertion and Belief." In J. Dancy, ed., *Papers on Language and Logic.* Keele: Keele University Library.

Snow, C. 1959 (1998). *The Two Cultures.* 9th Printing. Cambridge: Cambridge University Press.

Sosa, E. 1980. "The Raft and the Pyramid: Coherence Versus Foundations in the Theory of Knowledge." *Midwest Studies In Philosophy* 5(1): 3–26.

— 1988. "Beyond Skepticism, to the Best of Our Knowledge." *Mind* 97: 153–88.

— 1993. "Proper Functionalism and Virtue Epistemology." *Noûs* 27(1): 51–65.

— 2003. "The Place of Truth in Epistemology." In DePaul and Zagzebski 2003, pp. 155–80.

— 2005. "A Defense of the Use of Intuitions in Philosophy." In D. Murphy and M. Bishop, eds, *Stich and his Critics*. Oxford: Blackwell, pp. 101–12.

— 2007a. *A Virtue Epistemology*. Oxford: Oxford University Press.

— 2007b. "Experimental Philosophy and Philosophical Intuition." *Philosophical Studies* 132: 99–107.

— 2008. "Boghossian's Fear of Knowledge." *Philosophical Studies* 141(3): 407.

— 2009a. *A Virtue Epistemology*. New York: Oxford University Press.

— 2009b. *Reflective Knowledge*. New York: Oxford University Press.

Sosa, E. and Bonjour, L. 2003. *Epistemic Justification*. London: Blackwell.

Spirtes, P., Glymour, C., and Scheines, R. 2000. *Causation, Prediction, and Search*. 2nd edn. Cambridge, MA: MIT Press.

Stanley, J. 2005a. *Knowledge and Practical Interests*. Oxford: Oxford University Press.

— 2005b. "Fallibilism and Concessive Knowledge Attributions." *Analysis* 65: 126–31.

Starmans, C. and Friedman, O. (manuscript). "A Sex Difference in Adults' Attributions of Knowledge."

Steup, M. and Sosa, E. eds, 2005. *Contemporary Debates in Epistemology*. Oxford: Blackwell Publishing.

Sturgeon, S. 2010. "Confidence and Coarse-grain Attitudes." In Gendler and Hawthorne 2010, pp. 126–49.

Sutton, J. 2005. *Without Justification*. Cambridge, MA: MIT Press.

Swain, S., Alexander, J., and Weinberg, J. 2008. "The Instability of Philosophical Intuitions: Running Hot and Cold on Truetemp." *Philosophy and Phenomenological Research* 76: 138–55.

Swan, M. 2005. *Practical English Usage*. Oxford: Oxford University Press.

Taylor, J. 1991. "Plantinga's Proper Functioning Analysis of Epistemic Warrant." *Philosophical Studies* 64: 185–202.

Treanor, N. (manuscript). "The Measure of Knowledge."

Unger, P. 1971. "A Defense of Skepticism." *The Philosophical Review* 80(2): 198–219.

— 1975. *Ignorance: A Case for Skepticism*. Oxford: Oxford University Press.

Van Cleve, J. "Reliability, Justification, and the Problem of Induction." *Midwest Studies in Philosophy* 9(1): 555–67.

Vogel, J. 1990. "Cartesian Skepticism and Inference to the Best Explanation." *Journal of Philosophy* 87(11): 658–66.

— 1999. "The New Relevant Alternatives Theory." *Nous* 33(s13): 155–80.

— 2000. "Reliabilism Leveled." *The Journal of Philosophy* 97(11): 602–23.

— 2005. "The Refutation of Skepticism." In M. Steup and E. Sosa, eds, *Contemporary Debates in Epistemology*. Oxford: Blackwell.

Walley, P. 1991. *Statistical Reasoning with Imprecise Probabilities*. London: Chapman and Hall.

Weatherson, B. 2003. "What Good are Counterexamples?" *Philosophical Studies* 115(1): 1–31.

Wedgewood, R. 2002. "The Aim of Belief." *Philosophical Perspectives* 16: 267–97.

Weinberg, J. M., Nichols, S., and Stich, S. 2008. "Normativity and Epistemic Intuitions." In J. Knobe and S. Nichols, eds, *Experimental Philosophy*. New York, NY: Oxford University Press, pp. 17–46.

Wheeler, G. 2009. "Focused Correlation and Confirmation." *The British Journal for the Philosophy of Science* 60(1): 79–100.

— (forthcoming). "Objective Bayesian Calibration and the Problem of Nonconvex Evidence." *The British Journal for the Philosophy of Science*.

Wheeler, G. and Pereira, L. 2008. "Methodological Naturalism and Epistemic Internalism." *Synthese* 163(3): 315–28.

Wheeler, G. and Scheines, R. 2011. "Coherence, Association, and Causation." In Hartmann, Weber, Gonzalez, Dieks, and Uebe 2011, pp. 37–51.

— (manuscript) "Coherence and Confirmation through Causation." (under review).

Whitcomb, D. 2007. *An Epistemic Value Theory*. PhD Diss, Rutgers University. Available at: http://hdl.rutgers.edu/1782.2/rucore10001600001.ETD.16794

— 2008. "Review of *New Waves in Epistemology*, ed., Hendricks and Pritchard." *Notre Dame* Philosophical Reviews.

— (forthcoming). "Curiosity Was Framed." *Philosophy and Phenomenological Research*.

— (forthcoming). "Wisdom." In Bernecker and Pritchard, eds, *The Routledge Companion to Epistemology*.

White, R. 2010. "Evidential Symmetry and Mushy Credence." In Gendler and Hawthorne 2010, pp. 161–81.

Williams, M. 1991. *Unnatural Doubts*. Cambridge, MA: Blackwell Publishers.

Williamson, J. 2010. *In Defence of Objective Bayesianism*. Oxford: Oxford University Press.

Williamson, T. 1996. "Knowing and Asserting." *Philosophical Review* 105: 489–523.

— 2002. *Knowledge and its Limits*. New York: Oxford University Press.

— 2005a. "Contextualism, Subject-Sensitive Invariantism, and Knowledge of Knowledge." *Philosophical Quarterly* 55: 213–35.

— 2005b. "Knowledge, Context, and the Agent's Point of View." In G. Preyer and G. Peter, eds, *Contextualism in Philosophy: Knowledge, Meaning, and Truth*. Oxford: Oxford University Press.

— 2007. *The Philosophy of Philosophy*. Oxford: Blackwell.

Wittgenstein, L. *On Certainty*. Harper & Row: New York.

Wright, J. 2010. "On Intuitional Stability: The Clear, the Strong, and the Paradigmatic." *Cognition* 115: 491–503.

Yourgrau, P. 1983. "Knowledge and Relevant Alternatives." *Synthese* 55: 175–90.

Zagzebski, L. 1994. "The Inescapability of Gettier Problems." *The Philosophical Quarterly* 44(174): 65–73.

— 1996. *Virtues of the Mind.* Cambridge: Cambridge University Press.

— 2001. "Recovering Understanding." In M. Steup, ed. *Knowledge, Truth, and Duty.* Oxford: Oxford University Press.

Zollman, K. 2007. "The Communication Structure of Epistemic Communities." *Philosophy of Science* 74(5): 574–87.

Index